Desktop
Publishing
Bible

Anthony S. Tricoli

Related Titles

Personal Publishing with the Macintosh, Second Edition
Terry Ulick

The Best Book of: WordStar, Second Edition
Vincent Alfieri

Mastering WordStar®
Vincent Alfieri

Best Book of: WordPerfect®
Vincent Alfieri

dBASE III PLUS™ Programmer's Reference Guide
Ed Jones

Managing with dBASE III®
Michael J. Clifford

Best Book of: dBASE II®/III®
Ken Knecht

Best Book of: Lotus® 1-2-3®, Second Edition
Alan Simpson

Macro Programming for 1-2-3®
Daniel N. Shaffer

Discovering MS-DOS®
Kate O'Day, The Waite Group

MS-DOS® Bible
Steven Simrin, The Waite Group

MS-DOS® Developer's Guide
John Angermeyer and Kevin Jaeger, The Waite Group

Tricks of the MS-DOS® Masters
John Angermeyer, Kevin Jaeger, Rich Fahringer, and Dan Shafer, The Waite Group

Microsoft® C Programming for the IBM®
Robert Lafore, The Waite Group

C Programmer's Guide to Serial Communications
Joe Campbell

C Primer Plus, Revised Edition
Mitchell Waite, Stephen Prata, and Donald Martin, The Waite Group

Advanced C Primer + +
Stephen Prata, The Waite Group

For the retailer nearest you, or to order directly from the publisher, call 800-428-SAMS. In Indiana, Alaska, and Hawaii call 317-298-5699.

Desktop Publishing Bible

The Waite Group, Inc.
James Stockford, Editor

Anthony S. Tricoli

♫♫♫
HOWARD W. SAMS & COMPANY
A Division of Macmillan, Inc.
4300 West 62nd Street
Indianapolis, Indiana 46268 USA

International Standard Book Number: 0-672-22524-7

Library of Congress Catalog Card Number: 87-81109

The Waite Group
Developmental Editor: James Stockford
Consulting Editor: Mitchell Waite
Content Editor: Mary Goodell
Designer: Mark Ong
Managing Editor: Cynthia Pepper
Technical Reviewers: John Angermeyer, Kevin Rardin, Jerry Volpe, Cynthia Spoor, William Woodruff

H.S. Dakin Co.
Production Manager: Peyton Curlee
Graphics Coordinator: Kim Straitiff
Copy Editor: Jeff Novey
Style Editor: Carolyn Said
Production Assistant: Cindy Lamb
Indexer: Helen Berliner
Proofreader: Heather Leitch

Imprint! Press Typographer: Peter Lin

Howard W. Sams & Company
Acquisitions Editor: James S. Hill
Editor: Katherine Stuart Ewing
Cover Artist: Ron Troxell

Printed in the United States of America.

Contents

Preface

This book attempts to provide a basic introduction to desktop publishing. "Desktop publishing" is something of a misnomer; the term refers less to publishing than to production, a domain populated with specialists, including designers, editors, pasteup artists, typographers, proofreaders, even print brokers, production managing specialists, and more. The new field of desktop publishing has introduced even more experts to the amalgam: programmers, microcomputer systems specialists, and desktop power users.

We began this book project on the premise that no single professional could do justice to explaining the vast field of desktop publishing. We sought out experts from each of the many fields that make up PC and microcomputer-based publishing — graphic artists, typographers, designers, engineers, publishers, programmers, consultants — and asked them to write essays describing the fundamentals of their disciplines and some of the potential applications. Mirroring the diversity in the field itself, the voices of these contributors are also varied, and they occasionally repeat or contradict one another.

Our primary purpose in the *Desktop Publishing Bible* is to inform the person newly entering the field of desktop publishing, the typographer who must face PostScript, the designer who must master page layout software, the artist who must figure out how to manipulate pixels instead of ink, and other experts crossing into new disciplines. We review the production issues surrounding such subjects as magazines, comics, and music as a means to inform the reader of the possibilities that desktop publishing tools present. We offer these essays as beginnings to awareness: Each of those topics really deserves its own book.

Some purists limit the meaning of the term "desktop publishing" to the use of page layout software and laser printers; others may have somewhat more exotic views. In the *Desktop Publishing Bible* we have taken the broadest possible view: that desktop publishing concerns the use of microcomputer- and PC-based tools to create formatted printed matter for widespread distribution.

Each essay begins with a two-page spread that presents keywords, related essays in this book, an author biography, a synopsis of the essay, and a level indicator: introductory, intermediate, or advanced. These openers were included to allow readers to determine their reading paths both in terms of their interests and their experience.

We have divided the book into four sections. *Traditional Underpinnings* contains essays on traditional publishing savvy to help prepare you for the later essays. It reviews the entire process of print production, copyright laws, traditional typesetting, design issues, and compares the traditional to the new approach, with some startling results.

Systems and Hardware focuses on the hardware used in desktop publishing. The first essay examines using the Apple Macintosh for publishing, explaining such attributes as resolution, pointing devices, and the user interface. This is followed by a look at the hardware for the IBM PC, Microsoft Windows, graphic standards of add-in cards for the PC, printers, scanners, and high-end workstations.

Software contains essays illustrating the use of the basic programs used by desktop publishers. We examine graphics programs for artists, page layout programs, high resolution graphics editing, type encoding programs, PostScript programming, and finally the JustText editor.

Techniques and Special Applications discusses auxiliary techniques and programs designed to meet specialized publishing needs. Essays cover the production of newsletters, forms, magazines, comics, and even sheet music. The final essay describes the creation of a poster using an array of desktop publishing tools.

We designed, wrote, and produced most of the *Desktop Publishing Bible* using the publishing tools discussed in the essays. We used Macintosh Pluses as our main computers, the Apple LaserWriter to generate much of the art, the Allied Linotronic 300 phototypesetter with RIP interface to generate camera-ready pages, the JustText text-processing program to set the text, and most of the programs mentioned in the text to create the artwork.

The authors and editors of this book have struggled mightily to produce a collection of essays that does justice to this broad-based marketplace. If it's true that desktop publishing brings publishing to the masses, it is our hope that this book will help ensure that final quality of this work is as high as that of the traditional tools it is replacing.

Jim Stockford
Editorial Director
The Waite Group, Inc.
June 12, 1987

Acknowledgements

I am most grateful to the authors of the essays in this book; they have been generous in sharing their time and knowledge. I am grateful to Mitchell Waite for his encouragement and guidance throughout the project, to Mary Goodell for her dedication and support in development, to Cynthia Pepper for her ability to manage a great number of different people and problems at one time. I am grateful to Jeff Novey for his good-natured, very helpful editing, to Peyton Curlee and Carolyn Said for their hard work and expertise in editing and managing the production of this book, to Kim Straitiff for her skill and help in graphics and design, and to Kullok Kaughy for his wisdom, patience, and technical expertise. I am grateful to Peter Lin for his tireless contribution both as author and typesetter. Special thanks to Kathy Ewing at Sams for her understanding, support, and skill. Many thanks to John Angermeyer for his constant technical help, to William Woodruff for the help and education he provided me, to Mark Ong for the design of chapter openers, Cayenne Spohur for acquisitions, and to James Jaynes, Bart Anderson, and David Le for their contributions to the book in process.

We thank the people at Mindscape for the use of art from ComicWorks (Essay 24, Comics and Cartooning), those at Sigma Designs for the use of information on video displays (Essay 10, Monitors), and those at Adobe Systems for their help with printing the Sonata font (Essay 25, Music Desktop Publishing).

For Carol

Trademark Acknowledgments

I

Traditional Underpinnings

About This Section

W̲e start out with a caution — in the excitement surrounding desktop publishing we can easily forget that behind these wonderful new computer-based tools lies a deep tradition of publishing conventions and rules. These rules, standards, and basic criteria for acceptance cover a large body of knowledge, including letter forms, page composition and design, production, and even the very ownership of the printed word. It is unlikely that one person can be an expert at all these standards, but it is also likely that severe problems may result if they aren't well understood. This section presents some of this traditional publishing savvy to help prepare you for the later essays on desktop publishing. We begin with a review of the entire process of print production, followed by examination of the copyright laws as they pertain to self publishing. Features of traditional typesetting are explained next to provide a backdrop for later essays on the new tools that claim to replace typesetting. The subsequent essay reviews design issues so the reader understands the basic problems that occur in publishing. The section ends with an essay that compares traditional publishing to the new desktop publishing, revealing some surprising results.

KEYWORDS:

• Typesetting

• Pasteup

• Proofing

• Printing

• Production Management

Caroline J. Acker is a freelance technical writer and editor who lives in Marin County, California. A former editor of *Street Pharmacologist,* Ms. Acker has also edited college-level textbooks and taught writing courses at Florida International University and through UC Berkeley extension.

Essay Synopsis: The understanding of traditional print production is fundamental to any publishing effort, desktop or otherwise. The issues involved are preparing text for typesetting, placing text and graphics in an effective design, pasting up and caring for final art, tracking the job through printing and binding, and not least, negotiating with outside contractors. Throughout the process, critical checking and proofing points must be defined and implemented.

This easy-to-read essay presents an overview of traditional means of producing printed matter. It was chosen as the lead article because the principles of print production provide the foundation for desktop publishing and will prepare you for upcoming essays.

1

Printing Production

Caroline Acker

"We need a monthly newsletter to keep our customers abreast of our product development work."

"Would you write an instruction manual for the order entry staff? I want them up and running on the new file update system ASAP."

"If people really understood the commercial benefits of this technology, I think we'd have little trouble attracting investors."

Suddenly, you're a publisher. You have a message and you know who you want to deliver it to. It's up to you to get 2,000 newsletters or 25 manuals or 350 prospectuses developed, written, and printed.

This essay examines the role of the publisher and surveys the entire production process of getting something printed — from preparing the manuscript for the typesetter to deciding how the finished piece will be folded. It indicates the kinds of choices you are called on to make at each phase of the publishing operation. And it outlines how you must check the work at each of these phases to ensure that the finished job is accurate and that it is what you really want.

Like a movie producer, you, as publisher and production manager, are responsible for seeing that the job gets done. You hire the various kinds of creative talent and technical expertise to produce your published piece. Just as the film producer also can be the director, you can make many of the design decisions and do

5

much of the work that goes into publishing yourself, or you can hire out every part of it — except the ultimate responsibility for the quality of the result.

Also like a producer, you, as publisher, engage in a creative process. Printed matter communicates not just with words, but with color, line, shape, and texture. Whether the paper is shiny or dull, whether the letters are swirly or sleek, whether the layout is crowded or spare — every decision the publisher makes influences how effectively the published piece communicates.

Although publishing includes writing (or commissioning writing), this essay starts from the point when the words have been written in manuscript form. A manuscript is not a rough draft. It has been reviewed by everyone who has to review it as well as edited by someone with a good knowledge of grammar and of the writing style appropriate to the purpose.

This essay takes a brief look at the two basic phases of production: the typesetting and pasteup phase, and the printing phase. It then discusses these processes in more detail, emphasizing the choices you are called on to make at each stage and the kinds of checking you must do to insure the accuracy and quality of the finished piece. Although the decisions you make are discussed at the points where they are carried out in production, it is wise to have thought out these decisions before production begins. All aspects of the printed piece work together, and each choice should be made in light of your overall purpose.

Overviewing Production

When you contract for printing production, you get what you ask for. Anything you fail to anticipate is generally decided for you, either actively or by default. Thus, you avoid unpleasant surprises by visualizing as clearly as possible what you want and translating that vision into clear specifications as to format, design, size and style of letters, pictorial elements, type of paper, ink color, and folding and binding method.

What most people think of as printing consists of two phases. The first phase does not involve the application of ink to paper. Its objective is to produce the images that will be transferred to paper. This phase consists of typesetting and pasting up. Typesetting produces a copy of your text in the style and size of letters that will appear in the printed piece. The product of typesetting is called, naturally, "set type" or just "type." The art of designing and producing type is called "typography."

Pasting up is the process of affixing pieces of set type onto a stiff medium, such as cardboard, in exactly the positions where you want them to appear in the finished printed piece. Pasting up also incorporates any pictures or design elements the piece will include. This pasted up work is called a "board," and the board is photographed and used to make a "plate" for the printer.

Before we examine these activities in greater detail, let's briefly consider costs. It is important to take bids for publishing services. Prices vary widely, and sometimes with good reason, because they represent different kinds and levels of service.

Negotiating Prices

Typesetters generally charge a standard rate based on the amount of text to be set. Ask for the typesetter's policy regarding extra charges for making corrections to the set type. Ask also (or learn by experience when you submit your first job) how helpful they are about proofreading and correcting. Some typesetters do an initial proofreading after the type is set, and flag portions of your manuscript that are unclear. Others take no initiative in this regard. Whatever the arrangement, you, the publisher, bear the responsibility for the accuracy of the type.

Pasteup artists also may have standard page rates, but these are based in part on the complexity of the job. Again, check into what services you are buying. Are you hiring an artist to help design the printed piece or a technician who needs detailed specifications? The kinds of service you require will depend on the sophistication of the job and the degree to which you have thought through the design yourself.

Printing costs vary widely. Many print shops are small businesses, and they own a few presses that are suited to particular kinds of work. A print shop with the best equipment for your job can bid lower than a shop that must modify its equipment to meet your specifications. For these reasons, it is especially wise to request bids from several vendors for printing jobs.

Most print shops either perform binding services themselves or subcontract them. Unless you are dealing with very expensive and frequent jobs, it is usually worth the savings in time and energy to purchase these services through the print shop than to take bids and contract for them yourself.

Finally, a word about the least flexible commodity in publishing: time. Publishing projects usually have deadlines, and you must build into your schedule both how long it takes your vendors to do their work and how long it takes you to check it at each stage. Ask your vendors how quickly they can complete your job. The turnaround time they offer is based on the date when you say you can bring the job to them. It may not apply if you are late and they have already allocated people and time to other projects. Most vendors charge extra for rush jobs.

Now that we've gotten acquainted with the phases of printing production, we'll take a closer look at how you, the publisher, fit into the picture.

Preparing for Typesetting

The typesetting and pasteup phases of publishing require a high level of involvement. You must check the work of the typesetter and pasteup artist very closely to ensure the level of accuracy you require. You may consult extensively with the pasteup artist to determine exactly what your printed piece will look like.

The manuscript you bring to the typesetter should be typed or word processed, double spaced, on 8½ by 11 inch paper. Every word should be correctly spelled, every comma in place. Numbers should be expressed in digits or letters, depending on how you want them printed. Paragraph breaks should be clearly marked.

With the typesetter, you decide the style and size of the letters for your text and for any headings, bylines, or other freestanding text areas. Type styles are called fonts or typefaces. Each font is available in regular, italic, bold, and bold italic.

The size of the letters is measured in points; 72 points make up an inch. The larger the point size, the larger the letters. The type you are reading now is 11 point. Body text is often set in 8-, 9-, or 10-point type. Minor headings, headlines set in a larger size, can be slightly larger (12 or 14 point) and major headlines go to 24 or 36 points or larger.

The typesetter also needs to know the kind of columns you want the text to be set in. You determine column width by how many columns you want on a certain size page, allowing for margins and for space between columns.

Columns have either justified or ragged edges. Justified column edges are spaced so that each line begins or ends at exactly the same point: The column border is as straight as a ruler.

Ragged edges occur when the line width varies, depending on how word lengths happen to fall. The most common column styles are justified (both borders are straight lines) and ragged right (the left border is justified; the right column margin varies). An unusual effect can be created by having the left margin ragged and the right margin justified. Another variation is to have each line centered, so that both right and left margins are ragged.

Proofreading

When the typesetter has set the type, it is given to you in the form of text on long sheets of glossy photographic paper generally known as galleys. You must proofread it to find any typographical errors. Some errors are inevitable when text of any length is set in type. It is your responsibility to find them and mark them for correction. The typesetter then makes the corrections and you check again to verify that they were properly made. If necessary, you go through another round of corrections and checking.

Throughout the publishing process, the purpose of checking is to ensure that your specifications have been followed — not to introduce changes. The more advanced the stage of production, the more expensive it is to change the work that has been done. When you proofread, you are not judging grammar, style, and punctuation. You are looking for instances where the set type deviates from the letter perfect manuscript you gave the typesetter. (Of course, you kept a copy yourself, just in case of loss.)

You have the choice of marking errors directly on the set type or of working with photocopies of the type. The latter is the best choice for all except experienced proofreaders. If the typesetter prefers that you work on the type, make your marks with a pencil or pen that writes in the light blue shade called nonreproducing blue (because it will not be reproduced in the printing process).

Standard proofreaders' marks are listed in most dictionaries and in many other reference works. There is some variation in proofreaders' marks. What counts is that your marks must be absolutely unambiguous. Caret marks (^) must make clear exactly where (e.g., between which two letters, before or after a comma) an insertion goes. Until you and your typesetter have worked together long enough to have developed a deep mutual understanding, it is wise to go over the marks you have made before corrections are entered to be sure the typesetter doesn't misunderstand any instructions.

One method of proofreading is to go through the set type twice. The first time, compare it word for word against the manuscript. This process enables you to pick out any missing parts. A missing part might be a single comma, or it might be a whole passage if the typesetter's eye skipped some lines because the same word occurred twice in close proximity. You can also verify the accuracy of any words, letters, or numbers that you can't check just by looking at the set type. All numbers should be meticulously checked against the manuscript. Unusual or technical words that are not familiar to you (e.g., sphygomomanometer or meretricious) should be checked. Every character of set type must be checked, and every character on the manuscript must be looked at to verify that it wasn't omitted during typesetting. A common error of neophyte proofreaders is to check the body text with great care and to forget altogether to check the headlines, page header, and footer, as well as other pieces of text that aren't in the main body.

After checking the set type against the manuscript, read it again closely, checking for spelling errors. Look at *each word* and ask yourself if it's spelled correctly. You can pass quickly over the words and numbers you verified in the first reading. Look carefully at information (such as your telephone number) that is second nature to you. You're likely to overlook these items otherwise. As you proofread, be on the lookout for broken type — letters or numbers with gaps in them.

Finally, after you have proofread the copy, have someone else proofread it with the same two-step process. No one can catch all typographical errors, and sometimes errors even slip past two proofreadings by different people.

If there is only time for one person to proofread the copy, have someone other than the author proofread unless the author has had extensive proofreading experience. The person who wrote the words is often likely to miss errors because of an overfamiliarity with the manuscript.

Proofreading is a painfully meticulous chore, but with practice you will get better and faster at it. If you are indifferently motivated about it now, you'll become a fervent believer in its importance the first time a costly or embarrassing error slips through to print.

Your responsibility for the accuracy of the text is not over yet: You must check that the corrections are properly made. Either the typesetter gives you another printout of the copy or the corrections are applied directly to the pasteup. In either case, you need to check only the corrected areas. If you ask, the typesetter will indicate exactly which portions of the type were reset to make the corrections.

Pasting Up

After the type is set, pasteup begins. You now must indicate where on each page all the type, pictures, and other design elements go. Usually, you have a design in mind before the typesetting begins. If not, the layout is decided after the type has been set. If you hire a graphic artist to design the piece, this artist usually does the pasteup.

Each column of text, heading, byline, page number, and picture is pasted (usually with hot wax) to a piece of cardboard on which page and column margins are indicated in nonreproducing blue. Some additional typesetting may be required as pasting up progresses. Headlines may not be written until after space for them has been allotted. If an article is continued on a later page, the tag directing the reader there (called a jump line) must be set.

Photographs and Illustrations

Photographs are not pasted directly onto the cardboard. Instead, a sheet of rubylith, a reddish film, is cut to the size you want the photograph to be in the printed piece. The rubylith is pasted exactly where you want the photograph to appear. When you deliver the boards to the print shop, you should take the photograph as well.

Often, you do not want all of a photograph to be printed. For example, an expanse of blank wall may loom in the background, or you may want to include only one of three people appearing in the shot. To print less than the entire area of the photograph is to "crop" the photograph. "Crop marks" tell the printer which portion of the photograph you want reproduced. These are small marks you make in the margin surrounding the photograph to indicate the horizontal and vertical boundaries of the area you want printed.

Photographs are frequently enlarged or reduced when they are printed because of space or design considerations. There are risks in reducing or enlarging too much from the original size of the photograph. Too much enlargement causes the images to become fuzzy and unclear. Reducing a picture sharpens the images, but too much reduction makes images too small to recognize. You can reduce further than you can enlarge without compromising the quality of the printed reproduction of the photograph. Color photographs, if they are clear and sharp, can be printed in black and white if necessary, but even a little fuzziness or graininess in a color photograph can make it unsuitable for reproduction.

When a photograph or illustration is to be reduced or enlarged, you must know the exact dimensions of the reduced or enlarged version. A proportion wheel, an inexpensive tool available in most office or art supply stores, spares you the ratio calculations (e.g., 5 inches is to 4½ inches as 9 inches is to x) that may have been your bane in sixth grade math. This handy plastic wheel lets you see instantly what the new dimensions will be without any multiplication or division.

If the illustrations are black on white with clear lines and sharp contrast, and if, unlike original drawings, they are expendable, they can simply be cut and pasted on to the cardboard. Otherwise, they must be photostated with a process camera and placed.

If you don't have actual pictures to include in your printed piece, or even if you do, many design elements are still available to the impecunious publisher.

Negative Space Layouts

The least expensive design element is white or negative space: all the space on the page that doesn't have ink on it. Dramatic and interesting effects can be achieved by arranging the type, pictures, and graphics on the page in a way that exploits white space as a design element. (Of course, white space becomes expensive when generously deployed in a document of many pages with a large print run, and the more expensive your paper is, the more you're paying for white space.)

One easy way to come up with unusual layouts is to arrange three, five, or seven elements asymmetrically on a page. If you have body type, a headline and a photograph — bingo: You've got three elements to play with. "Play" is the operative word here. You can make photocopies of the set type, cut them into pieces, and move them around in different patterns on an area the size of your printed page. Endless possibilities reveal themselves. Experimenting with layout can be one of the most enjoyable facets of your role as publisher.

Remember that when brochures are folded, parts of both sides can be seen at once. If your project is a newsletter or book, work with double page spreads, and try to carry the same visual feel through the whole piece.

Rule Lines

Lines are available to you for the asking. Every pasteup artist has line tapes — thin rolls of tape with lines running along them — that can be incorporated into your layout. There are more varieties of lines than you may have dreamed of — double and triple lines, shaded lines, and more.

Line boxes can enclose author biographies or create sidebars: boxes of self-contained text that add a sidelight to the main article. Boxes are also useful for announcements in newsletters or for order forms in brochures. (Remember not to print information the reader needs, such as when and where an event is to be held, on the back of the mail-in registration!)

Clip art affords another inexpensive way to dress up your printed piece. Clip art consists of pages or books full of images that can be cut out, reduced, or enlarged, and included in your work. Pictures of various activities and things — such as computers or baseballs or cars — are available. Particular pictures appear in various sizes.

To include your company logo in printed matter, take a printed copy of it to your typesetter to have a photostat made. A photostat is produced by a photographic process that transfers the logo to photosensitive paper. Provided there are no halftones or screens in the logo, this photostat can then be endlessly reproduced in any size for inclusion in brochures, on business cards, and in marketing literature.

When the pasteup has been completed, you are presented with the pieces of cardboard on which the set type and illustrations have been pasted. The cardboard is larger than your finished page will be, and the page margins are indicated by short black lines (crop marks) just outside each corner. A cover flap of transparent waxed paper is usually taped along the top of the board to protect it from dust and smudges.

Proofing Finished Artwork

In the world of printing, artwork does not mean what Rembrandt did for a living or what Michelangelo produced during his stint as a ceiling painter, nor does artwork refer just to pictures. The artwork, also called the pasteup, the mechanicals, or the boards, is the original piece that you want reproduced through the printing process: in other words, the cardboards that the pasteup artist has given you. (A sheet of paper composed at your terminal and printed on your laser printer is the artwork, if no pasteup is required.)

In offset lithography, finished artwork is called camera-ready because it is ready to be photographed for the negative from which the plate will be made. Don't rush those boards to the print shop yet. First, you must check them for accuracy. The scope of what you check for at this stage is covered by five questions: Is everything there? Is everything where it's supposed to be? Is anything there that shouldn't be? Are corrections made to the typographical errors that occurred in the typesetting (if these corrections haven't been checked earlier)? Has any newly set type been proofread?

Where columns break or an article goes to another page, make sure that lines are not missing and that the new column or page picks up at the right point. Check that all pieces of body type have been put down in correct sequence. Make sure corrections have been stripped in at the right places. Check the alignment of columns and pictures to be sure the horizontals and verticals are true.

The boards are a valuable asset because future editions of the job can be printed from them. First, they must be transported to the print shop in perfect condition. They must be kept flat and clean. Because the type is usually affixed to the cardboard with paraffin, boards should not be exposed to high temperatures. Leaving boards in a locked car on a summer day can cause the wax to melt and your carefully arranged elements to begin swimming on the page.

For long-term storage, lay the boards flat where they will be protected from dust and, again, high temperatures. Cabinets with large, shallow drawers (like those in which maps are stored at the library) are appropriate; those made of sturdy cardboard are generally adequate and are far less expensive than wooden or metal models. An inventory taped to the top of the cabinet will help you to keep track of what you have stored.

Printing

At last, your job is ready to go to the print shop. Less is demanded of you in the printing phase than in the typesetting and pasteup phases because the checking you must do takes far less time.

Printing, in the strict sense, is the application of ink to paper. Although there are many printing processes, one of two printing methods — photocopying or offset lithography — will meet most printing needs, especially for the relative newcomer to publishing.

High-quality photocopying service is offered by "quick print" establishments. Photocopying is suitable for uncomplicated jobs that involve only one color and do not call for absolute precision in the width of margins or other technical specifications. Photocopying is less expensive and faster than lithography.

Lithography

Offset lithography is the most common printing process for books, magazines, and newspapers, as well as jobs calling for more than one color, sophisticated design, specially treated papers, and many other requirements. One-color jobs are also commonly done by lithography.

The printing process described in this chapter is offset lithography. Although lithography is more expensive than photocopying, it offers many more possibilities to the publisher, and it makes possible more professional looking results.

The first step in offset lithography produces a photographic negative of the images to be printed. From this negative, a plate is made. The surface of the plate is treated so that ink adheres only to those areas where the images appear. The plate is attached to a printing press, and as paper moves through the press, ink is applied to the plate and transferred to the paper.

After printing, the inked paper may be cut, collated, folded, drilled, stapled, or bound. These tasks fall under the category of bindery functions.

As a publisher seeking to buy printing services, you may work with one vendor that takes a job through the typesetting, pasteup, printing, and binding phases, or you may deal with different vendors for different services. A common arrangement is to have the typographer or graphic design shop set the type and do the pasteup then have a print shop handle the printing and binding.

Color

The most basic choice to be made about printing is whether the job will be a one-color job or will consist of two or more ink colors. This choice will have great impact on what the printing job will cost. For each ink color, a separate plate must be made. In many cases, the paper must make a run through a different press for each ink color. (Some presses are set up to apply two or four colors in a single run.)

Single-color printing offers you the full dark-light range of that color. For example, if the ink is black, your finished job can include any shade of gray. If the single color is blue, the job can include any lighter shade of blue.

Lighter versions of the ink color are applied by a process called screening: the application of tiny dots to the paper. The darkness or lightness of the shade is controlled by the size and density of the dots.

If you look very closely at photographs reproduced in the newspaper, you can distinguish these dots. Failing super acute eyesight, you can visit your local modern art museum and pause before one of Roy Lichtenstein's greatly enlarged comic book images.

In choosing the kind of paper (or stock) the job will be printed on, consider color, weight, and texture. Even among white papers, there are color variations: snowy white, slightly bluish or grayish or yellowish white, and many off-white shades such as ivory or pale beige. If colored paper will be used with ink other than black, ask whether the paper color will affect the printed ink tone.

Paper

Paper texture can be smooth or irregular. The paper may be dull or shiny. Highly reflective paper is called coated stock because a finish has been applied to it. Paper also varies in weight. Heavy paper, such as that used for booklet covers or tickets, is called card stock.

Many special effects can be created in the printing process at varying costs. These include reverse images, bleeds, and screens. A reverse image is a cut-out effect. If you print black ink on white paper and the letters show through in white with black ink surrounding them, you have a reverse image. A bleed occurs when the ink goes all the way to the edge of the paper. Printing is almost always done on large sheets of paper that are later trimmed to their finished size. For a bleed, the ink extends beyond the page margin and the excess is cut away.

Bleeds and reverse images create dramatic effects. A brochure panel might have a bold slogan in reverse image letters, with the ink bleeding off the three paper borders of the panel. On the fourth side, the ink goes to the fold, and exquisite coordination is required to keep the ink line and the fold perfectly aligned.

Screens, as we have seen, produce shading effects by spreading dots of ink rather than by covering larger areas of the paper. In the reproduction of a photograph, the density of the dots varies extensively to capture the three dimensionality and the color shadings of the picture. Screens can also produce uniformly light or dark shaded areas, as in boxes. If the screen is light enough, text can be laid over it (although very small letters are hard to read against a screen). Screens are measured by percent of the paper that is covered by a given density. A 10 percent screen produces very light shading while a 90 percent screen is almost as dark as complete coverage.

Binding

After your job comes off the press and the ink has had time to dry, the bindery functions are performed. Pages are cut to size, collated, drilled (for ring binders), folded, stapled, or bound.

Cutting can involve more than trimming the job down to size. A hole cut in a cover lets a picture on the next page show through. Tabs to divide chapters are produced by printing the title, then cutting away the rest of the margin. Tabs are expensive, check companies that specialize in producing binders and tabs. Booklets can have layered pages.

Before giving instructions for any folds, try out the fold you have in mind. How the paper is folded determines the sequence in which most readers see its various panels. Three-panel brochures can be folded in a Z fold (the paper edge forms a Z when looked at end on) or a letter fold (both end panels are folded toward the center).

For booklets or magazines, several forms of binding are available, from stapling for a few pages to stitching for jobs where durability is essential.

Some forms of binding allow the finished booklet to lie open on a table. This format is ideal for instruction manuals that the eye must refer to while the hands are busy learning new skills. For ring binders, indicate where on the page the holes should be drilled. True spiral binding and the similar plastic comb binding can produce slimmer volumes, but they lack the advantage of removable pages.

Checking the Printed Work

The kinds of checking that must be done during printing depend on the nature of the job. For single-color jobs, you check the blue line or brown line. After the negative is produced, an impression is made from it on blue or brown photosensitive paper. This impression is folded, collated, or stapled as the finished piece will be (but it may not be cut to exact size).

As when checking the boards, verify that no elements are missing from the blue line. Look for any flaws that may have been introduced during the making of the negative. These usually take the form of blotches where there should be blank paper, or blobs of blank paper where there should be ink. Carefully scan the entire surface of the paper to look for these flaws.

It's too late now to notice that a column margin is uneven. Layout errors should have been picked up when the boards were checked. Changes to content or layout at this point are prohibitively expensive in time and, especially, money, and they quickly fray tempers all around. Of course, if a piece has somehow come loose from the boards and fallen off or moved out of alignment, then the blue line might present the first chance to notice it.

For color jobs (i.e., more than one color), you are given a color proof to check. Here, you check not only the correctness of the hues and shadings, but also the registration or alignment of colored areas to each other. If the plates are out of alignment, colors are not placed exactly where they belong. Where two colors abut, or where two inks are applied to the same area to achieve a desired tone, the placement must be perfect to avoid overlaps, gaps, or fuzzy images.

Any minor errors you detect in the blue line or color proof — such as tiny flecks or blotches — are easily repaired on the negative. Correcting large-scale errors may slow down the job and require additional checking. You continue to be responsible for errors. Most print shops require that you sign a form indicating that you approve the job for printing (pending corrections to errors you have identified). The print shop is thus released from liability for errors that escape detection on the negative.

In most situations, checking the blue line or color proof is your last task before accepting delivery of your finished job (and paying the various invoices). For very sophisticated jobs, especially those where perfect registration is critical, you also perform a press check. Arrange to be at the print shop when your job is to be run, and check the first several sheets that come off the press. Final adjustments in color tone and placement and in ink density are made at this point.

Ownership of Art, Boards, and Plates

The artwork is your property, and the printer should return it to you with the finished job. If you want to reprint the job later with very minor changes (such as corrections to typographical errors that were discovered after the first edition was printed), these changes can be made inexpensively on the boards. (You do, however, incur new printing set-up charges — the making of a new plate and negative — if you change the artwork at all.)

The artwork can be cannibalized for future pieces. For newsletters and other periodicals, the masthead, copyright statement, publishing information, and other permanent portions can be lifted from the boards for one issue and pressed onto the boards for the next. Individual articles can be lifted and reformatted for mailing to customers as reprints and so on.

The negatives and plates made from your artwork belong to the print shop unless you make special arrangements to purchase them. The print shop should store them safely and, of course, they cannot be used or reproduced in any way without your permission. To reprint the piece without any changes at all to the artwork, have the print shop run it again from the plates made for the first run. You can make changes in the kind of paper, the ink colors, or the cutting, folding, and binding instructions if you wish. But if you decide you want a second printer to rerun your brochure, the first printer is unlikely to relinquish the negatives and plates without a struggle.

Managing Production

By now you have some idea of how many ways something can go wrong as your job moves through the phases of production that make up publishing. One way to improve the quality of your work and minimize the emotional strain that results when you bear the full brunt of Murphy's Law is to maintain good relations with the typesetters, paste-up artists, and print technicians you work with.

At the outset, provide clean copy to the typesetter and clear specifications to everyone. No one can set accurate type from tightly packed words with pencilled insertions, margin notes calling for passages to be moved around, and frequent misspellings. Similarly, no one can give you the finished work you want if you don't communicate clearly what it is you do want.

Allow enough time for each person in the production process to get the job done carefully and well. When you request cost estimates, ask for time requirements for the job. A good way to plan a publishing project is to work from completion day backward. Set the target date when you want the 1,500 brochures or 200 newsletters delivered. How long will bindery functions for this job take? Count back that many days from the target. How long will printing itself take, including time for the ink to dry and collating to be done? Note the date when printing must begin to make your target. Similarly, get time estimates for pasting up and typesetting. Remember to make realistic allowances for the checking you, and perhaps others, must do at each phase. When you work backward on the calendar, plotting the number of days for each of these functions and noting the dates when each phase must begin, you end up with a production schedule for the job. If you're new at publishing, you may be dismayed to discover the day you should have started this project was two weeks ago! With experience, both with different kinds of jobs and with different vendors, you'll develop a general sense of how much time specific projects need.

In situations where you really don't have enough time to get the job done at everyone's normal work pace, you can request a rush job at a higher cost. Most vendors have standard rush charges for jobs that must be completed in less than the normal turnaround time. But if every job is a rush job, if you're always dashing to your vendors with something that must be finished immediately, they, like the townspeople who heard the shepherd boy cry wolf too often, will cease to respond to your urgency. They'll suspect you're perhaps not terribly well organized. But if you usually bring jobs that reflect a good understanding of how long production takes, people who work with you will often work very hard when you bring them a rush job.

The best way to erode relations with printing vendors is to consistently require changes to work already done. The last minute reviser is the bane of the publishing world: the person who must revise the text after the type is set, change the headline size after the pasteup has been finished, switch to uncoated stock after half the job has gone through the printer. Of course, you must absorb the cost of any such changes — but these changes are very expensive, and it is hard to retain control of production and verify accuracy at each stage if you're constantly changing the specifications.

Don't abuse the bid-seeking process — the eloquent arguments for seeking several bids notwithstanding. Don't go overboard. As you work with the various vendors, you learn the kinds of jobs they can do best and most inexpensively. You come to trust that a vendor who has quoted you a number of competitive bids generally is pricing jobs well. It takes time and hard work to develop a cost estimate for a printing job. If you are a frequent purchaser of printing services, it is unwise to get several bids for every job you have, as it puts you in the position of constantly asking for estimates from shops that won't get the work. About the third time in a short period that you ask a print shop for a bid, and then take the job elsewhere, you have lost a friend. By the time you deign to let this shop do something for you, you are entrusting your precious job to potentially unfriendly hands.

Be aware of the 10 percent rule. It is general practice (and in many states a matter of law) that the print shop does not necessarily deliver to you the exact number of copies you order for large jobs (runs of several hundred or more). Usually, the print shop runs a small percentage more copies than you ask for so they'll have enough even if some copies are damaged during printing or at the bindery. These extra copies are usually delivered to you at no extra cost. Similarly, a job sometimes comes out a little short because of technical snags that chew up paper. The 10 percent rule says that the print shop can deliver up to 10 percent less than the quantity you ordered without incurring liability. Check the policy of your print shop in this area. And if it is crucial that you have 9,162 copies of your printed piece, order 10,000 copies!

Summary

Publishing is a lot of hard work (some of it is fun as well as hard). When the work is done, you have the satisfying experience of looking at, touching, reading, and showing off the printed piece you have produced. This tangible result of your labors will last a long time on the shelf or in your scrap book — an ongoing reminder of the creative endeavor you masterminded.

KEYWORDS:

- Fair Use

- Permissions

- Subsidiary Rights

- Public Domain

- Work for Hire

- Duration

John D. Goodell has been an organist for a silent film theater, an electronic designer, and a film director, John Goodell's achievements include creation of the first production line industrial robot, CBS cassette recorder, the conditioned-reflex teaching machine, several computer systems, and a 1973 documentary film *Always a New Beginning.* Mr. Goodell is currently the executive director of Knowledge Resources, a nonprofit educational corporation located in Saint Paul, Minnesota.

Essay Synopsis: The legal issues of copyright are fairly straightforward and most professionals in publishing should know them.

This essay is a thorough primer that reveals how and when you can use text from other sources in your own work and how you can protect the rights of the material you publish. The essay shows when to get permission and when not, when to file registration, how much of a protected work can be legitimately used, and what is in the public domain.

HOWARD W. SAMS & COMPANY

ℋℋℋ

Bookmark

DEAR VALUED CUSTOMER:

Howard W. Sams & Company is dedicated to bringing you timely and authoritative books for your personal and professional library. Our goal is to provide you with excellent technical books written by the most qualified authors. You can assist us in this endeavor by checking the box next to your particular areas of interest.

We appreciate your comments and will use the information to provide you with a more comprehensive selection of titles.

Thank you,

Vice President, Book Publishing
Howard W. Sams & Company

COMPUTER TITLES:

Hardware
- ☐ Apple 140
- ☐ Macintosh 101
- ☐ Commodore 110
- ☐ IBM & Compatibles 114

Business Applications
- ☐ Word Processing J01
- ☐ Data Base J04
- ☐ Spreadsheets J02

Operating Systems
- ☐ MS-DOS K05
- ☐ OS/2 K10
- ☐ CP/M K01
- ☐ UNIX K03

Programming Languages
- ☐ C L03
- ☐ Pascal L05
- ☐ Prolog L12
- ☐ Assembly L01
- ☐ BASIC L02
- ☐ HyperTalk L14

Troubleshooting & Repair
- ☐ Computers S05
- ☐ Peripherals S10

Other
- ☐ Communications/Networking M03
- ☐ AI/Expert Systems T18

ELECTRONICS TITLES:
- ☐ Amateur Radio T01
- ☐ Audio T03
- ☐ Basic Electronics T20
- ☐ Basic Electricity T21
- ☐ Electronics Design T12
- ☐ Electronics Projects T04
- ☐ Satellites T09

- ☐ Instrumentation T05
- ☐ Digital Electronics T11

Troubleshooting & Repair
- ☐ Audio S11
- ☐ Television S04
- ☐ VCR S01
- ☐ Compact Disc S02
- ☐ Automotive S06
- ☐ Microwave Oven S03

Other interests or comments: _____

_____

_____

Name_____

Title _____

Company _____

Address _____

City _____

State/Zip _____

Daytime Telephone No. _____

A Division of Macmillan, Inc.

4300 West 62nd Street   Indianapolis, Indiana 46268

22524

Bookmark

HOWARD W. SAMS & COMPANY

2

Copyright Law

John Goodell

If you are involved with creating original communications in the form of words or pictures, you should have some knowledge of copyright law in order to protect your own work and avoid infringement on material copyrighted by others. The following information is not intended to constitute comprehensive legal advice, but rather to provide guidelines and a general understanding of the highlights of the law. If you have reason to explore the law in detail, it can be found in any complete law library in Volume 17, United States Code Annotated, Section 100, *et seq.* (and sequence). The annotated version contains a great deal of useful relevant material.

As is true of most legal questions, there are gray areas involving copyright violations that can be settled only in court. The prime considerations in connection with the definition of the term "fair use" are developed in the following text. The basic question in such legal problems is whether, and to what extent, an action (such as quoting or copying a copyrighted work) constitutes some damage or loss of income to the copyright owner. To some degree such questions revolve around the extent to which material bearing the copyright notice is truly original and unique, hence truly copyrightable. If the content has appeared previously in published form, either it has been copyrighted already, or it is defined as in the public domain and cannot be protected by copyright.

RELATED ESSAYS:

1. Printing Production

21. Newsletters

Copyright Rights

The copyright law protects three basic rights. Only the individual who controls the copyright (or to whom it is assigned) legally may exercise these privileges. The most obvious is the literal inversion of the term "fair use": the right to copy. The next is the right to publish and to circulate the work so that it becomes available to the general public. The third right has to do with variations, such as condensations, language translations, and modified forms (e.g., making a motion picture from a book or a book from a motion picture). The copyright covers all parts of a work, including illustrations, pictures, maps, charts, and the like.

These rights belong exclusively to the author from the moment the material is expressed in an observable form. The original creator can sell, assign, rent, and dispose of these rights, partially or as a whole, to anyone or any organization with or without compensation.

Fair Use

This is a very important term because it defines the extent to which you may use excerpts from the work of others, and vice versa. The law does not explicitly define fair use, but the accepted principles — along with good judgment — are generally quite adequate.

The principal question is whether or not the use of the copied material has detracted from or minimized the author's material income from the publication or use of the work. The following are typical criteria.

Is the copy used for commercial, profit-making purposes? For example, a copy made in a library for purposes of study does not meet this criterion and is considered fair use.

Will the copy adversely affect the market for the copyrighted material? An obvious violation would be to publish a book that duplicates so much of an existing copyrighted book that the original book provides little or no additional significant information. Publishing quotations that encourage potential purchasers to buy the original does not adversely affect the market for the original, but may in fact expand it.

How large a percentage of the original work is contained in the copy? As much as a hundred or so words excerpted from a 100,000-word book is much less significant than the same number of words from a 1,000-word essay. The percentage of the amount copied is not a basic criterion, it is the effect the copy has on the commercial value of the original work. Thus, if you published 90 percent of a copyrighted formula, and your copy lacked one obscure, vital element that could be found only in the original material, the court might determine that you had not violated the copyright.

Is the material used out of context in such a way as to change or obscure the meaning intended by the original author, hence possibly harming its marketability? As an obvious example, if the original material appeared as, "Reading this book is a waste of time unless you have some reason to be interested in the content" and you were to quote, saying, "The first words in the book are 'Reading this book is a waste of time...' and that defines the quality of the writing," your quote would certainly be harmful to the sale of the book.

Permission To Copy

The author of a work that incorporates quotations or any form of copied material from copyrighted works has the responsibility to obtain permissions. These permissions should be in written form and constitute a simple, clear statement of the permission to copy, including a specific definition of the content as well as where and how permission is granted to copy it. Such a permission should include a statement of the form in which credit is to be given. The publisher should maintain files of all such permissions, together with statements of any special provisions. Such permissions may be, but rarely are, given in a form that allows the publisher to grant permission to others to extract and copy the material on a secondary basis, even though it may be incorporated in material for which the publisher owns the copyright.

Protection for Your Own Work

In order to claim copyright for your work, you must place a copyright notice in a location that brings it readily to the attention of anyone concerned. In the past, the rules were more rigid, but it is still common, though no longer mandatory, to place the copyright notice on the title page of a book, the first page of a journal, the title frame of a motion picture, and so on. There is an international agreement called the Universal Copyright Convention that requires that the notice include the circled ©, the word copyright, the year, and the name of the owner of the copyright. Generally in the United States, the © or the word copyright (or its abbreviation copr.) is sufficient to satisfy the law. It is certainly desirable to conform with these formalities. A number of Latin American countries do not subscribe to the convention, and adding the phrase "All Rights Reserved" at least puts potential infringers on notice in a way that can be defended as a clear statement in their courts, and therefore provides some protection.

Perhaps the most important, and certainly the least widely understood, fact is: You automatically own the copyright to your work from the moment of its creation in observable form.

Filing and Registration

United States law says that two copies of a work bearing a copyright notice are to be forwarded to the Copyright Office of the Library of Congress within 90 days of the publication date. There is no fee, and failure to comply in no way diminishes the legality of the copyright. Many writers rely on this basic protection and don't bother to file. The advantages are set forth below. If a question with respect to infringement arises, it may prompt the Register of Copyrights to request registration, and in this case you are legally required to comply.

Although registration is not required to obtain or maintain legality, most major works and published books are registered for two principal reasons. One is that registration establishes a public record of the details as set forth in the application form. The other reason is that registration is a required basis for an infringement lawsuit and, if made within 90 days of publication, provides some legal advantages. If you have not filed within the 90-day period after publication, there are some legal disadvantages. For example, if you file an infringement suit, you are required to prove the amount of the infringer's profit and that the infringer's profit did not come from a market that is uniquely available to the infringer and would otherwise have been available to you. You also must pay your own attorney's fees.

If you do register within the 90-day time period following publication, you may include your attorney's fees in the suit. Of greater importance, you may sue for statutory damages. This means that you need not prove the amount or source of the infringer's profit, but you may sue for an amount per copy that the infringer creates, and this amount is established by statute. In some instances, this can mean a great deal more income, more easily obtained, from an infringement suit.

The cost of registration is currently $10 and requires filing two copies in the Copyright Office. In the case of full-length theatrical motion pictures or similarly valuable illustrated books, the Copyright Office may return the copies to you upon request.

There are a number of different specialized copyright forms for purposes of registration. A list of nomenclatures as well as samples may be found in reference books or obtained by writing to the Copyright Office, Library of Congress, Washington, D.C. 20559.

Subsidiary Rights

There are a wide variety of subsidiary rights. Most should be covered in the agreement between the author and publisher to determine how to divide income from subsidiary rights. The subsidiary rights most commonly considered are as follows.

Paperback rights. When a book is launched in hardback form, subsequent publication in paperback form may involve another publisher, and the original contract should incorporate that possibility.

Reprint rights. Usually such rights involve collections, anthologies, and the like, which sometimes may have substantial value.

Serial rights. Sometimes a book or a scientific paper will be serialized prior to full publication under First Serial Rights. Second Serial Rights refer to serialization after the book or article has been published in complete form. Both are within the domain of the legal copyright that originally belongs to the author and, if anticipated, should be covered in a publishing contract. There are many other possibilities, including book club rights (generally at a price less than the published price). Every form of copying is covered.

Public Domain

When any work is said to be in the public domain, it means that it is free from copyright or patent, and thus is the property of the public. To copy any copyrighted work, it is prudent to obtain written permission unless the copied material is very clearly within the province of fair use. The law leans toward protecting the original author and publisher of a work, even though through some oversight the law has not been complied with rigorously. For example, it might be possible for an experimental press run to release a few initial copies of a book without the copyright notice. If you happen to copy from such a book, the lack of a copyright notice may not prevent an infringement suit. Hence it is important to check very carefully before taking such an action. The law tends to be lenient about almost any oversight with respect to the actual copyright notice, but it is so easy to comply that it would be foolish to overlook deliberately the © and other important details.

Where no copyright has ever existed, as in pamphlets, books, or other material published by the United States government, or when a copyright has expired and not been renewed, the work is clearly public property and no publication problem exists. However, there are some possible traps. The works of Charles Dickens are certainly in the public domain, but that designation does not necessarily apply to a translation into another language nor to annotations, footnotes, or any modification of the original material. It is important to bear in mind that even with works written centuries ago, any new versions, translations, notes, and comments may be subject to copyright.

Works published in the United States prior to 1906 are generally free of copyright problems because the copyright law specified a time limitation of 28 years plus a renewal for an additional 28 years. But this is not so in many other countries where copyrights from that era extend to 50 years beyond the death of the author. Thus a work originally published in the United States before 1906 might be in United States public domain but still protected in England, for example.

Works Made for Hire

The basic concept of this terminology is that when any copyrightable work is generated by someone who is paid to do so, the employer is the legal author and owns the copyright. It is not always obvious whether this provision is applicable. A typical exclusion might be an autobiography or even a fictional novel commissioned by a publisher. According to the most recent law (discussed at further length below) the duration of a copyright based on the made-for-hire principle is 100 years beyond the time of creation or 75 years after publication, whichever is shorter.

Duration and Legal History

On January 1, 1978, Public Law 94-553 became effective in federal law, incorporating substantial changes and eliminating for the future (but not with respect to the past) the common law copyright within the jurisdiction of the states. The most significant, but by no means the least complex, of the changes has to do with copyright duration. With a few complex and relatively unimportant exceptions, the basic new law is that a copyright is legally effective for 50 years after the death of the author. When two authors own the copyright jointly, it runs for 50 years beyond the death of the one who lives longest. If a work is published under an assumed name and the correct name of the author is unavailable, the duration is set to the shorter of the two terms set forth above for works made for hire.

There is an interesting aspect to the recent law having to do with the author's direct heirs. Independently of the terms of the contract with the publisher, the author's heirs may demand the transfer of ownership in the copyright to them 40 years after the contract with the publisher or 35 years after actual publication, whichever is the shorter time, provided their demand is registered in the Copyright Office two years before termination of the shorter of these two periods. Thus, if the author dies 35 years after the publication date, the author's heirs might own the copyright for 50 years. This law applies only to works published after January 1, 1978, the date it became effective.

Summary

Any and all use of copyrighted material should be considered and protected with great care. Curiously, the very act of asking permission, as a matter of courtesy, may mitigate against you in some instances because it may be viewed as presumptive evidence that you did not regard your publication as properly coming under fair use.

KEYWORDS:

- Typeface

- Hyphenation

- Justification

- Character
  Spacing

- Kerning

- Tracking

Donald McCunn has authored several popular computer tutorial books as well as the PC-based typesetting program ALEXANDER. He can be reached at Design Enterprises of San Francisco, P.O. Box 14695, San Francisco, California 94114.

Essay Synopsis: In typesetting the subtle variations of spacing between characters, words, and lines are critical issues. Indeed, powerful dedicated typesetting machines are needed to deal with these subtleties, and to produce final copy of high enough quality to be accepted for national publications, commercial packaging, and other highly competitive visual documents.

This essay offers a look at the rudiments of typesetting, with definitions of some important terms, examples of quality output, and comparison tables for typesetting equipment. In this essay you will learn about letterspacing, tracking, hyphenation, justification, and how typesetters view the trade-offs in choosing between traditional and desktop options.

3

Features of Conventional Typesetting Systems

Donald McCunn

Desktop publishing is the new kid on the block in a technology that has been evolving for hundreds of years. It offers some exciting new potential, but inevitably it must be measured against the time-honored standards of existing technology if it is to be accepted as a viable communication tool. The problem becomes: How do you establish standards to evaluate the capabilities of the software and hardware of desktop publishing?

Any graphic arts endeavor must combine subjective design decisions and the physical capabilities of the system. I will not attempt to discuss subjective design decisions like those that combine traditional principles of art with current trends and fashions. These decisions are largely a matter of personal preference, vary from year to year, and are dependent on the people who operate the equipment. What I will do is describe the physical capabilities of conventional typesetting systems and show how they affect design aesthetics.

You may be asking yourself, Why should I care about the capabilities of conventional systems? Doesn't desktop publishing represent a revolution that will usher in new techniques in communication and eliminate the need for the old systems? If you take this attitude, you are in fact attempting to reinvent the wheel, unaware that experience has shown round wheels function better than square ones. The art of publishing makes the hard work of writing, editing, designing, and producing a document seem effortless. If you want to be an effective communicator, you must discover what is involved in the hard work of traditional publishing in order to integrate the new technology effectively. You also must learn to evaluate the aesthetics of publishing, not from your own perspective, but from the perspective of your audience.

Evaluating Conventional Typesetting Systems

To evaluate the capabilities of conventional typesetting systems, I divide this description into physical attributes (such as resolution, speed, and font selection), control of design aesthetics (such as letterspacing and kerning), and formatting functions (such as margin indentations and tabular material).

The physical attributes can be determined easily by simply looking at the literature that describes the different systems. To understand the way systems control design aesthetics and format functions, we must examine the codes used by different typesetting systems.

Computer systems operate from codes that tell the equipment what to do. These codes either control the content of the output or the format. For example, the ASCII decimal code 65 tells a wide variety of output devices to produce an *A*. For the control to end one page and start a new one, printers respond to the ASCII decimal code 12 (or Form Feed), while PostScript devices require the code "showpage."

Although one premise of desktop publishing may be that the codes that control the format should be invisible to the operator, conventional typesetting systems require that you embed these controls in the text stream. This means that to understand the capabilities of conventional typesetting systems, all you have to do is to look at the codes they use.

Although the specific codes used by a given typesetting system may be different from the codes used by any other, the concept of what the code is supposed to do is universal. For example, to set the basic margins of the text to 27 picas of typeset length, the AM Varityper CompEdit requires **$LL2700**, the Compugraphic MCS/ACI uses **<LL27>**, and the MagnaType front-end for Linotype responds to **<CC27>**. Although some codes are universal, such as the line length control, others are unique to the capabilities of a given system. This discussion focuses on the typesetting concepts represented by the universal codes and the special functions revealed by the unique controls.

Physical Attributes

The physical attributes of conventional typesetting systems include the resolution and speed of the output and the range of available typefaces and special characters. These attributes are of primary importance to high-volume type buyers, such as book designers, magazine art directors, newspaper publishers, and type shops.

The future of desktop publishing will be markedly different depending on whether the desktop publishing industry attempts to woo these high-volume type buyers and the investment dollars they control, or whether the industry remains content with converting the corporate market from typewritten to typeset reports and documents.

High-volume type buyers are for the most part creating documents that are published in a commercially competitive environment. Compromise in quality or the uniqueness of a design may mean a significant loss in sales that quickly dissipates any economies or conveniences offered by desktop publishing technology.

Resolution

Resolution is the most obvious issue in examining the quality of type. Early typesetting systems used film masters created by photographing images three feet high and reducing this image to 11-point type. CRT Typesetting systems were introduced next and relied on digitally produced characters. Although the resolution of these characters does not match the earlier film images, CRT systems offer more control over the shape and size of the characters. The current resolution of CRT systems varies from 975 to 5,300 scan lines per inch.

The 300 dots per inch used by laser printers in desktop publishing clearly does not meet the lowest resolution of a CRT typesetting system. One of the problems with laser printers is the physical size of the toner particle. In order for laser printers to be capable of proofing copy prior to typesetting, they must achieve a resolution of 1,000 dots per inch and the toner must be ground to a finer size.

Speed

Conventional typesetting systems that offer optimum quality are usually fairly expensive, ranging from $50,000 to several hundred thousand dollars. To make a system such as this cost-effective, the speed must be adequate for a high-production environment. Typically these typesetting systems produce from 600 to 3,000 lines per minute. A laser printer operates at approximately 300 lines per minute, if graphics are minimal.

The problem with desktop publishing systems is that merging graphics is time-consuming. For example, a full-page halftone illustration at 300 dots per inch requires as much data to create as 333 pages of straight text. If you increase the resolution to 1,270 dots per inch, you quadruple the time required to set the image. It would take far more time to typeset this image than it would to use conventional camera and hand-stripping techniques.

At the request of their customers, Intergraphics, a typesetting service bureau, investigated adding desktop publishing capabilities to their current typesetting system. They discovered that a single page could take as long as 13½ hours to typeset. They considered that even taking a few minutes a page was too long in comparison to their current production standards. These time considerations would mean lower volume for fewer customers, which would force Intergraphics to raise their rates.

Typeface Selection

Desktop publishing systems simplify the process of merging text and graphics, but those systems currently are limited in the variety of text typefaces that are available. The type book for the well-established Linotype 202 lists more than 1,800 typefaces. Adobe Systems lists 20 typefaces for the new Linotype 300 that uses its PostScript system. They claim to be adding 20 new typefaces each quarter. At that rate of development, it will be 20 years before Adobe is able to match the selection of the older system. Figure 3-1 shows samples of a variety of typefaces.

Some designers are so spoiled by the riches available to them that they select the type shop for a given job based on whether it has a specific typeface. Other designers specify type based on the capabilities of the type shop they want to use. But most professional typesetting services usually have between 200 and 300 typefaces available to meet their customers' requirements.

Pi Characters, Swashes, Small Caps, and Non-English Characters

Related to typeface selection is the availability of special Pi characters, such as bullets, boxes, check marks, stars, and arrows. Some

SERIF FACES:

Times Roman, American Typewriter, Baskerville, Zapf Book, Caslon Antique, Melior, **Souvenir,** Century Schoolbook, Memphis, Benguiat, Bodoni, Clearface, Goudy Old Style, Korinna

SANS SERIF FACES:

Helvetica, Bauhaus, Serif Gothic, Optima, Kabel, Eras Book, **Fritz Quadrata,** Eurostile Extended

DISPLAY FACES:

Broadway, *Park Avenue Script,* **Rainbow Bass,** Linotext, **Nubian, Futura Black,** *Mistral*

UNIVERS TYPEFACE VARIATIONS:

Light, *Light Italic,* Medium, *Medium Italic,* **Bold,** ***Bold Italic,*** **Black,** ***Black Italic***

SPECIAL CHARACTERS:

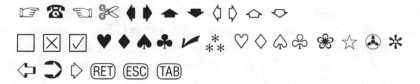

Figure 3-1. Typeface variations and special characters.

typefaces offer special versions of characters with swashes that can make an effective difference in display work. Small caps are specially designed uppercase characters that are the height of the body of the lowercase characters (the x height). And typesetting companies (such as Compugraphic and Linotype) have a variety of faces for non-Roman languages, such as Greek, Hebrew, Thai, Arabic, and Russian, as well as the phonetic alphabet.

Adobe is to be commended for its selection of Pi characters, the Zapf Dingbats, and Sonata Music fonts, but they still have a small sampling of the characters offered by conventional typesetting systems.

Controlling Design Aesthetics

Most typesetting systems offer a variety of codes to control design aesthetics. They can be grouped under the classifications of hyphenation, justification, and character spacing. Although simple systems have limited controls, more sophisticated systems provide the designer with a range of decisions to establish what is acceptable and what is not.

Hyphenation

Hyphenation is the process of connecting two words or dividing long words between two lines. In copy that is set with a ragged-right margin, hyphenation prevents excessive variation from one line to the next. In copy that is justified, hyphenation minimizes the amount of space added between words and letters to maintain parallel left and right margins. Figure 3-2 shows samples of text set with varying hyphen and spacing controls.

The most fundamental decision you need to make is whether you want hyphenation to occur. Typesetting systems allow you to turn hyphenation off and on at any point in the text. For example, you may have justified text with hyphenation enabled, but if you are going to include tabular material, you may want items within a column of the table to remain unhyphenated.

Another control is called a discretionary hyphen. It allows you to specify the appropriate hyphenation points for words that the typesetting system does not hyphenate correctly. These may include technical and foreign terms. Sophisticated systems allow you to add these terms

Hyphenation Off
This example implements evaluation of hyphenation and justification by employing exceedingly lengthy words contained within narrow margin parameters.

Hyphenation On
This example implements evaluation of hyphenation and justification by employing exceedingly lengthy words contained within narrow margin parameters.

Letterspacing Off
This example implements evaluation of justification and letterspacing by employing exceedingly lengthy words contained within narrow margin parameters with hyphenation disabled. Letterspacing is disabled for this paragraph.

Letterspacing On
This example implements evaluation of justification and letterspacing by employing exceedingly lengthy words contained within narrow margin parameters with hyphenation disabled. The maximum amount of Letterspacing allowed for this paragraph is ⁴/₅₄ of an EM Space.

Typesetting Spaces (12 Point Type)

EM Space| |, EN Space| |, Thin Space||

Spaces in Units: One |, Four ‖

Insert Space| |

(or) Insert | | Space

(or) Two Equal Width | | Insert Spaces | | In One Line

Figure 3-2. Variations of typesetting hyphenation, letterspacing, and fixed spaces.

to a hyphenation dictionary for the current job, while others require that you specify the discretionary hyphen in each occurrence of the word.

In addition to these basic hyphenation controls, sophisticated typesetting systems allow you to specify the minimum number of characters preceding and following a hyphen. There are also controls that allow you to specify the maximum number of sequential hyphens and whether the last word in a paragraph should be hyphenated to prevent forced justification of the next to the last line.

The better systems are able to perform automatic hyphenation in multiple languages. For example, the MagnaType typesetting front-end system supports hyphenation in English, French, Spanish, Italian, German, Danish, and Portuguese.

Justification

Justification is one of the standard options of typesetting systems. When it is specified, the space between words expands and contracts to make the right margin parallel to the left. However, there are limits to the expansion and contraction of the spaces between words specified as the minimum, maximum, and optimum (or ideal) word space. Loosely speaking, the optimum word space should be approximately the width of the capital *I*, the minimum should be half this width, while the maximum word space should be the width of the lowercase *n*. Studies have shown that exceeding these limits, called forced justification, reduces the legibility of the document. Compare this to the justification used in many word processing programs where multiple spaces are added between words to justify the margins, completely violating conventional design aesthetics and ignoring every study of legibility ever made.

The controls used to specify word spacing are usually given in fractions of an em space. An em space is the width of the type height. This means the physical width of the em space increases and decreases with the type size. For example, an em space for 12-point type is 12 points wide (there are approximately 72 points per inch), while an em space for 24-point type is 24 points wide. Because the word space control is related to the height of the type rather than the width of the characters, the word space control should be reduced for condensed type and increased for expanded typefaces.

One way to minimize forced justification in typesetting is to allow letterspacing. Letterspacing can be used in lines with loose spacing to add unit spaces (one-fifty-fourth of an em space) between each character in a word and minimize the width of the maximum word spaces. If a line is being set tight, negative letterspacing can be used to remove units of space between characters so that the minimum word spacing can be larger. In a line with negative letterspacing, the serifs of the characters may touch, whereas in a line with no letterspacing the serifs would not touch. Usually the range of letterspacing allowed is minimal.

All typesetting systems allow you to specify whether or not letterspacing is to be used. More sophisticated systems allow you to specify the maximum amount of positive and negative letterspacing.

Related to justification is the typesetting control that allows you to specify whether punctuation is to "hang" in the margin. Some characters, such as hyphens, periods, and quotation marks, are lighter in color than alphanumeric characters. When hanging punctuation is not used and these characters appear in the left or right margin, the margin appears to be slightly notched. When hanging punctuation is enabled, these characters are allowed to extend into the margin slightly to create an aesthetically pleasing margin. Hanging punctuation must be carefully adjusted for the particular typeface being used.

Character Spacing

Character spacing is used extensively in typesetting to control the amount of white space for paragraph indents, extra spacing between letters for headings, reduced spacing between letters for larger type sizes, and special adjustment between pairs of characters for kerning.

In order to control all the variations, typesetting systems have a number of codes for spacing as shown in Figure 3-2. Some of these controls indicate a space of a given width (the em space) while others control the general spacing between characters: word spacing and letterspacing for justification.

The controls for individual spaces include the following:

Em Space — A space that is the width of the type height.

En Space — A space that is one-half the size of the em space.

Figure Space — A space that is the width of the numeric digits "0" through "9." Most typefaces are designed with all of the numeric digits the same width for tabular applications. The figure space is used to keep these columns aligned. For example, the figure space can be used to align $1.00 under $10.00.

Thin Space — A space that is usually one-third the width of the em space.

Current Optimum Word Space — This may or may not be the same as the thin space.

Justifying Word Space — The space used between words that expands and contracts to justify the margins.

Fixed Space in Points — This control allows you to specify a given width in points. Some systems allow you to specify negative spacing as well. For example, the Compugraphic MCS control **<BP24>** specifies a negative width of 24 points.

Fixed Space in Units — Unit spaces are based on a fraction of an em. For most systems, one unit space is one-fifty-fourth of an em space. Older typesetting systems use one-eighteenth of an em. The fixed space in units allows you to specify either a positive or negative number of unit spaces. The physical width of this space varies with the type size just as the em space does.

Insert Space — The insert space expands as necessary to fill the unused space between margins. When an insert space occurs in a line, word spaces become the optimum width.

The terminology used to identify general character spacing controls is often misused. The following definitions are meant to correct this confusion.

Letterspacing — The spacing between characters that expands and contracts evenly to justify a given line when the word spacing parameters are exceeded. Some systems only add positive letterspacing; others use both positive and negative letterspacing. The amount of letterspacing used is calculated automatically by the typesetting front-end for each line as required.

White Space Expansion and Reduction — The amount of white space between characters is expanded and contracted by a specified amount at the designer's discretion. For example, a designer may specify that headings are to be expanded by three unit spaces between all characters. White space expansion and reduction are enabled and disabled by embedding controls in the text where the spacing is to be altered.

Tracking — Tracking is a variation of white space reduction and expansion. The main difference is that with the white space control, the amount of the expansion and reduction is specified in units, while tracking refers to a table built into the system for the typeface being used. Track 2 is the standard spacing between characters, Track 1 expands the spacing, and Track 3 reduces the spacing (see Figure 3-3).

Kerning — Kerning is the amount of space between a specific pair of characters. It is used to reduce the space between characters such as "Yo" and "To." For a more extensive description, read on (see Figure 3-3).

Kerning

Kerning requires very precise control of the spacial relationship between character pairs. It is accomplished by reducing the unit space between characters and it must be based on the specific typeface being used (see Figure 3-3).

Typesetting systems provide automatic kerning for text based on kern tables built into the system. For example, the MagnaType front-end supports up to 1,500 kern pairs for each typeface being used. This is essential if words such as "To" are to be consistently kerned.

It is also important to have a manual kerning capability for display type, such as chapter titles. This is important because the space between characters is more apparent in large type sizes than it is in small type sizes. The MagnaType front-end has two separate kern controls. One kern control adds to the value of the automatic kern table. The other kern control replaces the value in the kern table.

Another decision that must be made is whether the number "1" is to be kerned. For most typefaces, the numeric digits "0" through "9" are all the same width. This allows tabular material to be typeset with aligning numbers. However, all the numeric digits except "1" and "7" are composed of two vertical strokes: "0," "2," "3," "4," "5," "6," "8," "9." The diagonal stroke of the "7" and the single stroke of the "1" should occupy less space than the other digits. Sophisticated typesetting front-ends allow you to specify whether the "1" should be kerned. If it is being set within the text stream, the kern option should be on. If it occurs in a table, the kern feature should be turned off.

Another variation of kerning reduces the space between the characters fi, ffi, fl, ffl, and ff to create ligatures, a grouping of two or more characters on the same body of type. When the fi ligature is created, the dot of the *i* is left off. This reduces the visual confusion between the dot of the *i* and the ball of the *f*. Ligatures are usually special characters in the type font and are designed for optimum appearance. For some typefaces they are inappropriate.

It is important to remember that these variations of kerning must be used with discretion. For example, a ligature in a heading with ex-

Reduced White Space with a value of 2
Reduced White Space with a value of 1
Standard White Space
Expanded White Space with a value of 1
Expanded White Space with a value of 2
Expanded White Space with a value of 3

Tracking is disabled for this line.
Tracking with a value of 1 is used for this line.
Tracking with a value of 2 is used for this line.
Tracking with a value of 3 is used for this line.

Kerning Off:
AT AV Av AW Aw AY Ay FA LT LV LW LY OA OV OW OY PA P. TA Ta
Te TO To Tr Tu Tw Ty T. VA Va Ve Vi VO Vo Vu WA Wa We we WO Wr
Wu Wy Wo YA Ya Ye Yo yo Yu Y.

Kerning On:
AT AV Av AW Aw AY Ay FA LT LV LW LY OA OV OW OY PA P. TA Ta Te TO
To Tr Tu Tw Ty T. VA Va Ve Vi VO Vo Vu WA Wa We we WO Wr Wu Wy Wo
YA Ya Ye Yo yo Yu Y.

Kerning is Typeface Dependent:

VAT, VAT, VAT, VAT, **VAT,** VAT, VAT, **VAT,** VAT,

The CCI and MagnaType Front-Ends have a control that allows you to
specify whether the numeral 1 is to be Kerned.

No Kerning	Kerned 1
1900–1901	1900–1901
1911–1914	1911–1914
1914–1924	1914–1924

Ligatures are Typeface Dependent:
fi fi, fi fi, fi fi, fi fi, fi fi, fi fi, fi fi, fi fi, fi fi, fi fi, fi fi, **fi fi,**
fi fi, fi fi, fi fi, fi fi, fi fi, fi fi, fi fi, fi fi, fi fi, fi fi, **fi fi,** *fi fi,*

**Figure 3-3. Variations of typesetting white space, kerning, and ligature
controls.**

panded white space appears unnatural. Ligatures and kerning can create visual problems if you are using letterspacing.

Fractions in typed copy are frequently shown as "1/2." But in typeset copy this can be combined to create "½." In some systems the combined fraction is a special character while in more sophisticated systems, the front-end software can build fractions for any combination of numbers.

To people who have not set or purchased type, this fanaticism with kerning may seem excessive, but a local type shop in San Francisco that does a lot of advertising typography has one person proofing for kerning for every keyboard operator. You probably are exposed to their work and the work of others like them almost every day of your life but you are not aware of results, except at a very subliminal level.

Formatting Functions

Formatting functions establish the overall appearance of the text on the page. These controls affect the appearance of the main body of the text, individual lines used for headings, and extracts and lists within the text. This description divides these controls into text format, line format, margin indentations, and tabular material. Table 3-1 and Table 3-2 compare features between typesetting systems.

Text Format Controls

In addition to the basic text formats of justified and ragged-right copy, typesetting systems allow you to specify centered formats and ragged-left (flush left) margins (see Figure 3-4).

Line Format Controls

Headings are individual lines of copy that are made typographically distinct from the body of the document to indicate transitions in the text. In addition to changing the typeface and type size, format controls allow for extra line spacing above and below the heading; horizontal rules; and flush left, centered, and flush right formats that differ from the basic text style. A special control, called zero line spacing, allows multiple heads within a single line of text, such as a combination of flush left, centered, and flush right formats.

Table 3-1. Table summarizing sample hyphenation, kerning, and typeface enhancement controls.

	Autologic	CCI (Zeta)	Compugraphic	CRTronic	Itek Quadritek	MagnaType	MycroTek	OMNI	Penta	RayPort	Varityper
HYPHENATION & JUSTIFICATION											
Maximum Letterspace Expansion	•	•	•	•	•	•	•			•	•
Maximum Letterspace Reduction			•								
Maximum Consecutive Hyphens	•	•	•			•	•			•	
Minimum Chars. Preceding Hyphen	•		•	•			•			•	
Minimum Chars. Following Hyphen	•		•	•			•			•	
Minimum Chars. in Word	•		•	•			•			•	
Hyphenate Last Word in Paragraph		•	•			•				•	
Hyphenate Numbers			•			•					
KERNING											
Automatic Kerning from Table	•	•	•	•		•	•		•	•	
Automatic Kerning by Char. Shape										•	
Manual Kern Overrides Auto. Kern	•	•	•	•		•	•			•	
Manual Kern Adds to Auto. Kern	•					•	•			•	
Kern on Number One		•								•	
Create Ligatures Automatically	•	•				•			•	•	
Build Fractions Automatically		•				•					
Build Manual Shilling Fraction		•			•	•	•	•		•	
Build Manual Case Fraction										•	
TYPEFACE ENHANCEMENTS											
Pseudo Italic to Fixed Angle	•	•				•	•	•	•	•	
Pseudo Italic from 1° to 45°			•	•			•				
Pseudo Italic Slant Right Only	•	•				•	•	•		•	
Pseudo Italic Slant Left or Right			•	•							
Change Width of Type in Points	•	•	•			•	•	•	•	•	
Change Width Proportional to Height				•							
Underscore with Solid Rules	•	•	•	•		•			•	•	
Underscore and Skip Spaces				•							
Underscore Skips Descenders										•	

Table 3-2. Table summarizing some typesetting format capabilities.

	Autologic	CCI (Zeta)	Compugraphic	CRTronic	Itek Quadritek	MagnaType	MycroTek	OMNI	Penta	RayPort	Varityper
MARGIN INDENTATIONS											
Indent Left Margin for X Lines		•		•		•	•			•	
Indent Right Margin for X Lines		•		•		•	•			•	
Indent on Text from Left Margin	•	•		•		•	•	•	•	•	•
Indent on Text from Right Margin	•							•	•	•	
Indent on Text for X Lines				•					•		
Store Indent On Text Position		•				•				•	
Skew Left Margin on Diagonal	•	•				•				•	
Skew Right Margin on Diagonal	•	•				•				•	
Contour Left Margin Indent		•				•					
Contour Right Margin Indent		•				•					
TABLES											
Set Column Widths in Picas & Points	•	•	•	•	•	•	•	•	•	•	•
Set Column Widths Proportionally	•	•				•				•	
Set X Columns of Same Width	•	•				•					
Set Column Widths by Text	•	•				•				•	
Gutters with Vertical Rules		•				•					
HORIZONTAL & VERTICAL RULES											
Horizontal Rule of Fixed Length	•		•	•						•	
Justify with Rule	•	•	•	•	•	•	•	•	•	•	•
Justify with Double Horizontal Rules										•	
Vertical Rule of Line Space Height							•	•			
Vertical Rule of Specified Height			•	•						•	
Vertical Rules Set Baseline to Baseline	•	•				•				•	
Box Rule	•	•	•	•		•	•				
SPECIAL CONTROLS											
Size Type to Specified Measure	•									•	
Output Text for Color Separation										•	
Output Line Numbers of Text										•	

This is an example of text that is justified to create an even left and right margin. Hyphenation is allowed but letterspacing is disabled.

This is an example of text that is set flush left/ragged right. The ragged zone is controlled so all lines end within three picas of the full measure but no line ends within six points of the previous line.

This is an example of text that is set flush right/ragged left. The ragged zone is controlled so all lines end within three picas of the full measure but no line ends within six points of the previous line.

This is an example of text that is centered. The ragged zone is controlled so all lines end within three picas of the full measure but no line ends within six points of the previous line. The difference is spread evenly between the left and right margins.

This is an example of text that is set with contoured margins. This type of margin is frequently seen in advertising where the text wraps around illustrations. While it is rarely used in book work, it could be used to contour text around enlarged initial caps or decorations to create distinctive part openings. In order to create a contoured indent, you should xerox copy that is typeset to the full line length using the point size and line spacing of the text to be contoured. You can then draw the shape of the indent directly on this xerox and measure the appropriate indentation for each line.

This is an example of text that is Skewed from the left and right margins with a consistent angle. This could be accomplished using the same type of contoured indent as shown above, but that would require specifying the amount of indentation for each line. The Skew control allows you to simply specify the number of lines to be indented and the extent of the indent when the final line is achieved.

Figure 3-4. Variations of typesetting formats.

Indented Material

One measure of the sophistication of a typesetting system is in the variety of controls it provides to indent copy. These controls include specifying the indentation of the first line of a paragraph, indenting the left and/or right margins, indenting a margin for x number of lines, and creating hanging indents in which the first line of a paragraph is set to the full measure and subsequent lines are indented.

An advanced feature of MagnaType allows you to contour the text by specifying an indent of x number of picas for y number of lines. Up to 20 x/y combinations can be specified with full justification for smooth contours. Other controls include skewing margins to the left or right to create angled indentations.

You can also indent text by specific amounts by using a control that turns the typesetting system's flash (visual cue system) off and then back on. For example, if you have a dialogue occurring between three people, you may want their names to appear to the left side of the conversation. You can enter an initial line with the flash off that is the length of the longest name to be used, mark that location in the text, and turn the flash back on. To enter the conversation, cancel the indent, enter the name of the person speaking, restore the indent, and enter the comments of the speaker. This procedure would be repeated for each person's comments.

This same technique can be used to align outlines that use Roman numerals to identify individual items.

Tabular Material

Tabular material offers interesting formatting problems because the text within each element of the table can be of varying lengths, different line formats and type sizes, and surrounded by horizontal and vertical rules (see Figure 3-5).

Typesetting controls initially establish the width of each column. Items are then formatted within these columns using a flush left, center, or flush right control. Virtually any tabular format can be accomplished from these combinations.

Accessing Conventional Typesetting Systems

Conventional typesetting systems cannot be accessed through any existing WYSIWYG microcomputer program. This is because a

I. Basic Typesetting Values
  A. Initial Values
    1. Basic Controls
      a) Line Length (Measure)
      b) Line Format
        (1) Justified
          (a) Without Letterspacing
          (b) With Letterspacing
            (i) Minimum Letterspacing
            (ii) Maximum Letterspacing
        (2) Flush Left, Ragged Right
        (3) Centered
    2. Hyphenation
    3. Character Spacing Controls
  B. End of Paragraph Controls
II. Special Characters
III. Advanced Typesetting Features
IV. Advanced Typesetting Formats

Horizontal Table #9
Complex Table with Horizontal and Vertical Rules
(Graphics Character Set Alignment Controls)

Classes / Names	Group A			Group B			Group C		
	1	2	3	4	5	6	7	8	9
Section I									
Aaaaaa	●	○	●	□			●	○	√
Bbbb	○	□	√	○	●	○	□		○
Ccccccc		○	●		√	○	●	●	
Section II									
Xxxxxxx	√	●	○	○	□	●	√		○
Yyyyy	□		○	●		○		●	
Zzzzzz	●	○	○	√	●	○	○	□	○

Figure 3-5. Examples of text requiring special alignment controls.

WYSIWYG program must be able to make all the line-ending and page-depth decisions based on the same aesthetics used by the typesetting front-end. This would have to include all the controls described in this essay, the kerning and tracking tables as well as the character widths of all the typefaces you plan to use.

You can access conventional typesetting systems by preparing files using any word processing program. Many type shops work directly from microcomputer disks, while others prefer to have the files sent to them by telecommunications, which requires you to use a modem.

If you submit your file with only text and no typesetting codes, your savings over presenting the type shop with a computer printed manuscript will be negligible. If, on the other hand, you decide to code the document, you are responsible for any coding errors. For example, typesetting systems require a quad left at the end of every paragraph. If you miss a quad left, you have one paragraph where you wanted two. If you enter the type codes to start a chapter title but forget the type codes to restore the main text specifications, you have to pay to have the chapter set a second time. If you code the document accurately, you can save as much as 50 percent on your typesetting bills. On the other hand, if your coding is inaccurate, you may spend more by giving the type shop an electronic version of your document instead of letting them do all of the keyboarding.

I have addressed this dilemma with my multilingual word processing program Alexander by creating software that formats copy the way typesetting systems think. A conversion routine automatically merges type codes into the text to the specifications of the design of your document and the codes of the typesetting system you want to use. This allows you to verify the accuracy of the format using a standard computer printer, then typeset it on the finest equipment available using all of the aesthetics it is capable of addressing.

Summary

This is a minimal description of some of the more important functions offered by conventional typesetting systems. I trust it gives you some indication of the care, skill, and aesthetics that designers and typographers apply to their art to make it look effortless. As you approach your work, study the aesthetics of quality design, take every opportunity to learn from sources available to you, and develop an objective critical eye for the material you produce.

Production Notes

Typesetting from a microcomputer requires word-processing software for entering and coding text and a communication system for transferring the copy to the type shop. The type shop selects the typefaces they want to offer and controls aesthetic decisions through kerning and tracking tables. The typesetting front-end is the software that establishes how the text is to be formatted and output to the typesetting device. The output unit determines the resolution of the type and what typefaces will be available to the type shop.

The figures in this article were all created using Alexander for text entry on an IBM PC. The codes for the various typesetting systems were automatically embedded by this program. Four different typesetting systems were used to produce the actual art.

Type Shop: High-Tech Type, Alexandria, VA
Communication: Telecommunication via Modem
Front-End: Proprietary
Output Device: Linotronic 202
Figures: 3-1. Typefaces and Special Characters
3-3. Kerning and Ligatures from Different Typefaces
3-6. Table

Type Shop: H. S. Dakin, San Francisco, CA
Communication: Direct Media Reading
Front-End: OMNI International
Output Device: Linotronic 202
Figures: 3-2. Hyphenation On and Off
3-6. Outline

Type Shop: Mechanicals & Miracles, San Francisco, CA
Communications: Direct Media Reading (PC DOS Disk)
Front-End: MagnaType
Output Device: Linotronic 300 (Cora Coding)
Figures: 3-2. Letterspacing Variations
3-3. White Space and Tracking Variations, Kerning On and Off, and Kerning on the Number One
3-5. All Text Format Variations

Type Supplier: Design Enterprises of San Francisco, CA
Communications: Direct Wire Connection (with ASCII to 6 Bit TTS)
Front-End: Alexander
Output Device: Compugraphic Jr.
Figures: 3-4. Table Comparing Type Aesthetic Controls
3-7. Table Comparing Type Format Variations

Software Notes

Alexander is a multilingual word processing program with math, science, and music composition capabilities. The program automatically converts files for output to high-end typesetting systems such as the Linotype 202, Compugraphic MCS 8400, AM Varityper CompEdit, and Itek Quadritek 1600.

In addition to English, the program comes with character sets for more than 65 languages, including Western and Eastern European, Native American, African, Cyrillic, Greek, Hebrew, and phonetic alphabets. Additional language support features include right-to-left text entry (as well as left-to-right), key decals for non-Roman languages, and menus and prompts that can be translated into the native language of the user.

Science, math, and music support includes the capability of using a single keystroke to generate the multiple characters necessary for square roots, summation, integration, molecular structures, transformers, resistors, capacitors, musical staffs, and treble, bass and alto clef signatures. The special function keys are available for user assignment to support the editing functions, print enhancements, print formats, and the input of special characters or complete phrases.

A character generation program is included to meet the needs of the user with unique applications. The characters created are displayed on the screen exactly as they appear on the printouts using dot matrix printers, composite daisy wheel characters, LaserJet raster graphics images, or typesetting characters.

Alexander also allows editing by using a light pen or a mouse to control cursor moves, editing commands, and menu selection.

KEYWORDS:

- Layout

- Readability

- Hierarchy

- Grid

- Columns

- Visuals

Suzanne West, a graphic designer since 1971, is a partner in
West and Moravec in Palo Alto,
California specializing in the
needs of small businesses. Ms.
West's company produces
everything from eight-color
brochures to instruction manuals.
Ms. West teaches seminars
through UC Santa Cruz extension
on using the Macintosh as a
design tool, and teaches advanced typography at San Jose
State University. Her work has
won awards from AIGA, WADC,
and the New York Art Director's
Club.

Essay Synopsis: Good design is the result of the application of straightforward, easy-to-learn rules governing layout. Great design results from those rules applied with channeled creativity. The fact that desktop publishing now provides people with widespread access to page design means that many beginners may stumble.

This essay presents the basic rules of page design together with an illuminating perspective on our uneducated ideas about design: Most of us have been brought up with a monospaced typewriter mentality. In this essay you will learn about common misconceptions and preconceptions, about readability of type, the optimum line length, the correct proportion of white space to type, and the use of a grid to create columns.

4

Design for Desktop Publishing

Suzanne West

Desktop publishing tools are giving writers new capabilities which enable and sometimes require them to make choices about layout and typography. But exposure to the printed word hasn't necessarily prepared any of us to make page layout design decisions. We need a set of objective criteria — a structure — on which to base decisions. This need for structure becomes more critical as the size of the project (and the number of decisions) increases. A successful layout depends on how well we, as decision-makers, understand the intent of the author. In desktop publishing you are likely to be both designer and author — a distinct advantage over the old system.

Design advice abounds, and what makes a layout "good" often seems to be a matter of opinion. The most universal examples of good layout, though, tend to be simple and maintain a delicate balance between unity and diversity. This balance is easily upset — too much diversity, when we use too many of the options provided by the microcomputer, or too much unity, when we use the microcomputer as a typewriter.

The purpose of this essay is to provide the personal computer user with strategies for making appropriate decisions about typography, developing and maintaining the balance between diversity and consistency, and creating successful layouts — layouts that attract a potential reader and then don't interfere with reading. We will begin by defining terms, then develop two sample

RELATED ESSAYS:

3. Features of Conventional Typesetting Systems

5. Desktop Publishing: When It Makes Sense

15. Graphics Fundamentals

16. Page Layout Software

layouts so that you can see by example how we use a few rules of design to create different kinds of page layouts.

For about 500 years the printing press has carried on the Western tradition of the written word. Few changes have been made along the way in the approach to layout and typography. The traditional style that evolved continues to dominate the book layout to which we're constantly exposed and on which we base many of our (often unconscious) layout and typography decisions. For instance, our eye is trained to start at the top left of a page and move to the bottom right.

The typewriter has also had an impact on how we approach layout, and a formalized style based on typing has evolved. When we imagine creating a page of words, most of us will see widely spaced lines of type running the width of the paper with headings underlined or in all caps, the beginning of each paragraph indented exactly five spaces, and two spaces following each period. What we're seeing is the equivalent of a typed page, and the style of this page is a direct result of typewriter technology.

The typical typewriter offers a single weight and size of type. This type has a recognizable look because it has a fixed pitch (each letter is allotted exactly the same amount of space). It offers three choices of line spacing: single, one and a half, and double. We can emphasize information only by capitalizing, underlining, or adding extra space around a word. In order to get as many words as possible on a page, margins are small.

Because the typewriter has dominated communication in business and education, layout style has become centered and formalized around its technological limitations. And so while typewriters themselves have evolved, offering more options, our use of them has not. Even with the expanded capabilities of word processors and microcomputers, many of us still follow the rules dictated by the typewriter's technology. Many of us have unknowingly become locked into a typewriter mentality.

Making the Page More Readable

Legibility studies have been conducted off and on for over 200 years, although most have been in the nature of distance tests ("Can you read it from there, Fred?") and actually had little to do with reading. Early studies were not necessarily scientific in nature. Charles Babbage, for instance, "proved" that text set all in capital letters was the easiest to read — a conclusion contradicted by the studies performed both before and since. Another early conclusion was that serif type was easier to read than sans serif. In fact, some serif type is easier to read than some sans serif, but readability depends more on the shapes of the letter forms themselves than on serifs.

Newer, more accurate ways of testing readability factors are based on the structure of the eye and how it works when we read. Good design takes advantage of this information. For instance, we read a page best when the lines of type are between seven and ten words long (roughly 35 to 40 characters). The longer the line of type, the more the eye must move to reach the end of the line, and the more space must be added above and below the line. If there is not enough space between lines of type, the reader's eye jumps up or down a line. All of us have experienced reading the same line more than once or skipping a line entirely.

Armed with this information about readability, let's consider a typed page. With lines that go all the way across the page, double-spacing is needed for readability. With shorter lines, less extra space is needed between lines, and so we find that we are able to put the same amount of information on the page. The text lines are closer and the side margins are much wider. In fact, the page begins to look more like a typeset page from a book than a typewriter page, and we perceive the text as a column rather than as a texture covering the paper. Essentially we've squeezed the small chunks of white space from between the lines and combined it around the text. Now, because the text doesn't look as long, we may find that we're more motivated to read it. We even have space on the page for pictures and diagrams (see Figure 4-1).

Leaving the Right Amount of Space

In the ideal, classic book design of times past, text used up only about one-third of the page area. The other two-thirds were reserved for margins and an occasional reference element such as a page number. Books tended to be small and expensive — in the mid-1500's, a printed book cost about the same as a small farm. It was important to preserve the words by keeping them safely away from the edges of the paper.

Today, the generally accepted ratio of white space to text area is about half and half. This book, for instance, uses slightly more than half the page for text. A way of checking this easily is to measure the area of your page by multiplying the height by the width, then mea-

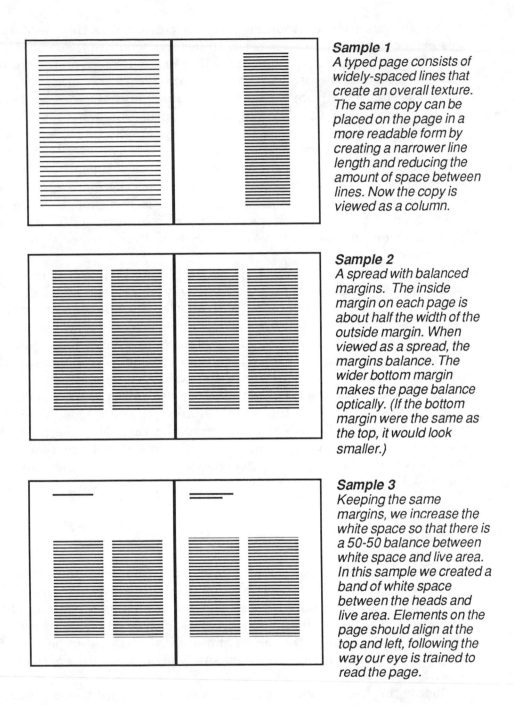

Sample 1
A typed page consists of widely-spaced lines that create an overall texture. The same copy can be placed on the page in a more readable form by creating a narrower line length and reducing the amount of space between lines. Now the copy is viewed as a column.

Sample 2
A spread with balanced margins. The inside margin on each page is about half the width of the outside margin. When viewed as a spread, the margins balance. The wider bottom margin makes the page balance optically. (If the bottom margin were the same as the top, it would look smaller.)

Sample 3
Keeping the same margins, we increase the white space so that there is a 50-50 balance between white space and live area. In this sample we created a band of white space between the heads and live area. Elements on the page should align at the top and left, following the way our eye is trained to read the page.

Figure 4-1. If you shorten the length of the lines of type so that they're more readable, you can also reduce the amount of space between the lines. The text now appears as a column rather than as an overall texture.

sure your live area, the area inside the margins where information is printed, in the same way. The live area should be about half the total area of the page. (*We tried this and were amazed to find that it's true. The margins of this book are one inch at the center gutter and side and three-quarters of an inch at the top and bottom. The area between the edges of the pages and the edges of the text is just about exactly equal to the area covered by the text. — Ed.*)

Often for the sake of economy, margins are decreased, causing the page to become crowded and less pleasant to read. There are many other variables besides margins to consider when economizing that won't interfere so much with readability or compromise the appearance of the page. We will take a look at some of these variables and discuss how they affect layout later in this essay.

Defining Layout Terminology

A layout is a composition of interrelated elements on a page. The term "elements" refers to each type of thing on the page. For instance, the pages in this book include such elements as the folio (page number at the bottom of each page), running heads (in italics at the top of each page), first and second level heads (large, boldface headings that structure the text), body copy (the bulk of the text), table headings, illustration captions, and so on. Because the elements are interrelated, a decision about one often affects decisions about others. Some of the terminology we'll be using may be familiar to you, but some of it may be new. And since design terms vary between specific fields of design, we'll briefly define our use of these terms.

Margins are the borders of space around the live area, the area in which most of the elements are arranged. The inside margin is the one closest to the binding or centerfold. The term gutter is often used in book publishing to mean the inside margin. In this essay we use gutter to mean the space between columns on a page. This isn't really a contradiction, since books seldom have more than one column per page — the inside margin is the space between columns as well. Reference elements, such as page numbers, chapter numbers, etc., are often placed in the margins. Within the live area are the text, visuals, and graphic elements.

Text refers to the body of type, which is generally in paragraph form. We use visuals as a catch-all term to includes photos, drawings, diagrams, and other nontext images. Graphic elements are content-free visuals such as bars, bullets, and boxes that help direct the eye.

Text is placed on the page in one or more columns. The formal structuring of the page into columns and fields is a grid (page layout software often refers to this as a template).

The layout may or may not have formal symmetry, equivalent or identical structure on either side of a central axis. Symmetry may be identical for every page, or mirror-image (symmetry by spread, facing pages).

In addition to the text type (under 14 points and readable as copy), there is display type (over 14 points and not necessarily readable as copy). The space between the lines of type is called leading. Within the columns, text may be aligned on both margins ("justified"), aligned on the left but not the right ("flush left"), or aligned on the right but not the left ("flush right"). An edge that isn't aligned is called "ragged."

Type Terminology

Type is a key element in layout, so we will discuss typographic terms briefly. Typographic terms, mostly remnants of metal type technology, persist in typesetting and desktop publishing.

Type is measured by points (a point is about $1/72$ of an inch), and layout is often measured in picas (a pica is 12 points). There are about 6 picas per inch. Type is referred to by point size. You can't just measure what you see because the point size actually refers to the height of the (now imaginary) block of metal (or body) that holds the letter. You can determine the point size of type only by comparing it with a preprinted sample. Even this may be inaccurate, since typeface designs with the same point size designation vary in the size they appear. Reducing standardization even further, each typeface manufacturer has its own version of a typeface. For instance, many of the typefaces used for laser printers are licensed from ITC (International Typeface Corporation). ITC typefaces may look larger than expected for a given size because the lowercase letters are larger than other versions with the same name and size (see Figure 4-2).

A benefit of desktop publishing is that when we specify a point size for a typeface we can see the results immediately — a definite improvement over sending it off to the typesetter with our fingers crossed. But be aware that these inconsistencies exist, since most microcomputers will continue to use this traditional system of measuring type and leading.

Some layout software offers the option of using points and picas. For instance, PageMaker has a menu item called "Preferences" that allows the user to specify points and picas for rulers. Many people prefer points and picas because they can work mostly with whole numbers rather than with fractions.

A Sample Project

We will discuss the design of a small brochure and develop two sample layouts to illustrate different ways to approach problems.

Our sample project is a brochure with an 8½ by 11 page size (a standard American paper size). Because we're printing on both sides of the paper, two pages will be viewed at once. This creates an 11 by 17 spread. We need to show a title, heads, subheads, and captions, and include from one to three visuals per page. These visual elements don't need to be located immediately below or next to a specific paragraph or sentence — just in the neighborhood on the same spread for easy access. Each visual has a brief, one-sentence caption.

Our concern here is to communicate specific information to a reader in an effective way. Just getting words on paper isn't enough

Alphabet
Alphabet
Alphabet

The texture of the page changes with the typeface being used. This example is ten point type with twelve point leading. This sample is Times.

The texture of the page changes with the typeface being used. This example is ten point type with twelve point leading. This sample is Helvetica.

The texture of the page changes with the typeface being used. This example is ten point type with twelve point leading. This sample is New Century Schoolbook.

These samples illustrate the differences between typefaces. All three samples of the word 'Alphabet' are 24 point type, but the visual size varies.

Also notice that each typeface uses a different amount of space because of the differences in their design. This affects the number of words that fit on a page, as well as the texture and overall look of the text.

Figure 4-2. Different typefaces available on the LaserWriter in the same nominal point size take up differing amounts of space.

today, as people are bombarded with printed information. We need to attract the reader first and then make reading as easy as possible. We begin by identifying the page and spread sizes, hierarchy (levels of information), relation of text to visuals, and number of visuals per page.

We will not address variables such as color, mood, or purpose. Here's why: Color should not affect layout, but rather enhance it. A good layout should be as effective in black and white as in color. Mood is something that should be reserved for art rather than communication, and is achieved as much by color as by layout. Specific purpose, beyond that of communication, is a secondary issue. This brochure layout could be used to sell high-pressure gas valves or handbooks for housebreaking iguanas.

Considering Hierarchy

Since most copy is divided into sections and subsections — a hierarchy of information — we need to identify the levels of the hierarchy (title, heads, first-level subheads, second-level subheads) before we begin. If we limit our hierarchy to four levels (including the title) it will be more readable.

Typographic decisions should be based in part on the hierarchy. Our variables include type style, size, weight, and space. We may augment these with graphic elements. The fewer the changes from level to level, the more consistent the page. Usually making two changes (such as size and weight) is quite enough. The changes can't be too subtle, or the reader will get confused. Creating samples before you begin working is a good strategy. With microcomputers this is a fast and easy way to compare ideas. Figure 4-3 shows two examples of visualizing hierarchy.

Examining the Grid

A grid is a preplanned network of guidelines that provides a system for organizing elements on the page. A page composed with a grid might be compared to a house built from blueprints, as opposed to a house in which the rooms were added randomly wherever they'd fit, with no particular plan in mind. Using a grid can ensure the consistency necessary to balance the diversity of items that will appear on the page.

Ready-made grids and templates are available. But, like ready-made house plans, they don't always suit your particular purpose, and

Heading

Subheading

SecondLevel Subhead

ThirdLevel Subhead Text aldilk ck
kldieus scilkdiek smc sl sdoek slnvn iekl ss
ien sdlfi ieskn vxlkvi eklnslij ilwns;ifnielcimei
die dm lx iekenrtixv ow weijfoisj viwlwjkd

Hierarchy Sample 1
*Each level is separated by
an additional line space
and is a progressively
smaller point size.
Leading is solid (for
instance, 18 point with 18
point leading) At the third
level, no extra space is
added and no new line is
started to separate it from
the text.*

H E A D I N G

SUBHEADING

SecondLevel Subhead

ThirdLevel Subhead
Text aldilk ck kldieus scilkdiek smc slsdoek
slnvn iekl ss ien sdlfi ieskn vxlkvi eklnslij
ilwns;ifnielcimei gkjk diedm lx iekenrtixv ow

Hierarchy Sample 2
*Only two point sizes are
used here. Hierarchy is
created by using all caps
and adding space. The
heading has extra spaces
between the letters. This
technique should be
used with discretion and
always separated by extra
line spaces.*

Heading

Subheading

SecondLevel Subhead

ThirdLevel Subhead Text aldilk ck
kldieus scilkdiek smc sl sdoek slnvn iekl ss
ien sdlfi ieskn vxlkvi eklnslij ilwns;ifnielcimei
die dm lx iekenrtixv ow weijfoisj viwlwjkd

Hierarchy Sample 3
*This example uses only
one size change and
relies on indents and line
spacing to differentiate
between levels.*

*In general, the fewer
changes made the better.
No change of typeface
was required for any of
these samples. Try some
samples of your own and
compare them.*

**Figure 4-3. These groupings are more similar than dissimilar. A few
changes can make a big difference in effect.**

since they can be interpreted any number of ways, it is important to learn the rules concerning their use. A grid isn't the final solution to layout, merely a device that helps you make some basic decisions about layout. For instance, the width of a column in a grid will determine your point size and even typeface, assuming your desired line length is 35 to 40 characters.

The larger the page, the more important it is to have a grid. Small pages, such as this book, usually allow only enough width for a single column. The larger the project (a manual versus a one-page ad), the more important it is to have a grid.

Creating Your Own Grids

Even if you're going to use ready-made grids, this exercise will help you understand more about why they exist. Our layout begins with the division of an 8½ by 11 inch page into columns. The columns and gutters determine the side margins. The columns, in turn, are determined by the typeface and size of text. Because column width and type are interdependent, you may need to go through the decision process several times before you achieve the desired result.

Text Type

First, let's be more specific in our definition of text type. Text type is usually between 9 and 12 points. More importantly, it is "normal" looking — no unusual characters (if you find that you are aware of the letter design as you read, that type style should not be used for text). The perfect text type is not only transparent (you aren't aware of it when you read), it presents an even texture on the page — you shouldn't see darker or lighter clumps of letters (one of the reasons Avant Garde is not recommended for text is that it creates an uneven texture). Most professional designers use few if any decorative typefaces. At best, decorative typefaces should be reserved for very specialized uses, and even then, never for paragraphs of text.

Some type has serifs (little "feet" on the letters, e.g., Times), and some is sans serif (no feet, e.g., Helvetica). Some people have a strong preference for one over the other. Each typeface is distinguished by variations in the weight of the stroke that makes up each of the letterfaces. The best choices for desktop publishing are serif typefaces that have very little difference between thick and thin strokes. Examples of these are Century Schoolbook, Palatino, Garamond, and Times. These have survived the tests of time and changing technology. If your preference is sans serif, the most appropriate (and perhaps only) choice for text is Helvetica.

For our example here we'll consider four options: Helvetica, Times, Palatino, and Century Schoolbook. Remembering that our most readable line length is 35 to 40 characters, we can look at a sample of each. Each of these has its own distinctive texture and look. Another difference is that each one takes up a different amount of space. Consider the examples. Helvetica and Palatino take up about the same amount of space. Times is the most space efficient, and Century Schoolbook the least. For our sample page we'll choose Palatino.

Column Width and Gutters

For our first sample layout we've chosen 10-point Palatino. To get 35 to 40 characters per line, our columns will need to be 12 to 13 picas wide. Either way, we can fit three columns onto an 8½ inch page width. The 12-pica column gives us more generous side margins, but the 13-pica column allows a few more letters per line. Both are reasonable choices. For our sample, we will use 13-pica columns. We'll choose to use 1½ pica gutters because these will prevent the reader's eye from jumping between columns (see Figure 4-4).

For our second sample layout, we've chosen 12-point Palatino. To get 35 to 40 characters on a line, our columns will need to be wider — 18 picas. This means that only two columns will fit on an 8½ inch page width. We'll use 1½ pica gutters here as well (see Figure 4-5).

(It is important to note that letterspacing may change with the type of software that is being used, affecting the number of characters that fit within a given line length. For instance, with the Macintosh there may be fewer characters per line in a MacWrite document than in a PageMaker document. The numbers we use here can only be general guidelines.)

Leading

The term leading originated in the days of metal type. The typesetter would insert strips of lead between the lines of metal type to increase the space from baseline to baseline. Leading is important — it affects the texture, readability, and amount of copy you can put on a page.

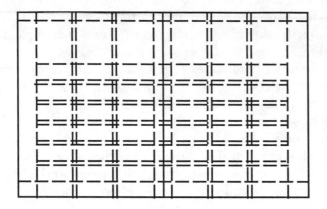

Three-column grid
Each page has 18 grid fields which can be used in different ways to create a variety of pages. This is a very flexible grid because it offers many placement options.

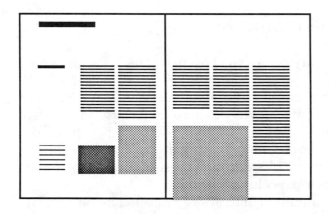

This thumbnail shows three visuals, captions, text, heading and subhead. The type 'hangs' from the grid lines. Text and visuals are separated so that the reader isn't blocked by a visual in mid-thought. The head jumps columns because it's out of the grid field area.

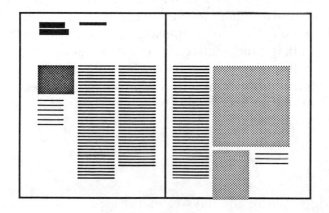

In this thumbnail the same elements are placed on the same grid. The text here is more continuous. The heading is split into two lines to maintain the column and the subhead lives at the top of the page in the second column.
In both samples the columns are ragged at the bottom—the new column starts with a new paragraph or subdivision.

Figure 4-4. Different text layouts on a three-column grid.

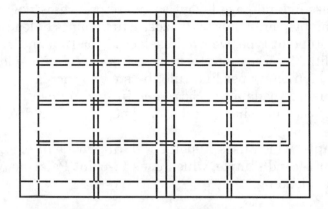

Two-column grid:
Each page has 8 grid fields which can be used in different ways to create a variety of pages. This is less flexible than the three column grid because it has fewer fields and therefore fewer options.
Some examples of how it can be used are shown here.

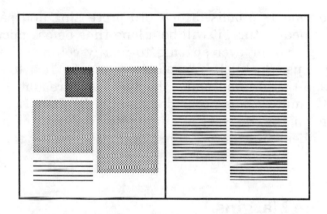

In the first sample, the left page has been used for the photos and heading so that it acts as an introduction to the text under the subheading on the right page. Because the grid fields are so large, many images don't fit neatly into them. The strategy here is to keep the gutters between the images equal.

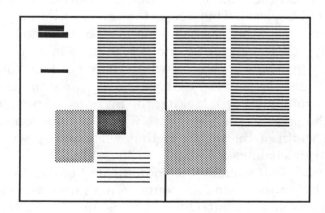

In the second example, the text hangs from the top margin and the visuals are forced to the bottom of the page. The subhead appears to float in space but is actually locked into the top left of a grid field. What sometimes looks like arbitrary placement isn't.

Figure 4-5. Different text layouts on a two-column grid.

Many word processing and page layout software programs now let you determine leading by points. For text sizes, 1 to 2 points of leading are standard. So for 10-point type, we would select 11- or 12-point leading. If you should find it necessary to increase your column width beyond the 35 to 40 characters-per-line rule, be sure to increase your leading as well to ensure readability. Extremes in leading can create interesting design effects for short blocks of type, but shouldn't be used for text.

For our first sample, which uses 10-point Palatino, we will use 12-point leading. For our second sample, which uses 12-point Palatino, we will choose 14 points of leading.

Justification

Even with the improvements promised for word processing and page layout software in the near future, it will be a long time before microcomputers have enough power over spacing to justify columns well. Therefore we choose to use flush left, ragged right type for text to ensure a more even page texture and make the type more readable. If your text isn't overwhelmingly long, consider manual hyphenation to get more regular line lengths. Be wary of automatic hyphenation, and don't have several hyphens in a row — this is very distracting to the reader.

Inside and Outside Margins

The inside margin (nearest the binding or centerfold) should never be less than ½ inch (about 3 picas). This keeps the text away from the binding and out of the curve if the page is bound in a book. Some laser printers automatically restrict margins to no less than ½ inch. Using wider margins not only gives the page more white space but helps hide the inconsistencies inherent in low-cost printing (uneven page registration, trimming, and ink flow). Making the margins asymmetrical adds interest to the page. For a spread, we want the outside margins about twice the width of the inside so that when the spread is viewed, the inside margins balance.

In our three-column layout sample, the columns and gutters left 9 picas to be shared between the inside and outside margins. We made the inside margin 3 picas and the outside 6. (This is about ½ inch for the inside and 1 inch for the outside.) In our two-column layout, we were left with 13½ picas for side margins. We made the inside margin 4½ picas and the outside 9.

Top and Bottom Margins

Our choice of type style and size has determined the columns that form the vertical lines on our grid. Now we can create top and bottom margins that relate to these. We will use a classic approach for our two-column sample, making the bottom margin match the outside (9 picas), and the top margin match the inside (4½ picas).

For contrast, we will use a more modern approach for our three-column sample, making the top margin one and a half times the inside margin (4½ picas) and the bottom three times the inside margin (9 picas). The bottom margins on both samples are much wider than the top. This is to correct for the optical illusion that causes the eye to see something placed in the measured center of a page as below center.

Ideally our page will have a 50-50 balance between margins and live area. Another way of saying this is that the ratio of the live area to page area is 1 to 2. Let's check the ratio of live area to page area on both our sample pages to see how close we are to these ideals. We can determine an area by multiplying the height by the width. For instance, the page area is about 51 by 66 picas, or 3,366 square picas. If we follow the same procedure for the live areas, we discover that if we used the entire live area we would be using about ⅔ of the page for each. The pages with this ratio would look organized because we have been systematic in our use of type and in our grid layout, but they would lack visual balance.

Grid Fields

The columns have determined the vertical lines for our grid, and these in turn govern our top and bottom margins. Horizontal lines between the margins will complete our grid to form boxes, or fields, on the page. There are a number of techniques for creating these grid fields — the most important thing is to make them uniform with gutters separating them.

For our two-column sample, we can create four grid fields in our live area, each 11½ picas high with 2-pica gutters. This gives us a page with eight grid fields.

For our three-column sample, we will create a section of grid fields, leaving a wide space between the fields and the top margin. This ensures that our ratio of white area to page area is maintained, and creates a horizontal flow. To allow more flexibility we want many grid fields. We will work from the bottom margin up to create six fields, each six picas high, with 1½ pica gutters between them.

Sometimes it is difficult to make grid fields fit into your margins exactly. Leaving a white area, as we did for our three-column sample, is one solution to this problem. Another is to adjust your bottom margin slightly. However you arrive at your grid, it's important that the field's area is consistent and that you know the basic rules for using it.

Using the Grid (Template)

Whether you use an existing grid or create your own, you need to follow some basic guidelines to use it effectively. The top and left of a grid field are the most important guidelines. Decide on a top field for your text and then be consistent.

If one of the columns will be empty, make it the column on the outside of the spread. On a single page, make it the column on the left. This creates the illusion that the blank space was planned — not as if you ran out of copy before you could fill the page.

The horizontal gutters between grid fields act as spacing guides between elements on the page. This gutter width would always be the governing space between visuals and visuals, visuals and captions, etc.

Avoid using arbitrary measurements. As a rule of thumb, use measurements created by your grid/margins, or multiples of them. Make elements fit completely into one or more grid fields when possible. If you create your grid before you create your visuals, you can format charts and diagrams to match. When visuals don't fit the grid fields exactly — for instance, if a photo needs to be wider than a single field but not as wide as two — try to make it end in the center of a field, and align it top and left.

Don't create an intricate alignment system. The simpler the system, the quicker the viewer can understand and "see" the structure and the relationships between objects.

Don't break the grid — that is, place an element arbitrarily on the page. The whole purpose of the grid, after all, is to ensure visual organization. Find other ways of creating interest on the page. Look at the examples carefully to see how the grid fields were used to create different effects, handle different amounts of information, and incorporate visuals and graphic elements.

Comparing Grids

Let's analyze our samples. The first has a three-column grid, asymmetrical margins, and text and visuals positioned within 18 grid fields (six fields high, three columns wide). A band of white space separates the title from the grid fields. The text is 10/12 Palatino. This grid offers us more flexibility but requires us to make more decisions. This would be a good multipurpose grid to use for many different printed pieces such as brochures, data sheets, and technical manuals. This one grid might be used to produce all the printed pieces within a small company.

The second sample has a two-column grid with eight grid fields (four fields high, two columns wide). The text is 12/14 Palatino. Bottom, inside, and outside margins on our spread are equal. This is a better grid for long sections of unbroken text and for more predictable content. It could also serve a wide variety of purposes.

Placing Visuals on the Grid

When visuals are introduced, page layout gets more complex but the results are often more interesting. A visual provides instant diversity (if only that it's different from the text), but too many visuals may create chaos. Here are some guidelines for using visuals on a page.

If you show a number of visuals, try clustering them, rather than spotting them evenly around the spread. You might even assign them a particular area — across the bottom or clustered in the center, so that the visuals have their own area.

Never interrupt a sentence or paragraph with a visual. If a visual must appear with a particular bit of text, try to place it next to the text, perhaps in an adjacent column. Do keep in mind that the viewer will be seeing the whole spread at once, not just a page, so you have many options for where to place your visuals.

If a similar image (such as a computer screen) appears regularly, especially if on sequential pages, find a consistent place for it. This way, your reader can find that particular kind of information easily. For instance, if your technical manual has several sequential pages with a screen image on each, make each screen the same size and put it in the same place.

If all the visuals are the same or similar in size, the spread will be too uniform. If two visuals must have the same emphasis, cluster them so that they're seen as a unit. Avoid stair-stepping (placing several pieces of art together so that their tops are staggered, one higher than its neighbor). This breaks the text and space into awkward areas that are difficult to deal with.

Using Graphic Elements

Graphic elements should be used sparingly, but can be very effective in breaking up text, emphasizing hierarchy, and adding interest to the page.

One of the most useful graphic elements is the rule line. Here are some examples of how the rule can be used: Use a wide rule above a main heading, a medium rule above a first-level subhead, and a fine rule above a second-level subhead. Or use a wide rule above a section heading and a fine rule after the last line of the section. (Note that we recommend placing the rule above the type rather than below, as an underline.)

Use rules above and below a block of text you want to segregate. This creates the same effect as a box, but doesn't require you to make your line length shorter as a box would. Limit your graphic elements to those that enhance communication rather than simply decorate the page (and possibly distract the reader).

Getting Started

It's important to get organized before you begin. You will not only work more efficiently, you'll be able to get the big picture before you begin. Collect everything that needs to be included in the printed piece before you begin. Create sample pages that include all or many of the elements you'll be dealing with, such as photos, diagrams, and levels of hierarchy. This will help you define problem areas before you actually get started, and help you select the best layout option for your particular problem. If you're working with an existing grid, make sure your elements fit the grid fields. If you're creating a grid, make choices that ensure that you have the flexibility you need.

Many designers create thumbnails — small sketches that help them think through the problem and let them see their ideas on paper. Creating sample pages is another way to get an overview of the project. Do thumbnails first because they take less time, then create sample pages of your best ideas to see if they will work for your particular project.

If you're restricted to a limited number of pages, make sure your copy length is realistic by doing some rough copy-fitting. Rather than relying on copy-fitting charts based on typesetting equipment that may not be accurate for a microcomputer, use your sample page to determine how many characters will fit per page.

Getting More on a Page

It's easier to create an attractive page if you don't have very much to put on it. If your document is copy-heavy, however, you need to consider some strategies for fitting copy onto the page without it losing its visual appeal.

Reduce the size of your visuals wherever possible and necessary. A smaller visual with white space around it has more impact than a large visual on a crowded page, although some visuals, particularly diagrams and computer screens, may need to stay a particular size.

Reconsider the typeface you've chosen. If it's a space gobbler, consider switching to something space-efficient, like Times. This can make a big difference over a few pages.

Consider how you're indicating paragraph breaks. If you're adding an extra line space, consider eliminating the extra space and using an indent instead. If you've used a point size for subheads that's larger than the text, consider reducing the subheads to the same size as the text and making them bold, at least if they appear in the columns. Often, reducing subheads to a slightly smaller point size reduces the number of lines they use.

If your copy is quite a bit too long and you have two extra points of leading, decrease this to one. If your copy is close to fitting, work with the line length. Sometimes hyphenating by hand will gain an extra line here and there. (If your document is a long one, this may be impractical.) Next, try increasing your line length by a half a pica — this, too, will gain you an extra line here and there without losing perceptible white space. If you really must reduce your white space, begin by decreasing the size of your bottom margin. Don't push the visuals down too far on the page, though, or the layout will get too bottom-heavy.

There are several things you shouldn't do to get more on the page, including making the bottom margin flush (which will probably mean having subheads near the bottom of the page), stepping up to a higher grid field with the text, reducing the point size so that there are too many characters per line, or reducing the gutter widths.

Summary

We have begun by discussing the effects of technology on our perceptions and sense of design. As microcomputers become more powerful, it is likely that our style of design will change as a result. Such a development in the rules of design will probably respect established rules of perception, especially of readability, such as having 35 to 40 characters per line, keeping half the page space live, and so on. The use of a grid is a powerful layout analysis aid, and it is important to match the inventory of your elements to the column widths and gutter and margin sizes of your page. Remember to keep your page layouts simple.

KEYWORDS:

- Cost Analysis

- Typography

- Design

- Production

- Print Specifi-
cation

- Quotations

Judith Maurier is an information designer and producer, and computer afficianado. She has had nearly 20 years experience developing and producing publications of all kinds, from magazines to software products — including user manuals, training materials, marketing collateral, and product packaging. She is co-founder of Publishing Power, Inc. (Palo Alto, Callifornia), which provides corporate publication services using both desktop and conventional techniques.

Essay Synopsis: There is a place for both traditional and desktop publishing. Desktop publishing systems are the cost-effective choice for small jobs without rigorous requirements for precision, and desktop publishing provides direct control throughout the production process. Traditional typesetting may be the preferred, less expensive approach for some types of jobs: those that require precision, those that are highly complex, or those that are very long. These are important and practical considerations for anyone shopping for a production company.

In this essay the author compares costs, production time, control factors, and quality, between a traditional typesetting house and a desktop publishing service. You will learn about pricing and comparing costs. The author provides a formal procedure for identifying and evaluating production phases in order to choose the appropriate process.

5

Desktop Publishing: When It Makes Sense

Judith Maurier

The desktop publishing revolution is upon us and, as with other revolutions, it is sometimes difficult amidst the revolutionary fervor to separate fact from fiction.

Personal computers are now capable of performing complex tasks of textual/graphic integration and page design that until now were the domain of computerized equipment costing upwards of $50,000. As the cost of computer systems capable of performing complex publishing functions has fallen below $10,000, we have watched the resulting rise of the new industry loosely called desktop publishing. Because of the relatively low cost of the hardware, many people have come to believe that desktop publishing is an inexpensive alternative to traditional publishing methods that rely on conventional typesetting and pasteup. In their enthusiasm, not many people have stopped to think about relative production costs. Desktop publishing is, after all, the most exciting development in the publishing industry since Gutenberg invented movable type!

Of course, for somebody with more time than money, out-of-pocket costs for an amateur publication created with desktop tools are cheap compared to professional typesetting. In the early days of desktop publishing, new systems were used to significantly improve the appearance of what would otherwise have been typewritten material. However, the emphasis on using low-cost desktop publishing systems has

RELATED ESSAYS:

1. Printing Production

3. Features of Conventional Typesetting Systems

changed from preparing materials that would otherwise be typewritten to preparing materials that would otherwise be typeset.

When amateurs use desktop publishing tools to create a "prettier" version of what they would otherwise produce using only a typewriter, they save substantially over having the material professionally typeset. However, when used by professionals for text/graphic integration and page design, desktop publishing methods do not necessarily guarantee the substantial and immediate savings that the great desktop publishing revolution hype would lead us to believe are possible.

Some Examples

When deciding whether to use desktop technology or traditional typesetting to produce a publication, there are complex factors other than cost that should affect your decision. While analyzing the comparative cost-effectiveness of available publishing methods, I will also explore a number of the more subtle (and powerful!) advantages that desktop publishing has to offer over traditional publishing. Here are two examples.

A Simple Job

A simple flyer can be produced with a Macintosh computer and LaserWriter printer. For the time being, let's omit from our figures the creative process of writing and designing the flyer. We first need to consider the costs of time it takes to type and lay out material that has already been written and designed:

Desktop Estimate:

Type and layout two pages:	.75 hrs @ $25/hr.	=	$18.75
Paste completed pages onto board:	.25 hrs @ $25/hr.	=	$ 6.25
Total cost of time:			$25.00
LaserWriter proofs:	2 @ $1.00	=	$ 2.00
Total Cost:			$27.00

Typesetter Estimate:

Typesetting:	.5 hrs @ $48.00/hr.	=	$24.00
Paste each piece of page onto board:	.5 hrs @ $38.00/hr.	=	$19.00
Total Cost:			$43.00

The rates used in this essay are in the middle range for representative professional services in the Palo Alto/San Francisco Bay Area at the time of this writing. You may find that rates differ in your area. You also may find that there are a number of publishing amateurs referring to themselves as desktop publishers who charge significantly less than the hourly rate used in the examples. You should also expect that these rates will vary over time — and not necessarily upwards. The point here is not to define what different publications should cost, but to offer a model for comparing the range of production options now available.

So far so good. The desktop alternative costs $27 and the typesetter $43: Going the desktop route represents a saving of almost 63 percent. Not exactly an insignificant cost saving over going the typesetter route! Our simple cost analysis of this job makes us favor the desktop publishing method over the typesetting method hands down. It makes one wonder what the result of a similar cost analysis would be for a more complex publication.

Complex Books

Our next example is about as complicated as the previous one is simple. I recently consulted with a publisher about producing a series of workbooks and guides, each one running around 200 pages in length. Each page would be filled with up to ten different art spots and type of different sizes and styles. The artwork was to be created in position on the page, thus reducing the total number of images that the computer would have to scan in order to digitize it. This would make it far easier to manipulate the artwork on the computer during page layout than if each piece of art were scanned separately. The author was to provide a typewritten manuscript. Different layouts would be designed for different exercises, but wherever possible, exercises would be written to fit within a common layout. Even so, each page was going to be unique.

The job was quoted in two ways: using a Macintosh-based publishing service and using a conventional typesetting house. Each outfit was given sample pages from the author and the same set of specifications. Each was asked to deliver typeset quality, camera-ready copy on boards marked up and ready for the printer. The Macintosh-based publishing service used a computerized scanner that retails for about $2,500 to digitize the art spots, a LaserWriter for initial proofs, and an Allied Linotronic L-100 for generating camera-ready copy. The typesetter used a more costly and more sophisticated combination of scanners and computers to generate camera-ready copy.

The desktop publishing service quotation averaged about $70 per page. The quotation included inputting all text, scanning the art, combining text and art together on pages, providing proofs generated on the LaserWriter, proofreading, Linotronic output, and preparing camera-ready boards.

The typesetter's estimate, including typesetting, digitizing the art, making up the pages, and producing the material through camera-ready copy, was closer to $50 per page — a savings of almost 30 percent compared with the desktop alternative!

Different Jobs, Different Costs

In our first example, using desktop technology saved us a lot of money over using traditional typesetting. But in the second example it was the other way around: The complexity of the job makes the desktop method more costly than the traditional alternative. In fact, the discrepancy will increase further as the jobs become more complex. This isn't really surprising. The logic behind why low costs are not a guaranteed feature of every job undertaken by desktop publishers is grounded in the facts controlling cost-per-unit efficiency in industrial mass production.

Consider for a moment some basic facts of industrialization. The newer, more sophisticated, more automated, and more expensive a piece of equipment is, the more effective it is at raising productivity and lowering the operating costs per piece. Although the sophistication of publishing tools now on our desks far exceeds that of typewriters, desktop systems are relative foot scooters compared with the computer-based publishing equipment that conventional typesetters and film houses use.

Desktop tools are slow performers in the world of professional publishing: Disk-access time, wait-for-print time, time for loading files — it all adds up. In addition, the small size of the computer screen means that much time is wasted traveling around on the screen and finding out where you are in relation to something else. The small screen size also makes it difficult to check one's work without taking the time to make a printout of the page. Furthermore, the output devices for desktop publishing that rely on a page-description language (such as PostScript), laser printers, and the Allied Linotronic typesetter (also a laser device) are notoriously slow. The Apple LaserWriter printer can print a maximum of eight simple text pages per minute. Add rules, symbols, graphics, and several typefaces, and that rate drops to as few as three pages per hour! When we stop to think about it, it is easy to see why the inefficiencies of the desktop method are compounded when a publication is more complex. If desktop publishing isn't as cheap as we are being led to believe, then why on earth would anyone choose it over the less costly traditional production method?

Advance Planning

The only reason to choose a more costly method is by demonstrating that there is a benefit to be had as a direct result of the increased cost. A common misconception about evaluating quotations of all kinds is to operate with the understanding that cheap actually means cost-effective. The purchaser of any good or service who only looks at the bottom line is doing their organization a huge disservice. Cost-effectiveness has more to do with the bang for the buck than it does with the buck itself.

To determine cost-effectiveness means simply to weigh estimated production costs against potential revenue. When considering desktop publishing, this involves analyzing your job costs in terms of the following six benefits.

Design Alternatives

The first phase of a project produced in the traditional method is the creation of sample pages. The designer organizes a few pages of the manuscript using different line widths, different spacing between lines, different type fonts, sizes, and styles. The sample manuscript is typeset and the designer then works with the galleys and pastes up sample pages. Such design explorations can sometimes cost as much as 10 percent of the total job.

In the hands of a professional designer, a desktop system can be used economically to explore a wider range of design possibilities, type fonts, sizes, and styles than is possible using the typesetter. In the time it would take to organize a sample manuscript for the typesetter, a desktop designer can indicate the specifications and see the results instantly on the screen. The net dollar cost of such an exploration, if it is extensive, might be higher, but ultimately the initial investment in design improvement is measured against the benefit of increased production quality.

Of course, in the hands of an amateur, this feature can be a double-edged sword. Because it is so easy to explore different alternatives, lots of time can be wasted looking at alternatives that professionals wouldn't waste their time considering.

Time Savings

The desktop method saves time in two ways. First, because the production process is integrated within one or two computer programs, there are fewer stages to go through. This significantly reduces the back-and-forth dead time involved in getting the results of different stages from the designer to the typesetter to the client and back again. Traditional methods involve going from manuscript to galley to pages to pasteup to confirmation proofs of camera-ready copy.

Using desktop methods I can go directly from the designer's manuscript/galley to page/confirmation proofs: The manuscript is prepared with the appropriate line length, type font, style, and size, and thereby acts as the galley; the pages can be made up with all art and graphic elements in position, thereby eliminating the pages stage of traditional publishing methods.

Second, typesetters can sometimes be a bottleneck when it comes to meeting tight schedules. Sometimes additional pasteup people can be brought in to speed up the task, but they are dependent on the typesetter to provide the type and corrections.

With desktop publishing, there need be no delay in waiting for revised type from the typesetter before the pasteup people can get to work. Minor type corrections can be made immediately in page layout on the computer.

Increased Control

In traditional publishing, the publication's creator must share control over how the information is presented with the designer and the pasteup artist. By putting page-design tools into the hands of the publication's creator, desktop publishing gives the creator more control than ever before over how the information is structured.

This advantage of desktop publishing methods is another double-edged sword. All this control in the hands of a nonprofessional can often have disastrous results: Everything may end up looking like a poorly done P.T. Barnum circus announcement. Good design is the product of training, experience, and talent.

Flexibility

Once material has been typeset and pasted in position on pages, the cost of revising it can be extensive. Even minor changes require a lot of expensive hand work.

On the other hand, desktop publishing tools offer a great deal of flexibility: Once text and graphics have been entered into the system, they can be manipulated inexpensively and in a multitude of ways. With a flick of the mouse, text and graphics can be copied from a flyer and pasted onto a layout for a postcard. With minor changes, the owner's manual for one model of your product can become the manual for another. Revisions of dated material are accomplished with ease. A manufacturer can respond immediately to customer feedback, for example, changing instructions to make them clearer. If a single product has several audiences with varying capabilities, it is no problem to create different versions of a manual to specifically address each level of understanding.

Economical Information Storage

Pasted up camera-ready copy doesn't have a long shelf life. Pieces of type fall off, boards warp or get bent, type gets creased. Furthermore, stored camera-ready-copy boards can take up a lot of valuable space, and the flat file in which they are most effectively stored is an expensive piece of office equipment.

The main storage medium for desktop publishing is the disk. It offers a compact and relatively safe alternative to storing camera-ready-copy boards. If storage space is at a premium and the cost of storage is an issue, you'll especially appreciate this feature of desktop publishing.

Adaptable Technology

People who now use desktop publishing are investing in a technological edge that could have a big payoff later when their experience enables them to use the more sophisticated tools that are being developed. However easy a personal computer is to learn to operate, there is a significant learning curve that must be traveled in order to use it effectively for desktop publishing. Desktop publishing integrates the use of word processing, charting and graphing, drawing, drafting, spellchecking, and page layout software, to name only a few of the programs. The learning curve for those who have no prior computer experience is growing steeper with each new software development.

Nonusers of the new technology may find themselves in the buggy whip business in a horseless carriage market. Many graphic designers are highly skeptical about using existing microcomputers during the design process. They regard the microcomputer as a newfangled horseless carriage, hampered in its prototypical infancy by a discouraging array of limitations: They are convinced that their old workhorses (the pencil, X-Acto® knife, and waxer) are more dependable and more predictable!

Other designers see the same limitations of the technology only as a temporary inconvenience. The small screen size, the paucity of fonts, the poor letterspacing because of a lack of kerning, the relative resolution of LaserWriter printers (300 dots per inch) for creating camera-ready copy — these technological problems are being attacked even as we work around them, and current users of the technology know they are shaping it by the demands they place on their systems. With experience, dedicated professionals are discovering ways to compensate for the weaknesses in their systems, and they are preparing for the next exciting generation of desktop publishing tools.

Desktop Publishing versus Traditional Typesetting

Although desktop publishing methods can approximate the quality that traditional typesetting achieves, they cannot yet equal that quality. An educated eye can easily tell typeset copy from microcomputer-generated copy: Both line spacing and letterspacing in typeset copy is far more refined, and there is a much wider range of typefaces to choose from when using traditional typesetting. A variety of different circumstances can affect your decision as to which method to use in producing a publication. The following are some variables to consider before determining which method you should use:

What is the purpose of the publication? Is your publication for information only, or must the publication also convey and sell the image of the company or product? Whenever your publication must represent your product or organization to the outside world, you need to consider involving professionals in the production process. Very seldom is the image of the publication not a consideration. All of the tiny details that comprise quality help give the reader a sense of the company that generated the publication. Professionally prepared information conveys a sense that the reader is important to the company and, no matter what the business, a quality publication indicates that the company cares about quality. Even companies that deal in commodities wrapped in brown paper bags cannot afford to give the impression that their business practices include compromises on quality.

What is the life of the publication? Will the publication be read once and then thrown away? Will it be read and then stored for possible future reference or will it be used for continual reference? Usually publications that will be read once and then tossed away can be of a lesser quality than those that will be around for a while and used for reference. Also, if the life cycle of the publication is a long one and someone is going to be living with it for a long time, higher quality is usually justified.

How many copies of this version will be reproduced? The answer to this question generally determines the answer to the next one concerning how the publication will be reproduced. When only a few copies of a publication are needed, printing is generally too costly an option per unit, and high-quality photocopies fit the bill. Quick-printing offers a better halftone reproduction than even the best photocopies, and with quantities of 50 or more is cost-competitive with the photocopy method. Even higher quality is available from offset printing. If price is an object, one usually needs a run of at least 250 to 500 to justify offset printing over these other methods.

How will the publication be reproduced? Will your printed product be photocopied, quick-printed, offset printed, or typeset? Photocopying does a fairly good job of reproducing camera-ready copy generated by the LaserWriter printer. The photocopy process tends to fill in the jagged edges that result from the 300-lines-per-inch resolution of the LaserWriter.

Quick-print methods are the unkindest to camera-ready copy generated by the LaserWriter, for two reasons. First, when generating film for printing, the photographic process tends to amplify the irregularities of the type because the camera has a more critical eye than the naked eye. Second, the printing process itself prints type that is fuzzier than the more expensive offset process. If the quick-print method is to be employed, I recommend that you consider the extra expense of Linotronic output as worthwhile.

Offset printing is the most expensive of the reproduction methods and produces the best results. Printing plates for the offset process are generally made of metal and offer better quality than their quick-print counterparts. If you will be printing your publication using an offset printer, you almost certainly will want the extra quality provided by the Linotronic output. Also, if you are printing your publication and dividing the costs into a larger number of copies, you are most likely producing enough copies to make the additional per unit cost for Linotronic output insignificant. You might at this point also begin to consider the additional quality that traditional typesetting methods can produce.

Traditional typeset copy reproduces solid letters that appear smooth to the naked eye. Only if you take a typeset word and enlarge it to many times its original size will you see some irregularities around the edges. Typeset copy also usually looks better than its desktop-generated cousin because typesetting equipment automatically kerns letters to reduce letterspacing between particular letter combinations, which makes them both more aesthetically pleasing to the eye, and easier to read. (However, simple kerning is quickly becoming a standard feature in desktop publishing software.) At present, typeset line spacing can also be more finely tuned than is possible with the desktop alternative. Aside from the niceties of letterspacing and line spacing, traditional typesetting currently offers a multitude of typeface options that are not yet available in desktop software. However, this too shall change.

How stable is the content? Will the publication not be revised after its initial creation? Will it be subject to infrequent revisions? Will it need to be updated frequently? If you are certain that the content of your publication will not change over time, and if you want the very best quality, consider the traditional approach. However, even infrequent revisions can be costly when using traditional methods. I once produced a revision of an educational textbook two years after initial publication. Even though there was only about a 25 percent change in content, the cost of the revision exceeded the original cost of production. No one was surprised. It is axiomatic in the publishing industry that a revised version often costs at least as much as the original to produce. And if you know in advance that your material will need to be updated often, do not pass "go." Instead, go directly to the desktop method.

How was the content created? Does the text already exist on a microcomputer disk? Does it exist as typewritten or handwritten copy? If your material already exists on a disk, the desktop method could have a cost advantage over the traditional method. It would not be unusual to pay a typesetter as much as $50 per hour for setting type. Even if you want your publication typeset, consider paying a word processor to put it on disk for you. Most typesetters today can convert your disk to their system with less work and at less cost than inputting it themselves. If your manuscript is on disk, you might consider using telecommunications (a modem and telephone) to send it to the typesetter or desktop publishing service to save even more time and money.

What is the schedule? Is there adequate time for all necessary steps of production, with an immovable final deadline? More typically, was the publication due yesterday or does there seem to be all the time in the world?

If managed well, the desktop alternative will save you time over the traditional alternative by reducing the number of steps you must go through, and by giving you maximum control over the production schedule. If not managed well, the desktop alternative will not only cost you valuable time, it may end up costing you more than the traditional alternative. Here are some things to keep in mind when managing desktop production.

First, budget a reasonable amount of time for exploring design and type alternatives and stick to it. It is easy to lose track of time when playing with possibilities.

Second, you will save both time and money by making sure that text and art are finished before advancing to the page layout step. (Even though the computer makes it relatively easy to change the pages once layout is done, adding to or deleting from the text will cause it to flow back and forth from one page to another. This often creates time-consuming quagmires of hyphenation, word spacing, and art location problems that result from the limitations of existing software.)

Third, be especially efficient when using the LaserWriter as a proofing tool, because wait-time for printing can be a killer. To do this means becoming accustomed to visualizing the page in reduced form as it appears on the computer screen. Use a spelling checker and read the entire page on-screen before printing. Try to catch errors at once by thoroughly checking your first proofs to keep the number of proofing cycles down.

Finally, there is no way to create an absolute model to follow when deciding which publishing alternative to choose. Each project is sure to present its own unique set of circumstances and considerations. Here is a list of the guidelines that I follow when advising clients.

Considerations:
- Quality image is paramount
- Publication has a long life
- Content is stable and unlikely to change
- Format is a complex combination of text and graphics
- Publication is to be offset printed in large quantities

Prescription: Traditional Typesetting.

Considerations:
- Quality is important, but not paramount
- Publication has a medium life
- Content is subject to small, periodic revisions
- Format is a combination of text and graphics
- Publication is to be printed in small quantities
- Schedule is a consideration

Prescription: Check Out Desktop Alternative

Considerations:
- Quality is not an overriding concern
- Publication has a short life
- Content is subject to many revisions
- Format is a straightforward, uncomplicated combination of text and graphics
- Publication is to be printed in very small quantities or photocopied
- Schedule is paramount

Prescription: Desktop Publishing

Comparative Cost Estimates

In some instances it will be clear to you that you need to go the traditional typesetting route, while in others it will be obvious that you require the flexibility of desktop technology. When the decision is not immediately obvious, you'll have to understand the potential advantages and costs of each method in order to make an informed cost comparison, and ultimately, a sound business decision. You're going to find that professional rates for typesetters and publishing services vary widely. If you are dealing with strangers, you should try to get individual prices for each necessary option from each outfit. You may even discover that contrary to our findings, desktop publishing services in your area are indeed cheaper than traditional typesetting, or vice versa. A proper publishing cost analysis begins by costing you some time and energy, but ends by saving you a great deal of grief and money. Here's how to do one:

Step One: Provide Thorough Content Samples

The more information you give the people bidding for the production of your publication, the more accurate their quotations are likely to be. Sometimes it is necessary to plan the production process completely before any of the manuscript has been written. When this is the case, prepare several written samples of the different kinds of information design that are required. For example, chapter openers (the first pages of chapters), often have a different layout from standard text pages. If your publication will be filled with charts and other graphics, make sure to include representative samples of the different kinds of art that will be required.

Step Two: Create Written Specifications

Before you give the sample content to those bidding for the job, you need to prepare written preliminary specifications for all aspects of the production. The specifications should include type specs, art specs, camera-ready-copy specs, and printing specs.

Type specifications include such information as the line length, type font, type size, line spacing (leading) for text, and different levels of headings within the text. Also be sure to tell how the copy will be provided. Will it be typewritten or on a microcomputer disk? If the latter, how will the disk be formatted?

Art specifications include answers to the following questions: Are there any repeating design elements on the pages? How many pieces of line art are there? Are there any photographs or illustrations that will be halftones? What art will be supplied? What art is to be prepared by the production service?

Camera-ready-copy specifications include information for preparing finished boards. When the publication is presented to you in its last form before printing, how do you expect the production service to format it for your approval? With typeset-quality type and the art in position? On single pages, or as two-page spreads (facing pages)?

Printing specifications include the final trim size of the pages and cover, the number of colors and how they are used, whether or not the copy bleeds off the page, and so on. Though you might wonder why the typesetter should be concerned with printing specifications in estimating final production costs, very often typesetters and production services use this information to figure how best to prepare your material for the press; this can save you a lot of headache-generating consultations during the final stages of a project.

Step Three: Request an Itemized Quotation

Give the production services your written specifications and ask them to supply quotations to you broken down by task. Having each outfit's costs itemized by task allows you to compare services more effectively than if you try to do so with only their bottom-line estimates.

Step Four: Try To Equalize Separate Quotations

Even if you get two quotations from suppliers with the same technology, they often slice and dice their estimates in radically different ways. When evaluating quotations from different sources, I cannot overemphasize how important it is to make sure you are comparing apples to apples. For example, you might find that the reason one quotation is significantly lower than another is that it doesn't include a vital task that it should. If one source provides an additional service within a line item, you will have to "break" the cost of that service out of the line item in order to compare it fairly with another estimate. Does one source include a proofreading charge at every stage, whereas another doesn't? You have to factor in your own cost for proofreading if it isn't included. Also, look at different quotations from your sources over time. When a source repeatedly overbids on a particular line item, it might indicate a weakness in their ability to perform that task.

Step Five: Include Your Own Costs

Often what you need to spend for nonproduction line items changes depending on which publishing alternative you choose. For example, when schedules are tight, freight and delivery charges can quickly exceed what any sane person would budget for them at the beginning of a project. The tighter the schedule and the larger the job, the more should be budgeted for this line item. And obviously, the farther a source is from you, the higher the potential costs for freight. Be sure to include all of the following line items in your cost estimates:

Typesetting
- Writing
- Editing
- Typing manuscript (not necessary if written on disk)
- Proofreading manuscript
- Designing pages
- Marking up manuscript (type specs)
- Typesetting galleys
- Proofreading galleys
- Laying out pages and creating dummies
- Illustrations and mechanical art
- Pasteup
- Final proofing and layout check
- Author's alterations
- Postage and freight
- Supplies
- Administration and overhead

Desktop
- Writing
- Editing
- Proofreading
- Designing pages
- Implementing type specs
- Illustrations and mechanical art
- Laying out pages
- Final proofing and layout check
- Author's alterations
- Postage and freight
- Supplies
- Administration and overhead

If you are producing a publication that has no existing model, be sure to factor in ample amounts for the inevitable exploration stage in the page design line item. Ask your sources to include the cost of sample pages as a line item in their quotations.

Only you can factor in the line item for author's alterations. Be sure to ask prospective production services for a definition of how they bill for author's alterations. Some sources are known for submitting attractively low bids and then socking it to you for alterations. Unfortunately, if you aren't careful you will find yourself the victim of this ploy after the alterations have been made and billed. Whatever you calculate to be a reasonable percentage of alterations, you might want to double it to be on the safe side.

Summary

Desktop technology can produce simple publications at costs far less than typesetting. The desktop publishing revolution is producing some valuable operational alternatives to traditional typesetting, but if you are producing a complex publication, don't make the mistake of assuming that desktop methods will necessarily save you money. Strip away the hype, measure the truth of desktop publishing's present state of development against your own specific needs, and you may find that the flexibility and control made available by the new technology still has too high a price.

To determine the appropriate production method for a particular publication, consider such variables as the purpose of the publication, the life of the publication, how many copies are to be manufactured, how the publication will be reproduced, and how stable the content is. Go directly to the typesetter when a combination of the following variables applies: A quality image is paramount; the content is stable and unlikely to change; the format calls for a complex combination of text and graphics; and the publication is to be offset printed in large quantities. Go directly to the desktop publisher when a combination of these variables applies: Quality is not an overriding concern; the publication has a short life; the content is subject to many revisions; the format is a straightforward, uncomplicated combination of text and graphics; the publication is to be printed in very small quantities or photocopied; and the schedule is paramount.

If you have any doubts as to which method to choose, spend some time working up a proper cost analysis of the alternatives. Estimate your project both ways. Make sure you are comparing apples with apples when you evaluate relative costs. Most importantly, don't blithely assume that one method is in all instances more expensive or less expensive than the other. Figure in your own costs relative to each alternative. And don't assume that the lowest cost alternative is always the best buy. The best buy is the one that not only suits your budget, but also offers the best chance of helping to promote your reputation for dependability, service, and quality.

Neither desktop publishing nor traditional typesetting can claim to be cheaper or more cost-effective than the other. Absolute rules about when to use one method rather than the other simply don't exist — yet.

II

Systems and Hardware

About This Section

The desktop publishing market consists of sophisticated software running on new and powerful personal computers connected to high-resolution printers. This section focuses on the hardware underlying the new publishing systems, describing the great range of choices that are available in computers, monitors, and printers. The first essay examines the computer most responsible for coining the phrase desktop publishing: the Apple Macintosh. This essay explains the computer attributes a desktop application requires in the way of resolution, pointing devices, and user interface. Subsequent essays look at the hardware of the IBM PC, and then at the software Microsoft Windows, an environment that makes the PC look and feel like a Macintosh. As understanding the graphic standards in add-in cards may help you in your purchasing decisions, we explore graphics boards that define the pixels in your PC system and then examine different kinds of monitors that display these pixels. Printers are the hub of desktop publishing, so we present an overview of both dot matrix and laser printers. Scanners let you capture images of forms, photographs, and artwork to use in your publication, and the next essay profiles the major types of scanners available. This is followed by a look at the powerful multi-user/multitasking UNIX operating system which the technical community has used for many years to perform publishing. Finally, if you want to know where desktop publishing is headed, we show you some high-end workstations from Sun, DEC, and Apollo.

KEYWORDS:

- Icon

- Window

- Pull-down Menu

- AppleTalk

- Mouse Pointing Device

Oren Ziv is communications manager of Micro D, a leading national distributor of microcomputer products based in Santa Ana, California. He writes about personal computers and their applications as well as manages the editorial production of the company's several national publications.

Essay Synopsis: Because graphics and text on the Macintosh are essentially the same thing, graphic images and text can be merged in the same file, manipulated there, and printed on the same page. Shortly after the introduction of sufficiently powerful tools to accomplish this, the phrase "desktop publishing" was born.

This essay provides an introduction and overview to the Macintosh computer and its powerful, integrated user-interface. You will learn why icons are an important file-manipulation tool, how windows help to organize your work, and how the clipboard and scrapbook allow information to be shared between files. The author will explain the important products that work with the Macintosh to make a true publishing system: the LaserWriter printer, Postscript, the AppleTalk network, word processors and graphics programs, font libraries, and more.

6

The Macintosh System

Oren Ziv

The Macintosh was first brought to the market with a very high-resolution, easy-to-read display screen, but instead of cursor keys, it used a mouse-type pointing device to accomplish tasks, such as selecting functions, marking text, and drawing lines. To make the point, Apple Computer bundled the Macintosh with a text editing program sporting many type styles and a capable bit-mapped drawing program. The Macintosh system was sufficiently integrated to allow data from nearly any application program file to merge into a file created by nearly any other application program. It was the first low-cost computer that could interchange graphics and a variety of typefaces between files. For this reason more than any other, the Macintosh has been the centerpiece of desktop publishing.

In this essay we present an overview of the Macintosh computer system, its software operating system, the computer hardware, and some of the major products that work with the Macintosh desktop publishing system.

The Macintosh User Interface

The Macintosh's graphic-based user interface makes it exceptionally suited for desktop publishing. By user interface we mean the manner in which different programs communicate and interact — the microcomputer's software working environment. The

Macintosh user interface has several distinctive features. It uses small pictures known as icons to represent directories, programs, and files; it provides "pull-down" menus that offer standard utility functions; it allows for "desk accessories" that are pop-up types of limited applications available at anytime; and it has two "capture" features, the clipboard and the scrapbook, which let you move either graphics or text information from one file to any other. It is important to mention that all software written for the Macintosh must respect this scheme, so the means of controlling any program has much in common with that of every other program. In other words, once you know how to use one program, you have learned a lot about how to use any new programs.

Icons

The Macintosh user interface was designed as a graphic metaphor: a desktop on which small pictures sit. The top of the desktop is bordered by a band in which you see banners for the pull-down menus. Along the right side sit pictures of a start-up disk and a trashcan (more about these later). The center of the desktop is a gray screen, the focus of most activity.

Each file stored on a disk is represented by an icon, a small picture symbol (see Figure 6-1). The reason behind choosing a pictorial representation of a file is that a picture can provide much more information in a limited space than can text. Figure 6-2 shows a text description of a file together with an icon depiction. Notice that the text takes up more room.

An icon may at first seem mysterious, but once you have learned its meaning, you can recognize it at a single glance. Its pictorial form allows a higher information bandwidth between the display screen and you, the operator, which helps speed up your work. At the operating system level are four main classes of icons: disks, folders, application programs, and data files generated by application programs.

By moving a small rolling box called a mouse, which was named for its slight physical resemblance to the rodent, you can direct a pointer arrow to select the icons that represent the programs and documents you wish to use. There isn't any vocabulary of command codes to memorize. Just use the mouse to move the pointer arrow to the icon you wish to open and click the mouse's button; the icon blackens to show that you have selected it for some function.

Each icon is associated with a "window." By window we mean a square on the desktop that includes an active interior area and some

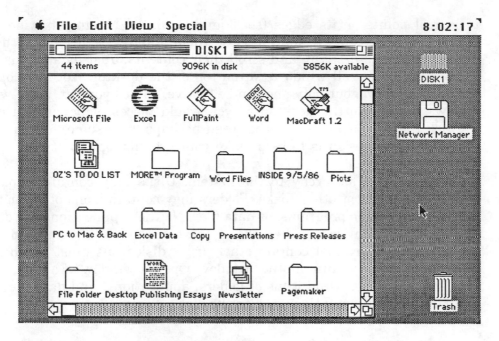

**Figure 6-1. Macintosh user interface, the window belonging to Disk 1 —
notice that the Disk 1 icon is gray, indicating it is selected.**

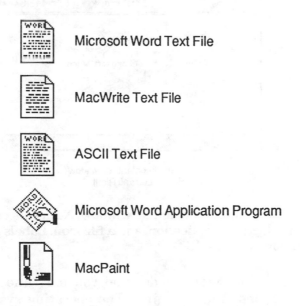

**Figure 6-2. Icons differ from one another. Notice that the text description
takes more space; familiar icons are instantly recognizable.**

control points on its edges (see Figure 6-3). All Macintosh windows have control points to let you close them, enlarge them, move them around on the desktop, and scroll their contents. Just as all icons sit on the desktop, all windows sit on top of the desktop. You may open many windows, but only one can be "active." Since you can move windows around on the desktop as you would pieces of paper, you can stack them on top of each other (and perhaps bury some). Again, the point to this design is to help make your organizing activity fast and accurate.

There is a hierarchy to the system. Disks may contain icons of everything except other disks. Folders may contain icons of other folders, application programs, or data files. Neither applications nor data files contain any icons; they are at the lowest level of relationships. Because disks cannot contain other disks, disk icons must sit on the desktop, never within another window. Open a window of a disk, and within it you may find icons of folders, applications, and data files — all of the data currently stored on the disk.

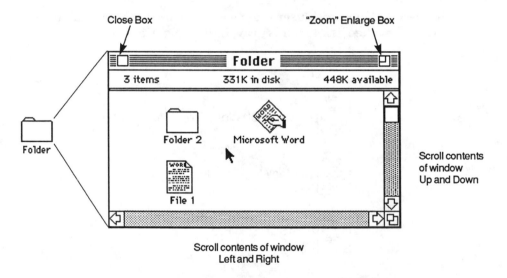

Figure 6-3. A folder icon and its window. Notice its contents include another folder, an application, and a file icon. Labels point to window control points.

Open the window of a folder and you may find icons of more folders, applications, and data files. The operating system lets you nest folders within folders within folders, and provides a powerful organizing environment.

If you open the window of an application, you do not find icons. Instead, the application program takes over the screen and presents its own window, headed by the pull-down menu banners and bordered by the controller "scroll bar." Scroll bar refers to the gray band at the right of the window (see Figure 6-3) that provides a means to scroll forward and backward through the contents of a file.

If you open the window to an icon for a data file, something interesting happens. Part of the Macintosh operating system includes the "Finder." The Finder has the job of finding which application generated the data file, loading that application into memory, and loading the data file so that it is ready to use. This is a handy shortcut if you recognize an icon as something you need to work on — just open it as you would any other window. Again, the design idea is to let you organize accurately and get to work fast.

Pull-Down Menus

The Macintosh's user interface also features pull-down menus. The pull-down menu bar sits at the top of the screen (see Figure 6-3). To open a menu, use the mouse to drive the pointer arrow over the menu title and select it (see Figure 6-4). Many of the pull-down menus include options that are standard to all application programs: Create a *new* file, *open* an existing file, *save* data to a file, *save* data *as* a different file, *print* this file, *quit* the application and return to the desktop. These are functions that all applications must invoke, and their standardization is one of the major benefits of the Macintosh design.

Desk Accessories

In keeping with the desktop metaphor, the accessories represent tools that are available to use at any time, much as pop-up programs in the MS-DOS environment. Whether you're working with file folders or within a file, you can call up such accessories as a clock, a calculator, a printer selector (the "chooser"), and a control panel. Third-party manufacturers have created some imaginative desk accessories, such as outliners, text processors, print spoolers, telecommunications programs, and a variety of finding and organizing aids. Again, these are available to the user at any time. Simply invoke them with the mouse pointer, and the system freezes your work while you operate whatever desk accessory you choose.

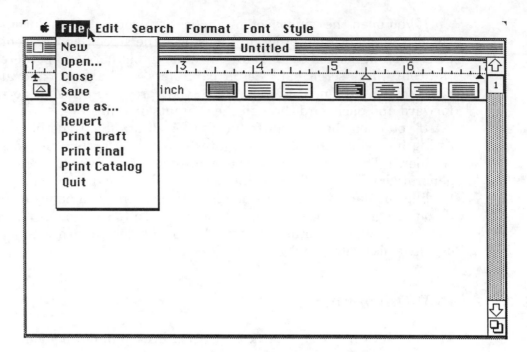

Figure 6-4. The pull-down menu is open for File choices; other pull down menus exist for Edit, Search, Format, and other functions.

Clipboard and Scrapbook

The clipboard and the scrapbook offer similar powers. They provide a system-wide neutral zone in which you can store data from one file for future use in another. The difference is that the clipboard is available from the Edit pull-down menu. Any cut-and-paste work is done with the clipboard; you cut or copy some data into the clipboard, move to another place within the same file or to a completely different file, and paste the contents of the clipboard into the target area. Every new cut or copy overwrites all previous material in the clipboard. You cannot append material to the clipboard, collecting here and there as you go.

The scrapbook is available as a desk accessory. The difference is that it stores its contents on a disk. Cut or copy a section of a file to the clipboard, then paste the material to the scrapbook for future use. You can scroll through the contents of the scrapbook and cut or copy whatever you choose for use in a file. You can do all this while you have a working file open.

Apple has promoted standardization of the way various software programs use the clipboard and scrapbook parts of the computer's system. This means that you can electronically clip text or graphics from one program, store it away, and place that same data into the document of a completely different program. For example, you can create an illustration using a graphics program, then place it in the middle of a word processing document.

The Macintosh Desktop Publishing Hardware

The Apple's costs are centered on the three or four pieces of hardware items in your system. The Macintosh is a closed environment. Although this limits you to the monitor and resident memory of the current version of the Macintosh Plus, it also means a limit to the amount of money you'll have to lay out to get started.

Although the Macintosh is described as being self-contained (the monitor, floppy disk drive, memory, processor, SCSI (Small Computer Systems Interface) port, printer port, modem port, mouse, and keyboard are all part of one unit), the Macintosh desktop publishing system is composed of several devices: the Macintosh Plus, the LaserWriter, a hard disk drive, software, an optional scanner, and other accessory items. Each item within the system works in cooperation with the others to provide a final, printed product of a quality that is far beyond the previous realm of affordable office equipment that has been available. Current software is being designed to take advantage of the Macintosh Plus's megabyte of internal memory (double that of the 512K model). You'll find that desktop publishing takes advantage of every bit of memory you can muster.

Three important additions were necessary to make the Macintosh a desktop publishing engine: the LaserWriter printer, the PostScript page description language, and PageMaker, the page layout program.

The LaserWriter Printer

The most expensive element in your desktop publishing system isn't the computer; it's the printer. Although it is possible to perform some page layout functions on the Apple ImageWriter and ImageWriter II dot matrix printers, the very basis of desktop publishing is the near typeset quality print that is the exclusive realm of the laser printer. When you first start investigating computer-assisted publishing, you might experiment with a dot matrix printer or a non-PostScript (we'll explain PostScript later) laser printer, but if you're serious about desktop publishing, buy the LaserWriter.

A laser printer is a microcomputer printer that operates and looks like a small copying machine. The difference between a standard copier and a laser printer is that instead of laying an object on a glass plate and transferring a photo image of the object onto the copier's light-sensitive drum, a laser printer recreates the image from your computer onto that same copier drum using electronics associated with laser technology. Once the image is inside the printer, it prints just like any other plain paper copier.

The LaserWriter is really the single greatest element in making desktop publishing a reality. The Apple LaserWriter differs from the laser printers that preceded its development (such as the Hewlett-Packard LaserJet) in that the LaserWriter's design emulates a typesetter. Earlier laser printers were designed to function as an advancement of dot matrix printing, the most popular type of business personal computer printer.

The LaserWriter uses PostScript (in fact, it is resident within the printer's read-only memory), which is an industry-standard page description language for commercial typesetting machines. A page description language is necessary for recreating graphic images on your laser printer's drum.

There are two different models of the LaserWriter: the LaserWriter and the LaserWriter Plus. The machines are very similar in that they both use the same MC68000 microprocessor as the Macintosh, and both printers have one and a half megabytes of RAM (random access memory). These printers print at a very high 300-dots-per-inch resolution. But the LaserWriter Plus differs from the original LaserWriter in that it also has a full megabyte of built-in PostScript language software, translating into more typefaces for instantaneous use. The LaserWriter is equipped to print four built-in type families: Times, Helvetica, Courier, and Symbol. The LaserWriter Plus comes permanently equipped with seven additional type families in its memory — Palatino, ITC Avant Garde Gothic, ITC Bookman, Helvetica Narrow, ITC Zapf Chancery, ITC Zapf Dingbats, New Century Schoolbook — providing the user with a greater selection of typefaces for a variety of publications. Both printers allow you to print in a nearly unlimited variety of type sizes and in either bold, italic, underline, outline, shadow, small caps, superscript, or subscript styles, depending on the limitations of the software you're using.

Is the LaserWriter Plus worth an extra $1,000? If you plan to create publications requiring a variety of typefaces, then the LaserWriter Plus will save you the time and irritation of downloading (reading information into your printer's memory from a disk) software typefaces. However, if Times and Helvetica are satisfactory typefaces for the majority of your publications, avoid the added expense of the Plus. If you find that later in your publishing career you could use the extra fonts, you can upgrade the LaserWriter to the LaserWriter Plus.

AppleTalk

Through the AppleTalk Personal Network up to 31 Macintoshes can share a single LaserWriter. Of course, 31 is a little crowded, but three or four Macintoshes per one LaserWriter is not uncomfortable at all. AppleTalk is a low-cost means of sharing devices that can perform advanced networking functions, like sharing data and software, when used in conjunction with a file-serving subsystem (see following discussion of hard disks).

The AppleTalk network is composed of a series of plastic connector boxes and cords that snap together so simply that anyone who ever used a Tinkertoy® or Lego® finds AppleTalk to be child's play to assemble. At its simplest, it lets several computers share a printer or a group of printers. An increasing number of low-cost products have been designed to enhance the use of this inexpensive cable-connecting system, notably allowing the transmission of file contents between workstations.

Hard Disk Drives

When dealing with the vast variety of software programs and large document files created in desktop publishing, you're far better off with a hard disk drive than another floppy drive. In choosing a hard disk you must consider several different features. You can spend anywhere from $1,000 to more than $7,000 for a hard disk drive; obviously, there are great differences.

Any hard disk you buy should be self-booting and connect to your Macintosh via the SCSI port on the back of the machine; this way you'll take advantage of the fastest path of communication between the disk drive and your Macintosh as well as keep your modem port free for telecommunications capabilities. As part of the Macintosh's start-up procedure, it first looks for system information at the internal floppy drive, then checks any external floppy drives, then looks to the SCSI port. If a hard disk is attached via the SCSI drive, it is called self-booting, because the software system that operates the Macintosh can be stored there; you don't have to use a floppy disk to start the machine. SCSI is an industry-standard interface that provides extremely high-speed access to your hard disk, or any other compatible peripheral device, such as tape backup systems or other high-capacity storage devices. The size (i.e., the amount of available memory) of your hard disk is determined both by the applications you plan to perform and by the number of users storing data on the disk. Ten megabytes may be too small for data storage in your desktop publishing system; if so, look into a twenty megabyte hard disk.

Hard Disk File Servers

If you set up your system to connect more than one Macintosh, you are probably interested in buying a larger hard disk and sharing it between several users through a networking environment. This requires a disk subsystem, an advanced hard disk unit that has the electronics necessary to support networking applications by working in conjunction with the AppleTalk network. The networking environment allows users to have their own private storage spaces as well as share files and applications with other users. Fifteen megabytes per user is a good memory capacity goal in choosing a larger drive. Iomega offers two sizes of high-capacity storage systems that work with the Apple-Talk network and feature the security and reliability of removable Bernoulli cartridges, a well-accepted alternative form of mass storage.

Hard Disk Backup

Other high-quality networkable hard disk subsystems, such as the AST 4000, come equipped with tape backup systems that prevent a devastating loss of important information caused by the dreaded hard disk crash. A crash is anytime the disk becomes permanently inoperable due to an equipment or software error. With a hard disk this is most often due to a head crash, when the head that normally reads and writes data to the hard disk from a suspended position, touches the surface of the disk because of an impact or power failure. Preventing loss of data is especially important in desktop publishing. If you should suffer a crash before you're finished with the final version of your publication, you would more than likely have to start at least your layout from scratch. And since a great deal of time can be spent on your computer before generating the final form of a publication, such losses can be devastating to both your nerves and your reputation. Purchase and use a disk backup system. If you can't afford one of the more convenient tape systems, there are several software programs that work with floppy disks. Although software backups will consume more of your time than tape systems, someday they too will redeem your investment.

Digitizers, Optical Character Readers, and Scanners

Desktop scanners digitize graphics and/or text and read them into your computer's memory so that you don't have to enter them by hand. The affordable desktop scanner is only about a year old. Desktop scanners for the Macintosh are scaled-down versions of expensive, optical scanners that exist for larger-format computers. But because the LaserWriter produces only 300 dots per inch of uniform-size dots, the image reproduced is not comparable to halftone print quality and may be unacceptable for some types of publishing. Optical character recognition software (OCR) necessary for scanners to read text, which may add $500 to the cost of a desktop scanner, are still in the infant stage of development and fairly limited in their capabilities.

Optical Character Recognition software for desktop scanners has difficulty reading different type fonts and columns of text. Presently, about the best you can expect from a desktop scanner is to reproduce line drawings and to read typewritten text. Desktop scanners also greatly increase the memory storage requirements of your system, affecting the size and cost of the hard disk you need to purchase. One scanner — the Thunderscan from Thunderware   uses an Image-Writer printer and includes software for reproducing graphics that sells for around $200. The Thunderscan is slow and produces a fairly low resolution image (72 dots per inch), but if you have an Image-Writer printer gathering dust, this is a good buy for the money. You still won't be able to produce good photographic reproductions, but transferring line art to a paint program, then touching up the image can produce an acceptable graphic.

The Macintosh Desktop Publishing Software

For desktop publishing, you'll need at least three programs to get started: a word processor, a draw or paint program, and a page layout program. Nearly every program that you'll use on your Macintosh will function in the same manner, so once you have learned to use one program, you can quickly learn just about any other.

Word Processors

You need the full power of a stand-alone word processor and a fully loaded paint program. Which word processor should you use? The two most widely available programs for the Macintosh are Apple's MacWrite Version 4 and Microsoft Word. The programs are similar. In spite of its popularity, MacWrite 4 is limited when compared with Microsoft Word. MacWrite 4's biggest shortcoming is that it doesn't allow multiple windowing: You can only have one document on the screen at a time. This makes it difficult to cross-edit between documents or write in one document while looking at another. Microsoft Word, on the other hand, lets you take advantage of the Macintosh's multiwindowing environment by opening as many as four documents at one time.

It is also very tedious to change margins or tab settings with MacWrite 4's process of inserting rulers to change paragraph attributes. And the lack of horizontal scrolling in MacWrite's windows makes it difficult to work with documents that extend beyond a seven-inch line (see Figure 6-5). Microsoft Word satisfies these as well as other MacWrite deficiencies and is truly a professional word processor on the same level as Microsoft's business-oriented products for the IBM. Word offers you far more keyboard-selectable functions (select them from the program's menu using the mouse or by pushing a combination of keys on the keyboard), which can accelerate your pace after you are familiar with the program. And Word offers a variety of advanced heading, footnoting, and layout options. And where MacWrite has no text/data merging functions, Word lets you take advantage of your computer's ability to produce personalized form letters.

Probably the greatest disadvantage to using MacWrite 4 as part of a desktop publishing system is that it is difficult to scan your typeface options. By pulling down the character menu in Microsoft Word, you can quickly view both your font and type size choices, then easily select both. MacWrite 4 forces you to use two different type selection menus: You must first select a font, and only then can you see what sizes of that font are available. Since type selection is very important to page layout, this can really slow your production.

MacWrite 4 has some advantages over Microsoft Word. It is easier to view and adjust pagination using MacWrite. And MacWrite imports text files from other formats better than Word (although Word does import text files and provides an application that easily imports files from the IBM version of Word). These are important features — ones we hope that Microsoft will improve on in upcoming versions of Word.

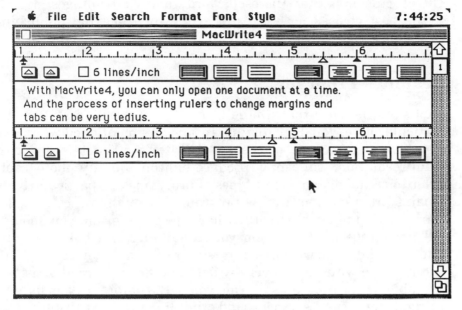

MacWrite

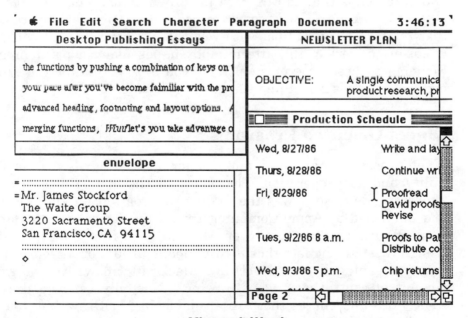

Microsoft Word

Figure 6-5. MacWrite vs. Microsoft Word. Notice that Microsoft Word displays contents of several files while MacWrite is limited to one file at a time.

The conclusion is that Microsoft Word's many advantages make it one of the best choices for word processing in a desktop publishing environment.

Graphics Programs

Publishing is more than words alone — you must create art. In this particular case, you'll create illustrations. As mentioned when discussing scanners, because of the LaserWriter's 300-dots-per-inch maximum resolution, you cannot produce halftone-quality photographs. In order to create artwork, two types of programs are particularly useful: a paint program and a draw program. Although you can adequately start desktop publishing with either type of program, you should take full advantage of the system you're building and buy both. In case you're not familiar with these sorts of programs, they equip your computer screen with tools generally found on a commercial artist's drawing table. Draw programs provide you with computer tools for drawing straight lines, curves, circles, and other line-oriented graphics. A paint program has computer tools that emulate brushes, pencils, erasers, and spray cans that can be used for drawing, shading, and blending patterns. In general, it is easier to use a draw program to create art that requires straight lines with vertical and horizontal alignment. It is easier to work with patterns and shapes using a paint program. Remember, these programs only give you tools — finding the artist to use those tools is something you have to provide.

Object-Oriented Programs

When choosing a draw program, look for one that gives you maximum utility and easy operation. The oldest of these programs is Apple's MacDraw. Because it was the first draw program for the Macintosh and published by Apple Computer, this program set the standard for this software category. However, MacDraft 1.2 from Innovative Data Design (despite the fact that it costs about $100 more) seems to have many advantages over MacDraw. MacDraft allows you a greater amount of control over your drawings. Not only can you draw the same lines and curves that are available in MacDraw, but you have additional tools for scaling, rotating, automatically setting line dimensions, and cloning as well as viewing your drawings from several different magnifications.

Make sure to get at least version 1.2 of MacDraft. It saves your drawings in the PICT format (a specific type of computer file) necessary for page layout programs. MacDraft helps you make graphs and simple illustrations for your publications. It also lets you generate forms that you won't believe. If you have a difficult time drawing a straight line, MacDraft is definitely the draw program to use.

Bit-Mapped Programs

There are two full-paint programs to choose from: Apple's MacPaint and Ann Arbor Softworks' FullPaint. Once again, as with MacWrite and MacDraw, MacPaint has set the standard for paint programs. And once again, the independently published software seems to have definite advantages, at least for desktop publishing. FullPaint offers greater features at a competitive price. It allows you to easily move, cut, and paste between up to four windows. FullPaint also gives you greater control over the screen by moving or completely hiding the tool palettes that block parts of the screen. The variable format rulers make this program especially suitable for desktop publishing. You might not even notice some of the features that FullPaint offers beyond MacPaint, but because it's the cheaper of the two programs anyway and is completely compatible with MacPaint, FullPaint may be the better choice for your system.

Page Layout Software

The next piece of software that you need to begin desktop publishing is a page layout program. This is the focal point of the software required for desktop publishing. Therefore, this category is covered in detail in another essay. For now, you should know that a variety of programs with a variety of features are on the market. The program that is the most well established, accepted because it is easy to use, and compatible with most other Macintosh software is PageMaker by Aldus. In fact, Aldus' founder Paul Brainerd is the man credited for coining the term "desktop publishing." Most of the Macintosh software programs are compatible with a page layout program, but check with a dealer to make sure that the software you choose saves its files in a format that is easily placed in the layout program you purchase.

Clip Art

You can buy a variety of other art-related software products for your Macintosh publishing system. For instance, various clip art programs are available that are collections of professional drawings in paint format. You can copy and alter these pictures by means of your paint program, then use them as illustrations, drawings, or embellishments in your publications. Clip art is a cheap and easy way to add some visual excitement to even the driest subjects.

Font Libraries

On the more technical side of the additional software category are font libraries. As mentioned when we first discussed the LaserWriter and LaserWriter Plus, each one is equipped with a limited number of typefaces within its resident memory. Those typefaces are created by means of Adobe Systems' PostScript page description language. PostScript literally tells the printer how to construct each character of a particular typeface from lines and curves. This is why the Laser-Writer is capable of recreating those letters in any size from four points to as large as the paper you're printing on. Non-PostScripting printers are much more limited in both typeface varieties and character sizes. It makes sense to turn to Adobe Systems when you need additional fonts. You may not need these additional fonts when you first start publishing, but if you eventually do find yourself creating a variety of publications, you'll need a selection of typefaces. That is exactly what you get with the Adobe Type Library. These are all well-known fonts licensed from professional printer typeface libraries. They can be downloaded (read) into your LaserWriter's memory, then used at your preference until you shut off the printer's power. Not only do Adobe's typefaces take full advantage of your LaserWriter's printing capabilities, but they also can be used with a professional PostScript typesetting machine, such as the Linotype Linotronic 100 and 300 image setters. You'll also find a variety of fonts and custom font-creating programs from other companies, but Adobe is the safest bet.

PostScript

Because the Macintosh must be able to generate PostScript command files in order to operate the LaserWriter, it can also create files that are readable by any other PostScript-compatible printer. This permits you to use your Macintosh and a professional machine, such as the Linotronic 100 or 300, to create publications that require professional typesetting. By transferring your Macintosh-created publication file via modem or floppy disk to a PostScript-compatible typesetting machine, you can print your pages at the ultra-high resolution of 1,270 or 2,540 dots per inch (the LaserWriter has a maximum resolution of 300 dots per inch). Currently, this type of typesetting ranges in price from $8 to $15 for a letter-size page, which is considerably less expensive than a comparable form of professional typesetting, which may cost from $25 to $50 per page. Therefore, with a Macintosh system you have the flexibility to print either near-typeset quality documents on your LaserWriter or to prepare documents to be typeset on a professional machine.

Summary

Macintosh users feel a sense of comradeship with each other. The computer's uniqueness as well as the pleasure with which it can be operated fuels this feeling. Several publications are available, such as MacWorld and MacUser, that discuss the latest applications and uses of the Macintosh. User groups also gather and communicate information about the Macintosh — Apple Computer can put you in touch with the user group closest to your home or business. Electronic bulletin boards are available, too, if you already have a microcomputer and a modem, where you can look for the latest information about the Macintosh. Any of these places probably can assist you in purchasing your system by providing the latest product information and tips to direct you toward the most helpful authorized dealers. If your budget is truly limited, begin with a Spartan system and add to it as you can afford to. You can start a complete publishing system with a single Macintosh Plus, a LaserWriter, a 20-megabyte hard drive, Microsoft Word, MacDraft, FullPaint, and Pagemaker for around eight thousand dollars — far cheaper than anything of similar quality and capabilities.

KEYWORDS:

- Expansion

- Configuration

- Architecture

- File Format

- Interface

Albert B. Margolis is a system manager and programmer with 14 years experience developing end-user and technical applications. He has been deeply involved in development and support of IBM PC applications since the introduction of the PC product line in 1981. He is currently responsible for development of PC and mainframe software for a major communications company and is involved in the startup of a mail order software company specializing in programming and desktop publication products, The Software Family, 649 Mission Street, San Francisco, California, 94105.

Essay Synopsis: With over ten million IBM and compatible computers installed worldwide, there is no question that these machines are ripe for desktop publishing software. But is the PC a viable choice; are there adequate peripherals; is it possible to exchange data? Or is the PC limited as compared to the Macintosh?

This essay presents an overview of the IBM PC/XT/AT family and MS-DOS compatibles, with an emphasis on the critical issue of file formats. You will learn why the MS-DOS machines differ from the Macintosh, what comprises a basic desktop publishing system, how various programs use formatting codes to store information on disk, how to interchange data between systems, and how to mix and match software and hardware to create a system tuned especially to your needs.

7

Desktop Publishing on the PC

Albert B. Margolis

This essay covers desktop publishing using the IBM Personal Computer and compatible systems, primarily in the office environment where most PCs are used to perform tasks ranging from preparation of correspondence to financial analysis to communications with other computers. Adding desktop publishing to the list of PC capabilities increases the effectiveness of written business communications and creates new business opportunities. It also increases the complexity of creating a working PC system by introducing even more variables into the process of selecting hardware and software, training staff, and producing the desired end product. This essay will explore the benefits of desktop publishing with the PC, the products required to implement it, and solutions to the problems you are likely to face.

Desktop publishing has the potential to significantly increase business effectiveness by improving the quality of written communications. Features such as integrated text and graphics, attractive page design, and high-quality print make possible the production of visually pleasing business publications that deliver their message more effectively than conventional word processing, and at lower cost and with greater ease than conventional typesetting and pasteup. Desktop publishing adds "punch" to existing publications, such as sales proposals and technical documentation, with little or no cost increase. It may provide a savings if typeset-

RELATED ESSAYS:

8. Microsoft Windows

9. Graphics Cards and Standards

10. Inside Monitors

11. Printers, Paper, and Toner

ting or other external services are currently used. Desktop publishing also creates new opportunities, such as making it feasible to establish product differentiation by customizing product documentation for small markets and even for individual customers.

Since we're discussing business use of desktop publishing, we will take a businesslike approach to the discussion. We will start by looking at the decisions required to establish business objectives for desktop publishing. We will then look at the options available to meet those objectives, considering both costs and the overall business computer environment.

The PC versus the Macintosh

Because the term desktop publishing was first associated with the Macintosh, many people have asked: Do I have to trade in my PC for a Macintosh in order to get involved in desktop publishing? The simple answer is no! The PC is a perfectly capable publishing system. We should go further, however, and take a short look at the whole truth and why publishing on the PC may never be quite as "nice" as publishing on the Macintosh — although it will certainly be at least as effective.

Simplicity versus Expansion

The Macintosh's designers wanted to produce a "computer appliance" that consumers could buy easily, plug in, and begin using immediately. To meet this goal, they designed the Mac according to strict standards for user simplicity and consistency in everything from plugging in the cords to using the most sophisticated programs, but with relatively little thought to ease of engineering. The PC, on the other hand, was intended to be the computer engineer's ultimate Tinkertoy™. The PC's designers established strict standards for engineering consistency in "bus interfaces," "software drivers," and other technical features, but gave little thought to simplicity of use.

As a result, relatively few hardware and software add-ons are available for the Mac, but they generally match the Mac's simple elegance and interact with each other and with the user in very predictable ways. PC add-ons have been introduced at a furious pace, with each product exploiting a different set of PC capabilities as well as interacting with each other and with the user in ways that reflect the product designer's personal view of what is "best."

The Macintosh's user environment can be compared to the quiet structure of a library, while the PC's is more like the frenetic interaction of a commodities exchange pit. The potential Macintosh publisher is presented with a relatively small number of elegant products, such as PageMaker and the LaserWriter, that smoothly perform their functions using the same hardware, software, and keyboard commands as other Macintosh programs. Publishers using the PC are forced to build their own systems, choosing from a bewildering array of system units, adapter cards, displays, disks, and programs that must be carefully evaluated for compatibility and completeness.

Display Graphics

In addition, the PC's hardware design short-changed graphics requirements, making the PC painfully slow and inadequate when displaying publication-quality type and graphics on the screen. The PC's display capabilities have improved significantly with the introduction of products such as the IBM PC AT, the IBM Enhanced Graphics Adapter (EGA), the Hercules Graphic standard, and integrated environments such as Microsoft Windows. But even if the latest generation of PC products provided a perfect publishing environment, the millions of PC users who would like to adopt desktop publishing but would not be willing to replace current systems are too large a share of the market to ignore. Most desktop publishing products, therefore, support both state-of-the-art PCs and their less graphically endowed predecessors. This backward compatibility allows manufacturers and publishers to reach the largest possible market, and also allows the majority of PC users to acquire some desktop publishing capability. Unfortunately, it also limits ease of use compared to the Macintosh, because the Macintosh's control techniques cannot be used in the mouseless, graphics-poor environment of most PCs.

Available Software Choices

The PC user faces an embarrassment (and confusion) of riches when it comes to selecting products. While the Macintosh user has virtually no printer choices, for example, the PC user must choose from dozens. He or she also must make such decisions as choosing between PostScript, DDL, or printer-specific formatting languages, and whether the printer controller logic should be implemented in hardware or software and whether it should be located in the printer or the Central Processing Unit (CPU), the microprocessor chip at the heart of the machine. While the Macintosh user is comparing the features of a relatively small number of word processing and page layout programs with the confidence that they will work together, the PC user is evaluating the architectures (the particular combinations of hardware making up a system) describing how many layers of software to use, how they should interact, and whether they will work with each other and with the available hardware. In addition to compatibility, the PC publisher must be concerned with consistency in order to minimize the difficulty of training and to avoid catastrophic mistakes like confusing one program's "help" key with another's "delete all" key.

Operating Flexibility

Although the PC's Tinkertoy design makes it difficult to set up and learn, the initial frustration will usually be justified by the long-term advantages of expansion and customization. Although Macintosh users have the luxury of picking systems from a handful of easy-to-use products, they have little flexibility if those products fail to meet their needs. The PC user, choosing from an array of functional components, can more easily evolve into a final system than a Mac user who must choose from "total solutions." A PC publisher, for instance, may start with a word processing program and later add a formatting program to provide more type styles and finally a paint program to add graphics. While the PC's incremental acquisition is less glamorous than the Mac's "turnkey" approach, it allows each part of a system to be chosen to fit the user's specific requirements and delays some choices until he or she has the experience to make an intelligent decision.

The PC's crude operating software (MS-DOS) provides certain advantages by providing access to individual software and data components. If a PC word processing program doesn't recognize a peculiar (but desired) feature of a printer, it is usually possible to solve the problem by "printing to disk" and directly entering printer control codes into the file. This type of operation is rarely possible on the Mac because of its absolute consistency — printer commands print to the printer, period — and "data intelligence," which makes files difficult to manipulate without special-purpose programs.

Although the process of developing a working PC system is neither cheap nor painless, the ability to evolve, to adapt, and to select from a variety of tools and methods to meet each situation will often be worth the cost. The PC's chaotic environment can be learned piecemeal as needs develop, so the training process is not as formidable as it might appear. The PC techniques are often kludgey, but the confidence gained from knowing that any problem can be overcome is worth the sacrifice of elegance.

Planning for Desktop Publishing

Your selection of a desktop publishing system will depend on your business and/or personal objectives. Do you need to produce commercial-quality publications or do you just want to spiff up correspondence? Do you have a large investment in hardware, software, and training? What economic payback will the system provide? Is the material you publish created from scratch or do you need to collect it from existing computer systems? Keeping these questions in mind as you make your product decisions will assure that the system you buy really does what you need it to do.

The tools required to produce professional-quality correspondence and reports are quite different from those required to produce professional-quality magazines and advertising. If you select the wrong tools, you are likely to create a lot of extra work for yourself and your organization, and may end up delivering your message in a form that confuses rather than explains. Desktop publishing is so attractive and looks so easy that you must take care not to become overly fascinated with the technology and forget what you are out to accomplish. There is no advantage in replacing an appropriately designed but visually boring publication that gets it's message across with a poorly designed substitute that is so visually exciting that no one notices the content. It is also important to remember that business publications are often boring because the subject matter is dry and the writing is poor: Time might be better spent improving the writing than in trying to sugarcoat it with graphic pixie dust.

Once you have decided what you want to produce, you need to evaluate your current equipment, software, training (if any), and the payback you expect from improving your current PC publication quality. Your investment decisions will be quite different depending on whether you expect to increase sales by millions of dollars, reduce advertising production expenses by a few thousand dollars, or just want to make your letters prettier. Pay particular attention to training requirements because the expense of staff training can easily exceed that of equipment and software.

A Basic System

A basic publishing system consists of an IBM PC with 640K memory, a Hercules graphics card with monochrome display, a hard disk drive, and an Epson FX-80 printer. Combined with a good word processing program (such as WordPerfect) and a formatting program (such as Fancy Fonts), this package can create attractive newsletters and documentation for internal company use. Most organizations would not use this type of system for correspondence, sales proposals, or other documents intended for customers because dot matrix printing is grainy and unprofessional looking. Some purists will question whether this should even be called a desktop publishing system, but the creative use of WordPerfect's column and line drawing functions and the addition of Fancy Fonts' type styles allows the preparation of documents that are significantly more interesting looking and attractive than typical word processing documents. A particular advantage of this type of system is that it requires very little training beyond that required for normal word processing. A complete system would cost from $2,000 to $4,000 depending on whether brand name or imported "clone" products are purchased.

Print quality can be improved significantly by upgrading the printer to laser technology. A basic printer, such as the QMS Kiss at $2,000, is a good choice for correspondence, sales proposals, and other text documents where dot matrix print quality is not acceptable but only simple text printing is required. These basic laser printers have minimum flexibility in font selection and graphics, so they are not a good choice for newsletters, advertising, or other graphically complex documents. These printers are as easy to use as dot matrix printers, so they do not add to training requirements.

A laser printer with additional memory, such as the Hewlett-Packard LaserJet Plus at $4,000, provides more choices in type styles and graphics. Full exploitation of the LaserJet requires additional investments in type cartridges or software (costing $50 to $200 per type style and size), a graphics program (such as PC Paintbrush at $100), and page layout programs (such as Polaris PrintMerge at $150 or Xerox Ventura at $895). The more sophisticated page layout programs will also require upgrade of PC memory to at least 640K and the addition of a hard disk at a cost of $400 to $800.

"Batch" style page layout programs such as PrintMerge are excellent tools for newsletters, technical documentation, and sales support materials. Because you do not see the formatted page until it is printed, however, they are not appropriate for precision layout, as required in most advertising materials — unless you are willing to live with a lot of trial and error. Batch style formatting programs allow you to add graphics and type style flexibility to word processing documents with little new investment or training.

What-You-See-Is-What-You-Get (WYSIWYG) page layout programs, such as Ventura, can be used to prepare consumer product documentation and camera-ready advertising, but at the cost of significantly increased complexity. WYSIWYG programs let you preview the page on the computer's display as you work, allowing precise adjustments of the layout before printing. Most WYSIWYG programs will run on an IBM PC with hard disk, but extensive use really calls for an IBM PC AT class system (costing $1,500 to $3,000) using the Enhanced Graphics Adapter (EGA) with Enhanced Color Display (costing an additional $1,500 to $3,000). The faster AT processor will make system response much snappier, so that movement of text and graphics occurs when you give a command instead of a few seconds later. The EGA provides a much more accurate representation of the final printed page. The EGA also reduces eyestrain compared to the standard IBM Color Graphics adapter and standard color display.

This type of configuration also calls for a pointing device, such as Microsoft's Mouse ($199), for rapid menu control and text selection. In order to get the best use of your investment, training in graphics design concepts will be at least as important as learning how to operate the hardware and sophisticated software.

By comparing your business objectives to the basic configuration and capabilities described above, you should be able to develop a basic idea of the type of system you will need and the approximate investment required. The rest of this essay will take a closer look at the components that make up the system and what you need to consider as you select each piece of your system.

If the manipulation of your page format is your primary concern, first select your page layout software, then pick a word processor and printer to work with that. This lets you tailor a system to maximize productivity and throughput. If print quality is your primary concern, you will get the best value for your investment by selecting your printer first, your word processing and page layout programs second, and everything else after that. This lets you pick your printer resolution and print speed first, then complement that decision with software that fully utilizes your printer and provides the formatting and convenience features you need. Decisions concerning selection of system unit, memory, display, and other components will be limited and sometimes dictated by the requirements of your printer and software.

Printer Selection

Printing options for the PC include dozens of products ranging from $200 dot matrix printers to $100,000 and higher phototypesetting systems. Although printer manufacturers love to publish page after page of confusing specifications, print resolution and print speed are the two factors that really affect the price of the printer and the quality of your final publication. Other features to consider include paper capacity, ease of use, cost of supplies, ease of programming, and compatibility with existing software.

Print resolution depends on the clarity and variety of type styles as well as the quality of graphics produced by the printer. Closely related to resolution for laser printers is memory capacity, which determines how many type styles and sizes can be used on each page and how much of the page can be filled with the printer's highest resolution graphics.

Print speed determines how fast you get your printed page and is generally measured in characters printed per second (cps) for dot matrix printers, pages printed per minute (ppm) for laser printers, and feet per minute (fpm) for phototypesetters. Actual print speeds vary significantly depending on how the printer is connected to the computer, whether you are printing graphics or text, and how full the page is. Most manufacturers consider printer speed measurement a creative art, so it is a good idea to do some testing if print speed is one of your critical requirements.

Parallel, Serial, and Bus Printer Connections

A parallel printer connection (often called an IBM printer interface or a Centronics printer interface) can transfer text faster than most printers can print. A serial connection (often called RS232C or "Com:") can operate within a range of speeds, most often limited to 300 to 9,600 baud (bits per second), which works out to approximately 30 to 960 characters per second. A low-speed serial interface is slower than many printers' print speed, reducing the rate at which you actually receive output. In addition, the serial interface specification includes dozens of options that create headaches during setup.

The only advantage of a serial interface over a parallel interface is convenience of connection. Serial connections allow cables up to 75 feet long; even longer cable runs are possible using low-capacity cable and/or special amplifiers called line drivers or modem eliminators. Parallel connections, in contrast, are generally limited to ten feet with no options for extension.

Serial connections also provide more options in "port sharing" devices, "printer sharing" devices, and "A/B Switches" that allow one PC to connect to several printers and/or allow several PCs to connect to one printer. Some similar devices are also available for parallel connections, but they are less useful because all the shared PCs and printers must be located within ten feet of each other.

A serial printer can also be connected directly to a modem for dial-up printer sharing. With a maximum speed of 1,200 or 2,400 baud and with a guarantee of communications problems during set-up and use, however, this type of arrangement is suitable only for the desperate and/or brave. It is usually much easier to exchange files from PC to PC using a communications file transfer program and then print normally at the receiving PC, which can use any sort of printer interface.

When printing graphics, a full page of 300 dots-per-inch laser printer graphics requires more than one million bytes of data. The page can be printed in approximately ten seconds on most laser printers, but the data transfer requires 18 minutes on a 9,600-baud serial interface. These delays can be reduced by using a bus interface, such as that provided as standard on the Cordata LP300 or added to Canon Laser Engines (used in the Hewlett-Packard LaserJet, QMS Kiss, and many others) using the Talltree J Laser. A bus interface can transfer over 100,000 characters per second and can transfer a page of 300-dots per-inch graphics in ten seconds.

Comparing Printers

The large number of printers on the market and the number of variables to consider makes it hard to shop for printers. To make the job more manageable, Table 7-1 groups printers into four basic categories and describes the range of specifications available by category. As you can see, there is a significant amount of overlap between categories. The most significant feature is resolution, since most of the other features are really a by-product of resolution. Print speed, the other major factor in printer selection, is much easier to deal with because each class of printer includes a broad range of speeds at each resolution, with price increasing proportionally with speed.

Table 7-1

	Dot Matrix Printers	Letter Quality Printers	Laser Printers	Phototype-setters
Print speed	30-1200 cps	10-60 cps	6-30 ppm	
Resolution	62-180 dpi	High (fully formed characters, not dot matrix)	300-400 dpi	1250-2500 dpi
Fonts per Page	1-5	1-2	1-20	1-20
Graphics	Line drawings with rough curves	Rectangular line drawings	Almost any line drawing; halftones with relatively low contrast	Line and half-tones
Cost	$200-$3,000	$400-$5,000	$1,800-$40,000	$25,000-$40,000
Notes	(1) Almost all software supports the Epson FX-80 printer which provides a reasonable set of text and graphics capabilities. You significantly limit your software options if you do not select a printer which is compatible with the FX-80. (2) The printing of most thermal printers and ink jet printers is too light to reproduce well with either xerography or offset printing. These printers should be used only for printing.	(1) Office quality daisy wheel printers now cost as much as or more than laser printers. Laser printers are a better choice for almost all applications. (2) Letter quality printers have many moving parts, making these printers the least reliable of the four categories.	(1) A minimum of 1Mb printer memory is needed to fully exploit a laser printer's capability for graphics and multiple fonts. (2) You will generally need to purchase several font cartridges or downloadable fonts and a font management utility program to fully exploit the printer's capability.	(1) Service bureaus are available to provide phototypesetting from PC files at a reasonable charge per page ($7-$11). Considering both cost and complexity, very few businesses will find it desirable to purchase phototypesetting

Letter-quality printers are virtually ignored in desktop publishing because of their inflexibility. Type styles for letter quality printers are changed by having the operator exchange print wheels. Dot matrix printers provide a lot of capability for very little cost, but the graininess of their output makes them inappropriate for publications intended to convey that the company is "high class." When matrix quality is not appropriate, laser printers are the most practical device for the office environment, considering cost, capability, and ease of use.

Phototypesetters provide the ultimate in print quality, but because of both equipment costs and the need for chemical film processing, they are likely to remain enshrined in the graphics department for at least a few more years. Depending on how frequently you produce publications, you might consider using either a dot matrix printer or a laser printer to proofread copy at your working PC, and a service bureau or a sharing arrangement for final typeset printing.

Laser printers and phototypesetters are capable of producing professional-quality, camera-ready copy including text, drawings, rules, and screens. The 300 dots-per-inch resolution of current laser printers results in photograph reproduction that is too grainy and too lacking in contrast to be acceptable in most applications. Photographs are not entirely practical even with phototypesetters, because of the lack of software and reasonably priced high-resolution scanners. Dot matrix printers are adequate for many applications and can produce attractive publications if you are willing to do some pasteup.

Matching Software with the Printer

In order to get the results you want and that your printer is capable of producing, you need software that produces the appropriate printer commands. While your first purchasing decisions probably involve printer requirements, you should avoid actually buying the printer until you have also selected your software. Unless your programs support your particular printer model and *all* its capabilities, you may end up paying for printer features that you can't easily use. The Epson FX-80 and FX-100 printers, for example, include italic and proportional type styles, but there is no way to use these styles using the standard set-ups provided with Microsoft Word, Samna Word III, or WordPerfect. The Hewlett-Packard LaserJet can print in hundreds of styles, but most programs recognize only a handful of Hewlett-Packard supplied type styles and sizes, resulting in improper justification if you try to use third-party-type packages.

If you can't buy the printer and software as a matched set, such as when you add desktop publishing features to an existing system, you will probably be forced to make compromises in both ease of use and final output results.

Text Preparation and Page Layout

In almost all situations, you will prepare your publication's text using a word processing program, such as Microsoft Word, WordPerfect, or WordStar. Your most difficult decision will be to determine whether or not you need to include a page layout program in your publishing system. The main determining factor is design complexity. If you are creating a simple document with one to three newspaper-style columns and some simple line graphics, you can probably do the entire job with your current word processor — this is particularly true if you are willing to do some pasteup for photos and more complex graphics.

Word Processing versus Page Layout

The most significant difference between word processing programs and page layout programs is how page formatting is specified. Word processing programs are text oriented, and they require that you describe your formatting, including the graphic elements, in relation to page margins and paragraph breaks. Text positioning floats freely as you edit the text, constantly changing where lines and pages break. Page layout programs are oriented to graphics and typesetting. You describe your formatting in terms of the page and column dimensions and place graphics where you want them on the page; you then "flow" the text around the graphic elements. If you add text to a word processing program, all subsequent graphic elements are shifted proportionately (and often incorrectly). If you add text to a page layout program, only the text positions are changed.

If you were preparing a financial report with a centered bar chart, for instance, you might use WordPerfect to prepare the text in normal word processing fashion including standard page margins and column widths. You could then insert some blank lines in the center of the page and use WordPerfect's line drawing function to create the bar chart. You would probably end up printing and re-editing several times before you managed to get the bar chart exactly centered. If the chart was not conveniently placed between paragraphs, you would have to use manual justification around the chart (with carriage returns at the end of each line) in order to avoid having WordPerfect's justification disturb the drawing. If you then had to significantly revise the text, you would have to repeat the trial-and-error centering process.

Using a page layout program, such as PC — Pagemaker, you would create the centered frame for the chart at the same time you set margins and columns. You would then place the text, most likely using text created with a word processing program. If you had to revise the text, you would simply make the changes and then "reflow" the text, letting Pagemaker take care of skipping over the chart and rejustifying the text.

If you are willing to do the work, it is possible to produce a magazine using only a word processor or to produce correspondence using a page layout program. The former case would require lots of trial and error to properly position column breaks and graphics. The latter case would require excess set-up time and less convenient editing than using a word processing program.

The decision as to what kind of program to use for which job depends on the frequency and economics of use. While the most functionally appropriate tools should be selected for routine activities, it may be more desirable to use a well-known tool for intermittent jobs, such as using your word processor instead of a page layout program to produce a one-page quarterly newsletter. While Ventura and Pagemaker can provide more flexibility, some users will find that it is more productive to make do with trial and error using their word processor.

Using Word Processors

A word processing program and a printer are the only tools required for many desktop publishing applications. This configuration is most appropriate for producing business documents, such as sales proposals, but to a degree it can be used for more complex designs. Word processing programs are designed to simplify typing, with only passing concern for graphic design. Since your programs won't provide much help, you should start with a simple design, a clear idea of what you want to produce, and knowledge of the word processing features you will use.

Nearly every printer on the market has its own unique combination of features and its own set of command codes to activate those features. In order to avoid having to make program modifications each time a new printer becomes popular, most word processing programs use the concept of a driver to translate control codes used within the program to the control codes required by a particular printer. Drivers are generally supplied as separate files that are read each time the word processing program is run. This makes it possible to support new printers without modifying the program. A few word processing publishers, such as Microsoft (for Microsoft Word), provide specifications for the driver file, allowing printer manufacturers (and even sophisticated users) to provide drivers for new printers. If the publisher of the word processing program must develop the driver, there is usually a long delay while the size of the market is evaluated and if justified, the publisher allocates a programmer to do the work.

In an attempt to advertise broad compatibility, word processing publishers frequently build incomplete drivers for large numbers of printers. It is possible, for example, to have a word processing program and a printer that support proportional fonts but an incomplete driver that prevents use of that feature, like the problem mentioned earlier when trying to use Epson FX series proportional and italic type styles. When selecting your configuration you must take care to verify that the printer features you want (not just the printer model) are *actually* supported.

Microsoft Word Version 3, WordPerfect, and Samna Word III all provide the capability to produce newspaper-style page columns. WordPerfect is the only one of the three to allow editing and display in the column format — the others display each column as a narrow page and format the columns when printing. PrintMerge can be used to create column formats from WordStar documents.

Some word processing programs, such as Samna Word III and WordPerfect, provide the capability to draw rule lines within a document. This feature can be used to draw borders, to create simple line drawings, or to draw frames for pasteup of separately prepared art. Rules are created by inserting graphics characters in the text, so they will shift in location as you add and delete text. If you draw a box, for instance, and then begin to insert text within the box, the right side will move as each character is added. While this problem can often be avoided by using "overwrite" editing mode instead of inserting, it can be quite bothersome if you are making trial-and-error changes to adjust centering and balance. In order to minimize rework, you should not insert rules until your copy is 100 percent final. You should then work sequentially from front to back, first inserting column-oriented rules, such as section separators, and then graphic frames. You should draw page borders only after you are completely satisfied with the rest of the document.

The rules created by word processing programs use up a full character position, so your margins, gutters, and text breaks must leave room for the rule characters. The insertion of rules will sometimes cause tabs to advance to the next stop, but you can minimize problems by being consistent in your use of tabs and spaces for indenting. If you do run into this problem, you can usually fix it in a few seconds by deleting the tab and inserting a few spaces — there's no need to panic, even though the initial appearance may seem catastrophic. The rules created by most word processing programs are centered within a character space, so you must use an odd number (e.g., 1, 3, 5) of characters or lines in any white space where you plan to insert a centered rule and place the rule as the centered character.

Formatting Programs

Some users may find that their word processing program almost satisfies their desktop publishing requirements. A formatting program can be used to add rules, screens, type styles, proportional spacing, and graphics without making the leap to WYSIWYG page layout systems. Formatting programs are available for both dot matrix printers (Fancy Fonts) and laser printers (PrintMerge). You use formatting programs by inserting control codes within your document and then print using the formatting program instead of your word processor's print command. Because they read the unformatted word processing file, some of these programs only work with specific word processing programs. Other formatting programs are resident programs that intercept the PC's printer port. These programs have the advantage of working with almost all word processors (and even other types of programs, such as spreadsheets) and let you use your normal print commands.

Formatting programs are most often used to add new features to older word processors, such as providing rules and proportional spacing for WordStar or to provide type style variety with dot matrix printers. Because they are more page oriented than word processing programs, however, it may be easier to use a formatting program for mastheads, borders, and other page features even if your word processing program has comparable commands. Table 7-2 lists features you should investigate when evaluating postprocessing programs.

Table 7-2

Question	Items To Consider
What word processing program does the formatting program support?	The formatting program should be able to directly read the files produced by your word processing program. It is also possible to convert your word processing files to ASCII to provide compatibility, but this extra step can be a headache if you need to make many trial and error adjustments. (Caution: some advertising claims of "works with all programs" means converting to ASCII.)
Does the formatting program calculate line endings and take care of hyphenation, pagination, and headers and footers?	Some formatting programs take care of only font control and graphics, requiring that you adjust the text with your word processing program. For all but the simplest designs, this will require excessive trial and error.
Does the formatting program provide an adequate selection of fonts at a reasonable cost?	Some formatting programs provide only a limited number of built-in fonts. Other programs require that you purchase each font separately. You should make sure that all required fonts are available and included in your cost evaluation.
Does the formatting program have a way of creating graphics and of merging graphics from other programs?	You must make sure that the formatting program is compatible with the graphic files you want to include in your documents. Some packages include a graphics editor for generating "hand drawn" drawings. Some provide compatibility with specific programs like AutoCad, Lotus 1-2-3, or PC Paintbrush. Some programs include a "capture" program to turn any PC display into a printable image. The formatting program should have the capability to turn any PC display into a printable image. The formatting program should have the capability to enlarge, reduce, and crop graphics before printing.

The most significant disadvantage of formatting programs is that they don't provide WYSIWYG display. Since your word processing program doesn't know about font changes and other postprocessor-controlled changes, the line and page breaks shown on your PC display will not necessarily match your actual output. This may require you to make several test print runs to get acceptable output.

Using Page Layout Programs

WYSIWYG page layout programs, such as PageMaker and Ventura, provide a great deal more flexibility in type style selection, graphics, and layout. The most critical concern from the business perspective is not whether these functions are useful (almost obviously they are), but whether or not they can be economically justified. While the programs are only modestly expensive, most business organizations will face a significant training expense before getting full use from the product. This includes both normal program training concerning the mechanics of the program and also graphics design training to use the program's features intelligently. In addition, while these programs almost always reduce costs compared to conventional typesetting and pasteup, they can raise costs compared to conventional word processing.

For infrequent office uses for which quality is not a prime concern, including occasional production of advertising flyers and newsletters, it probably makes more sense to use a word processing program with a postprocessor to add flair. Word processing programs have an advantage in familiarity that should not be given up lightly — especially if niceness is the only gain.

Page layout programs offer definite cost and convenience advantages compared to conventional graphic production services. In addition to reducing direct production expenses, page layout programs generally reduce turnaround time and errors by allowing designers to directly produce camera-ready copy. The biggest risk in converting from conventional methods to PC page layout is that design effectiveness may be compromised in order to live within the limitations of the programs. This is a particularly serious risk with page layout programs that are fairly new and have not had a chance to mature in either features or reliability. A more subtle risk is that much of the savings will be sacrificed to perfect designs just because it is so easy to make "just one more" change. Figure 7-1 illustrates one of the backbone differences between using a word processor or a page layout program to merge text with graphics. Note that a later text change in a word-processor file alters the graphics, in this case a box.

Graphics and Scanners

Graphics are classified as either line art or continuous tone art. Line art consists entirely of dense black and pure white patterns, such as most pen and ink drawings as well as most business graphics (e.g., bar charts and organizational charts). Line art can be printed on any of the dot printers. Higher resolution printers allow smooth curves and finer lines, but reasonable quality can be achieved even at low resolution, especially if the art is designed with the printer's limitations in mind, making art more rectangular for lower resolution printing.

Continuous tone art, such as photographs and shaded or stippled drawings, is made of black, white, and gray patterns and cannot be

Some word processing programs let you draw lines and boxes (rules) around text. This feature can significantly improve the appearance of your newletters. The box edge will move on lines where you add text.

Some word processing programs (like Samna and Word Perfect) let you draw lines and boxes (rules) around text. This feature can significantly improve the appearance of your newsletters. The box edge will move on lines where you add text.

a.

Page layout programs require that you first draw a box and then "flow" text into it. The program will justify inserted text to maintain the integrity of the box.

Page layout programs (like Ventura and PageMaker) require that you first draw a box and then "flow" text into it. The program will justify inserted text to maintain the integrity of the box.

b.

Figure 7-1. a. Adding to boxed text in a word processing document. b. Adding to boxed text in a page layout document.

directly reproduced with dot matrix black ink printing. Halftones are used to represent gray by creating an optical illusion: varying the density of small black dots so they appear to blur into shades of gray. Closely spaced dots appear black. Increasing the space between dots changes their appearance to gray and eventually to white. It is possible to create a halftone on a dot matrix printer, but the resolution is so low that only a few shades of gray can be produced and the resulting image is often unclear. Laser printers provide the minimum practical density for halftones, with a print quality slightly less than typical newspaper photographs. A density of over 2,000 dots per inch is required to achieve magazine-quality halftones. Unlike line art, halftones cannot be photographically enlarged or reduced because changes in dot spacing changes the perceived shading. Consequently, the original art must be reproduced at the required size and then the halftone process is repeated.

Computer generated graphics can be produced using either bit-mapped or vector technique. Bit-map graphics, such as those produced by Z Soft's PC Paintbrush or Microsoft's Windows Paint, are stored as a matrix of dots that mirror how the drawing is displayed on the CRT display and printed on a printer. These programs can only produce graphics with a resolution as high as that of the display used to create them, which is approximately 80 dots per inch horizontally and 40 dots per inch vertically for the IBM color graphics adapter (CGA) and 80 dots per inch by 60 dots per inch for the IBM enhanced graphics adapter (EGA). Bit-mapped drawings can be read by most page layout programs, including Polaris PrintMerge, Aldus PageMaker, and Xerox Ventura.

Vector-mapped graphics store drawings as a series of instructions, such as "draw a line from point a to point b" or "draw a circle of radius 3 around point a." Vector graphics can be redrawn for different resolution devices, making it possible to draw a rough image on the PC's display and a finer (higher resolution) image on the printer. Unfortunately, there are no widely accepted standards for vector formats, so none of the page layout programs directly read vector images, such as those produced by Lotus 1-2-3 and GCI Graphwriter. The PC Paintbrush package includes a program called Frieze that allows you to capture any display image as a bit-mapped graphic. This allows you, for instance, to display a 1-2-3 graph, capture it with Frieze, perhaps modify it with PC Paintbrush, and then merge it into a WordStar report using PrintMerge.

Existing graphics can be converted to computer format by using scanners such as Dest's PC Scan or Datacopy's Image Processing System. Most scanners produce a bit-mapped graphic at 300 bits per inch, which matches the resolution of most PC laser printers. These scanners can also create a simulated halftone during the scanning process. The images can either be printed directly or merged with text using a compatible formatting program or page layout program. They can also be modified with paint programs, such as PC Paintbrush. There are no strong standards for graphic file formats, so it is critical that you ask about and test for compatibility with your software and printer before selecting a scanner.

A scanned page is stored as a bit-mapped graphic, even if the image contains text. These files cannot be directly edited using word processing programs. Both the Dest and Datacopy scanners offer optional Optical Character Recognition (OCR) software to analyze the image and produce a text file. OCR software can recognize only certain type styles and sizes and requires fairly good print quality, so you should test with samples of the documents you need to scan before selecting an OCR unit.

Typesetting Services

Many phototypesetting services now produce type from word processing files. Most of these services work like formatting programs, requiring you to put type specification codes within your document. If you send your file by modem and request express messenger delivery, you can substantially reduce costs compared to conventional typesetting without sacrificing turnaround time or quality — even if the service bureau is across the country. Intergraphics provides this kind of service on a national basis, but it is also available from many local typesetting companies.

Some typesetting service bureaus will offer to read your word processed files and insert the typesetting codes for you. You should be cautious about this type of service because it provides little cost savings. While this sort of arrangement does reduce typographical errors compared to conventional typesetting, it does nothing to reduce the type specification errors that are the biggest problem in conventional typesetting.

Some of the new entrants to this field accept standard word processed files, allowing you to use your word processor's normal formatting commands. While a few of these services are geared toward PCs, most are intended for Macintosh users and expect files in the Adobe PostScript format popularized by Apple's LaserWriter. Microsoft

Word includes a PostScript driver, so even the Mac-oriented services are open to PCs if you use modem communications to transfer the files or if the service has a PC diskette reader.

Using Data from Other PC Applications and from Other Computers

The first generation of desktop publishing applications concentrated on newsletters and advertising material that were typed directly into the publishing computer. In the business world, however, many publications draw on data that is created or stored in existing computer systems, such as your boss's word processor, a distant correspondent's electronic mail system, or your company's customer proposal computer system. A great deal of time, money, and frustration can be saved by electronically transferring the data to your desktop publishing system instead of retyping from paper copies. Unless you consider compatibility with data sources before buying, however, you may find that the information you want can't be transferred at all or that it is "easier" to retype because incompatible format codes require too much editing.

The first data compatibility requirement is that you format the information so that it is acceptable to your desktop publishing software. This formatting is usually specified by the name of an interface format, such as Document Content Architecture (DCA) or by PC program compatibility, such as imports Lotus 1-2-3 files. It is important to check that your information sources are able to *write* files in a format that your publishing programs can *read*, and that both programs' documentation tell the *whole* truth about what types of files can be exchanged.

The second data compatibility requirement is that there be some way to move the information from the source computer to the publishing computer. This, of course, is not a concern if you are doing all the work on one PC. Data is most easily and reliably moved by exchanging diskettes from other PCs. It is also possible to exchange information by modem or local area network (LAN) communications, but this requires significantly more work as well as trial and error for the initial start-up. If you are exchanging data between unlike systems, such as between a PC and a mainframe computer or between a PC and a Macintosh, modem communications may be your only option due to lack of compatible diskette and LAN formats.

Introduction to Interfaces

Most programs store data and text in a custom file format that reflects the idiosyncrasies of the program and of the programmers who wrote it. If you typed the sentence "How now, brown cow?" into five different word processing programs and then used the MS-DOS "type" command to display the file, you would get five different displays — none of which is likely to be recognizable as your phrase. WordStar files are stored almost the same way they appear on the screen, except that the last character of each word is in hieroglyphics. Files from Samna Word III rarely print more than a few cryptic characters because the first part of the file contains formatting information in binary codes that the "type" command interprets as meaning that the end of the file has been reached. A different but equally bizarre story can be told for each word processor, spreadsheet, and database program.

A software translation interface is a standardized file format that allows programs to convert data. The conversion begins as a specification that describes the kinds of data that can be stored in the file, the format for storing the data, and the format for storing control information. The conversion is implemented in programs that "support" the software interface by providing commands that read and/or write in the interface file format. A simple word processing interface, for example, might state that the file can store only text using a carriage return control code to mark the end of paragraphs. A more complete conversion might include additional control characters for type styles, type sizes, justification, margins, columns, indents, and other document formatting information.

The main reason for using software translation is to preserve the structure of the information. In a word processing file, for instance, we would usually want to transfer not only the words but also structural information, such as the organization of columns, paragraphs, and sections. And for database files we want to know about the organization of fields and records. While identifying these structures may seem like a simple task (for a human), it is beyond the capabilities of many programs. Loss of structure makes it difficult to work with the data because the program can't tell where formatting breaks occur. It is possible to restore lost structure, but it usually requires that you edit every line of the file. To restore paragraph identity to a word processing file, you probably would have to delete a "hard" carriage return at the end of every line except the last line of each paragraph; other changes might be required depending on the complexity of the document and the formats you are using.

Some software translation interfaces, such as DCA for text and Data Interchange Format (DIF) for spreadsheets, were specifically designed for interprogram information exchange. Other interfaces are actually the internal program formats of popular programs (such as dBase III and Lotus 1-2-3) that are so widely used that other programs have been forced to support them. While interfaces greatly simplify data exchange, they are no panacea due to a number of practical problems. An interface is implemented with commands that convert files from one creating program's unique format to the interface format and vice versa. In order for an interface to work for you, the interface format must provide for all the data, structure, and formatting information you want to transfer; and both the sending and receiving program must fully support the interface. It is, unfortunately, fairly common for shortcomings in the interface or its implementation to require that you compromise your objective and/or use your creativity to work around problems.

Word Processing Interfaces

Almost all word processing and page layout programs can read some type of interface file. If this feature is included as a standard command or menu item it is usually called importing or translating. This is the case for Ashton Tate's Framework II, where importing is a selection on the "disk" menu, and for Samna Word III, where translating is a selection from the "do" menu. Many word processing programs also provide an "export" feature to create an outgoing interface file. If these features are provided in a separate program, the process is usually called convert, as provided with the WordPerfect and Microsoft Word packages.

The only difference between conversion and import/export is convenience. When import and export are included as standard commands or menu items, you can read and write interface files as easily as you do the normal files. When a separate program is used, you must exit the word processing program, run the convert program, and then run the word processing program to continue with what you were doing.

As with all other critical features, it is worth your time to test programs before making a purchase to assure that both the interface and the program support the formatting features you need. Incomplete conversion can result from use of unique program features, such as Microsoft Word's style sheets, that are not supported by DCA or most other word processing programs. Because style sheets are fairly unique, it makes sense that they can't be moved to other programs. Rational or not, this sort of shortcoming can be painful if not identified in advance. Microsoft minimizes this problem by providing the option to convert style sheets to embedded format codes before conversion to DCA, transferring your formatting but losing the flexibility of style sheets. Incomplete conversion can also be caused by program error or by design. Microsoft has chosen not to include "dot" commands in its Convert program that translates WordStar documents to Microsoft Word format, therefore ignoring WordStar margins, headings, footings, and other formatting information. While this shortcoming is documented in the manual, it would not be uncovered by asking the simple question "Can Word read WordStar files?".

The most basic word processor interface is an ASCII or text file. ACSII stands for American Standard Code for Information Interchange and alludes to the numeric codes used to represent characters within the computer and disk files. The ASCII interface includes only text with no structural or formatting information. When you import an ASCII file into a word processing program you will usually find that each print line has been interpreted as a paragraph and that print features, such as bold and underline, are either lost or misrepresented as duplicated and/or trashed strings of characters.

The only real strength of the ASCII interface is that it can be produced by almost every program in every product category (except graphics) and can be read by almost any word processing or page layout program. Many programs that do not specifically support data exchange allow "printing to disk," which produces an ASCII file — the only caveat being that the file may include printer control characters that cause odd results when read by some programs.

DCA is a set of interfaces developed by IBM for exchanging text between computer systems. It has been widely adopted by mainframe computer, minicomputer, and PC word processing systems, so it provides a convenient way to transfer text between unlike computer systems and unlike word processing programs. Revisable Form DCA provides hundreds of control codes to describe document formatting and is intended for transfers where the recipient needs the ability to revise the document. Final Form DCA provides only codes describing how to print the document, and is used for electronic mail systems to forward documents for printing.

The revisable form DCA format, for example, stores the page heading just one time, perhaps including a code showing where to insert the page number. A final form DCA file would have the heading repeated at the top of each page and the actual page number would be filled in. The revisable form DCA file stores text more or less the way you create the text with your word processing program (like a Word-Star **.he** line, for example) and the final form is similar to a "print to disk" file.

Revisable form DCA is supported by many mainframe, minicomputer, and PC word processing programs. DCA is probably the most thoroughly defined and documented PC interface, so it suffers less from inconsistencies than other interfaces. Nonetheless, it is still essential to verify that the formatting features you need are supported by all the word processing programs you are using and by their respective DCA import and export functions.

The most common PC text interface is probably still the WordStar file structure. This binary interface provides a reasonable way to move text without losing paragraph identity. Many WordStar formatting features are stored in final form rather than as control codes, limiting the amount of formatting that can be translated. The WordStar center and tab commands, for instance, simply insert spaces to position the lines within the current margins; there is no intelligence in the file structure to distinguish lines that should be recentered from lines that are simply indented. Only the formatting codes that appear on the screen, such as the dot commands and the Print menu control codes can be reliably interfaced.

Spreadsheet and Database Interfaces

The simplest interface between data sources (spreadsheets and databases) and documents involves moving unformatted data to the document and then manually adjusting alignment and formatting. Under the best of circumstances this is a tedious and error-prone process. Each time your source data is revised you are faced with the undesirable alternatives of either repeating the entire transfer and format process or manually editing the document to reflect the data changes. The more desirable approaches are to either do all formatting at the data source or to treat the data like a mail-merge file that is formatted automatically as it is read by your word processing program.

The simplest way to reliably include data in a document is to format the data with a spreadsheet or database report and then print to disk. The imported ASCII file will lack structural information, but this should not be a problem since it is "printed" by the spreadsheet or database in the format you want. Changes can be made by simply deleting the old data in your desktop publishing system and then importing a new version of the source report. You will not be able to include format codes, such as font selection and boldface, in the form required by most word processors, so this method is appropriate only for simple tables unless you are using a formatting program. Most formatters use embedded ASCII format codes that can be included in the interface file using the "print headings," "print constant," or "print literal" features of your spreadsheet or database report writer.

You will maintain the greatest formatting control and convenience for data by keeping the data's column structure intact when importing and then using your word processor's mail-merge function to read the raw data and apply all necessary formatting. This type of interface minimizes the interdependence between word processor formatting and spreadsheet/database programming, greatly simplifying change. This formatting independence is particularly valuable if the data is supplied by a different person or work group.

WordStar uses comma delimited files for its mail-merge data, and most other word processing programs have either adopted that format or provide a command to import comma delimited or WordStar mail-merge files to their internal format. Comma delimited files store each database record or spreadsheet row as one line and separates fields or columns by commas. Comma delimited files can be created by most database and spreadsheet programs including dBase, Rbase, Framework, and Lotus 1-2-3. Currently available page layout programs do not include mail-merge-like capabilities, so this type of interface is available only when using a word processor.

Summary

The virtues of the IBM PC and compatibles are that they are widespread, inexpensive, and expandable. Available monitors and printers range in price from one or two hundred to thousands of dollars, with corresponding capability. Software choices range from word processing programs featuring multiple columns, varying typefaces, and graphic-merging to elaborate and reliable page layout software. The variety of hardware and software available to the PC owner is the broadest of any microcomputer family and sometimes presents bewildering choices and issues of compatibility. The advantage gained is the possibility of designing a very finely-tuned system.

Because there are so many auxiliary products for the PC family — for instance formatting and conversion programs, graphic utilities, databases, and scanning systems — this area alone may justify the use of a PC-based system. Many choices exist, and it is possible to configure satisfactory systems at many price levels. The all-important consideration is to match the software to the hardware, and making the match depends on the trade-offs of operator comfort, production speed, and the need for software power.

KEYWORDS:

• Multitasking

• Operating En-
  vironment

• Tiled Windows

• Overlapping
  Windows

John Angermeyer is an independent consultant specializing in
microcomputer software
development, technical writing,
and desktop publishing.
Previously a software engineer
for a telecommunications company, Mr. Angermeyer has also
worked as a consultant in the
development of programmable
control systems. He is co-author
with other Waite Group authors of
*CP/M Bible, DOS Primer for the
IBM PC & XT, Understanding
MS-DOS, MS-DOS Developer's
Guide,* and *Tricks of the MS-DOS
Masters.*

Essay Synopsis: Microsoft Windows replaces the
MS-DOS operating system normally associated
with the IBM PC/XT/AT families of machines with
a new, easy-to-use operating environment based
on the idea of graphic panels, pull-down menus,
scrolling bars, and a mouse pointing device.
Within the Windows environment, unlike MS-
DOS, you can run more than one program at a
time. For desktop publishing, this allows convenient sharing of information in documents
generated by different programs.

In this essay the author explains what the
Windows operating environment is and why it is
unique. He discusses the program and its parts,
including the built-in word processor, paint program, clipboard, and cardfile. You will learn about
tiled windows, pull-down menus, multitasking,
and see how Windows creates an improved, integrated environment.

8

Microsoft Windows

John Angermeyer

Using an MS-DOS computer, such as the IBM personal computer series and its compatibles, for desktop publishing applications has many advantages and disadvantages compared to other types of systems. Compared to the Apple Macintosh, for example, an IBM PC or compatible system provides the benefit of being expandable, and gives the user a greater number of options for graphics display, printer output, and input devices, to name just a few. But at the same time, an IBM PC or compatible system has one distinct disadvantage for the desktop publisher: It does not inherently provide an operating environment that supports several compatible desktop publishing applications at one time.

Although there are a variety of MS-DOS programs that provide the tools needed for desktop publishing, they tend not to be compatible with each other when it comes to the easy interchange of formatted text and graphics between applications.

One approach to creating a compatible, integrated system is to add an operating environment to the MS-DOS system, as distinct from an operating system, such as MS-DOS. An operating environment is a program that is designed to work with the operating system, replacing many aspects of its user interface. For example, when an operating environment is added to an MS-DOS system, the standard MS-DOS **A>** prompt (in response to which commands

RELATED ESSAYS:

6. The Macintosh System

7. Desktop Publishing on the PC

9. Graphics Standards

10. Inside Monitors

are entered), is replaced with icons, buttons, and menus, and provides the user with a more intuitive gateway to the system.

There are several operating environments designed to operate in computers running the MS-DOS operating system. Some examples are Microsoft Windows from Microsoft Corporation, GEM (Graphical Environment Manager) from Digital Research, DESQView from QuarterDeck Systems, and Topview from IBM. Both Microsoft Windows (hereafter referred to as MS-Windows) and GEM employ bit-mapped graphics to display all data on the screen, whereas DESQView and Topview do not use bit-mapped graphics at all, relying instead on the standard characters generated by the system.

Operating Environments for Desktop Publishing

Although all four of the examples just mentioned are considered to be operating environments, only MS-Windows and GEM can be deemed appropriate for serious desktop publishing. Both environments provide the graphic interface necessary to support several graphics-intensive applications that can be used together to provide easy interchange of highly formatted text and graphics.

Why aren't text-oriented operating environments appropriate for desktop publishing? One problem is that they rely on a single non-proportional-spaced font. In the case of the IBM PC series and compatible systems, the single text font is stored in a ROM (read-only memory), and consists of all the ASCII characters (decimal codes 0 through 127) and the IBM extended character set (decimal codes 128 to 255), which contain several foreign language and other special characters. As the characters are displayed on the screen, they appear as they're defined in the ROM: Each character occupies the same amount of space as the next character, and the shapes of the characters are fixed. What does this mean to the desktop publisher? It means that if you're using a text-oriented operating environment or application, you won't have WYSIWYG (What You See Is What You Get) capabilities unless what you want printed is meant to look like the text on the screen. You won't have the capability of changing point sizes and fonts unless you embed special print codes within the text, although in some text-oriented applications, text can be seen on the screen in bold, underlined, and sometimes even in italics. A bit-mapped graphics program, on the other hand, can be designed to achieve WYSIWYG capabilities to the degree of the resolution on the screen and its relationship to the resolution of the output device. With today's equipment, it's virtually impossible to achieve true WYSIWYG capabilities. Generally, what you end up with is WYSIWYSOG, or "What You See Is What You Sort Of Get."

About Graphics

Although some stand-alone bit-mapped graphics programs can be used while running some text-oriented operating environments, they cannot run within the operating environment. This means that if a bit-mapped graphics program is run while in a text-oriented operating environment, the operating environment first must relinquish control of the system to MS-DOS so that the graphics application can operate. When a bit-mapped graphics program is loaded, it always takes over the screen because the various IBM graphics standards do not allow both text and graphics modes to coexist at the same time. When the graphics application is terminated, control of the system is returned to the operating environment. Although you may wish to exchange graphics data between several applications, such as between a paint program, a typesetting program, and a page layout program, it simply may not be possible if you're using a text-oriented operating environment combined with applications that weren't designed to be compatible with each other.

Some bit-mapped graphics programs include "snapshot" utilities that can be used to take pictures of graphic images displayed on the screen by another, incompatible application. However, in almost all cases, these snapshot utilities capture a displayed graphic on a pixel by pixel basis, ignoring any special formatting, such as object-oriented graphics or specially formatted text (treated as true text). What you get in the end is simply a picture of what's on the screen, in much the same way as a camera, digital scanner, or facsimile machine scans an image. MS-Windows has such a facility built-in. If you're able to run a non-MS-Windows graphics application under MS-Windows, holding down the Alt key and pressing the PrtSc key takes a snapshot of any image displayed on the screen and places it in a paste buffer for later use. This MS-Windows feature distinguishes between true ASCII (IBM ROM-generated) text and bit-mapped graphics. However, text that is manipulated within a bit-mapped graphics program is interpreted simply as bit-mapped images.

One of the main advantages of MS-Windows is that most applications which run under it are capable of interchanging most types of data between them. For example, a graphic image generated by the paint program provided with MS-Windows can be copied to other MS-Windows applications for further manipulation. Conversely, text generated by MS-Windows' text editor can be copied to other types of applications as true text. There are exceptions. For example, text generated by Microsoft Write (the word processor provided with MS-Windows) has special formatting associated with it, such that it cannot be transferred to Microsoft Notepad (MS-Windows' text editor) unless the text in MS-Write is first saved to a file as true ASCII without any special formatting. However, the existence of MS-Windows' "universal" paste buffer that works with all MS-Windows applications makes transferring data between applications considerably easier than among several incompatible stand-alone desktop publishing applications.

Features of Microsoft Windows

Of the two most popular graphics-oriented operating environments in use today (MS-Windows and GEM), MS-Windows seems to have gained the most popularity. When considering features such as paint programs and specialized word processors, both MS-Windows and GEM are comparable. They both provide windows and icons, make use of pointing devices (such as a mouse), and provide methods for the interchange of graphics data and text between applications.

One main difference between the two is that MS-Windows is a multitasking operating environment, whereas GEM is not. This means that you can run several applications designed to work within the MS-Windows environment at the same time. What's significant about MS-Windows' multitasking capabilities is that MS-Windows adds multitasking to the MS-DOS computer; MS-DOS, up to and including Version 3.2, is a single-tasking operating system, which means that at any one time only one program runs in the machine (although programmers have tricks to make it appear that several programs are running simultaneously on certain occasions).

Throughout the rest of this essay, we focus on how MS-Windows can be used as an environment for desktop publishing on an IBM PC series or compatible system. Once you know what the MS-Windows environment and its application programs can do for you, you'll get a good idea of how good MS-Windows will be as an environment if you're planning to use an MS-DOS computer for desktop publishing. Figure 8-1 shows the opening screen for MS-Windows. Note the disk drives labelled alphabetically.

Tiled and Overlapping Windows

MS-Windows supports two types of windows: tiled and overlapping. The main windows displayed by MS-Windows, including the windows in which most MS-Windows applications appear, are tiled windows (sometimes called tiles). They are called tiled because, unlike most windowing programs and environments, the windows do not overlap. As of the release of MS-Windows Version 1.03, MS-Windows applications can now be designed so that they use overlapping (nontiled) windows.

How do tiled windows differ from overlapping windows? When MS-Windows has only one window open, the window fills the screen. When a second window is opened, the first window has its size and position adjusted to make room for the next one, so that both windows exist side by side (vertically or horizontally), each occupying its own half of the screen. When a third window is opened, the existing two windows are adjusted again so that one window occupies one half of the screen with the other half divided into two quarters, or each window can occupy a third of the screen. As new windows are opened, all or most windows are adjusted accordingly. The size of each window

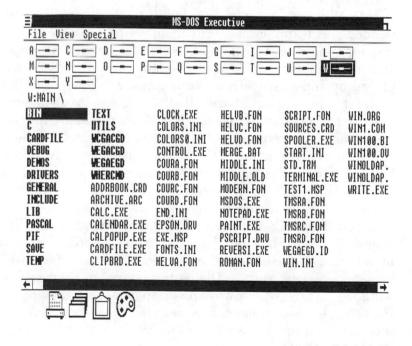

Figure 8-1. The opening window of MS-Windows.

and the way each window divides the screen can be manually adjusted. A window can be manually moved to any part of the screen, causing all other windows automatically to adjust. Up to a maximum of 15 windows can be opened within MS-Windows.

There are advantages and disadvantages to tiled windows. The main advantage is that you can have many windows opened at once and still get a glimpse of what's inside each one. No window covers up the contents of another window. Most applications provide "roll bars" that allow you to shift the contents of a window up, down, left, or right, without changing the position, shape, and size of the window. A window can also be "zoomed" at any time so that it fills up the screen. When the zoom is cancelled, the window reverts to its original state. If the screen gets too cluttered with tiled windows, any tiled window can be turned into an icon, which is placed at the bottom of the screen. An application that has been iconized continues to run, but the contents of the window are not visible. To open an iconized application, simply select the icon by moving the pointer to it and pressing the mouse button. While the mouse button is still pressed, move the icon to the desired position on the screen. The window opens once the mouse button is released, causing the rest of the open windows to adjust automatically in size and position.

MS-Windows handles overlapping windows differently from tiled windows. An application that displays in an overlapping window always is placed on top of any tiled windows currently open. When several overlapping windows are open, only the "selected" window is placed on top of the other overlapping windows (all overlapping windows remain on top of the tiled windows). A window is selected by moving the pointer to any portion of the desired window and pressing the mouse button once. A tiled window is selected in the same manner. However, if any portion of the selected tiled window is covered by overlapping windows, the only way to expose the covered areas is to move or close the overlapping windows or to zoom into the selected window so that it fills up the entire screen.

Almost all MS-Windows applications have what are called dialog boxes. A dialog box is displayed by some commands in pull-down menus and are used to contain options that can be turned on or off or be set to various values. Dialog boxes are, in themselves, overlapping windows. They will always overlap the contents of tiled windows. However, some of them can be selected, deselected, and moved around the screen in the same way as applications that are displayed in overlapping windows.

The MS-DOS Executive

When MS-Windows is first run in an MS-DOS computer, the first window that's displayed is called the MS-DOS Executive. The MS-DOS Executive can be viewed as the desktop part of the operating environment; it is the gateway to the system and its resources. The MS-DOS Executive essentially replaces the MS-DOS **A>** prompt with an icon- and pull-down menu-driven user interface to the system.

Notice that all the disk drives defined in the system are shown across the top of the MS-DOS Executive window, just below the title bar and the pull-down menu commands. MS-Windows is able to recognize not only real disk drives (floppy drives and hard disk drives), but also RAMdisks, external disk drives supported by device drivers, and virtual drives created with the SUBST command in MS-DOS Versions 3.1 and higher. The list of files displayed below the disk drives represents the files in the default directory of the selected disk drive (darkened). A disk drive is selected simply by moving the mouse pointer to the drive and clicking the mouse button once.

Individual files also are accessible in a similar manner: Move the mouse pointer to the file (the file underneath the mouse pointer automatically becomes highlighted), then quickly click the left mouse button twice. If the file is a ".COM," ".EXE," or a ".BAT" file, it automatically executes as if you had typed in the command at the MS-DOS **A>** prompt. It is from the MS-DOS Executive window that all other MS-Windows applications start.

Microsoft Windows Applications

One of the "gotcha's" with MS-Windows, as with most operating environments, is that to use it most effectively you need application programs designed specifically for MS-Windows. A true MS-Windows program is no ordinary MS-DOS program. In fact, MS-Windows applications do not run without MS-Windows. For an application to be most useful in the MS-Windows environment, it must be designed to make use of MS-Windows' windowing, pull-down menu, and icon facilities. It also must be designed so that it makes use of MS-Windows' data interchange capabilities — that is, the smooth transfer of bit-mapped graphic images or highly formatted text between applications.

MS-Windows provides a set of application programs, some of which are pertinent to desktop publishing, and others that are utilities for all situations. There are numerous standard programs supplied with MS-Windows, such as Windows Write (word-processing/typesetting programs), Notepad (general text editor), Windows Paint (basic drawing/paint program), and Cardfile (emulates an expandable box of indexed cards, each of which can contain a graphic or text) — all of which are very useful for desktop publishing. For general utilities, several other programs are included: Calc (general purpose calculator), Calendar (extensive calendar utility), Clock (analog clock), and Terminal (communications program). Control utilities for MS-Windows that provide intrinsic functions to all MS-Windows applications include Clipboard (temporary pasteboard for text or graphics "cut" from other applications), Spooler (print spooler), and Control (program to control different aspects of the MS-Windows environment and its applications, including printer selection, assignment of ports for printers and communications, and color changing).

You can get a good start at setting up a desktop publishing system with the applications that come with the standard MS-Windows package. Apart from the Windows Write and Windows Paint programs, the rest of the programs are appropriate to any MS-Windows applications you use with your system. That's not to say that Windows Write and Windows Paint are not appropriate for MS-Windows. However, their features are limited to fairly basic functions when compared to other commercial software applications designed for the MS-Windows environment. Both Windows Write and Windows Paint are useful programs for getting you started using MS-Windows, and for basic desktop publishing needs, such as WYSIWYG word processing, basic artwork, and limited page layout. Some of the standard application programs of MS-Windows are described in greater detail in the following sections.

Windows Write

Windows Write is a word-processing program that includes basic typesetting and page layout capabilities. It provides the features of most simple word processors. It can wordwrap; it allows you to set margins and tabs; it can copy and move blocks of text; and it can search for a text string and optionally replace it with another (once or globally throughout a document). It displays all text in WYSIWYG format, showing all changes in character attributes, fonts, and font sizes on the screen. All of its commands are available through the use of pull-down menus and dialog boxes. Table 8-1 shows the commands that are available in each pull-down menu. Note that some of the commands, when executed, display dialog boxes that are small windows containing further parameters for the command.

Table 8-1   Summary of Windows Write Pull-Down Menu Commands and Options

Pull-Down Menus	Commands	Keyboard Access	Dialog Box Parameters
File	New		none
	Open		drive & filename
	Save	none	filename, text-only make backup, Micro-soft Word format
	Print		(SPOOLER program)
	Change Printer		List of printers, each own dialog box
	Repaginate		Confirm page breaks
Edit	Undo	Shift-Esc	none
	Cut	Del	none
	Copy	F2	none
	Paste	Ins	none
	Move Picture		none
	Size Picture		none
Search	Find		Whole word, match upper/lower case
	Repeat Last Find	F3	none
	Change		Whole word, match upper/lower case, find next, change then find, change current, change all
	Go To Page	F4	Page number
Character	Normal	F5	none
	Bold	F6	none
	Italic	F7	none
	Underline	F8	none
	Superscript		none
	Subscript		none
	Font 1 (Helv)*		none
	Font 2 (Tms Rmn)*		none
	Font 3 (Courier)*		none
	Reduce Font	F9	none
	Enlarge Font	F10	none
	Fonts...		Fonts, font size
Paragraph	Normal		none
	Left		none
	Centered		none
	Right		none

Table 8-1   cont'd

Pull-Down Menus	Commands	Keyboard Access	Dialog Box Parameters
	Justified		none
	Single Space		none
	1 ½ Space		none
	Double Space		none
	Indents...		Left indent, first line, right indent
Document	Header		Distance from top, print on 1st page, insert page number
	Footer		Distance from bottom, print on first page, insert page number
	Rulers On/Off		none
	Tabs...		12 positions, decimal tabs
	Page Layout...		Start page numbers at ?, left/right/top/ bottom margins (inches or cm)

* The fonts shown in the table are default names for most types of printers. However, these three default fonts can be changed at any time by selecting the "Fonts..." command in the same menu.

As can be seen by the commands and options in Table 8-1, Windows Write provides several useful functions to the MS-Windows environment. In addition to the formatting and stylizing of text, Windows Write is also capable of accepting any bit-mapped graphics image that's been captured in the Clipboard program. Drawings created with Windows Paint and other MS-Windows applications can be copied into Windows Write as "pictures." Two commands in the "File" pull-down menu are used to control pictures inserted into a Windows Write document: Size Picture and Move Picture. These commands allow you to shrink or stretch a picture both horizontally and vertically as well as to move a picture to another part of the document. Pictures can be flush-left, centered, or flush-right, in much the same way as paragraphs. However, a picture always consumes entire lines. It cannot exist in a column or have text on either side of it.

Windows Write also accepts documents created with the Microsoft Word word-processing program. Although Microsoft Word is not a MS-Windows application, documents created with it can be read into Windows Write for further formatting and integration of drawings. Documents created by other word-processing programs also can be read into Windows Write if they are formatted correctly. As a general rule, a document created by a word processing program (other than Microsoft Word) first must be converted to straight ASCII, with all special formatting removed.

Although Windows Write may not be considered the ultimate tool for the serious desktop publisher who needs to do a considerable amount of page layout, it does provide many of the functions needed to get started. Several commercial programs are available now for the MS-Windows environment, some of which provide capabilities beyond those provided by Windows Write.

Windows Paint

Windows Paint is a paint/drawing program that provides an electronic canvas with tools such as a paintbrush, pencil, straightedge, and eraser. The canvas can be sized for portrait or landscape drawings for output on 8½ by 11 inch paper. Although not an extensive drawing program, Windows Paint provides several functions that allow you to make simple drawings for direct output or for inclusion in Windows Write documents.

The four boxes in the upper left corner of the Windows Paint window, just below the menu bar and above the canvas, are the "current status" boxes. They indicate the current drawing tool being used, the paint pattern, brush shape, and line width. The drawing tool is selected by moving the mouse pointer to one of the icons shown in the boxes to the right of the current status boxes and clicking the mouse button. The rest of the items in the current status boxes are selected by accessing the pull-down menus shown on the menu bar.

Drawing Tools

Selection Rectangle. The selection rectangle (shown in the upper left tool box) is used to select portions of a drawing for copying, moving, deleting, or for editing with the zoom function.

Selection Net. Just below the selection rectangle is the selection net. It's used to select nonrectangular shapes for copying, moving, deleting, or for editing with the zoom function.

Text Tool. Next to the selection rectangle is the text tool. The text tool allows you to insert text on the canvas by typing on the keyboard. Various fonts, font sizes, and character styles are selected with commands in the Font, FontSize, and Style pull-down menus. While the text tool is active, any text entered can be edited and changed. However, once another drawing tool is selected, any text previously entered is converted to bit-mapped graphics and no longer can be edited with the text tool.

Scroll Tool. Beneath the text tool is the scroll tool. It is used to move the canvas up and down in the window. The canvas is larger than what you see in the drawing window. The Zoom Out command can be used to see the entire canvas.

Pencil. Next to the text tool is the pencil. Use it for sketching in much the same way as you would use a normal pencil.

Eraser. Below the pencil is the eraser. It is shaped like a blackboard eraser and can be used to erase any part of a drawing.

Line Tool. Next to the pencil is the line tool. Use it to draw straight lines in any direction from any given point to another point.

Paintbrush. The paintbrush is used to paint in any shape with one of 24 different brush shapes and patterns.

3-D Tool. Next to the line tool is the 3-D tool, which is used to draw three-dimensional shapes by displaying axes to help you judge the correct perspective.

Fill Tool. Beneath the 3-D tool is the fill tool. The fill tool, which looks and acts like a paint bucket, is used to fill any enclosed shape with the current pattern selected from the palette. Up to 36 patterns are available from the palette pull-down menu.

Curve Tool. Next to the 3-D tool is the curve tool, which is used to make curves. It is used by first drawing a straight line (much like the line tool), and then selecting a point along the line with the click of the mouse button (or pressing the space bar) and "pulling" the line in the direction desired.

Airbrush. The airbrush, which is under the curve tool, is used to spraypaint any part of the canvas with the current pattern (obtained from the palette).

Geometric Shapes. The ten icons to the right of the screen contain geometric figures that can be created by moving the mouse to the desired position on the canvas and stretching the figure to the shape and size desired. Included in the top row is a set of clear icons: rectangle, rounded box, circle, oval, and freehand polygon. The lower row includes the same set of icons, except that they are solid. The clear icons allow the creation of shapes without any filler pattern or colors, whereas the solid icons allow the creation of shapes that automatically are filled with the "current" pattern (obtained from the palette).

Moving Images

By using the selection rectangle or selection net icons to select a graphic image drawn on the canvas, you can cut or copy the selected image. The cut or copied image can then be pasted in another part of Paint's canvas, to another MS-Windows application program, such as Windows Write, or to another canvas of Windows Paint running in a different window.

As stated before, Windows Paint provides the basic functions needed to create simple drawings that can be printed directly or included in documents. If you're going to use the MS-Windows environment to do a lot of artwork, especially technical artwork, consider some of the commercial packages available that can be added to the MS-Windows operating environment.

Windows Clipboard

The Windows Clipboard program has just one purpose in the MS-Windows environment: It holds any data, text, or bit-mapped graphics, that have been deleted or copied using the cut and paste feature in another MS-Windows application program. For example, if you delete or copy a block of text in Windows Write, that text is pasted to the Clipboard. You use the Ins key to paste the contents of the Clipboard into another document.

In some cases, the Clipboard can be run as a program to display its contents in a separate window. When you copy text or graphics from other applications, you immediately see the text or graphics displayed in Clipboard's window. Having three MS-Windows applications open on the screen at the same time (Windows Write, Windows Paint, and Clipboard) you can see readily how they can share similar data. First, create a document using Windows Write. Then draw a figure using Windows Paint, and copy it (using the selection net icon, then issuing the Copy command) to cause the drawing to be copied to the Clipboard. The drawing is then inserted into the spot in Windows Write using the Ins key.

Data, text, or graphics can be exchanged between applications in this manner by using the Clipboard program. Note that when text or graphics are captured in non-MS-Windows applications, the information is also copied into the Clipboard, and it is ready then for insertion into other applications. Unfortunately, the Clipboard cannot accommodate mixed real text and graphics. If true ASCII text is captured and copied into the Clipboard, then true ASCII text also is pasted. However, if text displayed in a non-MS-Windows-compatible, bit-mapped graphics mode is captured, then bit-mapped graphics are copied into the Clipboard. MS-Windows does not provide any facility to convert text in bit-mapped form to true ASCII text. Despite this limitation, the Clipboard is nevertheless a very useful utility for the exchange of data between MS-Windows and non-MS-Windows applications.

Windows Cardfile

The Windows Cardfile program provides the function of holding and sorting several "cards" in a "box." On each card, you can store a variety of types of information, such as text, addresses with phone numbers for autodialing, and bit-mapped graphic images. When text is stored on a file, it must be in ASCII format (such as that created with the Windows Notepad program) because the cards do not accept text from a Windows Write program. Apart from the obvious use of the Cardfile program for storing addresses and phone numbers, it is also very useful for storing small graphic images that you may want to use as "transfers" for other drawings created with Windows Paint. Figure 8-2 shows an example of what the Clipboard program looks like with a series of cards containing small graphic transfers that are useful for future drawings created with Windows Paint.

Nonstandard MS-Windows Applications

The following is a list of commercial MS-Windows application programs you may find useful for desktop publishing. These programs are available from companies other than Microsoft Corporation that have designed their programs to run in the MS-Windows environment. The following list is certainly not complete, but it should give you some idea as to what's available.

Drawing, Painting, and Design Programs:
Windows Draw, from Micrografx, Inc.
In*A*Vision, from Micrografx, Inc.
Big-Paint, from Hammerlab

Page Layout Programs:

PageMaker, from Aldus

Spelling Checkers:

Windows Spell, from Palantir Software

Communications Programs:

Windows in Talk, from Palantir Software

Miscellaneous Programs:

Windows GRAPH!, from Micrografx, Inc.
Scan-Do, from Hammerlab
Museum, from Hammerlab

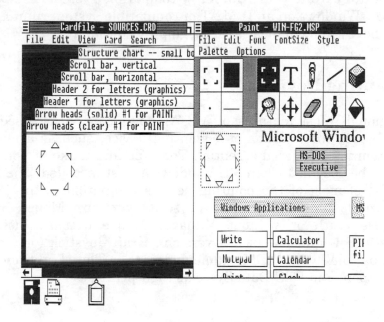

Figure 8-2. Using Cardfile as a source for graphics.

Hardware Compatibility

The following section describes some of the hardware that is compatible with MS-Windows. Although MS-Windows has certain requirements, most of the hardware described is optional.

System Level

MS-Windows is designed to run on an IBM PC that is running the MS-DOS operating system (Version 2.0 or higher) and is equipped with two double-sided floppy drives or a hard disk, as well as graphics display hardware. Other compatible systems include the IBM XT and IBM AT, and most close compatibles or clones. A system running MS-Windows must have at least 256K of RAM, although 512K to the full 640K of RAM is highly recommended. With the addition of an EMS "expanded memory" card, several megabytes of memory can be made available through a RAMdisk program, significantly increasing the performance of MS-Windows. The speed of the system's processor is also important: The standard speed of the processor in an IBM XT (usually 4.77 MHz) is generally not fast enough to run MS-Windows in an effective manner. It is highly recommended that you add an accelerator card to your IBM XT or compatible system. The performance of MS-Windows on an IBM AT or compatible system running at 6 MHz or above seems to meet with the approval of many users.

Pointing Devices

Although most features of MS-Windows can be accessed using the keyboard, the addition of a pointing device, such as a mouse, to the system is considered essential. The type and make of pointing device must be specified when MS-Windows is first installed. The following is a list of most of the pointing devices compatible with MS-Windows: Microsoft Mouse (bus card or serial version), Mouse Systems PC Mouse (with or without Manager Mouse option), VisiOn Mouse, Logitech Logimouse (serial version), Kraft Joystick (or other joystick compatible with IBM game adapter), The LightPen Company Lightpen, and FTG Data Systems Lightpen.

Display Hardware

MS-Windows requires bit-mapped graphics display hardware. The type and make of graphics hardware being used is specified when MS-Windows is first installed. The following is a list of the graphics hardware compatible with MS-Windows.

- IBM Color Graphics Adapter (CGA) or compatible, connected to a compatible monitor such as the IBM Color Display. This configuration yields a resolution of 640 by 200 pixels, with no colors (black and white).
- IBM Enhanced Graphics Adapter (EGA) or compatible, connected to an IBM Color Display or compatible display. This configuration

yields a resolution of 640 by 200 pixels, with 8 colors (128K EGA) or 16 colors (256K EGA).

- IBM Enhanced Graphics Adapter (EGA) or compatible, connected to an IBM Enhanced Color Display or compatible display. This configuration yields a resolution of 640 by 350 pixels, with 8 colors (128K EGA) or 16 colors (256K EGA).
- Hercules Graphics Card connected to an IBM Monochrome Monitor or compatible display, yielding a resolution of 720 by 348 pixels, with no colors (monochrome).
- FTG Data Systems Single Pixel Board

Several other graphics cards and monitor combinations may be used with MS-Windows. Many of them provide higher resolutions ranging from 640 by 480 to 1,024 by 800 pixels. The various manufacturers of this equipment can supply special device drivers that make them compatible with MS-Windows.

Printer Output Hardware

MS-Windows provides compatibility with a variety of printers.

Dot-Matrix Printers:
Epson MX-80 with Graftrax+, FX-80, FX-85, FX-100, and LQ-1500
Citizen MSP-25
NEC 3550 and P2\P3
Hewlett-Packard 7470A and 7475A
IBM Graphics, Proprinter, and Color Printer
Okidata 92, 93, 192, and 193 (IBM or standard models)
C-Itoh 8510
TI 850 and 855
Toshiba P1351
Star Micronics SG-10

Laser Printers:
Hewlett-Packard LaserJet and LaserJet Plus
Apple LaserWriter and LaserWriter-Plus (serial connection)
Most other PostScript-compatible laser printers

Summary

This essay has provided an overview of Microsoft Windows and how it offers an environment for using an IBM PC-series or compatible system as a desktop publishing tool. MS-Windows comes bundled with a word processor, graphics program, rudimentary file manager, and several internal utilities. One of the main advantages of using MS-Windows is that it provides a unified environment in which several application programs can run simultaneously and exchange data easily and smoothly.

KEYWORDS:

- Computer Graphics Adapter

- Enhanced Graphics Adapter

- Hercules

- Multisync

John Angermeyer is an independent consultant specializing in microcomputer software development, technical writing, and desktop publishing. Previously a software engineer for a telecommunications company, Mr. Angermeyer has also worked as a consultant in the development of programmable control systems. He is co-author with other Waite Group authors of *CP/M Bible, DOS Primer for the IBM PC & XT, Understanding MS-DOS, MS-DOS Developer's Guide,* and *Tricks of the MS-DOS Masters.*

Essay Synopsis: On the IBM PC/XT/AT and compatible computers, the meeting point between software and hardware is in the graphic standards that each supports. These standards are embodied in the interface cards that plug into the slots of the computer and control the display monitors.

In this essay the author explains the differences between the various display monitor standards currently in use on PC-type equipment. You will learn about IBM and non-IBM standards, tricks to using popular graphic interface adapter cards, and how to match desktop publishing software, such as page layout and graphics programs, with the correct system hardware.

9

Graphic Cards and Standards

John Angermeyer

One of the most important things to consider when planning to use an IBM Personal Computer series or closely compatible computer for desktop publishing is its graphics display capability. If you plan to use only a type-code program for output, graphics display capability probably is not a critical issue, but if MS-DOS-compatible WYSIWYG programs are your objective, you should consider carefully what type of graphics display hardware you need.

An important consideration for your desktop publishing system is the resolution of the graphics display. Obviously the higher the resolution, the more attractive desktop publishing becomes on your computer. We'd all like to have at least the same resolution as the Macintosh's 512-by-300-pixel screen. Or maybe you've been using a high-end desktop publishing system with a 19-inch, 1,024-by-800-pixel monitor for a while, and you'd like to have something similar on your personal computer. Even though high-resolution graphics are desirable, however, there are several other factors to consider. Having high-resolution graphics is nice, but it is important that what you see displayed on the screen closely matches what is printed, in terms of font styles, size, and character rendition (e.g., bold, italics). The following paragraphs describe the different approaches to adding display graphics to your system.

There are two basic ways to approach getting the optimum in display graphics for

your desktop publishing system. The first approach applies if you already have graphics display hardware installed in your IBM PC series or closely compatible system. Either you're happy with the present hardware or your budget doesn't permit you to upgrade to new hardware, and you're looking for the most capable WYSIWYG desktop publishing software that fits your needs and is compatible with your system's configuration. The second approach applies if you haven't yet purchased an IBM PC series or closely compatible system or if you're planning to upgrade the graphics display capability of your present system. You're trying to determine if the best WYSIWYG desktop publishing program you can find is compatible with the best graphics display hardware that can be installed in your machine. Best, in this case, means what you consider to be the best, based on features, personal preference, and cost.

As you explore the vast market of IBM PC hardware and software, the second approach to setting up your system for desktop publishing becomes more and more appealing. Considering the large number of available options for configuring your system, it is often difficult to decide what is the optimum hardware, although the choice of desktop publishing software is more limited.

Display Graphics Standards

To begin this discussion on display graphics standards, it's important to know something about the standards established by IBM, because almost all software that is designed for operation on the IBM PC series and closely compatible systems can be installed for use with one or more IBM graphics standards. The standards for graphics on an IBM PC or closely compatible system can be broken down into two groups: IBM standard and non-IBM standard. The IBM standard refers to graphics standards as defined and created by IBM and includes not only graphics hardware manufactured and endorsed by IBM but also hardware manufactured by other companies that adhere to the IBM standard. The non-IBM standards refer to standards that are not defined (and usually not endorsed) by IBM, but are designed for operation in an IBM PC or closely compatible system.

IBM Graphics Standards

As of the publication of this book, IBM has defined three graphics standards for use on an IBM PC series or compatible system. The three standards, in the order of increasing display resolution, are Color/Graphics Adapter (CGA), Enhanced Graphics Adapter (EGA), and Professional Graphics Controller (PGC), which is often referred to as Professional Graphics Adapter (PGA). These three standards are described in greater detail in the following paragraphs.

Color/Graphics Adapter

The Color/Graphics Adapter is the basic graphics interface used in the IBM PC series systems. Because the Color/Graphics Adapter has been around the longest of all the color graphics standards for the IBM PC, you'll find that it's also the most compatible. Almost all software written for the IBM PC series is compatible with the Color/Graphics Adapter. It provides two display modes: text and bit-mapped graphics. The text mode consists of ASCII and the IBM Extended Character set, but does not include bit-mapped graphics capability. If the MS-DOS ANSI.SYS device driver is loaded, up to 16 colors (from a palette of 16) can be assigned to any of the characters displayed on the screen. Text mode consists of 25 lines with either 40 or 80 characters per line.

The graphics mode of the Color/Graphics Adapter consists of two resolution modes: 320 by 200 pixels (medium-resolution) and 640 by 200 pixels (high-resolution). Depending on the display mode, the Color/Graphics Adapter can display from 2 to 16 colors simultaneously out of a palette of 16 colors. The Color/Graphics Adapter is compatible only with the IBM Color Graphics Display monitor or compatible monitor. Table 9-1 shows the character resolution and number of displayable colors according to the display mode.

Table 9-1   Color/Graphics Adapter Display Modes

Mode	Type	Resolution	Lines x Columns	Char. Box	Colors
0	Text	320 x 200	25 x 40	8 x 8	B/W
1	Text	320 x 200	25 x 40	8 x 8	16
2	Text	640 x 200	25 x 80	8 x 8	B/W
3	Text	640 x 200	25 x 80	8 x 8	16
4	Graphics	320 x 200	25 x 40	8 x 8	4
5	Graphics	320 x 200	25 x 40	8 x 8	B/W
6	Graphics	640 x 200	25 x 80	8 x 8	2
13	Graphics	320 x 200	25 x 40	8 x 8	16
14	Graphics	640 x 200	25 x 80	8 x 8	16

The Color/Graphics Adapter card has two output connectors: an RGB (red-green-blue) 9-pin D-shell connector and an RCA-type coaxial connector for composite video. The RGB connector is used for the IBM Color Graphics Monitor (originally designed for use with the Color/Graphics Adapter) and for most other RGB monitors compatible with the Color/Graphics Adapter. The RCA-type connector is used for composite video monitors, video cassette recorders, and television sets. Note that the composite video output of the Color/Graphics Adapter is "raw" video, so if the connected equipment does not have composite video input jacks (RCA-type connectors), then an RF modulator is required to convert the composite signal to the frequency of Channel 3 or 4 on a TV or VCR tuner.

Note that the RF modulator should output the correct type of signal for your TV or VCR. For example, in the United States and most other countries in the Americas, the standard is called NTSC; whereas in the United Kingdom, some other European countries, and Australia, the standard used is called PAL. Some countries have their own unique standards, such as France and the Soviet Union. None of the standards are compatible with each other, so it is important to select the right RF modulator for the video equipment you'll be using.

Enhanced Graphics Adapter

The Enhanced Graphics Adapter is the second-generation graphics adapter from IBM for IBM PC and closely compatible systems. It provides enhanced resolution and a greater number of colors than does the Color/Graphics Adapter: 640 by 350 pixels and up to 16 colors from a palette of 64. Because of its higher resolution and better color display, the Enhanced Graphics Adapter has been a welcome standard with which many users have enhanced their systems. Many application programs are significantly enhanced (visually) when an Enhanced Graphics Adapter is used. Table 9-2 shows the different display modes of the Enhanced Graphics Adapter.

Table 9-2   Enhanced Graphics Adapter Display Modes

Mode	Lines x Type	Char. Resolution	Columns	Box	Colors	Notes
0	Text	320 x 200	25 x 40	14 x 8	B/W	1
1	Text	320 x 200	25 x 40	14 x 8	16	1
2	Text	640 x 200	25 x 80	14 x 8	B/W	1
3	Text	640 x 200	25 x 80	14 x 8	16	1

Table 9-2   (cont.)

Mode	Lines x Type	Char. Resolution	Columns	Box	Colors	Notes
4	Graphics	320 x 200	25 x 40	8 x 8	4	1
5	Graphics	320 x 200	25 x 40	8 x 8	B/W	1
6	Graphics	640 x 200	25 x 80	8 x 8	2	1
7	Text	720 x 350	25 x 80	14 x 9	4*	2
8	Text	720 x 350	25 x 132	14 x 9	4*	2
9	Text	720 x 350	28 x 132	14 x 9	4*	2
10	Text	720 x 350	44 x 132	14 x 9	4*	2
13	Graphics	320 x 200	25 x 40	8 x 8	16	1
14	Graphics	640 x 200	25 x 80	8 x 8	16	1
15	Graphics	640 x 350	25 x 80	14 x 8	4	2
16	Graphics	640 x 350	25 x 80	14 x 8	4/16	3

Modes 0 through 6, 13 and 14 are IBM Color/Graphics Adapter emulation modes.

Modes 7 and 15 are intended for monochrome displays (compatible with the IBM Monochrome Display [MDA]), and therefore the four "colors" refer to shades of gray (or green, as the case may be).

In Mode 16, an Enhanced Graphics Adapter with 64K of memory supports 4 colors; an Enhanced Graphics Adapter with 128K or 256K of memory supports 16 colors.

One disadvantage of the Enhanced Graphics Adapter card is that it does not provide a connector for composite video output to composite monitors, television sets, or video cassette recorders. Don't plan to use your system for demonstrating screen images on large projection TV screens, unless the output device is RGB compatible or you have a separate RGB-to-composite video converter.

Enhancing the Enhanced Graphics Adapter

On the standard Enhanced Graphics Adapter card, there is a connector that is referred to by IBM as the "feature connector" and is "reserved for future use." As of the publication of this book, no particular attachment has been released by IBM for attachment to the feature connector. However, the general purpose of this connector is clear: By attaching certain types of circuit boards to the connector, you can modify the operation of the Enhanced Graphics Adapter to significantly enhance its performance. One type of addition consists of increasing the Enhanced Graphics Adapter's normal clock speed (normally 16-megahertz). A small board containing a 24-megahertz crystal that's wired to the proper contacts on a connector that mates with the Enhanced Graphics Adapter's feature connector can be added to increase the resolution to beyond 640 by 350 pixels: 640 by 480, 752 by 410, 896 by 350, and 720 by 350 (IBM Monochrome Adapter mode).

As of the publication of this book, there are no commercially available boards for the Enhanced Graphics Adapter's feature connector. However, if you're able to do some simple electronic wiring, you can easily build a 24-megahertz "feature card" yourself. The cost of all the parts is just under $10. Excellent information on how to do this is provided in the September 16, 1986 issue of *PC Magazine* (Volume 5, Number 15), a copy of which you can find in most public libraries.

The MCGA (Multicolor Graphics Array) and VGA (Video Gate Array) Standards

With the release of the Personal System/2 series of computers by IBM, two new graphics standards were introduced. Built into the system board of the Personal System/2 Model 30 is the Multicolor Graphics Array (MCGA) standard. In addition to all the standard CGA modes, the MCGA provides two modes of operation: 300 by 200 pixels with 256 simultaneous colors and 640 by 480 pixels with two simultaneous colors (monochrome). The MCGA includes a palette of 256,000 colors. The text character box generated by an MCGA is 8 by 16 pixels — double the resolution of the CGA standard. The MCGA does not support any of the EGA modes.

Built into the system boards of the Personal System/2 Model 50, Model 60, and Model 80, another graphics standard is provided, called Video Gate Array (VGA). In addition to supporting all the CGA, EGA, and MCGA modes, the VGA also has a graphics mode of 640 by 480 pixels with 16 simultaneous colors, and a text mode of 720 by 400 pixels with 16 simultaneous colors. The VGA also includes a palette of 256,000 colors. Both the MCGA and VGA standards require the use of monitors with analog interfaces. The analog connectors used in the Personal System/2 series are unique, and therefore require special connector adapters for most non-IBM monitors.

Professional Graphics Controller

Another graphics standard that was released at about the same time as the Enhanced Graphics Adapter is the Professional Graphics Controller card, which provides a resolution of 640 columns by 480 lines, with up to 256 colors from a palette of several thousand. The Professional Graphics Controller is unlike the other IBM cards in several respects. First of all, it is not designed to make use of the memory that is normally reserved in IBM PCs for graphics. It requires more memory than what is reserved and therefore has all its memory on the board itself. A separate 8088 microprocessor is used on the board to manage its memory and to communicate with the IBM PC. Because the Professional Graphics Controller has its own memory, it communicates with the IBM PC on a "serial" basis by using a piece of software called a Virtual Device Interface (VDI), which is a device driver that is loaded when the IBM PC is first booted (the definition for loading the device driver is placed in the CONFIG.SYS file). Any software you wish to run with the Professional Graphics Controller must be compatible with the Professional Graphics Controllers and its Virtual Device Interface. To date, very few software programs are compatible with the Professional Graphics Controller with the exception of Computer-Aided Design (CAD) programs.

Another difference with the Professional Graphics Controller is that it requires the IBM Professional Display or compatible monitor. The monitor must be RGB, have a display resolution of at least 640 columns by 480 lines, and it must have an analog interface; the Professional Graphics Controller is not compatible with the more common digital (TTL) interface found on most IBM-compatible monitors.

Unless you'll use your system for CAD-type programs that require the simultaneous display of many colors, you'll find the Professional Graphics Controller (and the handful of compatibles) prohibitively expensive. Because the Professional Graphics Controller is basically a computer on a board, its components are rather expensive. Another disadvantage with the Professional Graphics Controller is that it is slow. Because all display information sent from an application program to the board must pass through and be processed by the Virtual Device Interface software in serial mode, getting information quickly to the screen is no easy task. So unless you need high resolution with lots of colors for computer-aided design operations, the Professional Graphics Controller is not recommended for desktop publishing applications. If, however, you do want a display resolution beyond that provided by the IBM Enhanced Graphics Adapter card for desktop publishing applications, you should consider some of the special high-resolution (1,024 by 800 or more pixels) monochrome card/monitor combinations discussed in the following sections.

The IBM Monochrome Adapter

When the IBM PC was first introduced, the only display adapter available for it was the Monochrome Display Adapter (MDA) from

IBM. Although it displays high-resolution text (720 by 350 pixels), it is not capable of handling bit-mapped graphics. Even after the IBM Color/Graphics Adapter was released, many users preferred the Monochrome Display Adapter for word processing and other text-oriented tasks. Indeed, when the Monochrome Display Adapter is connected to the IBM Monochrome Display monitor, text that is displayed on the screen is very crisp and solid, because characters are formed in a box of 14 by 9 dots (as opposed to the Color/Graphics Adapter which displays a character in an 8-by-8 dot box).

Although the IBM PC is capable of supporting both the Monochrome Display Adapter and Color/Graphics Adapter at the same time, many users have found the combination to be a little extravagant. Other disadvantages of the Monochrome Display Adapter/Monochrome Display combination are that the characters are rather small (text mode is always 80 characters by 25 lines) and there's a high phospher persistence when text is scrolled.

If you're purchasing a system for the first time, and you want good-quality text display for word processing and bit-mapped color graphics capability, the IBM Enhanced Graphics Adapter (or a compatible board) works better coupled with an Enhanced Graphics Display or a high-resolution, multiple-synching monitor. Each character generated by the Enhanced Graphics Adapter is formed in 14-by-8-dot box, which is almost as good as the Monochrome Display Adapter.

Non-IBM Standards

Once IBM set its standards for display text and graphics on the IBM PC system, many companies jumped on the bandwagon, copied IBM systems, and developed compatible cards as well as new "standards." Most of the compatible cards made for the IBM PC were made after IBM released the Enhanced Graphics Adapter. Prior to this, many companies developed their own graphics standards, some of which provided a degree of compatibility with IBM graphics products for the IBM PC. Some popular graphics cards that provide direct compatibility with IBM graphics boards as well as others that provide completely new standards are described below.

Hercules Graphics Card

Probably the most popular non-IBM graphics standard made for the IBM PC is the Hercules card made by Hercules Technology. Although the Hercules card is monochrome, it provides 720-by-348-pixel bit-mapped graphics capability. The Hercules was originally designed to be compatible with the IBM Monochrome Display Adapter and the IBM Monochrome Display Monitor. Because the Hercules card is considered by some to have surpassed all the IBM cards in popularity, many programs — including desktop publishing applications — have been designed to be Hercules-compatible. If you aren't concerned with color and want high-resolution monochrome text and graphics, you might consider the Hercules card as a worthwhile addition to your system.

Hercules Graphics Card Plus

Due to the considerable popularity of the Hercules Graphics Card, Hercules Technology introduced a new version of the card called the Hercules Graphics Card Plus. The new card adds considerable text-mode capabilities to the original card by providing what are called RamFonts, a feature that provides the ability to create up to 3,072 unique characters rather than the standard 256 provided by the IBM PC and compatible systems. Additionally, the new version of the card is capable of displaying up to 90 columns by 38 lines of text. Although the new card is not compatible with either the IBM CGA or Enhanced Graphics Adapter, if you're content with monochrome graphics and high-resolution text, this card may be for you.

Multistandard Graphics Cards

With the recent plethora of Enhanced Graphics Adapter-compatible cards, many manufacturers are now making cards that support a variety of standards, in addition to the Enhanced Graphics Adapter standard. These cards are generically called multistandard cards. One reason why these cards are important is that many programs designed to operate with older standards, such as the CGA, do not always operate correctly with the Enhanced Graphics Adapter. Multistandard cards allow you to switch standards before running an application. Most multistandard graphics cards support the following standards: Color/Graphics Adapter, Enhanced Graphics Adapter, Monochrome Display Adapter, and Hercules. Most cards require that they be manually switched between modes, either by hardware switches or by a special program supplied with the card. A few cards are capable of detecting the display mode for which an application program is installed, and automatically switch to the correct mode. Some multi-standard cards are briefly described below.

Paradise Systems Autoswitch

The Paradise Systems PAEGA (Autoswitch Enhanced Graphics Adapter) was one of the first multistandard video cards capable of automatically detecting the required display standard for an application program as it is loaded and automatically switching to the correct mode. The PAEGA card supports the following display standards: Monochrome Display Adapter, Color/Graphics Adapter, Enhanced Graphics Adapter, Hercules, and Plantronics. The PAEGA card can automatically switch between Color/Graphics Adapter, Enhanced Graphics Adapter, and Plantronics modes, or between Monochrome Display Adapter and Hercules. The PAEGA cannot automatically switch between the Color/Graphics Adapter/Enhanced Graphics Adapter/Plantronics set of modes and the Monochrome Display Adapter/Hercules set of modes, because hardware switches must be set up first for the type of monitor being used: color TTL monitor for Color/Graphics Adapter/Enhanced Graphics Adapter/Plantronics modes, or composite-video monochrome monitor for Monochrome Display Adapter/Hercules modes.

Video-7 VEGA and VEGA Deluxe

The VEGA card manufactured by Video Seven was also one of the first multistandard cards made available as an alternative to the Enhanced Graphics Adapter card. The VEGA card supports the following display standards: Monochrome Display Adapter, Color/Graphics Adapter, Enhanced Graphics Adapter, and Hercules. A new version of the VEGA card, called the VEGA Deluxe, provides the same capabilities as the VEGA, including some higher resolution modes (640 by 480 and 752 by 410 pixels). The VEGA Deluxe is also capable of detecting the required display standard for an application program as it is loaded and automatically switching to the correct mode. The VEGA Deluxe card can automatically switch between Color/Graphics Adapter and Enhanced Graphics Adapter modes, or between Monochrome Display Adapter and Hercules. The VEGA Deluxe cannot automatically switch between the Color/Graphics Adapter/Enhanced Graphics Adapter set of modes and the Monochrome Display Adapter/Hercules set of modes, because hardware switches must first be set up for the type of monitor being used: color TTL monitor for Color/Graphics Adapter/Enhanced Graphics Adapter modes, or composite-video monochrome monitor for Monochrome Display Adapter/Hercules modes.

Almost all of the new Enhanced Graphics Adapter compatible cards being manufactured today support the Color/Graphics Adapter, Enhanced Graphics Adapter, and Hercules standards. However, not all of them support automatic switching of modes based on software needs. Some cards must be manually switched or must have a specially supplied program run to place the card in the right mode. The autoswitching feature found in some of these cards is a very useful capability to have, especially when a multisynchronizing monitor is also used.

High-Resolution Monochrome Graphics

If you've ever used a so-called high-end workstation before, more than likely the system included a higher-resolution, larger-screen display than the typical monitor and adapter arrangement of an IBM PC series or compatible system. Most high-end desktop systems, such as the Sun and Apollo general-purpose workstations and the Xerox 8010 and 6085 Star desktop publishing systems, use 15-inch or larger displays with resolutions of more than 1,000 by 400 pixels. Although the 12-inch screen size of a typical IBM PC series monitor (such as the IBM Color Graphics, IBM Enhanced Color Graphics, and compatible monitors) is considered adequate for most applications, desktop publishing (page layout) software users often desire larger screens with more resolution. Why does this desire for larger screens exist?

One answer is the general dissatisfaction with the display capability of a typical IBM PC monitor. For example, have you ever noticed that the image on a standard 12-inch IBM PC monitor looks less sharp and crisp than on the Apple Macintosh's 9-inch screen, even though the IBM PC's image is formed with more dots? Another reason for the dissatisfaction is because of the inability to display a large enough portion of an application on a 12-inch screen to make it useful. In particular, the use of page layout programs, such as Ventura Publisher (which runs under GEM) and PageMaker (a Microsoft Windows application), can be made considerably more efficient if a complete view of a layout page, or better still, two side-by-side pages, can be obtained.

With the knowledge of how beneficial large, high-resolution displays are to desktop publishers and CAD program users, several companies have developed add-on monitors for the IBM PC series and compatible systems. Almost all of the large display monitors available today are monochrome (black and white) monitors, and range in diagonal screen size from 15 to 19 inches. The resolutions of these monitors also vary quite a bit, although they all provide higher resolutions than the typical 12-inch monitors and IBM standard and compatible adapters (CGA, EGA, and PGC). The following paragraphs describe three popular large-display monitor packages that can be added to an IBM PC-series system. The three described are only a sampling of what's available, and more and more new and improved packages are being released every day.

Wyse WY-700

The WY-700 monitor from Wyse Technologies is one of the most popular add-on large-screen monitors for the IBM PC series. It consists of a 15-inch, horizontal aspect (landscape) monitor and special video adapter card. The WY-700 is a black and white monochrome monitor, and provides a resolution of 1,280 by 400 pixels. Included with the package are several device drivers that allow certain graphical environment programs to operate with it, including drivers for Microsoft Windows, GEM, and AutoCAD. The WY-700's adapter card can be used instead of, or in conjunction with, other graphics boards such as the CGA and EGA. The WY-700 is capable of displaying most application programs installed for use with the CGA, but it does not support the EGA or any other non-CGA graphics "standard." It is recommended that a standard graphics card and monitor remain installed in the system so that you don't get stuck not being able to run your favorite application. The WY-700 should only be used for those applications for which device drivers are available.

Genius

The Genius monitor from Micro Display Systems is a rather unusual monitor that fits into the category of large-screen displays. It consists of a tall-screen, vertical aspect (portrait) monitor and special video adapter card. The Genius is a black on white monochrome monitor, and provides a resolution of 736 by 1,008 pixels. The main advantage of the Genius is its ability to display a full "page" of text (66 lines) on the screen using application programs installed for a CGA display. Although the Genius is able to accomplish this feat automatically with some applications, most applications, such as many word processors and bit-mapped graphics programs, must be specially configured for use with the Genius. Many word processing programs can be configured so that 66 lines are displayed on the screen.

The Genius is accompanied by a setup program that allows you to place the Genius in various modes. A diagnostics program is also provided that can be used to identify and correct problems with the way in which the Genius displays applications. Another unique feature of the Genius is its ability to display two application programs in a "split screen." The screen can be split up into two upper and lower halves, and one can be used for displaying text while the other can display bit-mapped graphics. Without a multitasking operating system, however, only one application can be running at a time. Although the Genius is capable of handling applications installed for a CGA, it cannot handle applications installed for the EGA or other graphics standard. It is therefore recommended that the existing video card and monitor remain installed in the system.

Sigma Laserview

One of the most breathtaking large-screen monitors available today is the Laserview by Sigma Designs. The Laserview consists of a 19-inch horizontal aspect (landscape) monitor and a special adapter. The Laserview's screen is black on white monochrome, and provides a resolution of 1,664 by 1,200 pixels — one of the highest resolutions found in add-on large-screen monitors for the IBM PC series. When considering the larger size of the screen, the resolution is in fact only about 50 percent greater than the Wyse WY-700 and Genius. However, a significant difference can be observed when doing precision work with bit-mapped graphics programs. Like the Wyse WY-700, the Laserview is capable of running some application programs installed for the CGA, and requires device drivers for many programs, such as Microsoft Windows, GEM, AutoCAD, and other bit-mapped graphics programs. Because of the limited compatibility with other graphics standards, the Laserview requires that a primary display adapter (CGA, EGA) and monitor be installed in the system.

As mentioned, the three large-screen displays described are simply a sampling of what's available. When looking at each product closely, it's clear that no two are alike. They all vary in resolution, screen size, compatibility with other graphics standards, and, of course, price. For desktop publishing applications, the Wyse WY-700 provides good capabilities for its medium-range price. The Genius is ideal for text-oriented word processing, but not as nice as the other monitors for bit-mapped graphics-intensive desktop publishing applications. The Sigma Laserview is "top of the line," but, of course, is also one of the most expensive. If you want the high-resolution and large screen capabilities of high-end workstations, but want to keep the overall cost of your hardware and software down, adding one these large-screen monitor packages is definitely worth considering.

Monitors

Selecting the right monitor for your computer is often more important than the graphics adapter itself. The monitors available for use with microcomputers today vary according to screen size and shape, interface (digital [TTL/RGB] or analog [composite]), and supported display modes. Most of the monitors have fairly fixed modes in that they are usually compatible only with specific types of graphics cards.

What is the difference between digital and analog interfaces? Digital interfaces, also referred to as TTL interfaces, consist basically of three wires, along which precise (on and off) electrical signals are transmitted. The three lines are designated as red, green, and blue (abbreviated RGB), and it is through the combined use of these lines that a graphics board instructs the monitor as to what colors to display. Analog interfaces, on the other hand, rely on the transmission of a less precise nondigital color signal over one or more lines. Both televisions and radios receive information by means of analog signals. Because an analog signal is not restricted to the two states (on and off) used in a digital signal, it able to "carry" more complex color information. As result, and as a general rule, digital monitors provide color graphics precisely, easily, and at lower cost, whereas analog monitors are generally able to display more colors, but with a more complex interface, and generally at a higher cost.

Monitors Compatible with
Specific IBM Graphics Standards

Table 9-3 shows the compatibility of the various IBM monitors with IBM display cards. Many companies are now manufacturing monitors and display cards compatible with the various IBM standards. Therefore, you need to know what the standards are so that if you purchase a non-IBM product, you'll know what the compatibility issues are.

Table 9-3   Comparison of Monitors, Cards, and Interface Types

Monitor	Display Card	Type of Interface
IBM Monochrome Display	IBM MDA and Hercules	Analog
IBM Color Graphics Display	IBM CGA, and EGA in 640 by 200 mode	TTL/RGB
IBM Enhanced Graphics Display	IBM CGA, and EGA	TTL/RGB
IBM Professional Graphics Display	IBM PGC	Analog
IBM Personal System/2 Series Displays	IBM MCGA and VGA	Analog

Monitors Compatible with All IBM Graphics Standards

Recently, a handful of companies have begun to manufacture monitors capable of automatically switching display modes according to the graphics standard being used. These monitors generally have both digital and analog interfaces, and are easily adaptable to almost any system configuration. In particular, these types of monitors are most useful when connected to auto-switching multistandard display cards, such as the Paradise AutoSwitch Enhanced Graphics Adapter card. This card automatically switches between Color/Graphics Adapter and Enhanced Graphics Adapter modes, and the monitor automatically adjusts to the output signal so that the correct resolution and use of color is displayed. Most of these autoswitching (or autosynchronizing) monitors are compatible with all the IBM standards: Monochrome Display Adapter, Color/Graphics Adapter, Enhanced Graphics Adapter, and Professional Graphics Controller, in all display modes, including the Hercules graphics cards.

If you need to use color and if you want the maximum in compatibility and flexibility with your various application programs, you should consider choosing an autosynchronizing monitor. Most of these types of monitors support a display resolution of above 800 by 400 pixels, which is good enough for most applications. Generally, if you need higher resolution with color — 1,024 by 1,024 or more pixels — consider nonstandard, very high-priced graphics cards and monitors. If high-resolution monochrome monitors are acceptable, you can find several models that are more reasonably priced.

Table 9-4 summarizes the specifications of three autosynchronizing monitors with display resolutions more than 800 x 480 pixels.

**Table 9-4   Comparison of Specifications
of Three Popular Monitors**

NEC JC-1401P-3A MultiSync™ Color Monitor

Manufacturer:	Nippon Electric Corp. (NEC)
Diagonal Screen Size:	13 inches
Resolution:	800 x 560 pixels
Frequency Range:	15.75 through 35 KHz
Compatibility:	CGA, Enhanced Graphics Adapter, Professional Graphics Controller, MDA, Hercules
Interface(s):	TTL and analog color
Character Pitch:	0.31mm

SONY CPD-1302 Multiscan™ Color Monitor

Manufacturer:	SONY Corporation
Diagonal Screen Size:	13 inches
Resolution:	800 x 560 pixels
Frequency Range:	15.75 through 35 KHz
Compatibility:	CGA, Enhanced Graphics Adapter, Professional Graphics Controller, MDA, Hercules
Interface(s):	TTL and analog color
Character Pitch:	0.25mm

NOTE: SONY also manufactures the following autosynchronizing video projectors (compatible with the Multiscan™):
    VPH-103Q1 (for 100-inch screens)
    VPH-203Q1 (for 200-inch screens)

TEKNIKA MJ-503 Multi-Scan Color Monitor:

Manufacturer:	TEKNIKA (Fujitsu General, Ltd.)
Diagonal Screen Size:	13 inches
Resolution:	800 x 560 pixels
Frequency Range:	15 through 34 KHz
Compatibility:	CGA, Enhanced Graphics Adapter, Professional Graphics Controller, MDA, Hercules
Interface(s):	TTL and analog color
Character Pitch:	0.31mm

Summary

This essay has described some of the graphics and text display options available to you if you plan to purchase new equipment or enhance your existing system. Many more options are available than can be covered here, but knowing some of the more popular options often can help you decide what to get, not just from the hardware standpoint, but also from the standpoint of software compatibility.

KEYWORDS:

- **Monochrome**

- **RGB**

- **Resolution**

- **Flicker**

John D. Goodell has been an organist for a silent film theater, an electronic designer, and a film director, John Goodell's achievements include creation of the first production line industrial robot, CBS cassette recorder, the conditioned-reflex teaching machine, several computer systems, and a 1973 documentary film *Always a New Beginning*. Mr. Goodell is currently the executive director of Knowledge Resources, a nonprofit educational corporation located in Saint Paul, Minnesota.

Essay Synopsis: As printers take on greater powers of resolution, display monitors must keep pace. A person using a low-resolution monitor faces two problems: one, a greater number of trial print-outs; two, eyestrain.

In this essay, the author discusses the underlying principles behind the design of display monitors. You will learn about resolution and scan lines, graphic standards, phosphor decay, the value of color in an editing environment, sizes and orientations of monitors, and the nature of flicker, that annoying, low-level light variation that becomes apparent when you watch a display screen with peripheral vision.

10

Inside Monitors

John Goodell

In all desktop publishing it is essential to be able to "monitor" your work continuously in real time (essentially no delays) and make corrections as you progress. Waiting until the text comes out of the printer before making corrections and editorial changes largely eliminates the value of a computer word processor. Thus the monitor is a vital link between you and the computer and selecting it carefully to match your work is very important. The best monitor depends on the kind of work you do, the characteristics of your eyes, visual habits, and other personal factors. This essay covers these important considerations.

Many manufacturers offer complete desktop publishing systems in which the computer, monitor, printer, and possibly other peripherals are designed specifically to operate in combination. There are advantages and disadvantages to the customer in this packaging approach to equipment design, both with regard to cost and performance.

The advantages of manufacturing and marketing efficiencies lead to cost reductions, and the knowledge that a certain computer, printer, and monitor will be used together makes it easier for the design engineer to match typography, page layouts, and other design elements. The number of variables in desirable printer characteristics with respect to various publishing applications is enormous. The response of different operators to keyboard characteristics is not consistent, and the extent to

RELATED ESSAYS:

7. Desktop Publishing on the PC

9. Graphics Cards and Standards

12. Image Scanning and Processing

which a really large monitor is essential is not obvious. These are separate problems. No single package will resolve all of them for everyone. Consequently it is worthwhile to consider putting together individually purchased units versus the extent to which a given packaged system satisfies your needs. Another important consideration is the extent to which a particular package is capable of modification, and what kind of expense is involved in making changes. Intuition often misleads people into a lack of emphasis on the importance of monitors in connection with hardware upgrades.

A simple example concerns the video interface card (the card on which circuitry is mounted) that must be incorporated in the IBM PC (or clones thereof) in order to allow the computer to communicate with the monitor. The interface card for an IBM RGB color monitor will not function to couple the computer to an IBM monochrome monitor and vice versa. (The initials RGB — red, green, blue — applied to monitors mean that the digital signals for each color enter the monitor on separate lines and energize the corresponding colored phosphors on the screen directly and independently.) Inquiries about these matters and consideration of the pluses and minuses of operation, as well as cost factors, are worthwhile. You can't really find out the most vital answers by exchanging words with a salesperson or by just reading this or any other assemblage of words. You must experiment personally with a variety of equipment, and most stores are set up to allow at least a modicum of such activity.

Television Display

It is possible to use a television set as a monitor. For purposes of games and the like this works out quite well with various inexpensive computers. Cables for coupling with the required intermediate circuitry (discussed at greater length below) are readily available. For reading in general, as well as for any professional applications, even the best color TV set is not a satisfactory substitute for even the least expensive monitors.

There are several reasons that TV sets are unsatisfactory monitors. Many aspects of circuit design, especially the number of lines scanned horizontally on the screen, must conform in TV sets to the standardized characteristics of the signal from the transmitting stations. This places an unavoidable limit on display quality.

When a television set is used as a monitor, the digital signal from the computer must be changed so as to be transmitted to the television input in the form of modulated (analog) signals from TV stations. This introduces an additional opportunity for distortion to take place.

Home television circuits and viewing screens are deliberately designed to be somewhat "soft," or to use a term that is common in the industry, "forgiving." Minor errors and distortions in transmission and reception are smoothed over. The professional monitors used in the mixing and editing rooms of the transmitting stations and in the production of video cassettes are much more critical — much less forgiving — because the purpose is to *observe* faults rather than cover them up. Reading text or observing illustrations in a desktop publishing situation has the same critical requirements.

Service Life

Before going any further, it is important to point out that some of the problems and questions addressed in the previous paragraph, as well as in a number of subsequent paragraphs, are currently being solved by means of standardization. The advent of some recent products, such as the NEC model JC Multi-Sync and the Amdek 722 EGA Monitors, has contributed to increased standardization. These monitors introduce the capability of automated adaptation to both the IBM EGA (Enhanced Graphics Adaptor with a resolution of 640 by 350) and the IBM CGA (Color Graphics Adaptor with a resolution of 640 by 200) interface boards that couple the computer to the monitor. The Amdek monitor has a three-way switch that allows the choice of monochrome green, amber, or full color for text material.

The issue of standardization raises an interesting dilemma. There is a strong tendency to feel that standardization is a vital but often neglected factor in manufacturing practices. However, the other side of the coin is that standardization inhibits progress in the design of new, better, and possibly less expensive products. The computer industry is more likely to continue to progress with new and better products at this time than to freeze current designs. It would be wise to plan amortizing any equipment related to computers over only a few years. In one sense this is irritating, but in another it underlines decisions as short-term rather than long-term and thus renders them somewhat easier to make.

Monochrome Monitors

In the beginning, almost all monochrome monitors were created with white text on a black background; a little later green and amber screens became available. There has been some research indicating that green is more desirable in an environment illuminated by daylight or fluorescent light, and amber in the tungsten light that is common in homes. Intuitively one might expect the opposite to be true and personal preference is more significant than the results of this research. But it is worthwhile to make your decision in the presence of at least an approximation of the ambient light under which your work will be accomplished.

In monochrome monitor screens the decay time, the length of the period during which the image on the screen is vanishing, varies a great deal. When it is relatively long (on the IBM green monitors it is approximately one second) it interferes severely with readability for some observers, especially when scrolling is taking place. This is readily apparent with double-spaced text because the moving lines briefly light up the phosphor of the intermediate blank lines in the scrolling process. The effect is largely eliminated if the shift is in terms of changing to a page up or page down (a replacement rather than movement) instead of scrolling single lines. The long decay time is also obvious in the "ghost" image left behind by a moving cursor. Many viewers simply accept it as a necessary evil. It is not. It is a compromise between a number of factors, including brightness and the reduction of flicker in the design of the phosphor surface. Most amber monitors are designed with phosphors that are characterized by rapid decay times; and for many customers, freedom from the ghost problem is a prime consideration.

Color Monitors

It is widely believed that color monitors are less desirable than monochrome for writing and reading text material because monochrome monitors generally provide superior definition — outlines that are more solid and edges that are more crisp — but other advantages for reading and editing text on color monitors make them well worth exploring. For example, the default combination for color monitors is generally white letters on a black background. However, there are many desirable color variations available with WordStar, such as the ability to have a different background color for the text and for the menu, which separates them visually. With Microsoft Word, color becomes available if you start the program with WORD/C and then move to WINDOWS and the subprogram OPTIONS, at which point any one of the arrows will bring up a rainbow of numbered colors for selection.

The number you select will cause the background of the text to take on the corresponding color. The text will be white with the exception of gray or white backgrounds, in which case the letters are black. If you highlight a word when the background is in color, the highlight will be white with the text letters in black, and this creates a contrast that is very easy to observe. If you underline a word it turns green. The cursor is white and any text letter within the cursor becomes black. Bold type is displayed as a very bright green.

The white and gray backgrounds with black lettering are very comfortable, and the brightness can be easily adjusted. Looking at this kind of light source directly is quite different from reading black lettering on white paper by reflected light. In early devices, such as the microfiche, there was a disturbing granular surface in white backgrounds. This problem has been largely smoothed out in contemporary designs.

In Microsoft Word the color change takes place only in the document area, and the menu at the bottom of the screen continues to be distinguished by white text on a black background.

The advantage of all this color flexibility for reading document material is the periodic stimulation that always accompanies visual variations. In the use of color for the end result (the final printed material) in any application of communication with words and pictures, it is helpful to understand the kinds of value contributed by color. Color creates emotional and psychological responses as a consequence of experientially and culturally conditioned reflexes. Color grabs attention in much the same way as motion. Contrary to common expectations, color contributes very little to the transmission of verbal information. Information theory indicates that color increases informative content by approximately 15 percent.

In a few desktop publishing situations, color is a basic requirement in connection with illustrations. Aside from applications involving games, this has been the prime professional reason for purchasing color monitors. In RGB color monitors there is no readily observable screen persistence.

Size and Resolution

Soon, the monitor you are about to buy (or have just purchased) will almost certainly seem too small. At the usual working distances, the physical size of the screen is unimportant with respect to definition, the number of lines that make up an image. With television sets, the number of vertical lines is a constant 525 (some are actually off screen, hence not visible) and the effective visual definition of the images becomes dependent primarily on the dimensions of the screen and how close or far away it is. The smaller the screen (with a constant number of lines), the better the definition. The larger the screen, the farther away you should be for comfortable viewing.

In a desktop publishing situation, the distance from the screen is usually quite constant, and the constraints defined by transmission standards for TV are not present. Consequently, the design engineer can provide you with extremely high definition by providing a large number of lines spaced close enough together to simulate an engraving. In very high-quality graphic work on computers, e.g., motion picture production and creation, the monitors have as many as 4,000 lines. For reasonable comfort in desktop publishing with the usual relatively small monitors, a few hundred lines is adequate for text, and roughly 600 will provide reasonably satisfactory graphics. These terms are not expressed as values to satisfy a highly discriminating art critic, but rather to be adequate for a desktop editor to make composition and layout decisions.

The more important points with regard to size have to do with the very small window through which the operator views what is stored in the portion of random access memory devoted to visual display. In a high percentage of monitors, this window is limited to 80 characters in width and 25 lines in height. But in order to think more clearly about sequences and transitions, it is important in writing and editing to have as much text as possible available visually. A relatively large (19- or 20-inch diagonal) screen of good quality, such as the one supplied by Xerox with their desktop package, contributes substantially to efficient and effective working conditions. Obviously, for purposes of making decisions about layout, for example, it is essential to observe at least a full page. If two pages can be displayed at once in readable form, the effect is similar to conventional books and magazines.

Monitors come in two basic shapes. Those that are taller than they are wide are called "portrait mode" monitors, and they are used for display of single pages. Those monitors that are wider than they are tall are called "landscape mode," and they are used to display two pages side by side, known as a "page spread" (see Figure 10-1).

Monitors operating on principles involving the electrical switching of illumination from gas particles (rather than exciting phosphor surfaces into fluorescence) have been designed and offered in limited markets. This technique makes very large- and flat-surfaced monitors possible and could eventually lead to the development of full wall-size structures. This is entirely possible in the not-too-distant future and will help to satisfy some magazine writers and editors who commonly tape printed pages to an entire wall in order to be able properly to evaluate the flow and meaning of the information in their publication. Page juxtaposition and the verbal jumps in turning pages are important considerations. A reasonable analogy can be drawn between a slide presentation and a motion picture: The former is similar to turning the pages of a book; the latter to a well-spaced scroll.

Some available software creates a compromise by making it possible to pull back, as with a zoom lens, to wide-angle views on a small screen that at least allow the operator to see the geometric relationships between text and illustrations as well as between headlines and paragraphs. And while this is not ideal, it is a useful crutch.

It is important to realize that WYSIWYG (What You See Is What You Get) is never a completely true statement. The closer you can come to it, the less often you will find it necessary to print out sample pages before you push the button to start the high-speed laser printer.

The trend toward larger screens, which are at least capable of displaying a readable page, will undoubtedly continue. Radius has brought out a new, separate "big" screen as a peripheral product to be coupled to the Macintosh. The effective viewing area of the screen is approximately the same size and format as standard letterheads (i.e.,

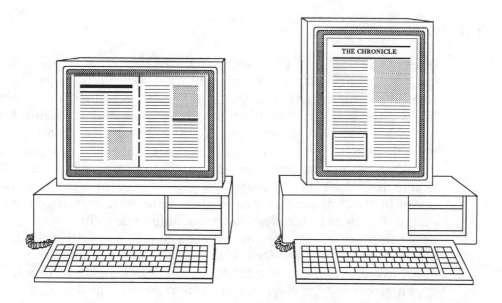

Figure 10-1. The landscape type display (left) is commonly used to view two-page spreads; the portrait type display (right) is used to view full-page work.

8½ inches wide by 11 inches high), and thus is capable of displaying a full conventional page of entirely readable text. Termed the Radius FPD (full page display), the definition of this screen is improved by slightly closer spacing of the pixels (75 per inch); and the sweep rate of 67 megahertz virtually eliminates any kind of flicker without resorting to interlacing.

Probably the most unusual aspect of the design for this truly rectangular flat cathode ray display (CRT) (864 pixels high by 640 pixels wide) is the way in which it can be combined and operated in conjunction with the standard Macintosh screen. The FPD can be placed adjacent to the Macintosh on either side, and the mouse can then cause the cursor to travel back and forth between the two screens with no effective information break between them.

One advantageous use is to set up the standard screen for the icons, tools, and operating notes, and put the document text on the full-page screen. You can move the mouse back and forth between them, selecting formats on the small standard screen and zipping back to insert, edit, and write document text on the large screen. It comes very close to having your cake and eating it too. This is not quite the same experience as having a full two-page screen available, but it is certainly an interesting and useful variation.

Flicker

Most of the equipment you will encounter that is appropriate for desktop publishing will use the presentation technique known as raster scanning. This means that the pixels (picture elements) are arranged in an orthogonal (rectangular) matrix of lines and are caused to light up by a beam that scans across them horizontally. In order to minimize flicker, the beam scans all the even-numbered lines top to bottom and then returns to scan the odd-numbered lines. The reason for this is that it is desirable to cause the illumination produced by the phosphors to turn off quickly rather than fade with a ghostlike hangover image. By the interlaced scanning technique described above, the time between placing new information on a given line is cut in half, and the effect of flicker, derived from blank times between displays, is reduced substantially. The vector technique, which is almost entirely limited to graphic rather than text material, is a process of drawing such that the phosphor surface is essentially continuous, and the electron beam moves in whatever configuration is required in order to draw lines as the shortest distance between points.

The conventional scanning rate is at 22 megahertz. Doubling that frequency would eliminate the need to interlace the lines. Apple has accomplished this by going to 50 megahertz with one Macintosh model. There is a special and curious kind of effect called "chewing" flicker that occurs if the observer operates the jaws in a chewing motion that affects the eye muscles, and Macintosh has gone to an even higher scanning frequency in a high resolution screen to eliminate the chewing flicker.

Summary

Monitors have various degrees of resolution, flicker characteristics, size, and cost. Medium resolution is sufficient for most desktop publishing work, but even small amounts of flicker can be disturbing, and while it may at first seem lavish, a very large screen size is quite practical and worth the investment for an active workstation.

It is worth emphasizing again that because the monitor functions as the window into the world of what resides in the random access viewing section of your computer, it is a vital and highly personal element in a desktop publishing system.

KEYWORDS:

• **Letter Quality**

• **Proportional Spacing**

• **Resolution**

• **Downloadable Font**

John D. Goodell has been an organist for a silent film theater, an electronic designer, and a film director, John Goodell's achievements include creation of the first production line industrial robot, CBS cassette recorder, the conditioned-reflex teaching machine, several computer systems, and a 1973 documentary film *Always a New Beginning*. Mr. Goodell is currently the executive director of Knowledge Resources, a nonprofit educational corporation located in Saint Paul, Minnesota.

Essay Synopsis: In publishing, the quality of the printed product is paramount, and in configuring a system, it is likely that the printer will dictate the choice of software rather than the other way around. But there are many variables to printing, including not only the device itself, but the choice of ink or toner, paper, and more.

In this essay the author discusses both laser and dot matrix printers, focusing on the mechanics of the machines, how they work, and why each serves its function. Having outlined this background, the author presents information on toners, inks, and paper. You will learn about impact and non-impact printers, reliability, resolution, bit-mapped fonts, and how a page description language controls the printer.

11

Printers, Paper, and Toner

John Goodell

Every aspect of desktop publishing is being affected by new techniques and new products. This is especially true of printers, but recent designs are rapidly approaching a plateau with regard to performance and price. Each approach is finding a niche in the marketplace, and the basic information that follows is likely to be valid for a long time.

In terms of desktop publishing, a printer is the output device that transforms signals from the computer into words on paper. Many contemporary typewriters are designed so that they respond to electronic signals from computers and can function as printers. Conversely, most desktop computers can be set up to drive a printer directly (i.e., in real time, directly from the computer keyboard), hence they perform like a typewriter. The significant differences are in the greater variety of typefaces and sizes that are available with printers and the way they respond to appropriate signals for creating illustrations of various kinds. Desktop printers can operate at speeds many times the maximum rate of any typist on a manual machine. The demand for speed and flexibility has sparked the development of a number of different methods for creating images on paper.

When you are shopping for a printer, ask the salesperson to let you look through one or more instruction manuals. The information in these booklets is designed to educate you rather than deliver the sales pitch inherent in advertising. Even a cur-

RELATED ESSAYS:

7. Desktop Publishing on the PC

19. Introduction to PostScript

sory reading of an instruction manual will help you make comparisons and ask intelligent questions.

Specifications are not included here in any comparative tabular form. Such data are readily available from dealers, but require careful evaluation. It is easy to manipulate lists of information to favor one product over another simply by selecting the items presented. Presenting such data in complete and entirely impartial form is difficult. The total amount of information is very large and most customers have at least slightly different needs.

When making any substantial purchase, "walk around the block" before writing the check. The following information is intended to provide some guidance with regard to what to think about while walking. The knowledge available to many readers is likely to be fragmented. Consequently only minimal assumptions have been made about the reader's existing knowledge.

Dot Matrix Printers

Until recently, dot matrix printers were almost entirely restricted to creating high-speed draft material. Today, even at astonishingly high speeds, some dot matrix printers are capable of very close to letter-quality printing. The output of these printers is a matrix, or pattern, of dots in which certain dots are eliminated in order to generate forms that approximate the corresponding coherent symbols.

Printing Heads

The printing head in a dot matrix printer contains a number of tiny solenoids, magnetic switches. Each of these consists of a very small coil of wire in the center of which is an element called a pin that is free to move lengthwise. When the coil is pulsed with an electrical current, it generates a magnetic field that causes the pin to hit the ribbon with a hammer blow. This strikes the ribbon against the printing surface and transfers ink in the form of a dot. In some dot matrix printers the pins are made of surgical spring steel so that they may travel through a slightly curved path that spaces them apart at the back and provides room for the coils. Most of the information that follows is applicable to all dot matrix printers, but it is related specifically to the Okidata line.

The Matrix

The nine pins in the Okidata 92/93 models are arranged in a vertical line and the term "matrix" relates to the printing pattern they produce as the head moves horizontally across the page. The dots are ¹⁄₇₂ inch in diameter and can be programmed to print horizontally at 72 dots per inch, in which case they touch, or 60 dots per inch with a very small space between them. The vertical spacing is a function of the actual mounting of the printing pins in the head and is always 72 dots per inch.

This dot dimension (¹⁄₇₂ inch) is the same as the standard units or points used to define the basic parameters of typography, such as the space between lines, the thickness of lines that separate text and graphic elements, and the vertical size of the type in a given font.

When using the Okidata 92/93 to print text with 12-point (pica) type at ten characters per inch, the 60 dots per inch is normal. For 12 characters per inch with 10-point (elite) type, 72 dots per inch is standard. For graphic printing, you can choose either 60 or 72 dots per inch for horizontal spacing. The latter has been made available primarily to provide support for certain software programs.

The number of pins in the print head of various dot matrix printers varies up to as many as 36, and the number 24 is becoming widely used. Increasing the number and reducing the diameter of pins results in a larger number of dots per inch as well as closer coupling of the individual dots, which substantially improves definition. One of the advantages in adjacent rows of pins in the horizontal direction is related to recovery time of the solenoid. With the single row of a nine-pin head, the movement of the head can be controlled to generate dots that are only half a dot apart, but once the solenoid fires, it cannot fire a second time with full energy until the pin has traveled back into the coil.

The half-dot spacing within adjacent points in a given horizontal row cannot be achieved with a single pass of the print head and only a single vertical row of pins. With a double row of pins the orientation and firing order of the pins with respect to the movements of the head can minimize this problem. Many patterns that require a double pass with a single line of pins can be accomplished with a single pass if two vertical lines of pins are available. This increased speed is accomplished in some Okidata models by using two nine-pin heads, but the dimension of the dots is unchanged and the definition is not affected.

Design and Reliability

Dot matrix printers have been remarkably reliable workhorses. Print head life exceeding 200 million characters, two years mean time between failures after operating eight hours a day for five days a week, and a mean time of 15 minutes per repair for the Okidata 92 is pretty impressive.

Design engineering involves making intelligent compromises. Theoretically it is possible to achieve almost any desired end result in designing a dot matrix printer provided it makes some associated sacrifices, such as manufacturing cost, operating speeds, and service-free performance. Unfortunately, no one can make truly reliable judgments about many of these factors until a device has been in the hands of end users for a substantial period of time — at least a year. Even with extensive in-house testing of equipment, quality is a moderately educated guess until actual field tests have taken place. Therefore it is important to determine whether a printer that has just been placed on the market has enough special advantages (and/or a strong enough guarantee) to warrant the gamble involved in purchasing it.

Print Quality

The flexibility of existing dot matrix printers is much greater than most observers realize. The quality of dot matrix printing has steadily improved, both by increasing the program capabilities and improving the basic designs. For example, the factor that has been said to make the difference between good typography and great typography is the proportional spacing of individual character pairs, called kerning. With a number of the dot matrix printers currently on the market, both proportional spacing of characters on a line and kerning between letter pairs can be accomplished via software or by creating your own typography.

It is almost always worthwhile, balanced against time and money, to purchase software that does things for you versus struggling through the learning process necessary to become a part-time technician. However, if you have the time, enjoy the activity, and can tolerate early disappointments, creating your own fonts of type can be rewarding.

The term "readability" — as it is commonly used concerning the characteristics of the output from various printers — is difficult to interpret without establishing some scale of values. If you have a reasonable understanding of the general field of knowledge covered by the content, it is surprising that the human brain requires so little information in order to understand the meaning of a written message. A printer may be operating very poorly and still generate enough legible marks on paper to be not only readable but understandable. It follows that increasing the speed of a dot matrix printer by reducing the letter shapes to very primitive forms is appropriate for purposes of printing and proofreading the content of draft material.

A moderate amount of technical information is helpful when selecting equipment, but questions about such things as clarity and definition are best resolved by direct side-by-side visual comparisons. Subjective evaluation must be the ultimate criterion. The interpretation established in the brain of the observer is influenced by many variables that are beyond discussion.

Laser Printers

The cost of the laser printers discussed here varies from $2,000 to $6,000. Until recently most of the laser printers in this price range used the engine designed by Canon, which brought the price of laser printers into the range of the desktop publishing market.

The most common dot spacing is 300 per inch, which provides very good definition for text and reasonably good graphics. The average observer, especially without an opportunity for side-by-side comparison, views the text results as comparable to high-quality periodicals. Speeds average around six to ten pages per minute, which is comparable to a dot matrix printer at 150 to 200 characters per second, and the cost per page varies between three and four cents. Other design parameters (described below) divide these printers into very different categories with regard to price and performance.

Laser printers are nonimpact devices and hence very quiet. The underlying principles of operation are essentially the same as for Xerox and similar copying machines. In fact, a large section of the hardware in many lasers is taken directly from electrographic copying machines.

How Lasers Work

The photosensitive phenomena associated with the element selenium were observed in the 1880s but were largely set aside, then rediscovered much later. Practical applications of xerographic copiers and laser printers did not surface in the United States until 1950. The significant effect is a very large change in electrical resistance for selenium in the presence or absence of light. In darkness, resistance of selenium is high, approximately one or two megohms. In bright light, the resistance drops to as low as 1,000 ohms. The high resistance in darkness causes a selenium-coated surface to be capable of holding an electrostatic charge for relatively long periods of time: up to several seconds or more.

Thus the selenium-coated drum in a dark laser printer, exposed to a high-voltage field, is raised to a high electrostatic potential capable of attracting a coating of toner (dry ink) (see Figure 11-1). When the laser light beam strikes the selenium surface, the electrical resistance of that area drops sharply, the electrostatic charge leaks off, and the ink is no longer attracted or held to the selenium surface. This basic phenomenon — the differential electrical resistance of selenium in response to light — makes the laser printer possible.

The prime phenomenon can be illustrated by withdrawing a vinyl phonograph record from a paper sleeve on a cold dry day. This creates an electrostatic charge that is almost sufficient to empty an ash tray of ashes if the charged record is held close to it in a flat position. In a laser printer, a rotating cylinder (or traveling belt) is coated with a material, such as selenium, that is capable of accepting and holding a high-voltage electrostatic charge. The surface of the cylinder is uniformly charged by passing close to a so-called corona wire. A "cloud" of microscopic plastic beads coated with black, dry ink (the toner) is created magnetically. The laser beam travels across the cylinder and is turned on and off at the rate of 300 times per inch of travel. The laser light beam is capable of discharging the electrostatic potential on the surface of the cylinder. At those points where the beam is turned on, the surface is discharged. At those points where it is turned off, the charge remains on the cylinder. At the points where the cylinder retains the electrostatic charge, it attracts the ink-coated particles — just as the phonograph record attracts dust. The result is a pattern of the powdered material on the surface of the cylinder that corresponds to the pattern of on/off switching of the laser beam as it scans the surface. Those tiny beads are then fused to each other and to the paper by heat and pressure. The black powder is condensed on the surface rather than absorbed into the paper, and it is possible to feel the raised type by passing your fingers over it. The end result is a very clean, clear image that is satisfactory for almost any desktop publishing application.

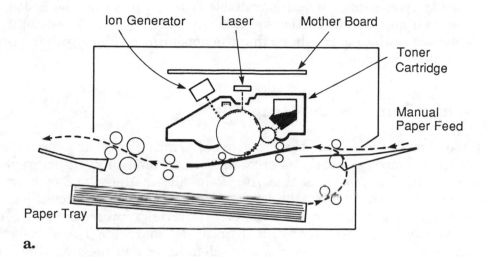

Ion Generator   Laser   Mother Board

Toner
Cartridge

Manual
Paper Feed

Paper Tray

a.

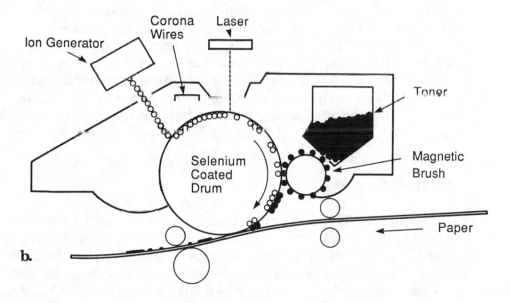

Corona   Laser
Wires

Ion Generator

Toner

Magnetic
Brush

Selenium
Coated
Drum

Paper

b.

Figure 11-1. Inside the LaserWriter the paper path (dotted lines) travels under the cartridge. Diagram b shows an exploded view within the cartridge.

Three hundred dots per inch is four times the number printed by the Okidata 92/93 printers, but still may seem inadequate when compared to the 2,000 to 5,000 dots per inch achieved in the highest-quality typesetting currently available. The truth is that the fusion of the extremely fine particles adds substantially to the definition achieved in the end result, so that the appearance of laser printed text is quite high quality.

Laser Printers and Graphics

You should realize that the problems of printing text considered high in quality are not nearly as great as the problems of printing graphic material. One reason is that the brain fills in the shape of a well-known pattern, such as the image of an alphabetic character, but is much less forgiving in the case of a pictorial representation where relatively long lines may flaunt their jagged character. The alphabetic characters are entirely symbolic, by definition, and need only be recognized in order to communicate their full meaning. Graphic material, at least theoretically, communicates as an actual pictorial representation rather than as a name that conjures up the picture.

The graphics from a laser printer are generally superior to the best available with dot matrix machines, but are still a far cry from the reproductions in most magazines. It is also true that the expectations from relatively short-run desktop publications are much less demanding. For purposes of printing graphs, bar charts, and explanatory drawings, both dot matrix and laser printers are adequate.

Printing Speed

Expensive ($150,000 and up) laser printers have been around since the mid-1970s, operating at high speeds of more than 100 pages a minute. It is considerably better to make comparisons on the basis of pages per minute than characters per second. The calculations used in this essay are based on an average of 5 letters per word and 250 words per page.

The speed of the best dot matrix printers is at least equal to the average desktop laser, but the quality is not. The speeds stated above — around six or seven pages per minute — can produce an average book in about an hour. Most daisy wheel printers would require an eight-hour day to print out the average book.

Types of Laser Printers

Among the first adaptations of the Canon engine was the Hewlett Packard Laserjet (introduced in 1984), the LaserWriter (offered by Apple in January 1985), and the LaserWriter Plus (reached the market a year later). The Plus machine is principally different in the number of built-in fonts available, and the LaserWriter can be upgraded to a LaserWriter Plus.

Additional print engines with various advantages and disadvantages are currently being designed and marketed. The Xerox Company, in cooperation with Fuji, has designed an excellent engine at a moderate price and incorporated it into its equipment. Toshiba's engine is in the Data Products machine that generates 12 pages per minute.

There are many variations of the basic technology described above, but at this time there is little difference in the end results. Perhaps the simplest way to categorize laser printers currently on the market, which also happens to correspond to a substantial price differential, involves the extent to which the program intelligence is built into the printer versus allowing it to reside as a separate entity that may or may not be integral to the computer.

The LaserWriter and PostScript

The Apple LaserWriter is in the former category and contains the same 32-bit processor that is used in the Macintosh, as well as 1.5 megabytes of RAM (random access memory). The latter houses the program command information called PostScript, a page description language written by Adobe Systems, as well as the typeset fonts that are effectively built into the system.

The LaserWriter, manufactured by Apple using the Canon engine, is controlled by the PostScript program stored in read-only memory (ROM) in the printer. The alphabets are stored in ROM in the form of algorithms for drawing the shapes of the characters available in a given font. In response to a demand from the operator, the PostScript program calls up the algorithms and equations that describe the alphabetic characters requested in the form of a 1-point font. When the required point size is specified, the instructions are scaled up and a set of digital bit-maps for that font in the required size is generated and stored in volatile memory. This technique makes it possible to have a very large number of fonts available from a relatively small amount of storage capacity.

The algorithms and equations that function in the PostScript mode of operation are also capable of manipulating the alphabets in a number of other ways that minimize the amount of storage required. Condensed or expanded alphabets can be created by applying differential magnification to the x versus the y axis. A synthetic italic font (termed oblique) simply tilts the y versus the x axis. The technique is also effective in accomplishing kerning, justification, rotation, and an assortment of other occasionally useful modifications.

Bit-Mapped Fonts

The other approach, which is more common and initially much less costly, is to store the information regarding each alphabetic character in a font in the form of a digital bit-map that defines the shape in a literal placement of dots. At 300 or slightly more dots per inch, the direct printing of such digital dot maps yields very good quality. The problems arise in the storage capacity required for a large number of alphabets in a wide variety of point sizes. The technique of enlarging directly in terms of dot placement and without mathematical manipulation is prohibited by the severe degradation of definition that comes when the bits are spread out by enlargement. For straight lines, filling in the gaps with extra elements is a simple solution, but the complex curves of a lowercase Times Roman *g,* for example, make a good end result almost impossible.

Although it is not practical to provide the required memory capacity for bit-maps of all the required faces in all the necessary dimensions in the form of ROM hardware, it is entirely practical to provide the fonts on disks to be downloaded to RAM in the printer as required.

Controller Location

In both approaches to generating individual letters, the alphabets currently in use are stored in volatile memory and must be restructured or reloaded at the beginning of a new session. Thus, the amount of intermediate volatile storage in a microcomputer is an important consideration, especially when it is necessary to call up a wide variety of typefaces during the processing of a document. But a number of programs allow a dozen or more typefaces to be used in a single page, and more are appearing all the time.

For printing applications involving reports, manuscripts, and the like, the high cost of PostScript and similar programs is not warranted. But there is an important advantage for complex typesetting that requires ultimate final quality. The PostScript program, for example, is entirely compatible for communicating data to typesetting devices, such as those available from Allied Linotype.

Apple's early introduction of the LaserWriter, with its excellent and broad spectrum of performance characteristics, generated the concept that incorporating the controller in the printer is correct design practice. Subsequent examination of the method of placing the control facility in the computer rather than in the printer makes it clear that there are good arguments for both approaches. It finally comes down to analysis of the features available for specific applications. A system design that places the controller in the computer reduces the cost of the system and can optimize the speed of the printer.

Industry Activity

As competitive pricing continues, laser printers with even less complete facilities than described here probably will become available, so this information should not be assumed to cover all possible laser design configurations.

Most existing laser printers have facilities for accepting downloaded type fonts recorded on disks. Adobe Systems has contracted with International Typeface Corporation and Allied Merganthaler, which own literally thousands of typefaces, to make their entire library of fonts available on disks. Fonts with various desirable characteristics are increasingly available from other organizations. Softcrafts Inc. markets a laser printing program with font editing and downloading facilities in sizes from 8 to 24 points and with more than 1,500 foreign language and mathematical characters and special symbols. The laser fonts run automatically with Microsoft Word and with Softcraft's own Fancy Font and Fancy Word programs.

In the few years since Canon introduced the engine that first made it possible to offer Laser printers in a size and price range that reached the desktop publishing market, more than 30 manufacturers have generated more than 60 different commercial models. Actually they aren't all that different, and by 1987, approximately three-quarters of them will be using the Canon engine. Prices that now range from less than $2,000 to around $8,000 are expected to drop substantially, but not below a retail list price of $1,500 — at least not in the reasonably foreseeable future. Several other engines have reached the market and more are under development. In the rush to capture the early excitement, the vast majority of manufacturers have made little or no effort to be truly innovative in their designs.

The most significant strength for the more expensive devices, such as the Apple LaserWriter, is the ease with which text in a wide variety of typefaces and graphics can be combined on a single page with high-quality printing results. The TurboLaser 800 from AST is in the same price class (actually a little higher), and performs at exceptionally high speeds as well as producing excellent graphics.

Purchasing Criteria

At least a dozen manufacturers offer equipment in the price range of $4,000 to $8,000. A wide variety of advantages and disadvantages exists in the approximately 60 different models, and what is trivial for one user may be vital for another. Thus it is wise and conserves time to review tabulations of characteristics in the trade publications and then actually examine only those machines that best fit individual requirements.

The first consideration is the extent to which graphics, in combination with a wide variety of typefaces, is important in a given application. If the vast majority of the work will be text designed primarily for verbal communication, the current price range, which is hovering between $2,000 and $3,000, is the place to look. If more elaborate facilities are needed occasionally, it may be worthwhile to use outside suppliers. This price range undoubtedly represents the most rapidly expanding market.

The other criteria of most significance are speed, print quality, resolution, and operating cost. It is interesting that the cost per page is approximately the same as it is for impact printers that use ribbons: roughly three to four cents a page.

The practical duty cycle is a factor that many observers may overlook. This determines the number of pages it is possible to print per month, which varies from an average of 3,000 or 4,000 using the Canon engine to a high of 10,000 to 25,000 using the Ricoh engine. The latter machines run at 10 to 15 pages per minute and the former at 6 to 8 per minute.

One other important factor that may be overlooked, especially in connection with graphics, is how large a portion of the page can be printed at the relatively high-quality resolution of 300 dots per inch.

Some machines can create full pages with this kind of definition, others are limited to half a page or less.

It is reasonable to predict that within the next five years, at least one new printing technique will appear. It will probably be at least as competitive in performance and cost, with respect to the lasers, as they are currently with respect to all other printing techniques.

In all printers using the Canon engine, a plug-in unit consisting of the photosensitive drum, the cartridge containing the toner, the corona wire, and the supporting structures, is replaced when the toner has been consumed, which is generally after printing around 3,000 to 4,000 pages, depending on the type and graphic dot density. Other printers simply replace the toner. In either case, the replacement-cost per page is at least as low as, and at some production levels lower than, the cost of ribbons for impact printers.

Output Media

Desktop publishing is different in many ways from conventional forms of commercial publishing and printing. Desktop publishing printers, for example, do not transfer liquid or viscous inks directly from type or lithographic plates to paper but most commonly, do so by impacting an ink or carbon-coated ribbon against the paper or by nonimpact transfer of dry ink (toner) to paper. Thus, some of the following information is not directly applicable but, as will happen occasionally, when the work spills over into conventional printing channels, a broader understanding is useful.

Symbolic patterns of ink on paper are the end product of desktop publishing, and consequently the techniques for the final production of hard copy warrant prime attention. The complex circuitry in computers, the carefully structured software programs, the large and clear monitor screens combined with well-designed printers are not very useful if the ink smudges, the characteristics of the paper are inappropriate, and the combination is unattractive and difficult to read.

If clearly communicated information is the objective, use hard matte finished paper with clean lines of matte black ink. The kind of black that produces the most readable printing has the light absorbing quality of the inside walls of an old brick chimney.

If the final run in monotone is to be accomplished via xerography or offset printing, some of these considerations become less important in creating the desktop original. The copy is often substantially better. Still, you have the privilege and responsibility of selecting the paper for printing. It is common to use reflective and glossy ink and paper for wedding invitations, for example, but elegance can be equally well achieved with appropriate design using high-quality matte materials.

Both Ricoh and Canon are said to have announced their color laser printers in Europe more than a year ago. In advertising and other applications where attracting attention is important, color has substantial impact. However, weigh the need for such facilities against the additional cost involved. Most desktop publishing applications have relatively little need for color.

Nonimpact Printing

The following material is largely derived from information supplied by the Electrostatics Business Group of the Olin Hunt Company in West Paterson, New Jersey. Olin Hunt is the largest supplier of toners to the manufacturers of impact printing equipment who distribute supplies, such as toners, under their own trade name.

In many desktop publishing systems, it is desirable and economical to have a copier as well as a printer available. The nonimpact technologies are essentially the same in copiers and in printers. Xerox has taken advantage of this by creating a copying facility in combination with the laser printer supplied in one of their newer, excellent desktop publishing systems. The printer and copier share most of the major components of the system. Most of the nonimpact systems described below are presented in formats applicable to copying systems, but the design principles for printers are the same.

The following information can provide a long-term reference for understanding and evaluating new units of equipment that are destined to appear in a steady flow in the next few years.

Toners

Designing toners is an intricate, largely chemical problem. Ideally, a toner is designed in cooperation with the manufacturer of a specific printer so that the parameters of the toner match the characteristics of the equipment with which the toner is to be used. In at least one instance the research and development program to create a satisfactory toner for a particular printer took more than five years.

In some respects, toners are merchandised in a highly competitive market, and independent manufacturers of toners attempt to keep their prices down by reducing distribution costs and by seeking less expensive components. In designing a competitive toner for a specific printer, the chemical analysis of existing products can be very difficult and includes the problem of determining which components are truly essential and which are not. When such products perform well, they may represent a worthwhile cost advantage. As with all competitive situations, the only sure solution is in trial and error. Unless the savings are quite substantial, it is usually better to stay with the product specifically designed in cooperation with the equipment manufacturer.

In the opinion of most experts in the field, nonimpact printing will dominate the future, especially in desktop publishing. The principal advantages are speed, minimum noise, high-quality hard copy, and successful printing on a wide variety of materials. The techniques described below are included in many existing products and ongoing research and development projects involving both printers and copiers.

Electrophotography

This technique, developed as a consequence of activity in the photocopy industry, is widely applied in order to obtain high-speed printed output in substantial volume. Siemens, IBM, Xerox, and a number of other companies are involved in these developments.

In the beginning, the photoconductor drum is sensitized by the application of a high-level surface charge. The drum must at this time be in the dark so that its electrical resistance is high enough to maintain the charge without appreciable leakage. The laser beam responds to digital control signals by applying light to the drum surface, increasing the conductivity and allowing the charge to decay in the lighted region. The positively charged toner particles are transferred to the discharged areas and are repelled by the areas on the drum that still carry a positive charge. Negatively charged beads are used to pick up the toner particles. As the drum continues to rotate, the paper is moved between the drum and a corona device that applies a negative (hence attractive to the positive toner particles) charge to the paper.

Paper

Initially created in China during the first few years of the second century A.D., paper has become the most widely used of all fabricated products. Annual consumption reaches 100 pounds per person in the highly industrialized nations. Paper remained exclusively in China for 500 years after its invention. Then, in the seventh century, along with the beautiful oriental game called Go, it reached Japan. Until then, the Japanese had no written language. Finally, via caravan routes, this useful, inexpensive, practical product was introduced into the Western world. Research continues constantly, but the basic methods by which paper is fabricated remain essentially the same after 18 centuries.

Many qualities in paper contribute to its desirability in connection with desktop publishing. Some of the same bond paper that was originally designed for use in typewriters is equally satisfactory for desktop publishing applications, but there are a number of special considerations in selecting paper for optimum results in various printers. The following are a number of the most important characteristics to consider in selecting paper.

Surface

Papers designed specifically for use with copiers or laser printers are developed within a specific range of smoothness to obtain the best results. Extremely smooth paper can cause problems in passing through complex pathways. Paper that is too rough often results in uneven ink or toner distribution and poor fusing of toners to the surface.

Thickness

Printers and copiers are designed to handle paper thickness within a specific range. Paper that is too thin causes multiple feeding and various kinds of jams. Excessive thickness can also cause handling jams as well as poor image definition. Variations in thickness between successive sheets, or even within an individual sheet, can result in blank areas and a mottled effect in dense areas.

Porosity

Highly porous papers cause feathered edges with absorbed inks, such as those used in impact printers. With any system, excessive porosity introduces feeding problems, especially where vacuum is used. Paper with extremely low porosity tends to curl and develop internal swelling points that distort the printing.

Transparency

Transparent papers allow visual bleeding through from back to front, which is not acceptable in paper printed on both sides. Papers coupled together must be opaque. Very dense opacity often indicates excessive filler content, and the release of fillers in the printing or copying process can cause operating problems in the equipment as well as poor definition.

Stiffness

Limp paper results in feeding errors and jams. Excessive stiffness can impede the paper from following a complex feeding path, can maintain bends and curls, and can flatten after printing.

Most equipment manufacturers are prepared to make recommendations on the best paper to use with their copiers or printers. A few make the mistake of claiming that any paper works with their equipment. Rarely, if ever, is such a claim completely accurate.

It is true that for rough drafts the principal consideration is price. Word-processing systems almost invariably consume, and ultimately waste, several times as much paper as facilities still devoted to typewriters. One reason is that it is so easy to turn on the printer and crank out sample copies. Another is that the printed word is far easier to evaluate and edit than the partial page of text available on most monitors.

Final drafts warrant the extra cost of smooth matte stock, heavy enough to slit thoroughly, hence separate easily and cleanly. Rag content has long been a criterion for high-quality paper but its only significance today is in terms of archival storage. Artificial fibers of many different kinds are beginning to expand the spectrum of available papers, and some of these synthetics are excellent in every respect, including long-term storage.

The principal design problems with paper have to do with moisture content, tendencies to slough off dust into the working parts of the printer, and the development of undesirable electrostatic charges on the paper. The end results with many varieties of paper not specifically designed for use in laser printers include curling, especially at the ends, poor definition, and streaking. The curling sometimes is sufficiently severe so that the paper will not feed smoothly into a copier. When only one or two sheets are involved, for example in a letter, the curling problem may not be serious, but when you have a manuscript involving 50 to 100 pages it can be intolerable. Sometimes, though quite rarely, the printer itself may be partly at fault if the heat applied in the fusing process is excessive.

Ink

The use of water as a solvent or suspension for pigments, hence as a means for depositing them to dry in patterns on various surfaces, originated more than 4,000 years ago in Egypt and China. Linseed oil, mineral oil, or varnish later became the base for inks used in printing. Primitive experiments produced desirable variations, but only in the 20th century did demand warrant full-scale research into the chemical design of inks for specific applications. Some notion of the magnitude of the market can be gained by knowing that the Sunday edition of a large newspaper may require a quarter of a million pounds of ink.

Today the supplier of inks and ribbons must take into account a great many operating variables, such as the basic kind of printer, the surface character of the paper stock, the reflective finish desired and so on to as many as 20 or more significant variables.

Ribbons, inks, and toners that are interchangeable among printers adapted to them almost all produce readable output, but even subtle differences can be important in an activity as sensitive as communication. The ink, or ribbon, recommended by the manufacturer of a printer is most likely formulated in terms of functioning efficiently with that particular machine. With toners, as has been emphasized earlier, it is even more important because the operating characteristics of laser printers involve more variations.

The rate at which ink dries is less important in desktop publishing than in commercial printing. In laser printing, the problem is resolved in the design of the final application of heat and pressure that results in fusing the particles of ink. The toner is not absorbed into the paper but fused on the surface, and the raised letters can be felt with your fingertips.

Summary

The two important families of printers are impact printers, of which the dot matrix is the workhorse and overwhelming popular choice, and non-impact printers, of which the laser printer is dominant. The composition of toner and paper has a bearing on print quality. Toners are specifically formulated for each make of printer, and while there is overlap, one must be cautious in substituting toners. The type of paper must be within a certain range of stiffness and porosity. Wide deviations in choices of paper and toner make for unwanted variations in print quality, especially in large black areas, shaded areas, and large sized letters.

Laser printers are becoming increasingly popular, and will be the dominant office printer before the decade is through. Prices vary depending on output quality, mainly a function of resolution, and features, especially the incorporation of a page description language such as PostScript and capacity for storing various fonts.

KEYWORDS:

- Scanning

- Resolution

- Windowing

- Compression

- Gray Scale

- OCR

James P. McNaul is vice president of Strategic Planning at Datacopy Corporation in Mountain View, California. He has more than 25 years of experience in engineering managment, marketing, and strategic planning with such companies as Harris Digital Telephone Systems Division, the Integrated Office Systems Division of Anderson-Jacobson, and Ford Aerospace and Communications Corporations. Datacopy Corporation designs, manufactures, and markets low-cost, high-resolution electronic digitizing scanners and image processing systems.

Essay Synopsis: Scanners are a broad family of machines that convert an external image to a form that can exist in a data file in your PC. They are used for scanning photographs, solid objects, and even text. One kind of scanner, the optical character reader (OCR), can read text directly off a printed page into a disk file, which saves the work of re-keying in that text. Some scanners are designed to read forms, saving the text in identifiable data fields in a database record.

This essay explores the technology underlying scanners and presents the major types of scanning machines available today. You will learn about the tradeoffs between imaging parameters such as gray scale, resolution, and file size, about different camera systems, and image capture and processing functions such as halftoning, windowing, scaling, and compression.

12

Image Scanning and Processing

James P. McNaul

Images are a form of information that is more pervasive in our lives than text or numbers. Yet traditionally when we think of data or information in offices, we think only of text or numbers. Images exist in many forms in offices. For example, a file cabinet is an image database, and a published document may consist of pages of images, even if they are only text and numbers. The human eye and mind have the unique ability to take an image and translate it into a learned concept: a letter, a number, a word, or a "thing."

Image scanning has become an inherent part of many office applications. Falling price, improved performance, and increasing ease of use are causing scanners and application software to be applied to such areas as electronic publishing, data entry, facsimile communications, and image management of records. This essay describes imaging technology, how it is applied as a system, and its current office applications.

Image processing is the conversion of an image of an object to electronic data so that it is in a form useful for a specific application. This usually involves three steps. One is the scanning process itself, where light energy is converted to an electrical signal representing the image. Next, the contents of the image may be changed in a specific way to meet the application's needs. For example, the image may be scaled in size or resolution, the edges may be enhanced, or the contrast or brightness changed. Fi-

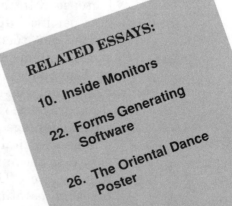

nally, the form of the data may be transformed, without deliberately changing the content. In this case, for example, the image of a page of text may be converted to standard computer ASCII code through a process called optical character recognition (OCR). In another instance, the image of a line drawing may be converted to vector form for a Computer-Aided Design (CAD) application by applying raster to vector conversion processes, which is presented later in this essay.

The important point is that image processing is application-specific. Some scanning methods are more appropriate for one application than for another. Similarly, the image processing that is applied is dependent on the final application and how that image is to be used in the application, for instance. There is no right way to scan or process an image. It all depends on what you want to do with the image and how much you are willing to pay in time and money (equipment) for a given level of quality. The following discussion covers some of the parameters that must be considered.

The Scanning Process

Images exist as light reflected off a physical object. This light contains information about color and intensity. To convert it to electronic form requires the use of a photoreceptor device that creates an electrical signal proportional to the intensity of the light falling on it. Light from the object is optically focused on the photoreceptor, which breaks it into a mosaic of dots called picture elements. A picture element that contains gray-scale information usually is called a pixel. If it is binary, containing only black or white information, it is called a Pel. Generally, the greater the density of picture elements (resolution), the better the image quality, but data storage and processing requirements increase with the square of the resolution. Resolutions of 200 to 400 dots per inch (dpi) are typical for office applications, but much higher resolutions, such as 1,000 to 2,000 dots per inch, are usually used in typeset-quality publishing. Figure 12-1 illustrates the process.

The analog signal for the photoreceptor is converted to digital form by an analog-to-digital converter. The analog signal for each pixel contains gray-scale information because it is a function of the light intensity, and ranges from white (full intensity) to black (no light). The analog-to-digital converter captures this gray-scale information by sampling the analog signal and describing it as one of a number of intensity levels. Usually from 4 to 8 bits of data are created for each pixel representing from 16 to 256 levels of gray, respectively. Most low-cost office scanners capture 4 to 6 bits of gray information, but higher-quality imaging systems convert the analog signal to 8 to 12 bits of gray-scale information. After it has been digitized, the information is ready to be processed like any other digital data. It represents the original image in what is called bit-mapped or raster form and appears as a series of dots.

The photoreceptor is usually a charge-coupled device (CCD) array, which consists of a fixed number of elements and usually is scanned across the image plane in discrete steps (or the image is successfully moved across the CCD array). Thus, the resolution must always be defined with respect to the object size. For example, a CCD linear array consisting of 1,728 elements captures 203 dots per inch over 8½ inches, usually rounded to 200 dots per inch. If the array is moved incrementally 2,200 times over the image plane, it would provide 200 by 200 dots per inch over an 8½-by-11 inch document focused on the image plane. Typical CCD arrays contain 1,728, 2,048, 2,555, 3,456 or 4,096 elements — representing 200, 240, 300, 400, and 480, respectively. Mathematical scaling can also be used to achieve a specific resolution from a given array size. Two-dimensional CCD arrays also are available, but they are economically constrained to about 512 to 1,024 elements, thereby limiting their resolution. The resolution's implication for the size of the resulting image file is discussed later.

Scanner Designs

Image scanners that are suitable for office applications consist of three basic types: camera-based, flatbed, and paperfeed. Each has its advantages and disadvantages, but virtually any application need can be

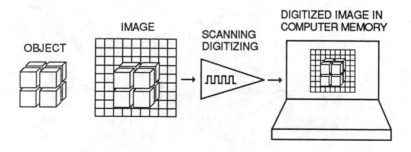

Figure 12-1. The image scanning process.

met using one type or another. These three configurations can be implemented in a variety of ways, and sometimes more than one approach is used in a single device.

Camera-Based Systems

Camera technology was among the first to be exploited for document scanning. The camera lens focuses the image of the object on the image plane where the film normally would be located in a standard camera. In an electronic digitizing camera (EDC), the film is replaced by a CCD array that is moved across the image plane by a stepper motor or a servo-drive system under the control of the host computer. As the CCD is moved in increments, information from each element is sampled for digitization. Typical sizes range from that of a 35mm camera to that of a view camera (see Figure 12-2). For office applications, they are usually marketed on a copy stand with appropriate lighting.

The electronic functions usually performed in an EDC include the servomechanism or stepper motor control, CCD sampling, analog-to-digital conversion, and control of communications to the host computer. EDC functions, such as the scan area and speed of scan, are typically under the control of the host computer. Scan times can run from as short as half a second to a few minutes. Often the time needed to complete a scan is limited by the ability of the host computer to accept the data into memory (see Figure 12-2).

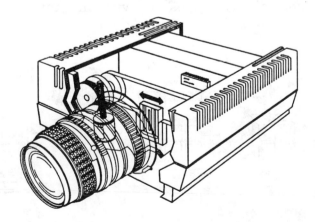

Figure 12-2. Digitizing camera.

The major advantage of an EDC is its application flexibility. Because most EDCs in use are mounted on a camera copy stand, camera operation is emulated. Lens selection can be made to match the application, and light intensity can be adjusted as required. Moving the EDC closer to the object increases the resolution (for smaller objects), and moving it farther away decreases resolution. Typical resolutions range from a maximum of 2,000 dots per inch over an area 2 by 3 inches to 200 dots per inch over 17 by 22 inches. Because of the copy-stand mounting, EDC systems tend to be somewhat more expensive than the fixed systems discussed later and they are more obtrusive because of their size and exposed lights. However, the flexibility is often required in scanner applications because of object size differences and the need to capture book or other types of manuscripts.

Flatbed Systems

Flatbed scanners are derived from office copier technology, where the document is placed in a fixed position on a glass plate and an optical path is scanned across the document face (see Figure 12-3). This allows precise positioning of the document, which in turn allows objects such as books or small three-dimensional objects to be scanned.

During scanning, a light is moved across the document face. Attached to the light bar is a mirror that reflects the incident light to a second mirror that moves at a slower speed to keep the optical path to the fixed sensor constant over the entire scan. The light/mirror combination is moved by a stepper motor, with the movement synchronized to the extraction of data from the CCD array (see Figure 12-3).

A flatbed scanner fixes the resolution over a certain maximum size document area. Resolutions are changed only by changing the way the data is sampled or by electronically scaling the resolution up or down. The flexibility to move the scanner closer to the object (as in an EDC) is lost, although movable optics are possible (as in a reduction copier). The fixed optics tend to simplify the design and keep costs down so that a flatbed scanner is less costly than an EDC and much smaller, typically having a footprint about the size of an office typewriter and being about five inches high. As in a copier, paperfeed mechanisms can be adapted to flatbed scanners to move successive sheets onto the glass plate. However, the document stays fixed during the scan.

Typical scanning resolutions are 400, 300, 240, and 200 dots per inch. The base resolution is determined by the number of elements in the CCD array. If a scanner has multiple resolution choices, it is done by electronic scaling. Scanning speeds range from approximately a second to 30 seconds. Again, the speed is often dependent on the data transfer rate to the computer. From 4 to 8 bits of gray-scale information for each Pel (16 to 256 levels of gray) are usually generated.

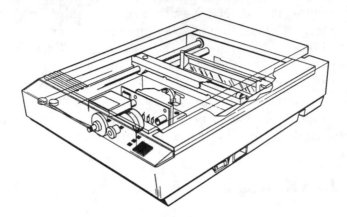

Figure 12-3. Flatbed scanner.

Paper-Moving Systems

An alternative approach, derived from facsimile technology, is to keep the optical path fixed and to move the document across the light bar and mirror (see Figure 12-4). This results in an even simpler mechanism and lower cost, but with somewhat less performance. There can be problems with paper skewing or jamming during movement, and only single sheets may be scanned. Other performance characteristics are similar to those of flatbed scanners. The paper skewing is an important consideration in publishing applications. Skewing causes horizontal and vertical lines to be broken (jaggies) in the scanned version. A flatbed scanner allows the original document to be precisely positioned during the scan and also allows multiple scans to be made without changing the position of the original (see Figure 12-4).

Variations on a Theme

The technologies discussed above can be combined in several ways. Sometimes an EDC is mounted in a cabinet with fixed optics so that it becomes an equivalent of a flatbed scanner. Mechanical movement of the optics can be done in a flatbed scanner to accomplish resolution (or

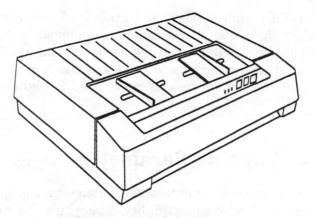

Figure 12-4. Paperfeed scanner.

size) scaling. This offers advantages in image quality, but tends to add to the cost of the scanner. In high-resolution scanners, very precise paper movement devices can be designed that eliminate the paper skewing; however they add considerably to the cost.

Finally, a type of scanner used in very high-resolution scanning combines several of these technologies in a design called a drum scanner. The original is mounted on a drum that rotates at a constant speed. The original is then scanned by a very narrow beam of light, typically from a light-emitting diode (LED) or a laser beam. This is reflected off the original to a single-element photoreceptor. The light beam and receptor then are scanned mechanically for the length of the rotating document. Obviously, this mechanical complexity tends to increase the cost of the scanner, while achieving high resolution.

Scanning-System Costs

Very-high-resolution scanning systems for high-quality publishing systems can cost from $25,000 to $100,000 or more. Adding color scanning and manipulation capabilities can bring these costs to $1 million or more.

Office scanners, with resolutions of 200 to 400 dots per inch, are considerably less expensive. Paperfeed scanners with 300-dots-per-inch resolution now cost from about $1,000 to $2,000 depending on the software and other features. Similar flatbed scanners cost from $1,500 to $3,000 with similar software. Camera systems cost from $5,000 to $25,000 depending on the way they are implemented.

Carefully analyze the application that requires the scanner before selecting one. Different scanner technologies are appropriate for different applications as well as levels of performance within applications. Both the scanner and the functions it performs with its image-processing software must be considered in light of a specific application.

Important Imaging Parameters

Two parameters in imaging are particularly important in regard to performance and output quality. These are the amount of gray-scale information generated and the capture resolution. Both are a result of the scanning process but have an impact on every function that follows.

Capture Resolution

A higher capture resolution tends to result in a higher quality image. However, two other considerations are important. One is the resolution of the output device and the other is the file size.

Most office scanners capture information at a resolution of 300 dots per inch because this is the resolution of the standard office laser printer. When the scanner resolution matches the printer resolution, the printed image stays the same size from capture to output. If the resolutions differ, the output image is scaled in size proportionately. For example, an image captured at 200 dots per inch is printed at two-thirds of its original size on a 300-dots-per-inch printer. Electronic scaling would have to be used to compensate for the size difference with some resulting loss of quality.

The image file size increases with the square of the resolution. At 200 dots per inch, an 8½-by-11 inch image file contains about 3.7 megabits (mb) of information if it is binary (i.e., does not contain gray-scale information). Each bit represents either a black or white Pel. At 300 dots per inch, the file size goes up to 8.4 megabits, and at 400 dots per inch it goes up almost to 15 megabits. Obviously, increasing the resolution has a significant impact on information-storage requirements and processing time.

Although the standard is currently 300 dots per inch, scanners and laser printers are available at 400 dots per inch. With the advent of more powerful desktop computers and lower storage costs, 400 dots per inch should become the office standard for both scanning and printing over the next year or so.

Gray-Scale Content

Another important variable is the number of levels of gray scale that are captured by the scanner. Gray-scale information is useful in publishing for a number of reasons, including the following. It allows higher quality scaling of images because the gray-scale information can be used to determine the level of gray of the inserted pixels. Better halftones can be generated using more gray-scale information to represent shades of gray on monochromatic printers. Image enhancement techniques can be used that make use of the gray-scale information.

As in resolution, you pay a price in file size with more gray-scale information. Most office scanners capture 4 bits (16 levels) of gray-scale information. This results in a file size of 4.2 megabytes (MB) at 300 dots per inch over 8½ by 11 inches. This increases to 7.5 megabytes at 400 dots per inch. At 8 bits (256 levels) the corresponding file sizes are 8.4 and 15 megabytes. Thus, one must trade off storage requirements and processing time to increase the level of gray-scale information in an image file.

Currently, four bits of gray-scale information is typical in office scanners. The tendency is to move to more levels of gray, with six bits becoming more common and eight bits available for special applications. As in resolution, decreasing storage costs and increasing processing power make it easier to deal with more gray scale information.

Image-Processing Technology

Image processing can vary from simple procedures to complex operations used for space-photo enhancement. Many image-processing operations are computation-intensive because of the large number of bits in an image file. Therefore, imaging systems tend to do some processing in special hardware for speed and some in the host computer.

Capturing the document page image through the scanning process is the first step in creating an image file. Basic control of the scanner is included in this, but three other functions are important.

Thresholding

An image file with four to eight bits of gray-scale information contains millions of bytes of information. While gray scale may be important in some applications, such as publishing or medical imaging, it can be discarded where only line drawings or text exist on the document. A process called thresholding can be used to convert the file to binary information.

In thresholding, a particular shade of gray is selected, either manually or automatically by the computer, and all pixels lighter than that shade of gray are set to white, and all those that are darker are set to black. Then the gray-scale information may be discarded and each Pel is represented by only one bit of information. This process is usually carried out in hardware in the scanner or computer interface to minimize the information that has to be processed by the computer.

Halftones

If the document being scanned has considerable gray-scale information, such as a photograph, a halftone may be used. This is a process, often used by newspapers and magazines, to create the impression of gray scale even though printing is essentially a monochromatic process (although multiple single colors may be used).

With halftones, the gray-scale information is processed to create a higher level pattern of dots that vary in number and placement. Each dot consists of a number of Pels. The larger the dots in an area, the darker the area looks, and vice versa. The human eye and brain integrate these dots and perceive shades of gray, but each Pel consists of only one bit of information: black or white.

Windowing

A scanner normally captures the full image of the objects as it is focused on the image place. However, it is frequently useful to capture only a portion of the image. For example, a page may consist of text and a picture. If the page is scanned using thresholding, the picture does not look good; it may not even be recognizable. On the other hand, if a halftone is used, the text may not be sharp and clear. With windowing, a first scan of the entire page is made using thresholding. Then a window is placed around the photograph, and a second scan is made using the halftone process. The resulting image file combines both types of information to result in a faithful reproduction of the page. In some cases, multiple windows may be set initially and the images within these windows treated differently during a single scan.

Image Processing Functions

Once an image has been captured and exists as a file in memory, various things can be done to it. Some of the more important ones are discussed below.

Scaling

Images of a particular size can be scaled up or down in size by adding or removing picture elements. Usually this is done by setting the scaling ratio in the x or y axis on the host computer or by creating a window on the display screen and having the computer scale the image to fit the window. There is a reduction in resolution as images are scaled down and Pels are discarded. Also, some distortion is apparent as images are scaled up, because interpolation is used to decide whether a Pel that is to be inserted should be black or white. However, for text or line drawings, reasonable scaling ratios work quite well. Scaling of halftones does not work as well because the algorithm for the halftone process and the scaling algorithm interact to create interference patterns in the resulting image. Scaling must be done using the gray-scale information, thus increasing the processing necessary. Then the halftone pattern is created.

Compression

Because of the large size of image files, they are usually compressed for storage or transmission and decompressed for processing, printing, or display. Compressing a typical 300-dots-per-inch image file in software on the host microcomputer can take 30 seconds to approximately a minute. Compressing in hardware is considerably faster.

The most common data compression technique is based on CCITT Group 3 facsimile standards and is called run-length encoding. Rather than using each individual Pel, a line of Pels is processed, and the number of continuous white or black Pels is encoded in the file. Thus, files with large areas of black or white can achieve significant compression. Compression ratios of 5:1 to 15:1 are typical for documents containing text or line drawings.

Little compression is possible with halftones because of their nature. Other more advanced compression techniques are available, but they tend to be more computation-intensive and are more sensitive to data errors. They will see considerable application in the future, however.

Optical Character Recognition

Text is usually represented in computer systems by a coding system called ASCII code, which represents each character by an eight-bit (or one-byte) code. This is a very economical way of representing characters in terms of storage and permits computer manipulation of the code. Images of a text character typically take about 100 times as much space as an ASCII character, depending on the size of the character image, and cannot be manipulated in the same way that ASCII code can be on a word processor, for example. A technique does exist that converts character images to ASCII characters; it is known as optical character recognition (OCR).

Various algorithms exist to convert images to text. In the process, the character images are first separated into individual images, then each is analyzed against a set of known characteristics. Based on this analysis, a new file is created with the equivalent ASCII codes. Error rates typically are less than 1 percent and the file is usually created much more quickly than an accomplished typist could type the same material. The software is usually "pretaught" to recognize specific character sets, where a character set is a specific type font style and size. For example, Courier 10 is a style of type often found in the office. It is a 10-pitch type (10 characters to the inch). Each style and size represents a different character set. The user can train some OCR software to recognize an unknown character set. Technology is currently becoming available that permits a wider variety of text sizes and types to be recognized, which increases the usefulness of optical character recognition in office applications.

Raster to Vector Conversion

A similar approach can be taken with line drawings. Computer-aided-design systems use a mathematical description of drawings called vectors. Lines are described mathematically (e.g., line coordinates, curve radius) rather than as bit-mapped images. The resulting file is much smaller than the corresponding image file. Software is available that converts a bit-mapped image file to a vector file. With current technology, considerable cleanup on the resulting vector file is necessary. However, raster to vector conversion should see future application as the technology improves and is more widely applied. Vector files are easier to edit than raster files and are preferred in engineering applications.

Imaging Applications

There are many office applications for image scanning and processing. As the cost of scanners for a given level of performance decreases and host processing power increases, scanners will become a standard peripheral on office workstations. At the present time, three applications are most prominent in offices.

Electronic Publishing

Document preparation is the most widespread use of microcomputers in business. The microcomputer has become the standard device for word processing, replacing dedicated word-processing systems. More recently, desktop publishing software, combined with laser printers, has significantly increased the quality of documents that can be produced on a microcomputer workstation.

Most documents can be enhanced through the use of images. Both appearance and readability can be improved. Electronic imaging systems, scanners and software allow image files to be created that can be placed easily in a document using desktop publishing software. Although most word-processing software is not designed to incorporate images, other software exists that interacts with the word-processing software to permit image insertion for display and printing. Electronic publishing at all levels, from desktop to in-plant, is expected to be one of the fastest growing applications for imaging over the next few years.

Data Entry

Although microcomputers have become the dominant means of creating documents in organizations, many documents are still created on typewriters where no electronic file is created. Also, many times a document comes into an organization in paper form and needs to be modified. This typically means that the entire document must be rekeyed, taking time and introducing errors.

Through optical character recognition many of these documents can easily be scanned and the text converted to computer code. Although some errors are introduced, the spelling correction capabilities of most word processors quickly find them. Generally, considerable time can be saved through this technique.

Optical character recognition is a useful adjunct to word processing and desktop publishing. The same scanner that is used for capturing line drawings or photographs can be used to scan the document for optical character recognition processing.

Facsimile Communications

As microcomputer workstations become the common method for creating pages of information, the need will grow to communicate information electronically to other locations. Now this is typically done by sending ASCII files from one computer to another or by sending page images by facsimile.

The technology exists to take information created on a computer or scanned into a computer and send it to a facsimile machine (or another similarly equipped computer) as a page image. The power and versatility of the computer has been coupled with the universal image communications standard, facsimile.

Summary

Imaging technology is improving rapidly while costs are falling and more applications are found. The major changes that will occur over the next two years include the following. The cost for a given level of performance will be reduced (basic scanners, with software, will drop below $1,000). Increased processing power will be built into scanners to improve quality and increase performance. Desktop publishing, in particular, has reached the point where very high-quality documents can be produced. This is increasing the requirement for even higher-quality images than those now available from low-cost scanners. Image databases, the "paperless office," will become an important office application. Optical disk storage, improved optical character recognition for text, and increased processing power will make economical image databases feasible. Image scanners will become a standard peripheral for microcomputer workstations, just as a printer is today. And, like printers, scanners will come in various sizes and shapes, levels of performance, and costs, depending on the application.

Truly, image scanning and processing is a technology whose time has come. It will have a significant impact on the way information is handled and will become a productivity tool in most office situations.

KEYWORDS:

- **Redirection**

- **Pipes**

- **Shell Commands**

- **Documenter's Workbench**

- **Embedded Commands**

Sarah Richey has worked in the computer field for fifteen years; for the last ten years she has worked as a documentation consultant. She became familiar with UNIX while doing work for AT&T. Her interests include literature, southwestern art, hiking, and almost any activity that takes place in the mountains. She is co-owner of Metro Documentation Service, located in Louisville, Colorado, near Denver.

Essay Synopsis: The UNIX operating system, available on mainframe and miniframe computers for more than 20 years, has been used primarily for text processing in multiuser environments. In these environments users work on terminals and share large-capacity disk drives and printers common to the system. Consequently, much powerful software has been produced that deals with text processing.

In this essay the author presents an overview of UNIX, with examples showing how to use standard tools to manipulate UNIX text files. She includes a survey of UNIX publishing application programs. Topics covered include creating shell command scripts to invoke spell checkers, creating tables and pictures, using embedded commands within a text file, and manipulating files within the system.

13

UNIX and Its Text Processing Tools

Sarah Richey

In the hotly contested arena of desktop publishing, debate centers around Macintosh and MS-DOS-compatible software and hardware. It seldom enters the world of UNIX. You may be reading this essay because you are curious about this lesser-known area of desktop publishing in the UNIX environment. Your curiosity could stem from a number of motives. You may wish to have a complete education in desktop publishing and to know all the options. You may need to know how to use UNIX as a desktop publishing system because it is the type of system you have available. You may wish to learn about UNIX because you currently know little or nothing about it. This essay addresses all three of these motives.

In this essay we will present an overview of the UNIX system, concentrating on the Documenter's Workbench programs which are the standard UNIX text processing tools. Later we will discuss some specialized software available for most UNIX systems.

Using UNIX as Your Desktop Publishing System

To some people, desktop publishing and UNIX seem to be contradictory terms because the latter is typically considered an "engineer's" operating system. In some circles, UNIX has been labeled as user unfriendly.

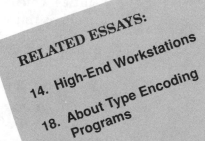

RELATED ESSAYS:

14. High-End Workstations

18. About Type Encoding Programs

Using the UNIX operating system to its full potential does require extra learning on your part, but you don't have to go to all that effort unless you want to. Learning the simple basics of UNIX is no harder than learning MS-DOS. The real point to consider is this: With UNIX, once you become comfortable with the basics, you still have room for growth and to expand your capabilities.

What Is UNIX?

UNIX is an operating system that runs on a wide variety of machines: everything from the smallest PC to the largest mainframe computer. It comes in three variations: UNIX System V, which is the version available from the creators of UNIX, AT&T Bell Laboratories; Berkeley UNIX, which is a version of UNIX produced at the University of California; and XENIX, which is a UNIX-based operating system created by Microsoft for PCs. These three versions mainly differ internally — in areas that are unapparent to the user. Your only concern should be that you know which version you have, because not all software runs on all three versions.

One strength of UNIX is its sparsity. Users have the ability to mold the system to their needs instead of molding their needs around what the system can do. In place of having utilities built in, UNIX supplies the tools for you to make your own. This gives you total flexibility in your operating system. For example, the standard UNIX publishing software does not allow you to preview your file in WYSIWYG form before you print it. But you can program in this ability — in fact, we will show how to do so later in this essay. You may not want that flexibility. You may want a utility that is already built. If this is true, you want to buy software that provides such utilities. One advantage of UNIX is that if your software does not have a feature you want, usually you can create it without much difficulty. UNIX is a multiuser, multitasking operating system. Multiuser means that more than one person can use the system at a time, and multitasking means you can perform more than one job at a time — some jobs can be run in background (they run without you really seeing it) and one job runs in foreground (the one you actually see running and can work with interactively). Large-system users find the first advantage particularly important. The second advantage, multitasking, helps you make the most of your time and of your computer resources. As you work to get documents out on time, this becomes a significant advantage.

UNIX runs on many different types of machines and you may find that to be a big plus in its favor. Because UNIX on a PC does not differ from UNIX on a large machine, files and programs created on a small UNIX machine can be used by any other UNIX machine, including the largest and most powerful. This capability allows you to create a file on a small system, a PC for example, then transfer the file to a large machine for processing. Larger machines process files faster and might have more sophisticated software and peripheral hardware than your PC. For instance, you could transfer a file to another machine in order to use a better printer.

Most of UNIX's fame rests on its versatility, which can give you a lot of extra capabilities if you are willing to learn how to take advantage of them. This versatility stems from a few UNIX concepts that no other operating system has and makes UNIX appealing to people who program and develop software. We can safely say that, in the past, the typical UNIX user liked to tinker with computers instead of using them just to accomplish a task. In fact, such a person might have purchased your UNIX system and so led you into the world of UNIX desktop publishing. But, as the computer loses its mystique, and users such as yourself learn more about how computers work and how to use them, UNIX should become popular among a greater spectrum of people.

UNIX Features

Let's look briefly at the UNIX "versatility-producing" capabilities and how they can help you as you go about your publishing tasks. You do not need to be a computer wizard to take advantage of UNIX. We will describe how you can use the following UNIX abilities: input/output redirection, piping program output, and the shell command language. When you have become comfortable with these three capabilities, you will be surprised at the "tricks" you can accomplish with them. After learning about redirection, piping, and shell scripts, we describe a few of these tricks.

Documenter's Workbench is the standard text processing package available with UNIX systems. This package contains several formatting programs. The text formatter, called *troff,* lets you change fonts for headlines, blocks of text, even for single words, or characters in your text. The fonts available depend upon capabilities of the system printer. A macro formatting program, called *mm,* is called as an option of *troff,* and lets you skip pages and set up paragraphs, headers, footers, and lists. There is a graphics formatter called *pic* that lets you create drawings, diagrams, boxes, and other graphic elements. A table formatter, called *tbl* lets you columnize data; and an equation formatter, *eqn,* lets you create mathematical symbols and formulas.

Each of the formatting programs works on a file that you create, so in creating a file you must embed the proper commands. Such commands as **.tl** and **\bu** and **.I** will prompt the *troff* program to form a title, make a bullet, or italicize text. When you have finished your file, you can invoke the formatting program to operate on your file. The *pic* formatter responds to such embedded commands as **boxwid**, **boxht**, **linewid,** and **arrow,** which do pretty much what their names suggest: Define box widths, heights, line weights, and create arrows. The other formatting programs operate similarly, each having its unique embedded commands. Although learning to be proficient is challenging, the command names are straightforward and the procedure is uniform.

Input/Output Redirection

UNIX has "device-independent input and output." This simply means that what goes into a program does not have to come from one particular source (such as the keyboard) and what comes out of a program does not have to go to another rigidly defined place (such as a printer). For example, when you run the program to check a file for misspelled words, the list of misspelled words prints on your screen. If you want to print a copy of the list, you can redirect the output to a file, then print that file. The world of UNIX has a language all its own, and in this language, the action just described is called "redirection." What are you redirecting? The output of the spelling check program. As a rule, UNIX assumes your keyboard to be the default, or "standard" input, and the terminal screen is the default, or "standard" output. Anytime you change the default input or output, the action is called redirection.

Piping Program Output

Another UNIX concept you can use while producing documents is "piping the output of one program into another." This allows you to issue any number of commands on one file at the same time. For example, here is how the standard UNIX publishing software, known as Documenter's Workbench, uses a series of formatting programs to format your files:

pic creates graphics;

tbl produces tables;

eqn typesets equations; and

troff typesets your text. (Documenter's Workbench is described in detail later in this essay.)

The three programs, *pic, tbl,* and *eqn,* must be run before *troff.* After your file has been processed by all of these programs, it may be printed. You could run each program separately.

```
pic myfile

tbl myfile

eqn myfile

troff -mm myfile

lp myfile
```

Or you could use pipes. Pipes get their name from the character that you type on a line to indicate that you want to use the output from a program as the input to another. You actually type the pipe character (which looks like this: |). If you type that character between program names, you are piping your programs. Rather than the five separate commands shown above, you will have one command that looks like this.

```
pic myfile | tbl | eqn | troff -mm | lp
```

Programmers and designers really like this feature, and as you can see, it makes your job easier as well.

Shell Command Language

The last UNIX concept we discuss is the shell command language. UNIX functions not only as an operating system, but also as a programming language. When you use UNIX as a programming language, you are said to be using the shell command language, and the programs you create are shell scripts. Programmers and designers find this feature extremely useful (and it is one of the reasons some people are almost fanatically fond of UNIX). You can take advantage of the shell command language in your publishing tasks. A shell script consists of little more than a series of UNIX commands that can be run by giving just one command, and that one command corresponds to the name of the shell script. Instead of typing that long line of pipes (shown in the previous example) every time you want to print a file, you can put all of it into a shell script and reduce your keying (and memory) to one command name. For example, the same job described previously, looks like this in a shell script.

```
pic $1 | tbl | eqn | troff -mm | lp
```

Let's say that you have typed this line into a file called *publish*. The *$1* tells the shell command language to substitute your file name after the word *pic*. Now, the entire group of programs is run on your file by typing the following: *publish myfile*.

Using UNIX When Publishing

Let's look at two examples that show how the power of UNIX can be used to help you in your publishing tasks. Our first task is checking for misspelled words. As we saw earlier, redirection allows us to send our list of words to a file, instead of seeing it print on the screen. We could print a copy and mark each word as it is corrected, but it is nice to use such a list interactively. To do this, we would follow these steps.

Table 13-1   Procedure for Running a UNIX Spell Checker

- Run the spell checker program and redirect the output to a file.
- Edit the file that we ran the spell checker on.
- Put the list of misspellings at the beginning of the edited file.
- Correct the misspellings within the file by giving a search command for the misspelled words. Correct the words. Then search for the words again. When no other occurrences of the words are found, your search takes you back to the first of the file, where the list is. Delete the word from the list. Continue this procedure until the list is completely deleted and all misspelled words are corrected.

All of these steps, except for number four, can be accomplished automatically by using redirection and a shell script. The shell script will look like this:

```
spell $1 > spell.out

cat spell.out $1 > temp

mv temp $1

rm spell.out
```

The first line runs the spell program on a file that you specify later (*$1*) and redirects the output (the misspelled words) to a file named *spell.out*. Remember that the *$1* tells the script to substitute your file name here. The second line uses a UNIX command called **cat** that combines your file and the file *spell.out* into one file. That file is named *temp.* The third line uses a UNIX command that renames a file. Thus, after this line is executed, the contents of the temporary file, *temp,* replace the contents of your original file, which is now just as it originally was except that it has a list of misspelled words at the top. The last line of the script simply deletes the file holding your misspelled words. You don't need it any longer because it has been put into your text file.

Now you have two steps to use your spelling list interactively: Run your shell script and repeat the fourth step as outlined previously. To run your shell script, type the name of your script and the name of your file at the UNIX prompt. For example, if you name the shell script *spellcheck,* type **spellcheck myfile.**

The second task we look at is proviewing a file. Because Documenter's Workbench is an embedded command system, we do not immediately see what our processed file looks like. Normally, you have to print a file to proof your formatting commands. However, we can modify the command described earlier, publish, so that we see a copy of the formatted file on the screen. This is what *publish* looked like:

```
pic $1 | tbl | eqn | troff -mm | lp
```

The **lp** sends the formatted file to the printer. If we take off that command, the output of this group of commands shows up at standard out — which is your terminal. However, that approach produces two problems. The formatted text doesn't show a screen at a time. It rolls by so that we can't really proof it. And the terminal doesn't know how to interpret all the line drawings that will be required of the processed tables. To eliminate the first problem, we add a command called **more** to the line of piped commands. This command will show you the output one screen at a time. Then we need to add a command called **col**, which helps your terminal know how to draw the lines used in tables. We can put all of that in a file called *proof* and then proof our files by typing **proof myfile**. The script proof looks like this:

```
pic $1 | tbl | eqn | troff -mm | col | more
```

Other Desktop Publishing Products
for UNIX Systems

As mentioned earlier, one area of monumental change in the field of desktop publishing is the list of software available for use with a UNIX system. To stay most current on the subject and to know what new software has been announced, you should look at the advertisements in the wide variety of magazines that deal with PCs. You should also look through the magazines that specialize in the UNIX operating system. Because desktop publishing under UNIX is a hot market item, you can be certain that the advertisements aren't difficult to spot.

We will look at a few of the products that are currently available. The descriptions provide a general look at the product and what it can do. At the end of this essay you will find a list of these products, what company supplies each one, and where you can write for more information. (The list includes Documenter's Workbench.)

A Description of Text Editors

Since much of the software available for UNIX is of the editor/formatter variety, we should mention the two most frequently used UNIX editors. Both are full-screen editors, which means that you can move the cursor around on the screen to position yourself at the place where you would like to add or change text.

The most common editor is *vi* (pronounced vee-eye). You use it to enter and edit text in a full screen mode. It also has a line command mode that lets you perform commands by line number, such as "move lines 100 through 200 to just below line number 850." Line command mode also gives you access to global commands, meaning commands that affect the entire document, such as "every time you see the word *house,* change it to the word *casa.*" This editor was created at AT&T by engineers. As a result, the commands are not always mnemonic or self-evident. You can find logic behind the *vi* commands, but the originators certainly came from a different environment than most desktop publishing users. For example, **t** is the command you use to copy lines. You see, "t" stands for transcribe, which means "to make a written copy of." And that is exactly what the command does! Despite its unusual command structure, *vi* functions as a perfectly good editor and many people use it with complete satisfaction.

If you are looking for an editor that is a little bit closer to the heart, and especially the mind, of an average PC user, try *emacs.* It has, among other things, on-line help, multiple windows (to edit and see more than one file at a time), and the ability to custom make your editor commands.

A Description of Formatters

As discussed earlier, with an editor/formatter system you first use an editor to enter text and formatting commands, then run the formatter program on the file to process those commands. In addition to the package already described (Documenter's Workbench), three formatting packages seem to provide decent support for publishing on a UNIX system. All three are built around the same formatting programs as Documenter's Workbench, but they include software that supports a wider variety of printers and expands the capabilities of Documenter's Workbench.

The product, *eroff,* is an enhanced version of Documenter's Workbench. It includes a formatting package called *grap* that allows you to insert graphic images into your text. With *eroff,* your graphic images do not have to come from the Documenter's Workbench graphics program. You can insert files created by a scanner, a paint program (such as MacPaint), or a CAD/CAM system. *Eroff* functions not only as your formatter package but also as the printer driver for the LaserJet and LaserJet Plus. As such, you can print frequently used symbols that are not standard on these Hewlett-Packard printers, such as bullets, mathematic typesetting symbols, and even foreign language characters. This package also comes for use with an MS-DOS system. Some people like Documenter's Workbench so much that it is their preferred publishing package, even if their system is not UNIX.

A package supplied by Image Network, called *xroff,* provides an enhanced version of *troff* that addresses some of the problems associated with *troff.* It also includes the processors and font software needed to use a wide variety of laser printers, and even phototypesetters. The font support provided by *xroff* contains Sanford Computer Modern, Computer Sans Serif, and Computer Modern Typewriter. All three font types come in bold, italic, and Roman and in point sizes from 4 to 16. This is a nice variety of fonts for any publishing system.

Enhancing Documenter's Workbench

A Canadian company, SoftQuad, offers another package that uses the Documenter's Workbench software as its base. This package is known as SoftQuad Publishing Software. As with *xroff* and *eroff,* the package enhances *troff* and its associated programs. The two most interesting changes supplied by this package are that it improves the error messages given by *troff* and changes the command structure so that it is now English-based and mnemonic.

One of the most frequently heard complaints about *troff* concerns its error messages. With an embedded-command system, problems can occur when you process the file, and you only know what went wrong by the error messages. With *troff*, you often don't get even a message. Your file simply stops printing at some point, and that point may or may not be the place in the file that causes a problem. When you do get a message, it seldom helps you understand what is really wrong. For example, the author of a programming book that described "dot commands" (such as **.print**) kept receiving the message: **Can't open file rt.** After some research, he realized that the problem came when a command name fell on the beginning of a line. Since *troff* interprets a period at the beginning of a line as one of its own formatting commands, it couldn't decide what to do when the line started with *.print*. The writer was able to correct the problem, but obviously the error message was of no help. SoftQuad has attempted to correct this shortcoming.

The formatting commands used with *troff* are shorthand and not always easily remembered. SoftQuad has expanded these terse and sometimes cryptic commands into an English-based, descriptive command language. For example, the command to insert a blank line is " for *troff* and **:space** for SoftQuad *troff.* This "long-name" capability, as it is called, proves especially valuable when you write your own macros. With SoftQuad *troff*, you might not venture into this area because the commands seem too much like programming and too hard to learn. With *SQtroff,* writing macros seems no more difficult than giving your instructions in English.

The SoftQuad Publishing Software can improve your output capabilities without even using a laser printer. It allows boldface and other typographic output on dot matrix printers that do not otherwise have such capabilities. It also supports an impressive list of laser printers and other types of printers. There are few printers with which this package cannot be used.

This software also allows you to tune individual fonts if you don't like the way they look. It tests for widows and orphans and eliminates them. It provides ways to debug your command file and consequently get the output to look correct more quickly. It provides a method to preview your file without having to print it.

Word Processors

Some users want WYSIWYG word processing programs to use with their UNIX system rather than a combination of editor and formatter. The WYSIWYG area is expanding, and more options should become available in the near future. However, more products are available now that should interest you.

The Lyrix Word Processing System has a number of nice features beyond being a menu-driven WYSIWYG system. To begin with, it lets you define "rulers," then displays these rulers on your screen. A ruler is a formatting line you embed in a document to define the format of a page. You can use it to set right and left margins, tabs, paragraph indentation, and the center point, and also to define whether your right margin should be justified or ragged. You embed the ruler in your file, but Lyrix does not count it as a line of text on a page and does not print it. If you want a ruler "turned off" temporarily (made invisible and inactive), you can do that, too.

Lyrix also lets you define your word-processing environment through the Lyrix Command File. You have a standard command file, but if you want to customize Lyrix, you can edit this file and change the messages displayed by Lyrix (you could make the system bilingual), the editing command names, and even change the menu. By changing the menu, you can include UNIX activities and new programs (such as your graphics or spreadsheet program) in your word processing interface. This makes it easier to use all of the components that make up your desktop publishing system. We mentioned earlier one drawback of a menu system: Once you are familiar with the commands, being forced to use menus can become burdensome. Lyrix allows you to define "invisible" menu selections that are shortcuts to the menu sequence, thus eliminating that drawback.

In addition, Lyrix has a "point and pick" feature that lets you use the arrow keys on your terminal to locate a document for editing. Out of a list of documents, you point to the name by moving the cursor with the arrow keys, then pick that document by pressing the Return key. Pointing and picking can also be used to move around in your directories (the "file folders" of UNIX).

Lyrix also has a spelling check program that shows you the misspellings in your file and lets you change them immediately. Furthermore, Lyrix has some special commands that make it easy to do many other things, such as moving through many pages of your document at a time, doing global search and replace, letting you "cut and paste" lines in your document, merging other files into the one you are editing, setting page numbers, and defining running headers and footers. Lyrix even prevents widows and orphans automatically. That saves time and energy as you prepare your final copy.

One more feature about Lyrix is that it creates a copy of your file before you edit it. If something happens to your file while you are editing, the original copy is still intact.

MARC Software International sells a WYSIWYG system known as WordMarc Composer. In addition to giving you WYSIWYG text entry, this package automatically creates an index and a table of contents, letting you pick from an almost unlimited number of styles for the latter. It also provides footnoting and automatic numbering for tables, paragraphs, and equations, along with automatic reference to these items, and it lets you write macros to customize the formatting commands.

MARC Software offers a less powerful version of Composer named WordMarc Author. This version gives you full text entry ability but does not have the formatting features of Composer. You can use this version if you want only to produce simple items.

If several people are involved in your publishing efforts, you can use both Composer and Author. Only one person needs to learn the formatting commands and capabilities of Composer. Everyone else can use Author to enter their text. When it is time to create a final copy, the "expert" (the Composer user) can incorporate all of the text into one compuser document, then put the finishing format touches on the material.

A Few Other Product Descriptions

Let's look at two other products that do not fall into a category. First, the Professional Writer's Package, a product of Emerging Technologies, and then devps, a product from Pipeline Associates.

The Professional Writer's Package is made up of a text editor (EDIX), a formatter package (WORDIX), a spelling checker (SPELLIX), and an index generator (INDIX). How does this package differ from the other editor/formatters already discussed? For one thing, you see all four formatting programs as if they were only one by using a menu-style interface known as the PWP Shell. More importantly, WORDIX can format a file and print it, show it to you on the screen, or send it to a special EDIX preview file. Because this package supports multiple windows, you can view the preview file and at the same time edit the unformatted file. This is an exciting feature. It gives you the best of both worlds: the power of an editor/formatter and the previewing abilities of a WYSIWYG system.

There are a number of other useful features to this interesting package, including on-line tutorials and help. It also uses multiple windows, and you can edit as many as four files at one time. You can read one document while editing another to compare the two, move or copy text between files, or preview a file in one of those windows.

In addition, you can use "wild card" characters when searching in your file. With wild card characters, you key in only part of a word, but the computer finds the complete word. You can say you want the search to find a word only if it is at the beginning or end of a line. And you can specify that you want the search to look for case-sensitive patterns (meaning an exact match of upper- and lowercase letters) or case-insensitive patterns (it will find a match of the letters, but not look at the case).

WORDIX can support any printer that can be connected to your terminal, with proportional spacing only on some printers. You can also define abbreviations to speed your typing. For example, if you are writing about the Documenter's Workbench package, you do not have to type the phrase each time you need it. Define an abbreviation and type only that abbreviation in your file any place you want the full phrase to appear. When the file is formatted, the abbreviation is expanded to the full phrase.

Moreover, a toll free telephone number gives you access to technical support people, and you automatically receive copies of the *Emerging Technology* newsletter.

Let's look at one last product. The package devps is a collection of programs that translates formatted *troff* files into the PostScript page description language. It turns formatted files (any formatted text file, including files from MS-DOS and Macintosh systems) into files that a PostScript printer can understand. The ability to turn *troff* files into PostScript files gives you two advantages.

First, the PostScript software resides in the printer and therefore can only process your file if it has been translated. For many years, each printer had its own language, so you could not use a file on a variety of printers. Now, many printers use PostScript, so you can use such printers regardless of your operating system or word-processing software. With devps, this versatility, usually reserved for MS-DOS and Macintosh packages, is available to you on a UNIX system.

Second, once a file has been converted to PostScript, you can edit the PostScript file (which looks somewhat like a programming file). You can add commands to it that you could not get from your *troff* formatter. For example, you can get textures, patterns, halftones, and images in any size and shape.

You can even define your own fonts if you need a font not supported by your software. With this software and the effort of learning the PostScript language you can go beyond your formatter's capabilities and use your printer to its fullest.

Summary

You should now have a better idea of what the UNIX operating system is and what options you have if you want to use it as desktop publishing system. Perhaps you are surprised at how many options you have! UNIX itself contains many flexible formatting utilities that are limited by the capabilities of the printers connected to the system. In addition, there are a growing number of products available that enhance the existing UNIX facilities. The UNIX operating system is available on many different machines and offers multiusing and multitasking powers now on a mature, proven system. Those of you for whom these features are important should take a close look at UNIX as a publishing environment.

KEYWORDS:

• LAN

• UNIX

• Multitasking

• Minicomputer

• Integrated Software

Mark Jaroslow is currently writing telecommunications software for a firm in Silicon Valley. During the past ten years, he has worked on minicomputers, microcomputers, and microprocessors. Mr. Jaroslow also has an abiding interest in desktop publishing, having spent much time as a newsletter staffer for the Society of Technical Communication chapter in San Francisco. A Knox College graduate in political science, he lives in Burlingame, California with his hiking boots and his library of science fiction books.

Essay Synopsis: Most of the interest in desktop publishing, and most of the information in this book, is concerned with the use of microcomputer-based hardware and software tools to set type, design pages, create graphics, and perform other production chores. Dedicating a single PC or microcomputer to an expensive laser printer and disk drive is a waste of resources. An alternative is to connect many powerful terminals to multi-user minicomputers (or super micros) and allow these terminals to have better graphics. Such terminals are called workstations.

This essay offers a snapshot look at the capabilities of high-end workstations, their increased resolution and speed, smoothly running Local Area Networks (LANs), and well-integrated software environments. You will learn about the ways in which Sun, Apollo, and DEC workstations behave differently from the Macintosh or the IBM PC, and a hint of the future.

14

High-End Workstations

Mark Jaroslow

The term "workstation" can refer to a terminal tied to a mainframe or to a personal computer. A high-end workstation, on the other hand, is a super personal computer that is designed specifically to work with local area networks (LANs) (see following). High-end workstations bring the power and graphics of minicomputers to the personal computer market with a vengeance. The software on these machines is fully integrated. Users can access whatever files they need without worrying about compatibility. As a result, desktop publishing software on these machines often comprises more than just page-layout programs. Surprisingly, though, desktop publishing programs on personal computers are still competitive in many respects with the software running on the high-end workstations. This essay explores some of the differences and similarities between the high-end workstation market and personal computers, such as the IBM PC and the Apple Macintosh. The three high-end workstations that are examined here — Sun Microsystems Sun-3, Apollo Computer Domain Series 3000, and the DEC MicroVAX II — represent almost 47 percent of all workstation sales for 1986. By 1990, the percentage is expected to grow to slightly over 52 percent.

RELATED ESSAYS:

13. UNIX and Its Text Processing Tools

The Hardware

Let's first examine the machines. Like PCs, they have a CRT display, a keyboard, a mouse, floppy disk drives, hard disk drives, and tape drives for backup. Inside, each has its own memory (Sun can make as much as 256 megabytes available to any one of eight programs, all running at the same time) and its own microprocessor.

As in the PC market, these workstation manufacturers coexist with a host of third-party vendors, who produce boards, software, and peripherals for their machines. Sun Microsystems and Apollo Computer actively work with the vendors so that software exists for their machines. Because the market for third-party products for DEC machines is already established, DEC only has to maintain its policy of open architecture, unlike Sun and Apollo, which must help promote the software for their workstations. Newspapers and trade magazines that cater to the DEC market have become the most efficient means for announcing products.

Workstations may be equipped with 80286 coprocessors to run MS-DOS programs, but they are also very different from PCs. One difference lies in the operating systems. Rather than MS-DOS, Sun and Apollo use UNIX as their primary operating system. Both companies support the AT&T System V and the Berkeley BSD 4.2 as well as their own versions, which are designed to take advantage of their machines' architecture. DEC, on the other hand, supports two different operating systems for the MicroVAX II. One is VAX, an operating system used by a wide variety of minicomputers as well as smaller models, and the other is ULTRIX, DEC's version of BSD 4.2 UNIX.

One capability both UNIX and VAX provide is multitasking, the running of multiple programs simultaneously. The process for starting each program requires users to open extra windows on their screens. Users can move data from window to window. For instance, one can start a word-processing program in one window and a spreadsheet in another. When users reach a point in their documents where they need some spreadsheet data, they can move the data from the spreadsheet window over to the document with the click of a mouse button.

Most PC operating systems are designed to run only one program at a time. They cannot provide users with multitasking. Such programs as DESQView and Topview allow multitasking by supplanting MS-DOS with their own enhanced versions. (*Ed.: IBM's OS/2, to be available at the end of 1987, will offer multitasking.*)

High-end workstations also have terrific graphics that run at high speed. Sun and Apollo offer palettes of 16 million colors, with 256 available at any one time. Their CRTs have high resolution screens, capable of displaying over 1,000 by 1,000 pixels, which compares quite favorably with PCs using color monitors and Enhanced Graphics

Adaptor (EGA) cards, which only display 640 by 350 pixels with 16 colors. (*Ed.: New VGA standard for IBM's PC/2 line offers up to 1,000 by 1,000 pixel options.*)

The most distinctive feature about these high-end workstations is that they are designed to work with local area networks (LANs). LANs allow individual computers to communicate with each other and with peripherals, such as printers, over a high-speed cable. The prime advantage of LANs is that they allow users to share expensive peripherals and valuable data on hard disks without relying on telephone lines that pass data back and forth at slow speeds.

By putting workstations on LANs, users suddenly have access to minicomputer power. They are no longer limited just to the files and peripherals on their system. Through the use of LANs, people can find programs and data on hard disks on other computers in the LAN, send electronic mail to other users, and communicate with distant computers regardless of the kinds of protocol they use, all at speeds faster than even the fastest modems. The best part of all this, though, is that users can still treat their terminals as independent personal computers, running programs and using data that only they have access to.

LANs let users communicate with the outside world by using gateways. Just as United Nations translators must understand many languages, gateways must be able to deal with the wide variety of LAN protocols that are transmitted today, the most important ones being SNA (IBM's System Network Architecture standard for mainframes), token ring (a standard that passes a single software token between LAN members to coordinate network use), and packet switching (a scheme for transmitting data in packets at high speeds).

Apollo Computer's Domain architecture implements LANs on its workstations by creating a dynamic net of resources that is available to any user, making it the most like a minicomputer of the three systems. Sun or DEC MicroVAX II workstations have access only to the memory inside them. Outside of disk servers (workstations with disk drives that allow other workstations in the LAN to access the files on its disk), these workstations can access only their own disk drives. On the Apollo system, though, users don't call on the memory in their machines, but use system memory, which is the sum of all memory available on all workstations in the LAN. Apollo users can also access any disk drive on any workstation in the LAN.

The advantage of the Apollo scheme is that it is very decentralized. Users who can look for files on multiple hard disks need not wait as long to access them as users who must jostle each other to gain access to the LAN's one disk server. The advantage of Sun workstations and

DEC MicroVAX II is that they can be treated as specialized stations. For instance, one workstation might be specially equipped to do graphics. This would allow users to run computer-aided design (CAD) programs producing figures for documents being written on another workstation. Then, when the CAD programs finish, their output could be brought over to be included in the document.

Peripherals

Desktop publishing depends on several peripherals: image scanners, laser printers, and phototypesetters. In most cases the same equipment that works on PCs works equally well on the high-end workstations.

An image scanner allows a user to read text from the page or to digitize any kind of graphics from photographs into simple line art that can be used in a document. Most image scanners work at 300 dots per inch, matching the output for most laser printers.

Scanners are not limited to 300 dots per inch. However, denser pictures make storing graphics information a big headache. The reason is that graphics tend to take up a great deal of room at 300 dots per inch — often more than what a single floppy disk can hold. As a result, if the dots per inch resolution is increased, file sizes quickly become unmanageable, even on workstations. For example, Interleaf, which sells ImagiTex scanners to the workstation market for use with its very popular UNIX-based desktop publishing package, recommends setting the scanners to 300 dots per inch rather than the scanners' maximum of 775 dots per inch.

The printers of choice for desktop publishing are laser printers, which generally work at 300 dots per inch. They receive their formatting commands from the computer in a special syntax defined by a page description language (PDL) that is used by the raster image processor (RIP) on board the printer. Several such languages exist. The most popular one is the PostScript page description language by Adobe Systems. This is what the Apple LaserWriter and the desktop publishing software for the Macintosh use. Other page description languages on the market are Imagen's DDL and Xerox's Interpress. In addition, Interleaf, the prime desktop publishing software vendor for high-end workstations, has its own proprietary RIP, which is much faster than PostScript, but not quite as flexible for such tasks as rotating and sizing characters.

Compugraphic and Allied-Linotype phototypesetters are the most popular machines at the moment. They can put out text at 1,270 DPI, which is quite an improvement over the laser printers' 300 dots per inch. They usually have their own page description languages. However that is changing, as Allied-Linotype can now read PostScript in addition to its own native language.

The phototypesetters work by using a laser to write to photographic film. Prices start around $50,000 and go all the way up to $1 million for devices that include laser color separations. Laser printers would have to double or perhaps triple the dots per inch they put out before they would be able to compete with typesetter quality.

Available Desktop Publishing Software

In the workstation market, desktop publishing layout programs fall into two categories.

The first is page layout programs, which import text from word processors, then allow users to format their documents in WYSIWYG environments. Two programs fall into this category: DECPage for DEC's VAX computers, and OmniPage, which is being ported over to Sun Microsystems and Apollo Computers machines from an AT&T workstation.

These programs have a great deal in common with many of the entries in the PC environment, such as Personal Publisher on the Macintosh, Ventura Publisher on MS-DOS-based computers, and PageMaker, which has versions for both the Macintosh and the IBM PC markets. All these programs allow users to cut and paste graphics and text into documents and to define page formats using style sheets that determine font types, point sizes, margins, number of columns, and so forth.

Users of DEC equipment have at their command the All-In-One Office and Information Systems software. It is a vast array of text editors, word processors, spell checkers, spreadsheets, databases, electronic mail, graphics, and time management programs. The system is totally integrated. It is very easy to include electronic mail memos or portions of spreadsheets into word-processing files.

Once a file is finished, it can be sent to DECPage, DEC's page layout program. Several fonts are available. Laser printers, letter quality printers, and typesetters are all supported. Users can specify the page format or style sheet that they want. Once they have chosen between the memorandum, letter, newsletter, or any in-house styles, the program handles font selection, margins, and text placement.

Omnipage is a page processor with strong graphics capabilities. The program can either import graphics files or create its own two- and three-dimensional graphics by using its VERSACAD drafting program. Omnipage also allows users to make light editing changes in the text and can cut and paste text files from spreadsheets and database programs into the document. It can import files from 35 different word processors.

Omnipage can also paginate, hyphenate, and justify. It can create a table of contents and index automatically. When outputing the text, Omnipage can send PostScript or DDL files to laser printers and phototypesetters such as Allied-Linotype models L100, L300, and L600 or Compugraphic models 8400 and 8600.

Word Processing/Page Layout

The second category of desktop publishing software combines the two functions of word processing and page layout into one WYSIWYG program. The company best known in this arena is Interleaf. Interleaf buys workstations from a vendor, installs its software, and resells the workstations under its own name. Its Technical Publishing Software (TPS) can work on any of the workstations of the major manufacturers in the market — Sun Microsystems, Apollo Computer, and DEC (MicroVAX II). Another company, the Alis Corporation, sells its desktop publishing software through Sun Microsystems, the two jointly calling it SunAlis.

Both TPS and SunAlis are capable of all the editing features that we have come to expect in word processors. They can search and replace, scroll, jump to different pages, and insert and delete. Their screens can display a full page of text. They can import files from spreadsheets, word processors, and graphics generators, whether they are MS-DOS-based PC programs or native workstation programs. TPS can import files from image scanners; SunAlis can receive database files, electronic mail, and appointment calendar files.

The Macintosh-like, mouse-driven interfaces of both packages are perfect for their page layout portions. Pages are formatted with a style sheet that controls the number and placement of columns, the sizes of the margins, headers, footers, type of justification, fonts, and point sizes to be used for the entire document. Pagination and hyphenation occur automatically. In addition, TPS can generate a table of contents semi-automatically, since the typefaces sometimes need to be edited. In Version 3.0, which will be released soon, TPS will be able to do automatic indexing. Both software packages allow users to alter the formats of individual pages to fit the inevitable special situations.

Both SunAlis and TPS have very strong graphics capabilities, which include MacDraw-like interfaces and clip art for free-style editing or brand new illustrations. Facilities also exist to create data-driven pie and bar charts from spreadsheets. TPS can import CAD drawings from other systems as well.

When it is time to print, both systems work with the PostScript page description language. This means that workstations can interface with many of the popular laser printers on the market today. In addition, Interleaf can also interface with Imagen's DDL page description language and with a language that Interleaf itself developed.

One problem with both software packages is that they do not give users the ability to letterspace or kern the letters in each word. As a result users cannot make the minute adjustments that produce true typeset-quality documents.

Summary

Workstation-based desktop publishing software tends to be either page layout programs or word-processing programs that also can do page layout. The programs are highly integrated in the sense that the data can easily be cut and pasted into documents. PC-based desktop publishing software, on the other hand, is made up mainly of page layout programs. Like workstation software, these programs can import foreign files, as long as they have compatible formats.

One of the biggest differences between workstations and PCs is the hardware. Workstation screen resolution dwarfs what is available on standard PCs. The amount of memory on PCs is small compared to that of workstations, which have hundreds of megabytes. Finally, workstations can run a great deal faster than PCs. IBM PC ATs run at about 8 megahertz, whereas Apollo workstations can zoom ahead at up to 25 megahertz.

Workstations have the memory, the speed, and the operating system to run multiple programs. PC-based programs, such as DESQView, can simulate multitasking, but if an application program is not written to work with DESQView or TopView, that program takes over the computer.

PCs may soon be able to remedy their hardware and operating system problems. New chips such as Intel's 80386 and Motorola's 68030 allow the memory and the speed to handle multitasking operating systems. Once the operating systems are written, software developers can write the necessary interfaces to allow their programs to coexist with others in a multitasking environment. Then the differences between PCs and workstations will revolve around marketing strategies and the families of application programs belonging to each operating system.

III

Software

About This Section

Be it a chart, newsletter, or brochure, there are many ways to produce a final desktop published work. This section takes you on a tour of the different tools that exist today for desktop publishing. Graphics programs are simple and fun to use, so we present how to use draw and paint programs, showing how some art programs allow manipulation of pixels while others treat graphics as objects such as lines and boxes. We then look at page layout programs such as PageMaker that offer friendly mouse- and menu-driven interfaces. High-resolution graphics can now be produced on the new 300-dot-per-inch laser printers, and an essay on laser art shows how that is accomplished. Following that is an essay on type encoding systems. These programs compete against page layout software, offering maximum control over the final look but also providing interfaces that are more difficult to use. Nearly all page composition and graphics programs produce files formatted for a standard printer language called PostScript. Knowing about this language can come in handy if, for example, you want to insert a simple PostScript routine into your letters to create a special effect, so we present a programing tutorial on the PostScript language followed by an introduction to JustText, a text processing program with typographic powers that allows direct access to PostScript codes.

KEYWORDS:

- Clip Art

- Image Fonts

- Paint Pro-
  grams

- Bit-Map

- Object-
  Oriented

Adele Aldridge is a freelance graphic artist who has worked on a range of desktop publishing projects. An art director, book designer, and publisher, she has written articles on creating graphics on the Macintosh as well as created her own ClipArt software called Magnetic Art Portfolios. She has contributed graphics to the software programs The Print-Shop and Yours Truly. She can be reached at Magnetic Arts in Sausalito, California.

Essay Synopsis: Although there has been rapid improvement since the introduction of early graphics programs such as MacPaint and MacDraw, the essential function of paint and draw tools have been established, and the genre is as well-defined as that of spreadsheets and word processors.

In this essay the author compares the convenience of microcomputer-based graphics with that of traditional graphics environments while explaining the various types of graphic programs available. Through examples you will see the difference between bit-mapped and object-oriented programs, clip art, image fonts, and borders, and you will learn how to use the graphic tools to create and manipulate images and patterns.

15

Graphics Fundamentals

Adele Aldridge

Art and graphics illuminate, highlight, illustrate, and help to communicate your printed message. Traditionally, to include art and graphics in a publication involved cutting, pasting, and designing each page by hand. In desktop publishing you use a microcomputer system that has the ability to typeset, design, lay out, and output camera-ready copy, thereby eliminating many of the older, more traditional production processes.

The key to desktop publishing is a page layout program that allows you to integrate text with graphics in your document. To do so, you need to use both word processing and graphics programs. The word processing program creates text; the graphics program creates images.

By now, many people are familiar with the advantage of a word processing program over an old-fashioned typewriter for ease and speed of making corrections or rearranging text, but they may not realize that the same techniques apply to graphics. You don't have to be an artist to take advantage of the new graphics technology! If you don't want to draw your own original graphic images, you can buy copyright-free clip art on disk to incorporate into your printed materials. Clip art is free artwork that is sold in books for you to copy and use as you like; newspapers and ad agencies use it all the time. The limitation is that you can't alter it — you have to paste it in as is. Clip art images on disk, however, can be altered

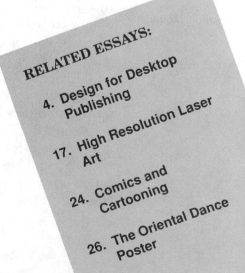

RELATED ESSAYS:

4. Design for Desktop Publishing

17. High Resolution Laser Art

24. Comics and Cartooning

26. The Oriental Dance Poster

with paint and draw programs to suit your own specific needs. You can keep the original image intact on the disk, make a copy, and alter it any way you like using graphics software programs.

This essay will tell you the kinds of graphics you can design with a desktop publishing system. It is not meant to be a tutorial on software, but rather to explore the possibilities of graphics software in general. Because graphics programs are changing rapidly to include new capabilities, references to specific software will be avoided. SuperPaint by Silicon Beach Software, for example, now offers a program in which you can switch from a draw mode to a paint mode — previously you had to use a separate program for each operation.

A New Point of View

The desktop publishing tools are revolutionary not only in their ability to create, transmit, and store information, but in being interactive. This is the quantum leap in creative productivity. People can now collaborate with each other on a piece of art or writing without leaving their separate studios.

If Michelangelo and Leonardo da Vinci were alive today, they would probably be using the latest desktop publishing tools. These two giants in the history of art lived in the same country and their lives overlapped in time. Leonardo would probably be designing new computers as well as creating art with them. And Michelangelo would design his Sistine Chapel first on disk and then print it out at a blown-up scale to be used as a guide for his painting.

A dialogue might go as follows:

Leonardo calls Michelangelo on the phone and says, "Hey, Angelo! I just did this picture on my Macintosh that I'm putting in a newsletter to send to my friends inviting them to come to my new flying machine demonstration. I want to show it to you to see what you think, but my car is broken and besides there is a blizzard out and I'm coming down with a cold."

Michelangelo: "No problem, Leo. Send it over your modem, and I'll copy your picture onto one of my disks and get back to you in an hour with my suggestions. You don't have to leave your studio."

Leonardo then sends his image from his computer to Michelangelo's computer over the phone line with his modem. The image received and stored on Michelangelo's disk is an exact duplicate of the image that sits on screen in Leonardo's studio. Unlike other art forms, the copy cannot be distinguished from the original.

Michelangelo saves the original image he just received in his microcomputer and names the image, *Leo's Picture*. He then creates some new pictures by making changes to Leo's picture, keeping some of the original. He creates a number of variations of the work on his disk as suggestions he has for Leo's design. Angelo has been careful to save Leo's original picture so that it is not lost.

After Michelangelo adds his comments by way of making several drawings, he then prints all of these drawings on his dot matrix printer. The image he gets is not as crisp as what he sees on the screen, but it's a good proof and he can print it later on a LaserWriter if he wants a clearer image. Perhaps he creates five variations as alternative designs. Michelangelo keeps what he has created, has his printouts to look at which are original works in themselves, and then with the use of his modem wires his work back over the phone to Leonardo. Now both artists have the original work as well as the additional edited work. Neither artist has left his studio.

Leonardo, having received Michelangelo's suggested variations, now electronically "pastes" one into another piece of his work on his studies of the human body and another into the theories about navigation. What exists now is an integration of the work of the two artists in one document. Leonardo adds more changes to the work so that after a while, one cannot tell where Leo's or Angelo's art begins or ends. Both artists still have the original work on disk, however, as well as all the processes in between to keep or "dump." In addition, they have a record of their unique creative interaction.

Leonardo is satisfied with his invitation and is ready to have it printed. If Leo didn't have his computer, he would go to a typesetter so he could achieve a professional-looking invitation. Instead, Leonardo wires his work via his modem from his country house to a place in the city that will then send his image through the LaserWriter. The result is called almost typeset quality. He could have used the Linotronic printer, which provides even better resolution, but he decided that the LaserWriter is good enough for his purposes. At his convenience, Leonardo goes to the place that received his work on the modem and picks up the camera-ready copy that can go to press immediately.

Although Leo had the choice of wiring the material directly to his printing shop without leaving home, he decided to photocopy it instead of having it printed because he didn't need enough copies to warrant the price of setting up a press run. The place that did his laser printing had the copies of his invitation completed and ready for him when he arrived later that same day.

As a by-product of the work Michelangelo did with Leonardo, they eventually sell this disk of original art so that other people can buy it to use as clip art!

Using the New Tools

Computers allow artists and untrained artists alike to do things that would be impossible with any other single tool. For example, commercial artists who design newsletters, brochures, invitations, books, advertisements, pattern designs, or any product requiring type design and/or images on a page, may need to do some or all of the following functions: cut, paste, reproduce, shrink, enlarge, or rearrange. They may also need to use the following tools: paint, ink, charcoal, pencil, brush, glue, eraser, airbrush, and type. The graphics software enables the user to emulate all these functions without any tools other than the computer and printer. And the flexible editing capabilities for graphics enable graphic designers to experiment with many variations in a relatively short period of time compared to the old methods of pen, ink, and other conventional materials.

Besides the speed in creating graphics with a desktop publishing system, you can combine the operations of entering data, typesetting, and graphics in one process. It's a far different procedure from typing a page, going to a typesetter, pasting it up, and changing it. When using traditional typesetting, if you want to change the type style, you have to pay for every change; such experimentation is very costly. With a desktop publishing system, you can change the type with a flick of your finger and experiment with different styles and sizes before printing. Page layouts can also be altered in the same way, without actually cutting and pasting.

In addition to all the above advantages, the use of a desktop publishing system saves the artist a great deal of work space. With a computer, disks, and printer, the work station can reside on one table. All the tools are in the computer program. Doing the same work without a computer requires much more table space to draw, cut, paste, and lay out, not to mention all the pens, ink, and other tools that may be used. "Saving" an image on a computer is accomplished in a matter of seconds. This process enables you to keep the original picture intact, as well as make many instant variations, saving as many of them as you like.

Another "space" advantage to working on a computer is being able to store a number of documents on a disk approximately 3½ inches square and ⅛ inch thick. It's easy to transport ten such disks, whereas the same information in hard copy would require a heavy portfolio. Of course, you'll need a computer at the other end of your travels to print the work, but these days that's not a problem. People who hire artists to do graphics for desktop publishing purposes usually have the systems.

Finally, besides speed, flexibility, and efficiency, the interactivity of desktop publishing tools allows you to communicate with clients over great distances. For example, suppose you work in San Francisco and have a client in New York. You don't even have to print out your file — you can transfer the data immediately over the phone. A job can be done in one day that would otherwise take at least three or four days, depending on the kind of delivery service you use.

Artists and publishers who are prejudiced against the new graphics technology often have rejected it automatically without knowing what the tools can accomplish. After reading this essay and playing with the possibilities offered by paint and draw programs and clip art, you can decide for yourself.

What Are Graphics and Why Use Them?

Graphics are elements that add interest to your page or highlight your point to clarify your text. A graphic element can be a pie chart in a business proposal, an illustration for a story, a fanciful border for a special invitation, or a specially designed letter for personal stationery. If you can't create your own images, you can buy clip art and either insert these ready-made pictures into your work or change the images to suit your needs.

White space is a graphic element and an important consideration in design. What you leave out of a page is as important as what you put in it for graphics. For example, a page full of type, top to bottom, single-spaced, with no margins, no white space, no images, and no special emphasis on any aspect of the content will not invite anyone to read it. The same information can be presented with illustrations or sidebars, margins with a border, or other elements to bring it to life. Don't use all of the above, though. You need to strike a balance between white space and clutter!

What Is Clip Art?

Clip art consists of copyright-free images, which purchasers can use to cut and paste into whatever they want. Commonly used images are borders, trademarks, symbols, signs, and human figures. Clip art is often sold by subscription and is also sold in paperback book form in art supply stores.

Clip art on the microcomputer for desktop publishing is designed for the same purpose as printed clip art: as an accompaniment to enhance or illustrate another piece of information. The purpose of using clip art is the convenience, and it is especially handy for those people who do not have drawing skills and need to "borrow" the images that other people have created.

Press-type is a form of clip art that is sold in sheets. These sheets are made of decals of alphabetic letter shapes in a particular font. They are transferred onto a page by rubbing. These sheets also come with rules and borders. A desktop publishing system completely eliminates the need for using fonts or borders clip art. That process simply cannot compare with the accuracy and speed that can be achieved with a computer.

There are a few programs that take the ability to use clip art in a different direction. These programs allow you to use images in a prearranged format designed to have a particular function. They are extremely easy to use and have the ability to turn out a variety of images where you have some control over the input. These programs require no actual ability to draw on the part of the user.

Mac-A-Mug, published by Shaherazam, is designed so that the nonartist can create a composite face from the hundreds of separate features stored in the graphics database of the program. Mac-a-Mug was designed to be used by police departments for creating frontal views of men and women. The program is simplicity itself to use. There is a menu to choose from a variety of eye glasses, mustaches, sideburns, beards, heads, eyebrows, eyes, ears, noses, mouths, chins, and hats. You can even choose how many wrinkles you want to put on the face, and you have the ability to change the left or right side of the face independently. With all these variables, the number of faces you can create is vast. This is a wonderful tool for illustrators as well as police forces. It is also fun to click on the different parts and see all these faces appear in front of you as if by magic.

A second program in this genre is The Print Shop, which is published by Brøderbund Software. This program is designed to let you create greeting cards, signs, banners, or letterheads with preset formats. The Print Shop has a disk full of clip art, such as borders, and small, medium, and large graphics to load into your sign, banner, greeting card, or letterhead. The program allows you to edit the art provided or use it as is. You can also load other clip art or your own graphics into the program. Even if you don't want to add your own graphics, or those of another clip art disk, The Print Shop allows for the individual's creativity within the preset format because you can move the graphics around, type in your own words, and generally have a lot of freedom to play.

Yours Truly, published by Looking Glass Software, is a program designed just for Christmas cards. It is similiar to The Print Shop but doesn't have the flexibility of allowing you to add your own graphics or edit the images. The program comes with an assortment of images and another assortment of greetings. You can mix them as well as make up your own greeting. While this program doesn't have the sophistication of The Print Shop, it is very inexpensive and does its specific job very well.

Clip art can also be used in more creative ways than just pasting an image "as is" into a document. For the time being we will limit this discussion to ready-made images that do not require the user to do anything to them except paste them into a document. Editing clip art is discussed later in this essay.

Borders

Clip art borders can be electronically pasted into paint, draw, and page layout programs. You can also create borders in paint and draw programs with the use of the patterns and tools for creating lines and rectangles. Page layout programs provide tools for making borders and are very useful when you want to lay out your page by transferring your document from a word processing program and creating borders after you have your copy set.

Image Fonts

A font is a set of all the characters on the keyboard in a specific typeface. Character fonts are made up of letters. Image fonts are made of images, and like any other font can be installed with the desk accessory Font Mover into any program. You can use these image fonts in word processing programs as well as graphics programs.

Image fonts can be considered a form of clip art, the difference being that images on fonts are accessed through the keyboard, and clip art is usually accessed through a paint document. The size of the image in a font is limited to the size font that your program allows.

Image fonts combine well with other clip art to create larger pictures. Cairo is an image font published by Apple. Borders is another image font, made by T/Maker in Mountain View, California. Figure 15-1 shows upper and lowercase typefaces of Cairo and Borders and part of a border made by typing out letters QWWWWWWWWWWWW WWWE.

Cairo-lowercase

Cairo-uppercase

Borders-lowercase

Borders-uppercase

Figure 15-1. Image fonts Cairo and Borders compared against their equivalents in the standard alphabet; notice that Q and E corners mate with repeated W lines to begin a frame.

Editing Clip Art

As an artist, I have found editing clip art to be a more exciting use of computer graphics than using an image "as is." Whether I use another artist's work or create my own, I can save it, file it, rearrange it, or let others create with it. I can retain the original work, so I don't have to treat it as precious. This allows a freedom of play that generates more creativity. Being able to interact with others' art on disk is one of the benefits of creating on the computer, as compared to creating directly on paper.

Here is a vision of an artists' clip art chain letter. Create a picture on your computer and send it (on disk or by modem) to ten different artists. Ask each of the ten artists to interact with your work in some way and then mail it on to ten more artists. Each artist could send a disk to the top name on the list. If all artists cooperate, you will eventually receive back thousands of disks full of work that had originated from you and yet had been interacted with and changed in some way.

Whether you are an artist or not, the ability to edit other people's art is immeasurably valuable for adding to your desktop publishing skills. If you want to edit commercially available art to suit your specific purposes, you should have an understanding of how to use the tools of a paint program because almost all clip art is accessed as a paint document. Paint documents may be transferred into draw programs, word processing programs, and page layout programs.

While all the graphics in this essay have been created on the Macintosh computer, the basic capabilities of the electronic tools in a paint, draw, or page layout program are similar.

Tools of Paint Programs

The tools in computer graphics programs are derivatives of tools that existed in the graphic arts before computers were invented. The images are created on a monitor and can be printed out with either a dot matrix printer, a LaserWriter, or Linotronic printer. The results often cannot be distinguished from a pen-and-ink graphic. Creating black-and-white graphics on the Macintosh gives an effect similar to drawing with pencil, charcoal, or ink.

MacPaint provides a good example of a paint program. Figure 15-2 shows the tools on the left side of the page, with a pattern bar on the bottom. When someone asked me how I did my drawings on the Macintosh, whether with the mouse, a pen, or digitizing device, my response was, I spend most of my life in a place called fat bits. The fat bits feature of paint programs allows you to edit details pixel by pixel in blowup size. All paint programs will provide some kind of magnification feature that allows for editing tiny details.

Figure 15-3 shows the enlargement of a portion of a face in fat bits. Notice the smaller inset on the right. The small section is the actual size of the piece being worked on. The black square shapes are the pixels and can be changed from black to white by clicking on the pencil. In this diagram I am focused on working on a detail in the eye.

The Paint Bucket: The paint bucket acts as a vessel that you load with a pattern and then dump into an enclosed area. This fills in any confined area on the screen with any of the patterns chosen from the pattern bar (imagine that you are going to paint a room and while

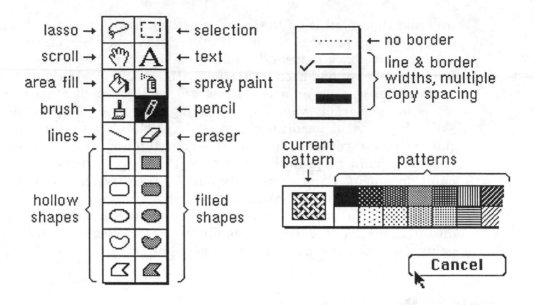

Figure 15-2. Symbols for graphic tools and patterns found in MacPaint.

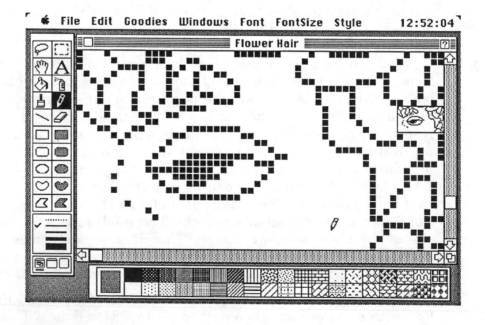

Figure 15-3. Pixels in an enlarged MacPaint image; notice the reduced image inset at the right.

using the paint bucket out comes a pattern, like wallpaper, instead of one color). In addition to the patterns that are embedded within the paint program you can also create your own custom patterns.

The Lasso: By enclosing the outline of an image with this tool you can move it or copy the image as often as you like. The image of the three horses (see Figure 15-4) is an example of how I took the figure of one horse and pasted it three times and filled two of the horses each with a different pattern. The lasso is very useful for transferring parts of drawings within a drawing, or adding them to new drawings, as will be demonstrated in the section about illustration.

Figure 15-4. Duplicates of the same image can be filled with different patterns.

The Rectangle: The rectangle is a useful editing tool that can copy an image and/or move it on a page as well as enlarge, shrink, invert, color, flip horizontally or vertically, and rotate it. The rectangle encloses an image and, while over-printing into another area, will erase what it is pasted over. In Figure 15-5 notice that in contrast to the image of the horse copied and moved in the lasso mode, the image blocks out the image beneath it. When an image is selected in the rectangle edit mode, the artist has much more freedom to play with the images than could ever be done by hand.

Figure 15-5. The rectangle tool captures an image and can be used to paste over another image.

The Spray Can: The spray can tool allows you to spray in small amounts of black, white, or any pattern over an area. Similar to a real spray can, the spray can sprays a small amount of pattern at a time. The end result can be the same as the paint bucket, covering an entire area with a pattern, or it can be used like a piece of charcoal, leaving random white spaces.

The Brush: The brush is much more powerful than any ordinary brush. The size and shape of this brush may be changed and can be used with any pattern. Figure 15-6 shows a brush menu from the MacPaint program, demonstrating the available brush choices. The brush shapes can be custom designed and combined with your choice of patterns. The fact that you can edit your own patterns, plus the fact that you can use all this with a device called brush mirrors, is an amazing combination of variables just within the brush tool of the program.

Brush mirrors is a magic tool that can create kaleidoscopic designs quickly by allowing you to draw two, four, six, or eight sides simultaneously. The diagram in Figure 15-7 is a dialog box for brush mirrors from the program FullPaint.

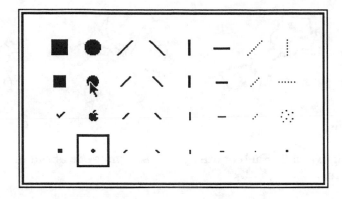

Figure 15-6. Each pattern can be chosen as the tip of the brush. The stroke mark of the brush varies upon the tip pattern selected.

By using the variety of brush shapes, combined with the choice of brush patterns, you can create an endless number of symmetrical designs that are ideally suited for fabric or tile patterns. The designs or pictures can be ironed onto fabric, which can then be painted or sewn over. There are manufacturers who make special printer ribbons for iron-on transfer. You can use these designs on T-shirts, a canvas for a painting, or whatever you can imagine.

In the diagrams on the next page Figure 15-8a shows an image drawn with one diagonal; Figure 15-8b is an image drawn on the opposite diagonal; Figure 15-8c is an example of both diagonals turned on at once; Figure 15-9a is an image drawn with all the diagonals; Figure 15-9b demonstrates filling in some of the areas of the design with the paint bucket; and finally, Figure 15-9c shows how a background was also filled in with the same tool.

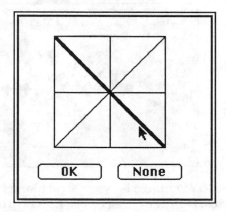

Figure 15-7. The dialogue box for the mirrors tool.

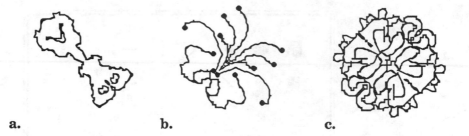

a.   **b.**   **c.**

Figure 15-8. Each of the figures is symmetric about one or both diagonal axes.

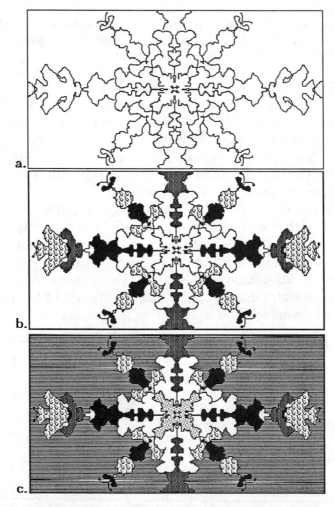

a.

b.

c.

Figure 15-9. This image is symmetric along both the horizontal and vertical axes. Different areas were filled with various patterns using the paint bucket tool.

Figure 15-10 is an example of creating a pattern suitable for fabric design. A pattern was created in brush mirrors. The checkerboard effect was achieved by copying the first pattern in the rectangle mode, and alternately reversing and pasting the images together.

Figure 15-10. A pattern suitable as a fabric print generated by brush mirrors and inversions.

Editing Patterns

Graphic programs offer you a variety of patterns that can be used with borders, brush, paint bucket, or filled shapes. By clicking the pencil over a pattern in the pattern bar you can change the pattern. Then by clicking the paint bucket over any enclosed white space the pattern will automatically fill in the space. Creating your own patterns can be fun, and editing the patterns can be as simple or as complex as you like.

There is an easy way to create a pattern. Take the spray can and scribble a design at random on the right-hand side of the page window. Next, click the arrow into any one of the pattern squares. A window will appear where you can take the arrow and change the design. Click the arrow at any spot in the scribble and you will see a pattern appear in the window. If you move the arrow and click again the pattern will change. When you find one you like, click "OK" and you will have a quickly made new pattern. The following examples are ones I made in a few seconds to demonstrate how quickly this operation can be done. Note that I didn't draw a thing; the tool did it (see Figure 15-11).

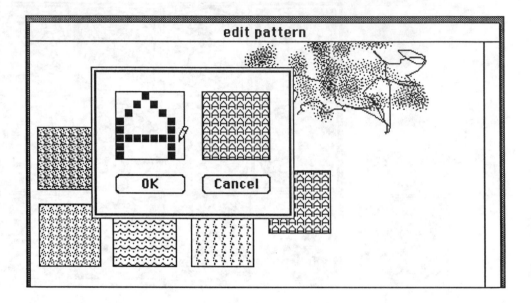

Figure 15-11. Create a pattern such as repeated A's or capture a fragment of a random pattern such as the scribble and repeat it.

You can also draw any shape you like in the pattern window, eight by eight pixels. You might want to make a pattern of your initials to use as a subtle background for whatever reason you can think of. An example of creating the letter *A* as a pattern is also shown in Figure 15-11.

Text in Paint Programs

In paint programs text doesn't function as in a word processing program because letters are treated as images. The text tool allows you to type words with or without your image and to edit words the way you edit pictures, pixel by pixel. The text tool is useful for graphic designers who want to create special effects with individual letters. When you want to edit the details of a letter or word, you will want to use a paint program so that you can make changes in shapes.

A paint program will also allow you to overlay letters for design purposes. Before these programs were available, a graphic artist would have to use press type for designing, which is slow and costly. The other alternative was to have type set and then, if you wanted to change the type style, pay for another version. The computer allows you to try many different type fonts and styles quickly and cheaply before committing your final decision to print.

Text in Draw Programs

It would be more accurate to call paint programs draw programs, because the effect produced is much closer to drawing than it is to painting. The word "paint" suggests color and fluidity. However the word "draw," as in the program MacDraw, has been adopted as a name for object-oriented programs. Paint programs are bit mapped. The images of a bit-mapped program are made up of black-and-white dots and can be edited pixel by pixel. If an image in a bit-mapped document is placed on top of another image, it erases the one beneath it, or adds to it (see Figures 15-4 and 15-5).

With draw programs, images as well as letters are object oriented. Each shape created is stored in the memory of the computer rather than the individual dot. This means that images can be layered one on top of the other and shifted, allowing for great flexibility in moving the objects. Words in draw programs are also treated as objects and can be moved with the same kind of flexibility. Words can also be edited in the same way as in word processing programs, giving greater flexibility when you want to change something.

If you want to create or alter images in detail, pixel by pixel, then a paint program is the one to work with. If you want to use only text and geometric shapes, as in drafting, a draw program will best suit your purposes. Draw programs are very useful for creating small ads because you can create pieces of text that can be moved around as objects. You can also edit the text if you need to as well as paste images from paint into draw programs, and in that way work with both.

Illustration

All images on disk can be changed. Images from a clip art package can be changed slightly and then pasted into larger formats. Now let's focus on the medium itself as a tool for desktop publishing illustration. By illustration, I mean pictures that artists create to be sold as electronic clip art, pictures created to be put into a desktop publishing venture (such as a book), or pictures made as personal fine art to be shown in galleries.

The process of interactivity in the scenario between Michelangelo and Leonardo da Vinci also applies for the artist working alone. You can rework your own art and interact with it in a variety of ways to speed up the process of making pictures. The best way to create original illustrations is to build your own image library. You can use smaller images to build larger pictures by saving the pieces you use in one illustration so that you can later alter them or paste them into other illustrations. The cutting, pasting, and rearranging of images on computer is a simple task. It is creating the original forms that takes some time and skill.

The following examples illustrate the process of building complete images. We'll begin with an illustration called Eve's Garden, where you will see, step-by-step, how separate parts were placed in the larger picture. All the stages are saved and the separate parts can be reused.

First I built a winter tree (Figure 15-12a). To then place some leaves on it, I drew several little leaves and, copying them with the lasso, I pasted them on the branches of the tree (Figure 15-12b). Next, I added more leaves with the same method and created an apple by using an image from a font (Figure 15-12c). I added apples to the tree and placed some on the ground, also by pasting them with the lasso (Figure 15-12d). Then I built a wall to surround a garden and created a woman to sit there. I added some plants and finally completed Eve's Garden (Figure 15-13).

I created a series of illustrations starting with a set of three illustrations I had created for a Christmas card program by Pixillite called Yours Truly (Figure 15-14). Some of the elements from these illustrations were saved and used to create some larger pictures in the series that follows.

I took one of my landscapes, *Desert Moonlight*, and pasted an image of a sleeping woman (called *Love Asleep*, from the disk Magnetic Art Portfolio Romantic Images) along with some horses taken from the Christmas card, to create an illustration called *Desert Dream* (Figure 15-15).

In the picture *Santa's Runaways* (Figure 15-16), two of the horses were borrowed from another card and manipulated by turning their heads slightly and enlarging the horses in the front, to give proper perspective. Then they were dropped into the reversed images of the same *Desert Moonlight* illustration.

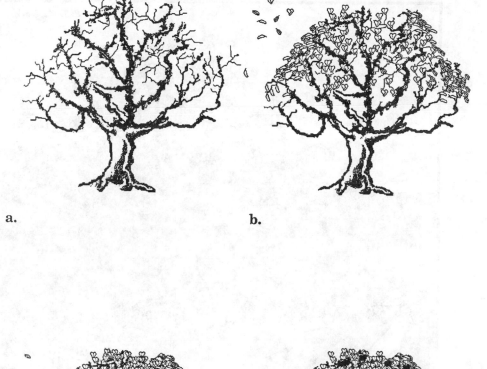

a.

b.

c.

d.

Figure 15-12. Adding elements to a sparse beginning.

Figure 15-13. Eve's Garden

Figure 15-14. Images created in Pixillite's card generating software, Yours Truly.

Desert Moonlight

Desert Dream

Figure 15-15. Adding images together

Figure 15-16. Santa's Runaways

Summary

There are several advantages of using computers to produce art. Because you work in an electronic media, you can make changes very quickly, keeping the original and each of the generations for future use. You can add images from other sources with just a few keystrokes. Clip art is one source of art; a recorded image from a scanner or video camera is another. Storage of finished electronic art is much simpler than that of conventionally produced art.

The two major types of graphics programs are bit-mapped and object-oriented. Bit-mapped programs store graphic shapes as clusters of dots; object-oriented programs store shapes as a list of directions for drawing lines and filling shapes with patterns. Some graphics programs are designed for one task only, for instance, making greeting cards. You can use graphics programs to images to text and vice versa, but once you add text to an image, you can't edit it; it becomes part of the image. In addition to business applications, you can use computer graphics for illustration and fine art.

KEYWORDS:

- **Templates**

- **Ruler Guides**

- **Viewing Modes**

- **Column Grid**

- **Master Pages**

- **Nameplate**

Oren Ziv is communications manager of Micro D, a leading national distributor of microcomputer products based in Santa Ana, California. He writes about personal computers and their applications as well as manages the editorial production of the company's several national publications.

Essay Synopsis: A page layout program is like an electronic drafting table on your computer screen. It creates files that are formatted as discrete pages, and the program itself must be able to import text and graphic information from paint and draw programs. Page layout software gives the user tools to manipulate the positioning of the elements on the page.

In this essay, the author describes page layout software in terms of its functions and system requirements, then offers an overview of the process of producing a newsletter. You will learn about the various features of page layout programs and techniques on how to import and manipulate text and graphic files, set up master pages and templates, and use such attributes as viewing modes, rulers, and grids.

16

Page Layout Software

Oren Ziv

Page layout software created desktop publishing as a computer application. The Macintosh, laser printers, hard disks, word processors, and graphics programs existed for several years before anybody ever uttered the words "desktop publishing," coined by Paul Brainerd of Aldus Corporation to describe the purpose of PageMaker, a relatively inexpensive program that allowed the Apple Macintosh and Laser-Writer to operate like page layout equipment that cost more than $50,000.

Using a computer to perform typesetting and layouts is nothing new — newspapers and typographers have been doing so for years — but the availability of the application on a microcomputer budget was a technological breakthrough.

What can you actually produce with a microcomputer system and page composition software? Many people have already produced tabloids, magazines, brochures, handbills, advertisements, and business forms using this relatively new application: Imaginative microcomputer users are discovering new ways of applying the unique tools provided by page layout software everyday.

From its microcomputer beginnings on the Apple Macintosh, page layout software has moved firmly into the big blue IBM world as well. Programs such as Xerox's Ventura Publisher, coupled with a variety of add-on enhancement products (such as

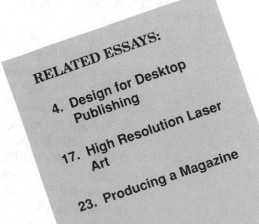

RELATED ESSAYS:

4. Design for Desktop Publishing

17. High Resolution Laser Art

23. Producing a Magazine

high-resolution video graphics boards, WYSIWYG monitors, mice, and laser printers), provide page composition capabilities similar to the Macintosh. Now, anyone who can afford a reasonably high-end micro-computer system can afford a page composition system capable of producing near typeset quality text and near professional quality graphics layouts to produce a wide variety of printed publications.

What Does a Page Layout Program Do?

A page layout program allows you to perform on your microcomputer almost all of the functions of a graphics production artist. You can create publications that consist of pages of near typeset quality type and graphics. The publications producible with a page layout program can combine text and graphics to come very close to the same graphics quality found in a professionally produced newsletter or magazine.

Using word processing software, such as Microsoft Word, along with the improved graphics handling capabilities of the Macintosh and IBM, you can type in columns and mix your words with graphics. However, Microsoft Word's column formatting still has very limited applications. Such formatting limitations led software developers to create page layout software to complement the already existing word processor.

Most page layout programs accomplish their tasks by allowing computer users to bring onto a page text that is produced with a word-processing program and graphics that are produced with a paint program. Page layout programs allow the user to combine and manipulate both text and graphics in one document.

Who Uses Page Layout Programs?

As desktop page layout programs advance, they assuredly will become capable of completing the entire process of producing even the most professional-quality publications. However, at the present time they are not perfect for every publishing job. For the most advanced applications, page layout software can function more as a tool than a solution — always keep in mind that if it is easier or faster to complete a task by hand, go ahead and push your computer aside. For instance, it is still easier to perform some steps in producing a magazine by hand, yet editors and art directors are using computerized page composition for the jobs that it performs well. A magazine editor might produce all the body copy for a publication using a page composition program and a laser printer, avoiding both the time and cost of having the majority of the copy professionally typeset. This does more than save hundreds of dollars, it gives the editor an increased amount of control over the copy, allowing changes all the way through to the final layout. However, the same editor may still wish to have the headlines professionally typeset, thereby providing a professional look to the larger graphic elements.

When you use professional art and photography, microcomputer page layout programs cannot fully complete the job of illustrating the publication. Yet, an art director may still use a page layout program to design a publication, leaving spaces for artwork. Using a page layout program in this manner produces a working dummy necessary for the complete process, but the final layout will still be cut and pasted in a traditional manner. In the same way, advertising agencies have reported using page layout software in all steps leading to a design's approval. These agencies create computer generated artists' composites in order to help their clients visualize the final layout — which is then professionally produced. Many businesses are using page layout software as a means of producing high-quality paperwork. A microcomputer, page composition program, and a laser printer can become a forms-generating machine. The wide variety of type sizes and the ability to easily manipulate both text and graphics makes page layout software capable of producing exceptionally high-quality forms.

Page layout software can be applied to dressing up a standard proposal or bid. Using different typefaces and styles, graphics, bullets, and a variety of advanced page formatting elements (such as horizontal and vertical rules, shading screens, and superimposing graphics and type), a page layout program can contribute greatly to getting a proposal or presentation the attention it deserves. The ability to create high-quality forms and graphics helps convince even the greatest skeptic that a desktop publishing system quickly pays for itself.

The Features To Look for When Choosing a Page Layout Program

When it comes to the nitty-gritty of choosing a program, consider not only the software's features, but decide which program suits the method by which you produce publications. Each program takes a slightly different approach to assembling a page, and you should be aware of these differences when selecting the correct program for your purposes.

System Requirements

Different programs have different system requirements. Besides the most obvious difference of being written for either an IBM or a Macintosh, there are various memory and data storage requirements for specific page layout programs. Although most Macintosh programs require at least 512K of memory and a minimum of two disk drives, there are exceptions. MacPublisher II from Boston Software Publishers only requires a 128K Mac, making it one of the few capable page layout programs available to owners of the earlier Mac who haven't upgraded their machines. You shouldn't assume that a program is less powerful because it uses less resident memory.

Optimally, you should choose the program that has the features which best serve your purposes, as well as a program that operates in a manner that matches your method of production — then match it with hardware that meets the system requirements of the page layout program. Ventura Publisher for the IBM requires only a 512K IBM PC or compatible processor (8088), whereas most other high-end MS-DOS-based page layout programs require an AT compatible processor (80286) because of the 80286's higher speed and data processing capabilities. And since the AT has become the corporate standard for IBM format machines, most publishers have aimed their programs toward this processor. Ventura has developed a product that is compatible with the PCs and XTs already in use as well as the relatively low-priced PC Asian clones that are readily available.

Both IBM and Macintosh programs, in spite of their minimum data storage requirements, need at least ten megabytes of hard disk space. The programs themselves tend to fill at least one floppy disk. Because page layout involves importing comparatively large amounts of data from other programs, you'll find that without a hard disk you'll be shuffling disks in and out of your computer's floppy drives at a level that will frustrate your ability to quickly perform the application. Because a hard disk has become practically standard equipment on most microcomputer systems, advanced software (page layout included) is written to take advantage of the hard disk's conveniences. It is possible to operate using only a floppy disk system, but you'll feel as if you're pedaling a bicycle on a freeway.

What size hard disk is best suited for a page layout program? Twenty megabytes seems to be the current standard for hard disk mass storage. However, determine how the particular program you choose stores data files. Some programs copy files created from other software, then store them in a reformatted file of their own, thus requiring a good deal of storage space. Other programs, such as Ventura, require substantially less storage space by making changes directly into a file originally created by another program.

You must also consider how much data storage you need for other software programs that you wish to have readily available on your hard disk. Be sure you know what is required for software-hardware compatibility before you purchase.

Ease of Use

How easy a program is to learn and use is another important factor leading to your individual choice. All of the programs readily available for the Macintosh use the Mac's graphic interface. Many of the tools in these programs are similar or identical to other popular Mac word-processing and graphics programs. However, some programs are easier to learn and use than others. Orange Micro's Ragtime uses several unique tools that require some getting used to. MacPublisher's many options require a new user to flip back and forth in the reference manual more often than most people like. Yet all Mac programs have a degree of consistency that is far beyond the IBM software. Because there is a distinct lack of standardization in IBM format software, you can expect to find a wide variety of tools and methods for these programs. Most IBM programs are designed to operate using one of the Macintosh-emulating software environments, such as Microsoft Windows or Digital Research's GEM. This provides a modicum of standardization in an otherwise confused arena. Therefore, judge IBM programs for ease of use on an entirely different scale than for the Macintosh. Anyone who has managed to learn to use a program such as Lotus 1-2-3 with any degree of efficiency finds Ventura Publisher, with its pull-down mouse-controllable menus, a breeze.

Apple or IBM? From its inception, the Macintosh proved itself to be a very special computer. Not only was it easy to use, but a user could combine text and graphics using its scrapbook and clipboard features. With the Macintosh, someone could produce a great looking graphic, then insert it right in the middle of a business proposal. Word-processing programs, such as Microsoft Word, even allows you to print text in several columns. The IBM software and enhancement product industry did not ignore these very important capabilities. Software companies began creating IBM software environments, such as Digital Research's GEM and Microsoft's Windows, that provide both ease of use and text/graphic merging.

Electronic mice that allow the user to quickly and accurately move the computer's cursor in order to work with graphic elements, such as lines and shading, are absolutely necessary for desktop publishing, and have become readily available for the IBM.

The ultra high resolution necessary to perform the detailed graphic alignments required by desktop publishing is available for the IBM format by using the most advanced video boards with the latest enhanced color and high-resolution monochrome monitors.

Therefore, with the proper mix of enhancement hardware and software, an IBM-compatible machine can come very close to the Macintosh's graphics handling abilities.

Importing Data

Most page layout programs are designed to easily import data initially produced in other software programs. More often than not, you'll want to create documents or graphics using a word-processing or graphics program, then import the file into your page layout program. Once again, because of the similar file format of Mac programs and inconsistency in IBM file formats, this is a much easier proposition for Mac page layout programs. Even so, some Mac programs only import an unformatted ASCII file, while other programs, such as PageMaker, also accept files formatted by MacWrite and Microsoft Word. The ability to maintain already existing formatting saves the time it takes to change both the type and paragraph characteristics of an unformatted file.

Almost all Mac page layout programs accept only PICT formatted graphics files (saved with the same structure as MacPaint), making it critical to select a graphics program (such as FullPaint, MacDraw, or MacDraft), that saves files in this format. If you need to import a graphic that is not saved in the PICT format, you can still cut and paste between programs using the Mac's clipboard and finder, but it is a tedious process.

One of Ventura Publisher's strongest points is that despite the IBM's lack of standardization, it is capable of importing formatted files from a wide variety of popular word-processing and graphics generating programs. A unique feature of Ventura is that once imported into it, a formatted file can be exported into a variety of other IBM formats. Importing formatted files is a feature that should not be overlooked when selecting a page layout program.

Page Size and Document Length

Some programs are limited in the size and number of pages they can compose and print. You must verify that the program you consider is capable of printing the page size and document length that you require. For instance, Ready, Set, Go! 2.1 by Manhattan Graphics Corporation only prints an 8½ by 11 inch page but it easily handles files up to 40 pages long. Other programs print in several page sizes but have a difficult time dealing with single files longer than 20 pages.

Of the Macintosh programs, Ragtime excels in this area, handling an almost unlimited range of page sizes depending on your printer, and it can create documents of 100 pages or more.

Ventura supports a large variety of page sizes and the ability to print double-sided pages. Ventura also gives the user the ability to print a document from first page to last or from last page to first, which can be critical in time-restrained situations, because you can print a copy of your layout collated correctly rather than in reverse order.

Viewing Modes

Look at how a page layout program allows the user to view and access the created page of a document. This can be critical when trying to maintain a well-composed page design. Ready, Set, Go! and Ragtime use a "Show Page" function copied from MacPaint for viewing a page from either close up or far back. Although this works well in a paint program, it seems inadequate for page layout. When laying out a page, you need to look at the page from several different magnifications. For instance, when deciding the basic design elements of the page, you want to look at the whole page at once. However, when you're placing text in columns, you might want to view the page from a smaller magnification so that you can actually read the text in order to decide exactly where the columns should break. When you are aligning the various graphic elements on your page, you want to view them at as much as 200 percent magnification so that you're assured of accuracy. The wide variety of easily accessible views found in PageMaker and Ventura is an important feature.

The ability to easily scroll horizontally and vertically within a document also is important to the layout process: Check how easily the page layout program you're selecting lets you move within a page and between different pages. Viewing and accessing a page is a very important aspect of the page layout application.

Graphics Capabilities

Most page layout programs offer similar graphics handling abilities but very different text manipulating capabilities. This doesn't mean that you can create illustrations with your page layout program: You need a paint program for that. However, once you've created a graphic and imported it into your page, you need to stretch, crop, or size the graphic to fit into your layout. You might also want to place a border around something or shade an area of your page, and the graphics capabilities of most page layout programs allow you to do this.

Page layout programs usually have a variety of simple graphics tools for creating lines and borders and shades. Verify that the program you choose allows you the greatest freedom with the type of graphics that you intend to use in your publications.

Text Processing

Different page layout programs vary in their ability to alter and manipulate text once it has been imported into the layout. It is difficult to change text once it is imported into PageMaker. Ragtime includes its own word processor that allows the user to change textual elements easily as well as to search and replace particular words or phrases in an entire layout. MacPublisher excels beyond similar programs in its adjustable line spacing (leading) and character spacing (kerning) capabilities. Most programs offer discretionary hyphenation and word wrapping but vary in the ease with which these processes can be adjusted.

Once again, as with other features, match the text processing capabilities of a page layout program with your particular publication needs. If you need to make textual changes quickly as you're publishing, choose a program like Ragtime, which gives you that ability. If you are planning to wrap text around graphics of various shapes — as is often done in advertisements — kerning may be a necessary feature; if so, choose a program that gives you that ability. The text processing features of a particular page layout program can be judged only on how well they fit your particular publishing requirements.

Style Sheets or Templates

Style sheets or templates are reusable selections of page formatting options and design elements. These are files that allow you to make certain basic design decisions about your publication (such as nameplate, column grids, and page numbering) then save them as a foundation for each new issue of that publication. This aids in maintaining design consistency in each issue. Templates don't prevent you from customizing each document. However, they do save the time of reinventing the wheel each time you create a new document with your page layout software.

Ventura Publisher comes with a selection of 50 style sheets readily available. Preformatted style sheets provide the novice page designer with a solid foundation for developing a professional looking publication. Ready, Set, Go! and Ragtime allow users to save master documents to be reused and altered for specific issues. Templates, style sheets, and master documents can be an important feature when you are working with several different publications, each with its own distinct design.

Command or Shortcut Keys

Another important feature not available in all page layout programs is command key accessible commands. Command key options allow you to perform a function with a combination of keyboard strokes and/or mouse clicks rather than using the pull-down menus found in most page layout programs. Once you become familiar with your page layout program, these options dramatically increase your ability to produce documents. The ability to access PageMaker's different viewing magnification by means of command key options is particularly advantageous. Whereas Ready, Set, Go! is noticeably lacking in these options, Ventura Publisher allows command key options to be programmed using software utilities, such as ProKey and SuperKey, to perform a variety of functions with a minimum of key strokes. When purchasing software even the novice computer user must consider such power functions as command key options, because such advanced features are required fairly quickly. In addition, as you become accustomed to using the various tools provided by your page layout program, you'll probably look for shortcuts to increase your production speed. Command keys are a way of increasing your speed. If you plan to use your page layout program only sporadically, you'll probably stick to using commands from the pull-down menus, and command keys are an unimportant feature.

Program Speed

Speed of operation — the actual time it takes your computer to process the information generated by your page layout — is another important factor to the power user. Some programs are faster than others, and when minutes become critical — for instance, when publishing an investment newsletter — program speed is vital. Ready, Set, Go! is sluggish when compared to similar Mac programs, which could make it frustrating to use. Among IBM programs, Ventura Publisher takes advantage of the run-time version of the GEM operating system's speed, which makes it faster than Microsoft Windows-based programs.

Operating speed is also a function of the computer you are running the program on. With the Macintosh, for now, you are limited to the maximum resident memory of the latest release Mac. With an IBM-compatible system, the processor that the machine uses and the resident memory of the system can affect the operating system of your program. Frequently, processing accelerators and memory enhancement products maximize the operating speed of the page layout program you choose. However, these products must be checked for compatibility with the particular software that you are using. Double-check with your dealer or the products' manufacturers to make sure that they won't cause you compatibility problems.

Production Methods

Before making a final decision on which page layout program to choose based on the features it offers, consider the overall method that the program is based on and how closely that method matches the way that you intend to produce your publication. Both Ready, Set, Go! and Ragtime use a method that is designed to build pages from individually created elements — the overall page is manipulated to fit the elements.

For example, if you were intending to follow the method suggested by these programs, you would bring both your text and graphics into the page layout, adjust the relative size and location of these two elements, then add rules or other elements to round out the overall look of the page. With Ragtime these separate elements are created within the layout, then moved and sized to create the document's pages. Using this method could make it difficult to maintain a consistent design throughout a publication. Traditionally, each element composing a page is dealt with individually during the early stages of a publication's production.

Once the layout process has begun, pages are designed based on the completed elements and the basic page design (the number and size of columns and rules, as well as other elements, such as the publication's name and date that appear on practically every page). The tension between the elements and the overall design may influence the designer to make modifications that create an individual page which satisfies both influences.

Ready, Set, Go! and Ragtime's method seems best when one person is creating each element of a publication and at the same time is laying it out, thus adding some design elements to what would otherwise be a traditionally word-processed document.

Users familiar with traditional print production methods will probably be happier with one of the page layout programs that emulate those methods. Both PageMaker and Ventura Publisher try to automate well-known graphic production procedures. A basic page design is created in the program, which includes master items that are copied on to each page of the document. Then, text and graphics are imported and placed within the established design of each page. Finally, each page is altered to fit in those elements that it includes. But this is an oversimplification of the process. For now, it is important that you choose a page layout program that suits your production style.

An Example Using a Page Layout Program

To give you a more detailed examination of how a page layout program works, we go through the steps necessary to produce a simple newsletter using Aldus' PageMaker. Newsletters are particularly well-suited for the way a computerized page layout program operates. Once again, PageMaker tries to follow the same procedure that someone designing a newsletter in a traditional manner might follow. However, these steps are very different from what is traditionally considered editing. The actual text has only a small part in the graphic look of the printed piece. The initial newsletter design must be created as an independently well-designed frame into which your text and graphics (created in a word-processing program and graphics program) can flow.

Begin with the Design

PageMaker is a capable tool, but the actual design depends on you. It is a good idea to gain some rudimentary page layout skills through a seminar, class, book, or by consulting with a professional designer. PageMaker was designed with graphic page design in mind: The more you know about the principals of this field, the better you are able to take advantage of this program's features. Even if you do have some graphic design knowledge, it is still advisable to seek assistance from a professional graphic designer or art director. Even if you can't afford to have an art director design your newsletter layout from scratch, consider contracting a couple hours of a designer's time to tweak your own design.

Templates

Collections of newsletter layout templates are available for Page-Maker. These templates (as mentioned earlier) are newsletter designs that can be easily modified to fit your particular needs. By following the tutorial program included with these templates, you'll learn to manipulate PageMaker's various tools.

Make It Simple

Whether you begin with a template or create your own design, make sure to use elements easily recreated by PageMaker. For example, use rules and shading that can be produced using PageMaker's graphics tools, and use graphics that are produced or easily duplicated by a computer paint program. Different page layout programs have different graphics capabilities. You might print a "palette" of the things easily produced by the program you choose, then have a designer work exclusively with those elements. By using only those elements easily reproduced with your program you maximize your production speed. Therefore, begin your newsletter with a simple but solid design, then constantly build on that foundation, slightly improving the newsletter's look with each new issue.

Design Consistency

What makes a good newsletter design? One thing is consistency in style. PageMaker will assist you with this. You'll begin setting up your newsletter with PageMaker by selecting your page size, page orientation (wide or tall), margin widths, single or double sided page format, and publication length (the number of pages and pagination). Page-Maker provides the page sizes that are most frequently used: US letter, US legal, A4 letter, and tabloid. PageMaker limits the maximum number of pages in one document. However, you can begin the page numbering with any number sequence, making it easy to create larger publications from a combination of several PageMaker documents. Figure 16-1 shows options available from the page setup menu; Figure 16-2 shows the resulting layout blank.

Measurement Options

PageMaker allows you several measurement options. First pull down the edit menu and select preferences. This gives you a choice of which measurement system you prefer to work with, such as inches, millimeters, or picas and points. Picas and points is the default setting because it is the standard for print production. Next, pull down the tools menu and select "show rulers;" this presents vertical and horizontal rules that indicate the current location of your cursor, thereby allowing you to reference the exact location of each element of your design and maintain consistency. Although you can change the zero point of PageMaker's rulers, it is a good idea to leave them at their default setting at the corner of the working area of your page layout, because it's a good perspective on how much actual space you have to work with.

Viewing Modes

Another tool that helps you maintain the consistency of your design is PageMaker's several viewing options. You can view and work on your publication in a variety of different magnifications selectable from the page menu. Fit in window; actual size; and 50, 70, and 200 percent. The fit-in-window option centers your page on the screen and allows you to view it in its entirety. The actual-size option provides the closest approximation to how the page actually prints. However, because the Macintosh screen has a 72 dots-per-inch resolution and the LaserWriter has up to 300 dots-per-inch resolution, discrepancies occur, and things that appear to be aligned on your screen print ragged.

The other magnifications are useful for different tasks, depending on how much of the page and what degree of accuracy you need for your particular purpose. For instance, using the 200 percent view can

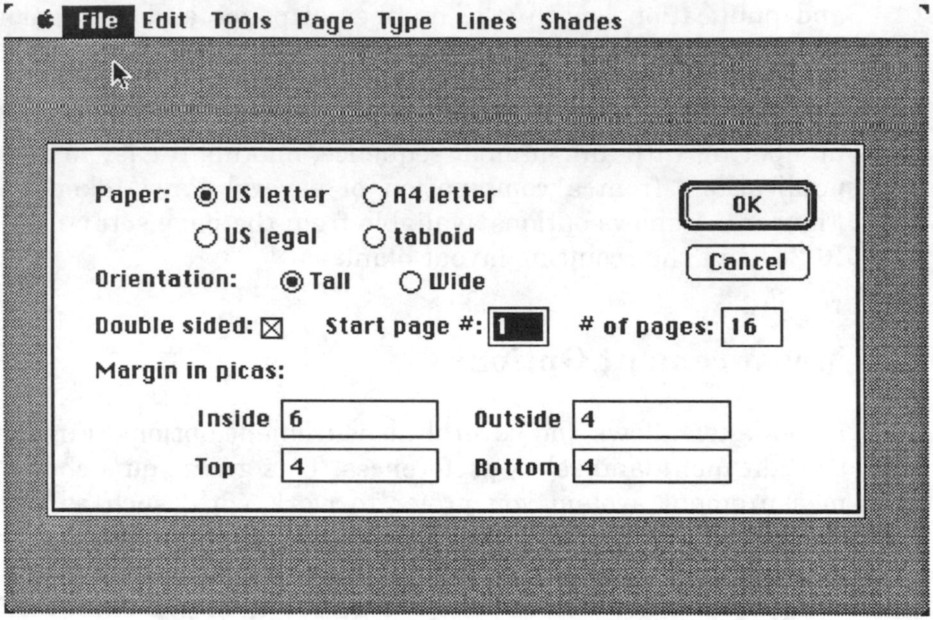

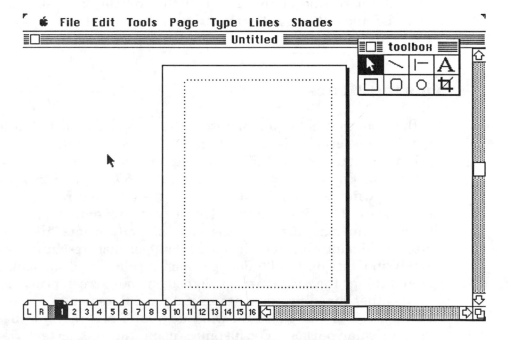

Figure 16-1. Page Setup menu.

Figure 16-2. Opening PageMaker layout.

help clean up graphics created within PageMaker. Selecting "show facing pages" allows you to view how the opposing pages of a double-sided publication look, although this is the only view in which you cannot change anything — you must switch to another view to make any alterations. Also, by selecting thumbnails from the print menu, you can print on one page up to 16 miniature or thumbnail-size pages of your publication, providing an overall look at your entire design. Judiciously using all of these viewing options should assist you in maintaining design consistency.

Creating Master Pages

As soon as you make these initial selections, PageMaker presents a visual representation of your newsletter page on your screen, displaying your page as if it were actually sitting on a pasteboard (see Figure 16-3). Of course, at this point it will be mostly blank except for a large frame in the center of the screen and several small representations of pages on the bottom of the screen. Among these small pages, you find that the first one or two pages read "L" or "R," indicating that they are master pages for your left or right formatted pages. (In a double-sided

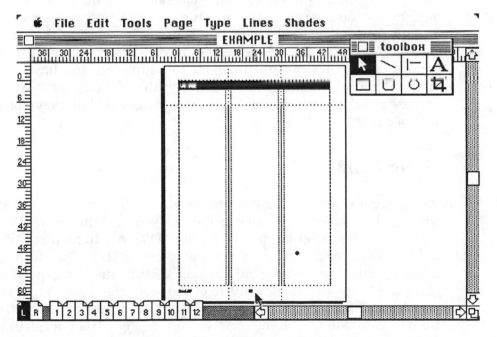

Figure 16-3. Creating a master page.

publication — folded so that pages face each other, the left- and right-hand pages should be almost mirror images of each other. However, PageMaker allows you to format the left or right page as you wish.)

This is the stage where you can indicate the major design elements of each formatted page, including your column grid, page number, horizontal and vertical rules, publication name and date, and any other element that is repeated on most inside pages. By creating master pages, you are actually placing your design into PageMaker. The master pages that you create is the design foundation for your newsletter, and the overall quality of each issue is greatly influenced by the attention you pay to maintaining your design. Remember that the elements on your master pages is repeated on every page. However, PageMaker also allows you to remove the master items and customize any individual page.

Column Grid

Your first choice on the master page is the format of the column grid for your pages. Pull down the tools menu and select "column guides." Then you must select the number of columns you wish and the spacing between columns. PageMaker automatically divides the master page into equal columns based on your selection. How many columns to use and how wide a space between columns is an important part of your design. You adjust the size of the columns by varying the size of the gutter between them. PageMaker automatically makes the column guides equal. You can use unequal columns, but you have to adjust manually the column guides that are already created. The column guides affect the placement of various elements, but they don't print on your page.

Ruler Guides

Next, create on your master pages any horizontal or vertical ruler guides that you desire to be a part of your column grid. Like your column guides, ruler guides don't print: They are to help you maintain a consistent design throughout your newsletter. Specifically, ruler guides assist you in placing various textual and graphic elements. With the "snap to guides" feature of the tools menu activated, text and graphics automatically align within the grid you create with these guides. Activate the "guide lock" feature to keep from accidentally adjusting your guides.

Adding Elements

Once all of your column and ruler guides are set on your master pages, create on the master pages the graphic elements that are repeated on most inside pages. For instance, you'll probably want to place actual printing rule lines (of various widths) on some of your horizontal and vertical rule guides as part of your master page design. Any textual items that are to appear on every page should be included on the master pages. For instance, the name of the newsletter, the newsletter's date, and the page number probably should be somewhere at the top or bottom of each page.

PageMaker handles pagination especially well: By simply selecting an insertion point and pressing "Option #" on the Macintosh, you can place an automatic page number marker on a master page, thereby putting the page number in the same place on every page. Remember, you want to reverse the location of textual items on opposing pages for a mirror image.

Setting Up a Title Page

The title page of your newsletter is not a master page for many of its elements appear only once in each publication. However, because of its prominence, the title page demands a great deal of design attention. By carefully structuring its various elements, you strengthen the initial impact of your newsletter. Stick with a set number of elements on the title page, then fill in the text and art for each specific issue to help give your readers a structure on which they can depend for easy, reliable reading. The title page is unique regarding both the page elements that it includes and the elements that it does not include. Because the title page traditionally indicates the publication's date near the top of the page, there is no need to include it at the bottom of page. Because the publication's name is easily identified, there is no reason to list it also at the bottom of the page. A page number is redundant on the title page because it is the first page.

Creating a Nameplate

Obviously the element that sets the title page apart from the rest of the pages of your publication is the title or nameplate. To identify it graphically, the nameplate is often referred to as the masthead for newsletters, newspapers, and periodicals. Because the nameplate is the first thing that anyone sees in your newsletter, it is very important that it represents, in both words and graphic appearance, what the publication is trying to communicate. Once you have a clear conception of what you are trying to say with your publication, work with a designer to create a nameplate that conveys a unified message in your title graphic. Figure 16-4 shows a title page with nameplate.

There are at least two ways of producing a nameplate. It can be produced manually by a graphic artist. Then you can have several camera-ready stats made that can be pasted in place each time you produce your newsletter. Second, using a paint program you can work with a designer to create a nameplate. Once created by the latter method, your nameplate easily can be placed on your newsletter with PageMaker. You also can crop, stretch, or size your nameplate using PageMaker's various graphics tools. Of course, the latter method of producing a nameplate is preferred because it saves time by taking advantage of your computer's graphic-handling capabilities.

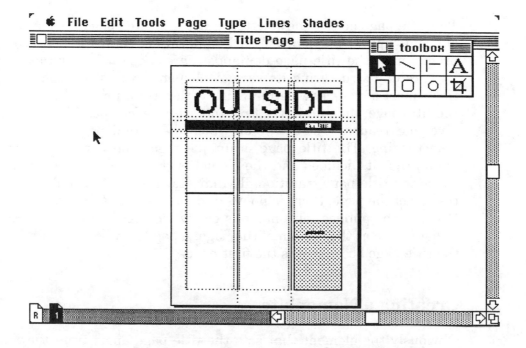

Figure 16-4. Title page with nameplate.

Choosing Typestyles

Another consideration when you design your newsletter is the type selection. This is one area where you are a bit constrained with desktop publishing. By limiting your type selections to those that are either resident or easily downloadable (produced with software that is read by your computer and then communicated to your printer), you will avoid mixing an inordinate number of typestyles — a sure sign of amateurism. Many beginning desktop publishers go crazy using every possible type face and style in their publications. Typestyles (such as italic, boldface, and outline) should be used consistently, and adhere to an accepted rule of style. Italic and boldface typestyles should mean something to your readers; don't dilute either graphics or contextual importance by overusing type style options. Look at any major magazine and you'll notice that a very limited number of type faces are used. A very popular combination is to use a serif typeface (the letters with the little tails on them), such as Times-Roman, for the body copy and a sans serif typeface (letters without little tails on them), such as Helvetica, for headlines. Typefaces can reflect a good deal about a publication: They should enhance the publication's image, not fight it.

The type selection available through desktop publishing still provides you with some exciting creative possibilities. Depending on which laser printer you're using, you can print type in a wide variety of sizes. Those laser printers operating with a page description language (such as Adobe Systems' PostScript, used in the Apple Laser-Writer) print characters from 4 to 127 points in half-point increments. And most page layout programs provide autoleading, the capability of varying the space between lines of type. You also can use reverse type, overlapping type, and graphics so that the letters appear white against a dark background. Using these options, you can maintain a consistent type style but still make your publication visually interesting. Once again, the advice of a professional graphic designer can be useful when selecting typefaces, styles, sizes, and effects.

Headline Size and Style

Once you've selected typestyles, you should also select the size and style of your headlines. This includes deciding which size of type you'll use for such things as main heads, subheads, and call-outs. It is important to use the same size and style of type consistently for each headline category, because this allows your reader to develop an expectation of the relative importance of the information conveyed in these elements.

Saving Your Master Pages as Your Own Template

It's a good idea to first create your entire newsletter as a template without any articles or pictures. You'll create every page with the elements that will appear in each issue of your publication. You'll begin every newsletter layout session by opening your template document, then using PageMaker's "saving as" feature to duplicate the file in order to work with it. Any changes that you decide to make a permanent part of your overall publication design must be changed on the original template file. Otherwise, each individual issue will be worked on strictly from the duplicate document.

Placing Your Stories into the Layout

After you create a template that reflects your design, it is time to place the stories and art that you've developed for a particular issue in your layout. Placing stories and art created in other programs is a simple procedure that is explained well in PageMaker's manual. You simply choose the "place command" from the Edit menu, select the file you wish to place in your layout, then, using the placing tool that this command has initiated, indicate where that particular item should fall within your column guides. PageMaker automatically aligns the text or graphics with the column guides that are are in place on your page. Once a particular column is full, a plus sign appears at its end: By clicking on the plus sign, you can direct where the text should continue. You simply fill your pages with the stories and art that you developed prior to beginning the layout process.

Wrapping Text

Text placed within PageMaker can be manipulated easily. Once you've placed a story within your column guide, you can change where that column begins or ends by simply pulling up or down the markers (which function like window shades) that indicate a column's beginning or end. PageMaker automatically adjusts the text in any other columns that are a continuation of that same story. To readjust a particular column width of a column that is filled with text, you must move the text within that column to the pasteboard (off the page), pull the bottom column marker all the way to the beginning of the column, then place the text again within your readjusted column guides by clicking on the collapsed column's plus sign. Figure 16-5 shows text entered ("poured") into columns.

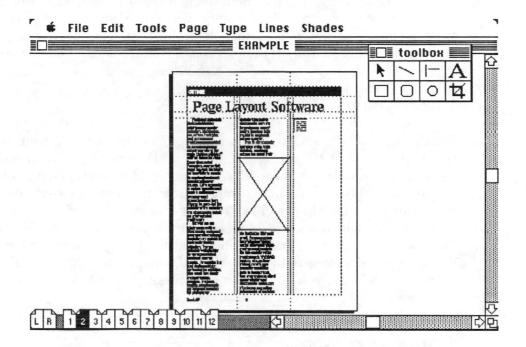

Figure 16-5. Wrapping text.

Wrapping Text Around a Graphic

If you decide to wrap text around a graphic, place the graphic on the page first. Next, place text in the column guides above the graphic — the text automatically stops when it reaches the graphic — then continue placing the text beneath the graphic. Temporarily adjust the column width to fit the side of the graphic, click on the plus sign where the text stopped flowing just above the graphic, and place text within the column space alongside graphic. The column above and below the graphic, which you placed before adjusting the column guides, doesn't adjust in width, but the text adjusts to fill all three spaces — above, alongside, and below the graphic.

Textual Changes

Although it is easy to manipulate text within PageMaker, as stated earlier, it is not easy to make extensive textual changes, such as editing and changing typestyles and sizes. And although you can make textual changes within your layout, it is much more difficult and time-consuming than if you made them using a word processor. If you need to make extensive changes to a story that has already been placed in your layout, it is often best to delete the text, change the original word-processing document, then once again place it into your layout.

Discretionary Hyphens

PageMaker recognizes discretionary hyphens that only appear when the word breaks at the end of a line of text. Discretionary hyphens can be created with Microsoft Word, or you can add discretionary hyphens within your layout. To add discretionary hyphens to text already placed in columns, simply place the cursor where you wish to add the hyphen and hold down both the command key and the hyphen key. You should use discretionary hyphens rather than regular hyphens to divide a word between lines so that if you adjust the flow of text within the column, you don't have unnecessary hyphens in the middle of lines.

Including Graphics

PageMaker allows you to place paint documents created with a paint or draw program within a PageMaker file. PageMaker also allows you to create several types of graphic embellishments in your layout. Once a graphic created by a paint program is placed within your layout by selecting "place" from the file menu, you can resize it by selecting one of the handles that appear on the border that surrounds it. By holding the Shift key when resizing a graphic, you maintain the original proportions of the graphic. Otherwise, you can distort the graphic by stretching or compressing it. PageMaker also has a cropping tool that can be used to trim the graphic to only the portion you wish to use. Once trimmed, the graphic can then be sized to fit your layout. However, you cannot actually change a placed graphic within your layout — all changes to the actual picture must be done within a paint or draw program.

Drawing Tools

PageMaker has several drawing tools, similar to those of MacDraw, that can be used to draw lines, circles, squares, and rectangles. These tools can be used for creating embellishments, such as vertical and horizontal rule lines, outline boxes, or background screens. When creating a rule line using PageMaker's line tool, you can select the width and style of the line from the selection offered on the Lines menu. Boxes drawn with PageMaker's rounded corner tool can have different shaped corners, which you select by choosing rounded corners on the Tools menu.

Shading and Reverses

Once a frame or circle has been created using one of PageMaker's drawing tools, the area within that frame can be shaded by selecting one of the variety of shades or patterns available on the Shades menu. PageMaker offers white or nonlines for indicating shaded areas that are to print without a line border. And there is also a white shade for reverse graphics. Reverse graphics are created by covering a graphic element with text or another graphic. These are manipulated by using the "bring to front" and "send to back" selections within the Edit menu.

Graphic Embellishment

By learning to manipulate PageMaker's graphics tools, a variety of graphic embellishments are available to you. Clip art programs are available that provide graphics that easily can be placed into your layout. Although it is not yet feasible to use photographs within a desktop publishing layout program, you can draw frames indicating the size and location where photographs can be manually placed within your final, printed boards. A good tip when manipulating graphics is to take advantage of the pasteboard portion of the program's screen. Because of the restrictions of your column grid, a graphic can be easily sized, cropped, or drawn on the pasteboard, then moved within the column guides on your page.

Printing Your Publication

Once you've placed and manipulated all of your text and graphics, you should be able to print a camera-ready master for the pages of your newsletter. Depending on your circulation, you can photocopy or send to an offset printing shop the actual pages printed by your laser printer for reproduction.

Reducing Your Final Page

When printing a layout that includes MacPaint formatted graphics, you must print your layout at 96 percent reduction (which is selectable from PageMaker's printing "dialog box"), to achieve the highest quality graphic reproduction. This reduction is advisable because of the difference in resolution between the Macintosh's screen and most laser printers.

Using a Professional Typesetter

PageMaker takes advantage of Adobe Systems' PostScript page description language. This is the language that it uses to operate the Laser-Writer and some Allied Linotype typesetters. Because of this, Page-Maker can be used to perform a variety of type-fitting functions that would normally require the services of a typesetting firm. Using a PostScript printer, you can reduce or enlarge a PageMaker document from 15 to 1,000 percent. When a LaserWriter's 300 dots-per-inch resolution is not enough, PageMaker also gives you the option of easily printing your document on a Linotron 101P or a Linotronic 300P professional typesetter, which print at 1270 and 2540 dots per inch, respectively.

Summary

Page layout software takes the place of the artist's paste-up board. The main purpose of a page layout program is to let you mix text and graphic images on a page in a multiple column format. Generally you should create your text using a word processor, create your graphic elements using graphic software, and then set up the page format and "pour" the text and graphics into the page set up.

Different page layout programs have differing capabilities. Some can handle large amounts of data, some let you create graphics or text, some are faster, have different viewing modes, come with varying kinds of templates, and so on.

It is in the page layout program that you determine the design of your publication, so be sure to establish simple rules of design for your format. It is good practice first to set up master pages, defining columns and rulers; then you can make copies of the masters and load text and graphics into them.

Page layout software can be a powerful companion to other application software, but developing skill takes practice.

KEYWORDS:

• Jaggies

• Icons

• PICT Image

• Transparency

• Laserbits

Mitchell Waite is a coffeecake hound who spends most of his time in bistros flirting with women and dreaming of being a famous publishing magnate who lives on a beach in the Bahamas. He is the well-known originator of the "parachute" look, and claims to be able to go hang-gliding just by waving his arms.

Essay Synopsis: In this essay the author leads us along the trail of progressively more sophisticated paint and draw programs on his quest for a way to create high resolution images on a LaserWriter. There is an implicit promise of ease in using graphics software, so the various hidden limitations of each program come as a sudden and jarring frustration. He presents a problem of creating a bar graph made of stacks of book icons and examines the powers and limitations of popular paint and draw programs applied to this task. You will learn how to transfer images between paint (bit-mapped) and draw (object-oriented) programs, how to side-step the "staircase" effects of low resolution curves, and how to place a foreground image over a background image without the effect of transparency.

17

High Resolution Laser Art

Mitchell Waite

The number of Macintosh illustration programs is increasing at such a furious pace that it is almost impossible to keep up. Some of the most exciting of these programs are the ones that use the high-resolution 300 dots per inch of the Apple LaserWriter. In comparison, the original ImageWriter offered only 72 dots per inch, so this is a significant advance.

We wanted to prepare a brochure to present to our authors and publishers, and we wanted to use our Macintosh and LaserWriter combination as much as possible. PageMaker made perfect sense for creating the text and the simple rule lines. But the choice for a sales graph was more difficult to make. We chose to use a chart in the brochure that represented the number of copies sold of The Waite Group's four best-selling books. We wished to show the sales volume of these four products and also the retail dollar sales that each book has generated.

Our idea was to make a stack of little book icons, created in MacPaint, with each book representing 20,000 copies. We wanted the shadow cast from each stack of books to represent the retail sales for that book, with the name of each book appearing in white type in the shadows. When the project was finally done, we found that the idea is the easy part. How did we turn this idea into a reality using the Macintosh, LaserWriter, and their various tools? That is what this essay is about. It is also about

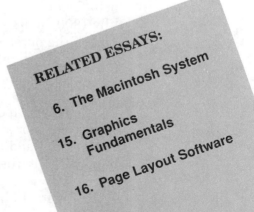

RELATED ESSAYS:

6. The Macintosh System

15. Graphics Fundamentals

16. Page Layout Software

using the high resolution of the LaserWriter to draw extremely realistic images.

Pick Your Tool, Watson

Because the market was crowded with software for drawing on the Macintosh, we had a large selection of tools from which to choose. Some of the tools we had to play with for this project included Page-Maker 1.2, MacWrite, MacPaint, MacDraw, MacDraft, FullPaint, SuperPaint, and Cricket Draw.

We learned a lot in producing our previous book, *Desktop Publishing on the Mac* (Kevin Rardin. Plume/Waite. New York: New American Library, 1986). For instance, the best way to approach using art with PageMaker (assuming that it is too complex to draw in PageMaker itself) is to create it in MacDraw.

Why MacDraw and not MacPaint? The reason is that MacDraw creates graphic "objects" as opposed to MacPaint's bit images. A box, its fill pattern, thickness, and other drawing elements are all a single object rather than a collection of dots.

The point is that these objects generally show up much better on the LaserWriter than do MacPaint bit images. Here is why. MacDraw stores graphic objects as a large collection of "QuickDraw" instructions. When they are sent to the LaserWriter, the QuickDraw instructions are converted to PostScript code. PostScript code is a device-independent language that can draw at the maximum resolution of whatever device it is used with. The PostScript code emitted from MacDraw and other similar programs is interpreted by the PostScript engine in the LaserWriter and converted finally into a high-resolution bit map for the laser printing process. The resolution is 300 dots per inch. On an 8½ by 11 inch paper, this translates to 2,500 dots horizontally (300 by 8½) and 3,300 dots vertically (300 by 11). You have to remove the outer ¼ inch or so around the page where the LaserWriter won't print, so call it 2,400 dots by 3,000 dots. It's certainly a huge number of dots.

As an example, a shadow made in MacDraw is simply four corners of a weirdly shaped polygon that is filled with black. Because graphic things are stored as objects, PostScript is able to use its internal routines to build amazingly fine sharp lines on its high-resolution bit map, without the jaggies, those stairstep, ragged edges of bit-map curves.

If you send MacPaint images to PageMaker, you end up sending a pure bit map of dots that are pretty big (¹⁄₇₂ inch) to the LaserWriter, rather than a set of QuickDraw calls. The result is that the Laser-Writer produces a crude looking, jagged drawing. If you turn "smoothing" on when you print a MacPaint drawing (from PageMaker or MacWrite), you sometimes get better effects. It was with this knowledge that we approached our problem. In the following example, we see the effects of smoothing and how it can wreak havoc on our ideas.

Start with MacPaint

The approach that we first thought of was simple. First, create the little book icons in MacPaint, paste them into MacDraw, organize them in MacDraw as little stacks of books and finally into a chart, save the chart as a PICT image, then open PageMaker and "place" the chart into the page. In case you don't know, PICT images are a way to store object-oriented drawings in a standard format that can be read into some other Macintosh programs, such as MacWrite. It's sort of like saving your drawing on the clipboard permanently in a file, but it's a different version from the regular MacDraw document. When you do a "Save As" from MacDraw, there is a button called PICT. Press it and the icon for the saved file looks different from the normal Mac-Draw document icon as an indication that its contents are now stored as a graphic object rather than a bit map.

First, we had to know the final size of the drawing. The artist for the brochure (we were smart enough to hire an independent graphic designer to design and produce the camera-ready art for the brochure) made up a dummy with the exact dimensions for the chart graphic area. This made it fairly easy for us to figure out how big each individual icon could be. Our first trial icon is shown in Figure 17-1.

Figure 17-1. Original icon for book used in chart.

Once we had drawn the icon, we saved it in a file (so we could modify it later) and copied it to the clipboard. Then we quit MacPaint, opened up MacDraw, opened a new document, and pasted in the little book icon.

Next we duplicated the icon and used the mouse to drag the new copy to sit exactly above the first one, only then releasing the mouse button. If you move and place an object this way in MacDraw, the program remembers the number of pixels you moved it. Then, when you do the next duplicate (clover-D), MacDraw places the new object exactly the same number of pixels away as you did in the first move. Thus, it stacks the books perfectly equidistant, one above the other. The final result is shown in Figure 17-2.

Figure 17-2. The stack of MacPaint icons in MacDraw.

It is not easy to get such little objects to line up. The handles on the objects are so small, it is hard sometimes to see where and how to move them. Sometimes the arrow cursor in MacDraw obscures an important point in a line you are trying to connect.

We made four stacks of books and drew a surrounding grid for the graph. Things were beginning to look great. Next we drew in the shadows for the book stacks. The shadows represented retail sales, and because each book had a different cover price, the height of the shadows was not proportional to the height of the stack. We used the polygon tool in MacDraw to make these shadows. The polygon tool might be the most important tool in MacDraw. It lets you use the mouse to create multisided figures that close up when you connect the end to the beginning of the shape. Once you have drawn a polygon, you can put it into the edit mode, in which case each vertex becomes a "handle" that can be moved independently. You then pull the four corners of a four-sided polygon into the shadow shape and place it at the base of the stack. You have to use "Send to Back" to get it to go under the bottom book on the stack. We spent a lot of time trying to get the shadows to line up with the bottom of the stacks. That is when problem number one set in.

Transparency

We noticed that when we put the shadow polygons behind the book stacks, the shadows showed through the books; the books were actually transparent wherever they appeared white (see Figure 17-3a). This was a drag because real books are not transparent, and the appearance of having the shadows come through was ugly. After thinking about it for a while, it began to make sense why this was happening. MacDraw treats everything as an object. When it takes an object from a MacPaint bit map, it sees only the black bits of the pasted bit map. If a bit is not black, it is considered transparent: not there. We could not find any way around this. Our solution was to create a "mask," a polygon that followed the outline of the stack of books, fill this area with white, and put it behind the books to block the shadows.

Distortion of Small Bit Images

We slaved over this method for about a day, totally immersed in getting the masks to fit properly. Our eyes were killing us. How we wished for a "fat bits" function in MacDraw that would allow us to zoom up on an image and edit it at four or eight times its real size. When we finally had our creation finished and ready to print, we ran into problem number two. We had assumed, correctly, that what printed from MacDraw would be similar to what printed from PageMaker. So we saw no reason to paste into PageMaker and add the text, until we had done it right in MacDraw.

But when we printed our creation the first time, we were very disappointed. The jaggies were obvious, and our illustration looked like a stack of alligator jaws, not books. When we turned the "smoothing" feature on, it got worse (see Figure 17-3b).

Why didn't it work? Basically the icons needed more detail than MacPaint could provide. To see why this is so, you need to understand the difference between dots on the LaserWriter and the dots shown on the Macintosh screen. There are about 72 dots per inch on the Macin-

a.

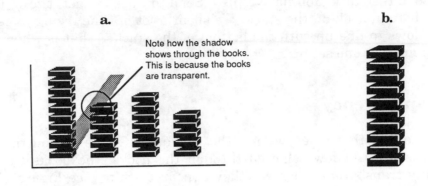

Note how the shadow
shows through the books.
This is because the books
are transparent.

b.

c.

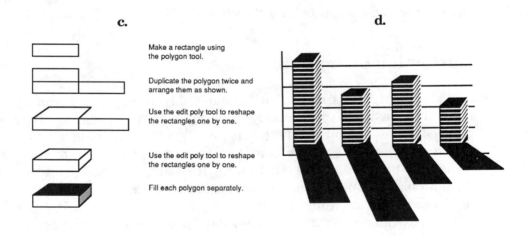

Make a rectangle using
the polygon tool.

Duplicate the polygon twice and
arrange them as shown.

Use the edit poly tool to reshape
the rectangles one by one.

Use the edit poly tool to reshape
the rectangles one by one.

Fill each polygon separately.

d.

Figure 17-3. Evolution of the simplified MacDraw chart.

tosh screen; one dot is about $\frac{1}{72}$ inch square. We say the ImageWriter and Macintosh display in 72 dots per inch (dpi). If the printer has a similar resolution, if it can resolve at least one dot every $\frac{1}{72}$ inch, then What You See displayed on the screen Is What You will Get printed on the printer. This is the ubiquitous WYSIWYG (pronounced "wizzy-wig") mentioned throughout this book.

The resolution of the LaserWriter is *higher* than that of the Macintosh screen, and there lies an interesting situation. There are 300 dots per inch on the LaserWriter, so there are more than four times as many dots per square inch than on the Macintosh screen. You can think of a single Macintosh pixel as being made of approximately 16 LaserWriter dots arranged in a four-by-four matrix.

Now, because we pasted the small book into MacDraw, we pasted a MacPaint bit image with limited resolution of large, 72-dots-per-inch pixels. There is no way that MacDraw can tell the LaserWriter how to take advantage of its much higher resolution. A 72-dots-per-inch pixel ends up being a large fat dot, just like it appears on the ImageWriter. We can turn on smoothing, but when the image is small, the larger Macintosh screen dots connect in ways that distort the actual shape that is intended (on large MacPaint bit images, smoothing can have a satisfying result). That is why smoothed images look so different from the unsmoothed images.

Forget MacPaint, Draw Your Entire Image in MacDraw

The solution to problem number two, distortion of small dot images, was to explore other ways to draw the books without using MacPaint. This would get us around the sticky transparency problem as well. We were, as you might imagine, a bit discouraged at this point. Why didn't anyone tell us that this would be so hard?

Our first attempt was to build little book shapes using MacDraw's polygon tool. We figured out the minimum number of corners we would need for the polygon. We found several ways to draw the book. The one that worked best was to make the book out of three four-sided polygons. Figure 17-3c shows how this is done. We then filled the polygons and duplicated them to make a stack. This worked pretty well until we built up a lot of books in a stack. Then we discovered a third problem.

Too Many Objects in MacDraw

When we tried to move a large stack to a line or relocate it, we found it very difficult to move the objects. MacDraw slowed way down, reacting very poorly to mouse movements. It would sometimes take five or six seconds after moving a stack of these objects for MacDraw to draw them all in their new locations. We were fighting the sheer limits of the Macintosh's processor speed.

Each object in the MacDraw document is stored in memory somewhere with its coordinates, its line thickness, fill patterns, and everything else. These objects are spread out in all kinds of places in memory. When a collection of objects is moved as a big group in MacDraw, all the coordinates must be updated to the new locations in memory. This takes time. Using the MacDraw "grouping" function (clover-G) did not speed things up. We were fighting the program, so we decided to take a fresh approach. (Give yourself this escape option when you experiment with a new Macintosh art idea: If it's too hard, it's probably the wrong way to go, so sit back and try some other approach.)

The new approach was to reduce the number of polygon objects that made up a stack of books. We used one black-filled polygon that followed the contour of the outline for the entire stack, then used a two-sided polygon (two connected lines made with the polygon tool) with white for the line pattern to make up the front edge and the right side of the book. The result was much easier to manipulate because it was made up of fewer objects, and it looked pretty good. We decided to make the shadows come out of the page rather than go behind the stacks, because that was easier to draw, was more dramatic, and we could put the names of the books in the shadows with white Page-Maker type. Figure 17-3d shows the final result.

Seeking a Higher Resolution Graph

After we thought about the final result for a few days, we decided this was just not good enough. Our image did not look like books stacked up; it looked like wafers of some kind. Someone in the office told us it looked like apartment buildings. It looked like problem number four.

We simply were not happy with the limited detail of the MacDraw book objects. The minimum line thickness for the borders was as small as we could make in MacDraw, but they were much wider than they needed to be for LaserWriter printing. Because the resolution of the

LaserWriter is 300 dots per inch and that of MacDraw is only 72 dots per inch, we knew it was not the LaserWriter's problem, but Mac-Draw's. Because PageMaker can make thin, one-point-wide lines, we suspected there might be a new drawing tool for the Mac that allowed access to the high resolution of the LaserWriter.

We investigated MacDraft, which acts a lot like the original Mac-Draw program. We fell in love with it when we discovered it could zoom an image up and down two and four times. That feature would make it much easier to edit polygons and move their infuriating handles. But MacDraft would not let us make lines any thinner than would MacDraw. We felt trapped between old and new technology. The LaserWriter was developed by Apple after MacDraw and MacDraft, so it is no wonder those programs don't access the full capabilities of the LaserWriter.

We looked at FullPaint, which is a really beautful product. Its highlights are that it can open four MacPaint documents at the same time and can perform stretching, twisting, and distorting of bit images. Clickart's Special Effects, which installs in MacPaint as a desk accessory, does the same thing. FullPaint has rulers, a grid, and a feature called LaserPrint that lets you edit at the LaserWriter's high resolution. The LaserPrint utility divides the document into either four or sixteen new documents, each representing a subsection of the original document. You can then edit each subsection in detail, then recombine them all into one enhanced drawing for laser printing at 150 or 300 dots per inch.

That meant we would have to draw the entire graph in one of the 1/16 LaserPrint documents in FullPaint, make the whole thing up as a giant bit image, laser print it, and finally paste it in by hand as the last step. (You can't paste a FullPaint image into PageMaker, only a PICT.)

But using a paint program to make an entire graph did not seem right; a chart is more object-oriented. We wanted a draw program with the ability to talk to the LaserWriter's high resolution 300 dots per inch. We were down to our last possible choice.

SuperPaint Does Laser Drawing

The answer came from a product called SuperPaint. We found Super-Paint to be a super deal of a program: It combines the features of MacPaint and MacDraw into one program that opens both paint and draw type windows and lets you draw in either. You can easily move paint bit images into the draw window and vice versa. SuperPaint also is the only paint program so far that gives 32 shades of gray for the LaserWriter.

The laser-bit editing feature of SuperPaint was what we were after, however. The way it works is a little difficult to understand at first, but after a while it makes beautiful sense. The program lets you draw a section of a regular paint or draw type document in a blown up 300-dot-per-inch resolution. First you have to select a section of a regular paint document and save it as a special "LaserBits" document. This file now contains the 300-dots-per inch version of the section of your original drawing. The manual claimed that we could edit a piece of a MacPaint rectangle as large as 2 by 2½ inches. This comes from 2 x 4 = 8 inches, which is the maximum width of a MacDraw document, and 2½ x 4 = 10, the maximum length of a MacDraw document. This size limit may be a problem for another project, but it was far bigger than what our little books needed to be, in 300 dots per inch. That would let us give the books incredible detail.

Now, after you make up your 300-dots-per-inch paint elements, you "place" them in your regular draw document. We couldn't get Super-Paint to place the high-resolution object into the paint window, and there was no reference in the manual to this being allowed. We could save the SuperPaint draw document in PICT form, and it would be suitable for pasting into PageMaker, or we could put it on the Clipboard, if we understood things, and paste it into the PageMaker document.

A special feature of LaserBits is that any change you make to the original LaserBits document is automatically reflected in the normal draw document where the objects are assembled. That makes it possible to build the chart in the draw window, edit the single book icon at 300 dots per inch, and have the change appear in all the books made of this object! You can create a single book icon as a laser bit image, paste it into the draw document, and duplicate it there. Each book is then linked to the 300-dots-per-inch object drawn in the LaserBits document. When you look at the objects in the regular draw document, they look kind of dark, and the detail is missing — even when you blow them up. When they are clicked on, they have different kinds of handles that identify them as LaserBits objects, not regular draw objects. We created a LaserBits version of the little book icon. Figure 17-4 shows how the book looked when we drew it in the Laser-Bits window.

We used Helvetica Bold uppercase for the typeface. To get it perfect, we had to touch up the type using the SuperPaint fat-bits editor.

SuperPaint features a little magnifying glass function. When you click on your drawing with this tool, the image jumps two times larger and presents a second scrolling window with the fat-bits view. Another click on the fat-bits object zooms it out another two times to give a four times fat-bits image. By the way, both FullPaint and SuperPaint allow horizontal and vertical scrolling, a feature absent from MacPaint.

Figure 17-4. The book icon in LaserBits mode. Pixels are each 1/300 inch.

We made the lines that represent the edges of the pages 45 degrees so that there would be no jaggies at all, thinking that this would give us the highest quality lines (not necessarily true, as it turned out). We played with the paint image until the pages and the spine of the book appeared to be curved. Next we placed one of these into a SuperPaint draw document, duplicated it, moved it, and repeated until we had formed the final stacks. We then added the polygon shadows to produce the final image. Figure 17-5 shows how the final image looked.

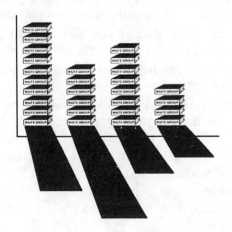

Figure 17-5. The actual SuperPaint output of the chart on the LaserWriter.

Take a close look at this baby; it's hot stuff. The most immediate thing is the fact that the resolution is so high you can see the pages on the side of the little book. The type WAITE GROUP on the spine comes through loud and clear.

A Last Hurdle — The Grid

We ran into another problem when attempting to add the grid. When draw lines were added to the high-resolution chart for axes, the transparency problem came up again. The books were still transparent, so lines that were supposed to be behind them actually showed through, like the shadows did. And we found that the axis lines were too darn fat for the fine quality of the books, now at 300 dots per inch. It then dawned on us that the grid for the object could also be made in 300 dots per inch, then line thickness could be controlled down to one LaserWriter pixel ($\frac{1}{300}$ inch). That was a great idea, but when we tried to implement it, we discovered the limits of LaserBits' 2-by-2½-inch rectangle. We could not get a full line for the graph. Instead it had to be made out of two sections and slid together. That finally worked, but it seemed less than ideal. It finally dawned on us that we could use the thin line of PageMaker to form these grid lines, and use the Draw line to make the thicker axis of the graph. We dropped the idea of making the finer grid in SuperPaint. All we needed to do was paste this final drawing into PageMaker and add the text around it. This turned out to be super easy. Using PageMaker's 200 percent mode it was easy to place the text.

Unfortunately the final result in PageMaker, with the text attached, could be output only from PageMaker. Once a picture is in PageMaker, we can't change the SuperPaint LaserBits image and expect the PageMaker version to change as well because the link doesn't exist. To make any changes you have to go back to SuperPaint, modify the icon in the draw document, save it as a PICT, and place it back in PageMaker over the old image. You can easily make up a set of different LaserBit icons, however, or use ones from clip art that others have made. As long as they are not too large (3 by 2½ inches) you can use them for high-resolution effects. One thing to remember is that if you convert something made in MacPaint to LaserBits, you can't erase the black bits in the original — you can fill in the white bits only with black LaserBits. Thus, clip art has to be copied manually to get high-resolution versions.

Taking LaserBits to the Cutting Edge

You could draw up a plan for a building and make up trees and shrubs for the landscape objects in LaserBits. Then you could paste these into the final Draw document for absolutely incredible results.

How about designing the plumbing, conduit, or electrical drawings for a large building? Using LaserBits you could make up dozens of shapes to represent parts and move them around in the draw window, attaching them with draw-size pipes, wires, tees, and so on.

You could digitize your face with MacVision. Then you could take some portion of it, like your eyes and mouth, and turn them into LaserBit objects. You could have some bewildering effects by using contrasting levels of detail. How about fitting your entire face in a 2-by-2½-inch square with 300-dots-per-inch resolution, which is enough for a passport photo.

Summary

If you want to do high-resolution illustration with your LaserWriter, and if you wish to have lots of detail in your final output, experiment with SuperPaint's LaserBits mode. There probably will be many new programs coming along with LaserBits ability. Apple, Aldus, and Microsoft offer sophisticated high-end paint/draw/CAD programs that use the LaserWriter's 300-dots-per-inch output. Aldus has announced Illustrator, which promises to add beautiful Bezier curves and handles to its final output, something impossible with the current tools.

Epilogue: Enter Cricket Draw

Just as we finished writing about these different approaches to drawing our chart on the LaserWriter, a copy of Cricket Draw from Cricket Software showed up at the office. This program was different enough from the others that we decided to give it a try and see whether our chart would come out better, and how much work the process would take.

Cricket Draw differs in several ways from the other products described so far. Cricket Draw is object-oriented like MacDraw, Mac-Draft, and SuperPaint, and the objects will be familar to users of those products. There is one new fantastic object: Bezier curves — but we'll get to that later. Cricket Draw goes further than the other programs in that it allows incredible control over the objects that are drawn (remember SuperPaint lets you edit a fat-bits version of a drawing at 300 dots per inch, but that is not the same as editing a draw object at 300 dots per inch). All the objects can be shaded in gray tones or in color from zero to 100 percent (apparently they anticipate color laser printers and screens). The shades can be painted with a simple but powerful fountain tool, and the rate at which the shades vary can be made logarithmic, linear, or radial. When you double click on any object, you get a dialog box full of selections that you can use to change the intensity of the fill, the thickness of borders, and so on. You can vary the thickness of lines down to .05 of a pixel, an inch, a centimeter, or a pica.

The tricks to Cricket Draw are that it generates a complete PostScript code listing of the image you make in a draw window and it lets you edit the code as a PostScript file. Because it generates PostScript directly, the accuracy of the final output is set by the limits of the output device, not the image itself. When you print on a LaserWriter, you get 300-dots-per-inch images. On a Linotronic, you get up to 4,500 dots per inch. The drawing looks the same on the screen in both cases.

Figure 17-6 shows what the original book for Cricket Draw looked like before it was shrunk for the actual size. We did not use this in the

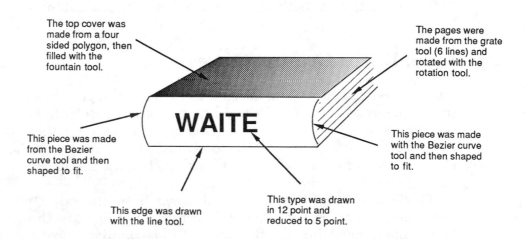

Figure 17-6. How the Cricket Draw book was made.

final brochure because we were limited for time, but if we had had more time we certainly would have proceeded with it further. Several unique aspects of this graphic deserve mention. The Bezier curve tool alone is worth the price of the program. This tool is like some of the tools provided in Macintosh font programs. It puts anchors that look like little dots near but outside a curve, and it lets you pull the curve into the shape you want with the mouse and these handles. You have to use it to see its power, but the best way to describe it is to imagine that the curve is an easy-to-bend wire that has ropes attached to key locations. When you pull the rope, you bend the curve, which always stays smooth.

The left and right sides of the book spine were made with two Bezier curves. A horizontal line connects them and forms the bottom edge of the book. The top of the book is made from a four-sided polygon, then filled with the fountain tool. The fountain tool fills an object with a shading that varies from black to white. On the screen, it looked like a custom pattern from MacPaint and appeared where the tool was used, but underneath the fill is actually PostScript code for generating the smooth variations in shading. You can set the shading to vary from zero to 100 percent, and you can make the shading logarithmic or linear. (These are some examples of special effects that can be done with PostScript. As these tools mature you will see more and more of these kinds of effects.) Figure 17-7 shows the shading in 300 dots per inch, which is not as good as it would be on the Linotronic 300. *[We may as well mention here that there is a limit to the resolution and fineness that an offset print shop can accommodate. If you're preparing camera-ready mechanicals for offset printing, be sure to find out from the print shop what resolution to use. The Linotronic 300 can produce art that is of much finer resolution than many offset shops can duplicate. If they were to try to print an image at too fine detail, the result would be a drippy smudge, for the ink would run together. — Ed.]*

The type was drawn at 12 point and reduced to 5 point. Cricket Draw did not handle text well, and when it was reduced it could not be edited because the individual characters could not be differentiated on screen. You have to blow the text back up to a size that allows the cursor to click between letters. According to Dennis McFerren, one of the key programmers of Cricket Draw, the problem is a limitation of Apple's text routines, not Cricket Draw. He assured us that they would endeavor to find a way around the problem.

The pages of the book were drawn with the grating tool. This tool draws a series of parallel lines. You set the number of lines and the way they are spaced, from linear to logarithmic. You can rotate the grate, as we have done, so that the lines are all at an angle, then you can stretch the end points by pulling on the edges of the grating object. This ability to treat everything as an object is one of Cricket Draw's chief strengths.

Figure 17-7 shows a single bar of the stack of Cricket Draw books. The shadow was added as a five-sided polygon, then shaded with the fountain tool. Note that you can see where the shadow shows through the bottom book. This is because the book's page side is not a white-filled object but is transparent. Another white-filled polygon placed behind the grating would cure this.

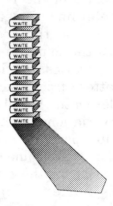

Figure 17-7. Output from Cricket Draw.

We originally felt that we needed a draw program like Cricket Draw to create the detailed image for the brochure. As we got further into Cricket Draw it became obvious that this is an incredibly powerful and precise tool. It gave us almost too much power, too much freedom of control. For that reason Cricket Draw should become very popular with developers who need to create object-oriented drawings with lots of detail and precision down to the resolution of the printer (300 dots per inch and greater). But to learn to work well with Cricket Draw takes lots of time and skill. For simple 300-dot-per-inch-resolution artwork, where you want quick results, SuperPaint is a better choice.

KEYWORDS:

- **WYSIWYG**

- **Kerning**

- **Ligature**

- **Hyphenation**

- **Paragraph**

- **Drop Cap**

Malcolm Brown is a computer consultant at Stanford University. Although interested in all aspects of digital typography, he is particularly interested in typesetting and page description, having worked with a variety of typesetting programs on the PC, the Macintosh, and UNIX-based systems.

Essay Synopsis: Type encoding programs use special codes that must be embedded in text to accomplish typesetting. These encoding programs actually predate the newer "What You See Is What You Get" (WYSIWYG) page layout programs, and consequently are more familiar to people coming from traditional dedicated typesetting environments. Type encoding programs give the greatest degree of control over page layout without resorting to programming in a page description language such as PostScript.

In this essay the author discusses the principles of type encoding programs and compares features of three popular such programs, JustText, TeX, and DeskSet. You will see in what ways the embedded command codes control the placement of text on a page and accomplish automatic hyphenation, kerning between letter pairs, special treatment of initial capital letters in paragraphs, control over breaks between lines and paragraphs, and much more.

18

About Type Encoding Programs

Malcolm Brown

Computer programs designed to do word processing and typesetting take one of two approaches.

The first approach is called WYSIWYG (pronounced "wizzy-wig"), meaning "What You See Is What You Get." These programs attempt to display on the screen what your text will look like when it is printed. Additionally, these programs permit you to manipulate sections of text visually. Using a pointing device, such as a mouse or a cursor, the arrangement of text can be altered with immediate visual feedback on the results.

A second approach employs special codes to govern the position and style of characters, graphics, rules, and other marks on a page. We can refer to this kind of program as a type code program, although such a label can be misleading. Since the introduction of electronic phototypesetting in the 1950s, the term "type codes" has referred to a convention of markup instructions used with phototypesetting equipment. As we will see, present-day typesetting programs may use very different conventions for their typesetting codes.

Given these two approaches, the question arises: Which is better, the WYSIWYG or the type code system? As natural as this question seems to be, it is in fact quite misleading, and answering it in the abstract does more harm than good. To simply oppose WYSIWYG and type code programs is short-sighted for at least four reasons.

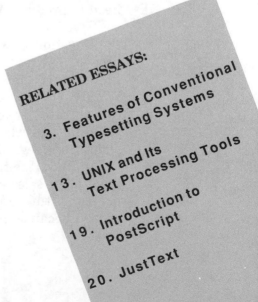

First, there are type code programs that have a WYSIWYG component, in that they can display their output on the computer's screen. The notion of a WYSIWYG versus type code opposition could cause you to completely overlook the previewing capabilities of some type code programs.

Second, to conceive of type code and WYSIWYG considerations as an opposition invariably makes an objective consideration of the two approaches impossible. The very context encourages you to take one side or the other. There is an inclination to apothesize one's subjective favorite as objectively better, which, in turn, can lead to a simplification and/or misrepresentation of the "opponent." It is doubtful that anyone is helped very much by such an approach, especially when faced with the decision to acquire a program that will cost hundreds or even thousands of dollars.

Third, the question fails to differentiate among WYSIWYG and type code programs with respect to their quality. Some WYSIWYG programs are better than others, just as there are better and worse type code programs. Indeed, even if you hated WYSIWYG programs, you'd probably be better off using a good WYSIWYG program than a poor type code program (and vice versa).

Finally, the question to WYSIWYG or not to WYSIWYG is merely one of many considerations you must take into account while deciding what sort of software to acquire. Indeed, it may actually turn out to be one of the least important considerations. Before buying a program, you should have asked certain questions, such as: What equipment do we have or are we likely to get? What experience do the people who will be operating this software have in areas such as page composition, design, document production, and typography? What computer experience have these people had? What kinds of documents do we need to produce? What level of quality must the final product achieve?

Given these considerations, it seems warranted to dispense with the question of which is better, and instead take a more fruitful approach. The first step is to become acquainted with the way these programs work, and with what they can and cannot do. In as much as WYSIWYG programs are covered in other essays in this book, we will concentrate here on the workings of type code programs. Once we have some idea of what type code programs are like, we can turn to considerations regarding the appropriateness of such a program.

To illustrate the operations of type code programs, three programs have been selected: TeX, DeskSet, and JustText. This selection does not constitute an endorsement of these programs. They have been chosen because they run on microcomputers and are representative of typesetting programs that employ some kind of type code system. While representative, they differ in several respects, and some of these differences will become apparent in the course of the discussion.

How Do Type Code Programs Work?

Almost all programs of this type operate similarly. The user prepares a file that contains the text to be typeset and the codes that govern the way in which the text will be set. This file is often called the input file. The codes that it contains are instructions for the typesetting program. When the input file is sent to the typesetting program, these codes are not printed, but are interpreted by the program and then discarded.

You can use any text editor to prepare your file as long as the editor can produce a file in a standard (or generic) format. Such a format (often called an ASCII file) is simply a file that contains nothing but the letters, digits, and punctuation marks found on the standard typewriter keyboard.

Here is an example of input, using the TeX convention. Examine the line of input: **Is Boswell's \itLife of Johnson\rm a difficult work?** You will notice the curious notations **\it** and **\rm.** These are instructions to the TeX program. In the TeX system, each instruction or code begins with a blackslash: this character (called an escape character in computer jargon) acts as a flag to TeX, informing the program (and the user) that what follows is an instruction and not text to be typeset. When TeX encounters such a code, it looks up the instruction in its memory and carries out the action associated with it. If TeX can't find it, it assumes that the instruction has been mistyped and reports an error.

In this particular example, the first code **(\it)** instructs TeX to shift to the italic font and to set everything from that point on in italic. The second instruction **(\rm)** tells the program to return to the Roman font. Depending on the font that is being used, the output of the above might be: Is Boswell's *Life of Johnson* a difficult work?

If you examined the input and output closely, you will have noticed that TeX made one alteration without being told to. The apostrophe in the input line was a straight one, but TeX automatically typesets it correctly as a closing, single quotation mark. TeX also changed the "fi" in "difficult" to the fi ligature. Most encoding systems will perform certain basic operations like this automatically, or by default. In a well-designed system, these default operations are appropriate in the majority of instances, but can be altered should special circumstances require it.

You may have also noted that the commands **\it** and **\rm** suggest the names "italic" and "roman." Type code conventions are often (but not always) mnemonic. The codes that a program uses constitute a vocabulary, and mnemonic codes help you to master it more quickly. In the case of TeX, as we will see, you can even generate your own system of codes. Table 18-1 gives a comparative overview of the codes that the three programs use to perform certain typographical actions.

A glance at Table 18-1 also shows the different conventions used for differentiating type codes from normal text. TeX uses a backslash character (although even this can be changed), JustText uses matching curly braces ({ and }) and DeskSet represents its codes either symbolically or inserts them between matching angled brackets (< and >).

Table 18-1   A Comparison of Typesetting Commands

Action	TeX	JustText	DeskSet
end paragraph	\par or blank line	{ql}	F10 key + <enter>
line length to *n* picas	\hsize—*n*pc	{m*n*}	<LL*n*>
page break	\eject	{pb}	<ALT>+F7
advance *n* points	\hskip—*n*pt	{a*n*}	<FP*n*>
leading	\baselineskip—	{l*n*}	<LS*n*>2
em dash	—3	{md}	
center *text*	\centerline {*text*}	*text*{qc}	*text*F8+ <enter>
shift to italic and back	\it text \rm	{f4}text{f6}	<FT7>text<FT5>
kern backward (once) 1.5 points	\kern -1.5pt	{ms-1500}	<BU8>4

Processing and Output

Once a file has been prepared, it is processed by a typesetting interpreter that is the heart of an encoding program. As it processes the input file, the interpreter may give the user some error messages if it "thinks" it has encountered a mistake, such as a misspelled instruction. Depending on the severity of the error, the processing may continue or be halted. In most cases, the user then corrects the mistakes in the input file and runs it through the interpreter again. This process is repeated until all errors that have to do with the syntax of the type codes have been corrected.

DeskSet is slightly different in this respect. Because the program's editor automatically inserts codes for you when you press function keys, it is unlikely that you will have syntax errors when you send the input file to the typesetting program. This, then, would spare you the debugging described in the previous paragraph.

Getting rid of syntax errors does not, of course, eliminate any genuine typesetting errors, such as accidentally setting an entire page in italic. The only way to correct these is to examine the printed result and make the corresponding changes in your input file.

The output that the interpreter produces is a sequence of instructions for the printing of the page. These instructions can be saved as a file on a disk or, in some cases, can be sent directly to a printing device. Additionally, TeX (on microcomputers) and DeskSet offer a WYSIWYG component: Their output can be previewed on the screen prior to printing, giving the user a chance to see a facsimile of the printed pages.

JustText generates a PostScript file that is intended for any device that has a PostScript interpreter, such as the Apple LaserWriter or the Linotronic 300. DeskSet can also produce a PostScript file, but has an option to generate code for Compugraphic phototypesetters. Accordingly, the output that these programs produce is intended for a specific set of printing devices.

TeX's output, on the other hand, is device independent, meaning that it describes a printed page without reference to any kind of printing device. These device-independent files (or DVI files, as they are called), can be moved to any computer environment and then processed for display on the screen, or for printing on laser printers or phototypesetters. The advantage of this approach is that TeX will always produce the same results no matter what kind of computer environment it is run in. TeX has been implemented on more than 50 kinds of computers worldwide.

Before we go on to discuss these programs in greater detail, it may be helpful to clarify the difference between a page description language (such as Adobe's PostScript, Imagen's DDL, and Xerox's Interpress) and a type code program. In most instances, page description language code is generated by a computer and is sent to a printing device. Its use is largely automated; hence the computer user will only rarely (and perhaps never) see the page description code or have to deal with it. Programmers, of course, will deal directly with page description languages. In most cases, however, their task is to write a program that will take care of the automatic generation of page description code. Once done, it will (or should) require no further human intervention. A type code program, on the other hand, is anything but automated. It is intended to be used directly by people who are not necessarily programmers. In short, a type code program furnishes a set of typographic tools for creative use.

The Finer Points of Type Code Programs

Now that we have some idea as to how type code programs work, we can turn our attention to some of their capabilities. It would be pointless merely to list all the things a type code program can do. Because such a program is capable of putting a glyph, or any possible typographical character, anywhere on a page, the limits of the program are set much more by human imagination and aesthetics than anything else. Given the right fonts, a program such as TeX or DeskSet can be used for extremely complex formats. It has been used to produce camera-ready copy for numerous books, essays, articles, and newsletters.

Rather than merely present a list or table of capabilities, it would seem much more useful to emphasize aspects that tend to make type code programs especially useful.

Dimensions

A general characteristic of type code programs is the capacity to place glyphs on a page with a high degree of exactitude using very fine dimensions. Since the program doesn't have to represent what it does on the screen, it can allow you to use finer increments. The importance of this point can be appreciated if you compare the resolution of a computer's screen and various printing devices.

Resolution is usually described in terms of pixels per inch. The term "pixel" is an abbreviation for "picture element" and is the smallest dot that a device is capable of turning on or off. The resolution of the Macintosh screen is 72 pixels per inch, hence it almost exactly corresponds to a printer's point. By contrast, the resolution of most desktop laser printers is 300 pixels per inch, slightly more than four pixels per printer's point. A phototypesetter may have as fine a resolution as

2,400 pixels per inch, which means that it can place roughly 33 pixels in a single printer's point. Accordingly, we can characterize the Macintosh screen as having a coarse resolution, the laser printer a low resolution and the phototypesetter a high resolution. This comparison makes it apparent that the results from any typesetting system that is bound to coarse resolution will be crude when compared with those from a system using low or high resolution.

For many (perhaps even most) of the operations performed in typesetting text, specifying placements — such as the length of a line — in terms of points or picas is adequate. Nevertheless, there are times when a finer placement is necessary. Most of the JustText commands, for example, require dimensions in picas or points. For the purpose of a more exact placement, the program provides a microspace command, allowing the specification of a movement that is one-thousandth point.

TeX allows its users to specify dimensions in a variety of ways. You can use the English system (inches), the metric system (centimeter and millimeter), or picas and points (for the classically minded, you can even specify dimensions in ciceros and Didôt points). You can specify fractional parts of any dimension; TeX doesn't "mind" being requested to move things one-thousandth point. Internally, TeX uses scaled points for its calculations. A scaled point is an unusually fine measurement, as there are 65,536 scaled points per single printer's point (and 100 scaled points is the length of a wave of light).

The dimensions considered above may be called absolute, because — in theory, at least — a dimension such as three picas will always be the same length. Often you can also specify relative dimensions as fractional portions of an em or an ex. These are dimensions whose actual length is relative to the font size currently in use, which means that specifications using these dimensions may work across a wide variety of fonts and font sizes (the TeX logo is a good example of this).

Kerning

Of what use are such fine dimensions? One important use is kerning. In order to improve the appearance and readability of words, the letters comprising them are sometimes moved closer together (or farther apart) than their natural width would allow. Kerning is the process of altering the natural spacing between letters.

Kerning is important for text type as well as for type sizes used in headlines and logos. You are probably already familiar with the concept of kerning in text type. Certain pairs of letters (such as *T* and the *y*) become more readable if the *y* is moved slightly closer to the *T*. Compare these two renderings of the same word.

AVAST   AVAST

Some type code programs will perform kerning automatically. DeskSet provides a table of kerning pairs for each font it works with. As the DeskSet interpreter examines the text of the input file, one of the things it looks for is a pair of characters that matches a pair in its kerning table. Once it has made such a match, it will kern the two characters in accordance with the metrics in the kerning table. You can activate or deactivate this feature, or even modify the kerning table. TeX operates in a very similar fashion, gleaning information on kerning from its font information.

The kerning command in JustText operates differently. Activating kerning reduces the white space between all letters, not just selected pairs. It is therefore a kind of universal kerning. This may be useful when space is a premium, or when an airy look is important.

The capacity to specify kerns anywhere in a document is important when working with computer-generated typefaces, particularly in the larger point sizes. Some computer printers will generate larger point sizes of a font using the same descriptions employed for the smaller sizes. While this approach has many advantages, its weakness is that distortions may be introduced at both the very small and very large sizes.

An example of this is PostScript. In the PostScript system, a font is stored as a set of outlines. To generate a font at a particular size, the outlines are expanded using certain ratios and then filled in. Accordingly, PostScript uses the same outlines to generate a 7 and a 700 point size of the same font. Note here the difference between 12 point and 54 point, using PostScript's Times-Italic.

FAST *FAST*

The large white space between the *F* and the *A* becomes easily noticeable in the larger point size (although already apparent in the 12 point size). Here then is an instance in which the employment of a kern is quite important: A user could reduce the white space and produce a more attractive result.

Since no automated system will cover every instance, type code programs often will allow you to kern by hand, that is, to explicitly call for a kern. To specify a kern in TeX, for example, you simply type **\cs{kern}** and give some dimension. A negative number would move backwards or to the left and a positive number would move to the right. For example, you might type **F\kern -.2em ast** in your input file, and the result would be that the letters *ast* would be moved two tenths of an em space closer to the *F*. (The example above shows the effect of a gradual increase in the amount of kerning.) JustText and DeskSet provide features that would permit you to produce the same result.

Ligatures

A topic related to kerning is that of ligatures. A ligature is a combination of letters that have been merged together to form a single unit. The improvement that a ligature offers may be apparent using an example.

find   find

Which one has the ligature? Obviously the second one does, and, just as obviously, the ligature enhances both the appearance and the readability of the word.

The most common ligatures used for English are the combinations *ff, fi, fl, ffi,* and *ffl.* Depending on the font it is using, TeX will automatically spot these combinations and substitute the corresponding ligature.

JustText and DeskSet do not provide such automatic support for ligatures. You can, however, substitute them manually in JustText by using a text editor's search-and-replace function.

Strangely enough, Adobe Systems provides only two ligatures in its PostScript fonts (the *fi* and *fl* combinations). Accordingly, programs that specifically support PostScript devices will not be able to provide for more than the two ligatures named above.

Macros

The entry of typesetting instructions can be wearisome, especially for repeated actions. For example, in JustText, you must take care to type the quad left command (**{ql}**) at the end of every paragraph, otherwise all your paragraphs will merge together. As you can imagine, this can become very repetitive. Although a text editor's search-and-replace function can relieve much of this tedium, a much more powerful approach is the use of macros.

Macros are a way of encoding a set of instructions under a single name. You can think of the name as an abbreviation for the set of instructions. When the typesetting interpreter encounters the abbreviation, it looks up the set of instructions associated with it and executes those instructions. These abbreviations are called macros. Both TeX and DeskSet have macro capability, although TeX's is much more robust.

Another advantage of the TeX macro system is that you can call your abbreviations anything you wish. Moreover, if the way a code is named doesn't make sense to you, you can very easily rename it. If, hypothetically, it was easier for you to think of the command **\italic** (instead of **\it**) to switch to the italic font, you can simply type **\let\italic=\it** and it's done.

Another advantage of the macro system is that it is often very easy to produce sweeping changes simply by defining a single new macro. Here's an example (taken from the *TeX book*): Suppose you have typeset a lengthy manuscript using an oblique font for emphasis. Now your tyrannical editor demands that you change all occurrences in the oblique font to italic. In a WYSIWYG system, you might well have to make each and every change individually. In TeX, you need to simply type **\def\oblique=\it}** at the beginning of your manuscript, and you're done (assuming that **\oblique** is the command to switch to the oblique font).

Using the macro facility, you can design commands that are very useful and powerful. Let's consider a second example: If you typeset a book, an operation you would perform fairly often is starting a new chapter. In TeX, you could define a macro (that you might call **\beginNewChapter**) that would do all of the following: insert a page break; make sure that the new chapter begins on an odd-numbered page; leave out the running head for the first page; set the chapter's title, leaving extra space above and below; adjust the running headers and footers for the new chapter; reset the footnote numbering to one; and make an entry for the chapter in a table of contents file. You can also define macros that act as "boilerplates," which are formats that are used repeatedly for such things as memos, letters, and tables.

The macro system in DeskSet is somewhat different. The program allows you to record as many as 1,000 keystrokes and save the "recording" under 1 of 8 function keys. Thereafter, pressing a function key will replay the recorded keystrokes in the file you are currently editing. Additionally, DeskSet can record your macros on disk, allowing you to reuse them for other files. You can then construct a macro that would be functionally equivalent to TeX's **\beginNewChapter**, although you would have to remember which of the 8 function keys you used for it.

Hyphenation

A key point concerning the readability of text is controlling the amount of whitespace that occurs. Generally, the amount of space between words should be fairly regular and not stretched or condensed too much. When justifying text, particularly with shorter line lengths (such as columns), it is important to be able to hyphenate words so as to reduce the amount of stretching and shrinking that is required.

All three of the programs under consideration approach hyphenation in a similar manner. In fact, JustText borrows TeX's hyphenation routines directly. In each case, the program is armed with rules for the hyphenation of English words and an exception dictionary. The dictionary is a collection of special-case words, and you can add words to it when necessary.

When TeX analyzes a paragraph and decides that it needs to hyphenate, the program will first look in the exception dictionary for the word. If it fails to find it there, TeX will consult its hyphenation patterns to select the hyphenation point. These patterns were the result of much study, and they appear to operate flawlessly for the 700 most common English words.

The English patterns are not built into TeX. Users can substitute their own patterns, which is obviously important if a language other than English is used.

The exception dictionary is important for a number of reasons. TeX's hyphenation rules are quite accurate for the most common English words, but writers will very often employ a special vocabulary that the rules may not cover accurately. In addition, because hyphenation rules for English may vary due to context, not all hyphenation points can be found by an automated system. For example, the word record can be hyphenated in two ways, depending on whether it is a verb or a noun. To make matters worse, certain dictionaries may sometimes disagree with others on where to hyphenate a word.

In TeX, you have two ways to assist the program to find the correct hyphenation points. The first is to type a discretionary hyphen, which acts much like a "soft" or condition hyphen in many word processing programs. You can type **re\-cord** or **rec\-ord**, depending on how you want TeX to position the hyphen. The second method is to add to the exception dictionary, which saves you the tedium of having to place a discretionary hyphen in every occurrence of a word. With TeX, you only need to type **\hyphenation{Nietz-sche Mon-taigne}** once in your file. From that point on, TeX will be able to correctly hyphenate the names Nietzsche and Montaigne.

The hyphenation capabilities of these programs may not be as important for short documents, in which you can carefully take care of hyphenation by hand. For longer publications, however, these hyphenation capabilities will be invaluable.

Special Effects

Special effects don't necessarily have to be spectacular, rarely used typographical feats to be important. For example, one of TeX's most important "bells and whistles" is so common that it's employed on nearly every page it typesets: TeX's system for breaking lines into paragraphs.

Most programs determine line breaks on the fly: When they arrive at right margin, they simply choose a breakpoint (or hyphenate) and then move on. As straightforward as this seems, this approach has a severe drawback: The program has no notion of the paragraph as a whole when it chooses a line break in this manner. It cannot, for example, detect that a breakpoint in line two may result in a bad line break in line nine. Indeed, such programs may have no notion at all about what constitutes a good or bad breakpoint. The result can often be a right margin that is too ragged, or a white rivers effect (vertical paths of white space that reduce the readability of the text).

TeX takes a different approach to this problem: It reads in all the text associated with a paragraph and then begins to decide the best way to place the line breaks. This means that the final words of a paragraph can influence the appearance of the first few lines (and vice versa). This enables TeX to distribute spacing adjustments over an entire paragraph (as opposed to a single line) and thereby minimize large, unsightly white space.

TeX's method for computing all this is a finely woven system of checks and balances, and Don Knuth, the author of TeX, has called this method "probably the most interesting aspect of the whole TeX system." This system consists of some 20 parameters that establish

TeX's standards for good and bad breakpoints. TeX uses these parameters when computing the best appearance of a paragraph, and a user can adjust any number of these parameters to suit the necessary requirements.

While such a feature is important, there are certainly instances in which a more razzle-dazzle effect is called for. Most typesetting programs offer some useful razzle-dazzle effects.

One example of this is the drop cap, the use of a large initial letter to begin a paragraph. Although TeX can do this, JustText conveniently provides a single command for this: {dc}. To use this command, you simply type the number of lines that should be indented and the letter to be used as the large capital. JustText computes the rest. For example, to specify this paragraph, you could type {dc20}.

A type code system will do many things by default; that is, it does things a certain way unless explicitly told to do otherwise. In a well-designed typesetting system, it is possible to suspend the defaults for special effects. TeX, for example, will allow you to change nearly all of its defaults (although, obviously, you should know what you're doing, or you may create a typographical monster). One of the defaults TeX permits you to alter is the shape of a paragraph. By using the **\parshape** command, you can specify paragraphs formatted in any arbitrary shape.

Obviously, the TeX code required to perform such typographical feats is not simple, and you need to have had some experience in working with TeX before taking on such a maneuver. It would be necessary, however, to have had experience with any program when attempting more challenging typographical constructs.

One use of such strange paragraph shapes might be for wrapping text around graphics, as the TeX examples suggest. A powerful feature in JustText, called art wrap, does exactly that. You can position a MacPaint file on a page, and JustText will indent its lines so as to avoid the MacPaint section of the page.

The inclusion of graphics is another important special effect. The development of page description languages, such as PostScript, has been very important because it allows the introduction of graphical elements on the typeset page with a facility that was not possible before.

The combination of text and graphics, however, calls for two types of expertise: You need both a typesetting program as well as a page description language. It would be highly inefficient, for example, to ask PostScript to perform the mathematical calculations associated with typesetting. While PostScript could do it (it is in fact a Turingequivalent language), that is certainly not what it was designed for. If, on the other hand, you combine the imaging capabilities of a language such as PostScript with a good typesetting program, the result is a very robust system indeed.

All three of the type code programs that have been mentioned in this essay take this approach. JustText has an "include any" command {**ia**}) that allows you to include or import up to two PostScript files per page. The program also includes some conversion utilities that convert files created by some graphics programs (such as MacPaint) to Post-Script format.

DeskSet can accept graphics files from a number of different devices and programs, including Lotus 1-2-3 graphics, and input from several desktop scanning devices. The user imports these files using the "virtual picture" command and specifies coordinates for the location of the graphics.

Although TeX produces device-independent files, it has a **\special** command that enables the user to pass on instructions directly to the printing device. In many of the microcomputer implementations of TeX, you can use this tool to include PostScript code and in this way supplement TeX's typesetting capabilities with PostScript graphics. Implementations of TeX on the Macintosh have taken advantage of the Mac's graphics capabilities. TeXtures, for example, includes a "picture window" with each TeX file, which makes it quite easy to include any Macintosh graphic item in your TeX documents.

WYSIWYG and Encoding

Now that we have become acquainted with type code programs, we can consider their usefulness in a broader context. Indeed, the notion of usefulness is the key issue, so our question might be: Under what circumstances and to whom would a type code program be useful?

Some type code programs will appeal to those who have had previous experience with phototypesetting equipment. Such a person will feel at home with JustText's and DeskSet's codes, such as quad left, superior (superscript). If you have had such experience, you will be able to learn to use JustText and DeskSet productively in a short period of time.

More generally, a type code program will appeal to those who like to have direct control over the fine points of their work. In other words, those who like "doing it themselves." In the JustText manual, William Bates makes an important point in this regard:

This is not a consumer product, and may never be. I'm not sure professional-quality graphics arts production can be "made simple." I think of the Macintosh user interface as something akin to an automatic transmission on a car. For a lot of people — perhaps the majority of people — it's fine. But there are a few people who need and want the level of control that a stick shift provides. This system — JustText — is for people who must have control over the LaserWriter and who care that extra percent about the quality of their output. The analogy of a car's transmission is apt. We have seen some of the ways in which type code programs allow you to "change gears" manually, instead of having a machine or somebody else make the decision for you.

Another consideration has to do with the abstract approach to typesetting that an encoding system entails. Since your input file contains text, codes, and numeric parameters, you are not visually constructing a page but rather doing it abstractly. It is analogous to the computer programmer who must imagine the way in which a program operates as the code is being designed. Obviously, this approach won't appeal to everyone. Typographer Richard Southall writes:

> Because graphic designers think visually, they need visual objects to think with: if the first task a designer has is to analyze the conceptual structure of a document, the second is to sketch out possible graphic embodiments for it.... The primitive concepts that are handled by computer text-formatting languages, the terms the languages use to describe them, and the commands with which they are manipulated, are all completely alien to the experience of traditionally educated designers.

This is an important point: The abstract or quantitative approach that characterizes encoding systems may not be appropriate for someone who must "think" in terms of visual objects. This is a key consideration, one which should weigh heavily in the decision concerning which program to buy.

Yet it would be well to make a further distinction. The term "desktop publishing" is actually a fuzzy concept, since a variety of different tasks are lumped together under a single term, and this can be misleading. Professional book and document production calls for the teamwork of a variety of experts, such as a designer, copy editor, production editor, and perhaps an illustrator. A single person rarely has the skill to accomplish "publishing" all alone.

Hence you must keep in mind which of these tasks is going to be done by the person using the typesetting program. While it may be important for a designer to work in visual terms, it may actually be more advantageous to implement the designer's specifications using a nonvisual system. Since a designer delivers a set of specifications, it may be easier to implement them using a type code system that makes it very easy to encode the designer's specifications: regarding line length and leading, for example.

The appeal of an on-screen typesetting program is obvious. Yet it is possible to become obsessed with the WYSIWYG aspect so as to lose sight of the actual goal, which is the printed page. We have already seen how coarse most computer displays are when compared even to low-resolution printers, such as laser printers based on the Canon LBX engine. A screen representation can only convey a facsimile, that is, convey an impression of the final product. This is not to deny the usefulness of on-screen representation, but nevertheless, the proof of the pudding remains the printed pages. Given current display technologies, is it impossible for the screen even closely to represent the final printed result. This means that for all the on-screen work you might do, you will always have to proof your work by printing it out. Some WYSIWYG programs limit their printed output to what they can display on the screen, and in this case WYSIWYG may become "What You See Is All That You Get."

Another factor concerns the kind of document you will be producing. Type code systems are particularly useful for longer documents, such as books, monographs, and essays, in which you must produce a large number of fairly uniform pages. As we have seen, it is relatively easy to use type codes to set up a set of specifications that the program will follow automatically page after page.

Summary

A type code program is a system in which you use a command structure to determine page layout, as opposed to moving typographic units that are visually represented. Currently, the advantages that a type code program generally offers are a finer control of the placement of typographic elements on the page, an abstract approach to page construction that encourages consistency, macro facilities, automatic hyphenation, and the capacity to change system defaults directly.

When considering the acquisition of any kind of computer equipment, a rule of thumb is to first identify the programs that will enable you to get your work done and then acquire the hardware and additional software needed to make those programs run. This rule certainly applies to page composition software. The key is to match the capacities of the program to the skills, training, and preferences of the people who would be using it, as well as to the level of typographic quality you must achieve.

This is why, in the end, it is a mistake to think of this choice merely in in terms of WYSIWYG versus type encoding. Rather, the important point is to make a successful match so that you can do productive and satisfying work.

About the Typesetting Programs

TeX is a computer-based typesetting system developed at Stanford University by Professor Donald Knuth. The name of the program consists of the uppercase form of the Greek letters tau, epsilon, and chi, the Greek word for art and technology. While TeX may be used as a general typesetting program, its particular forte is its capability to typeset mathematics and other technical notations. Until 1984, TeX was available primarily on mainframe and minicomputers. Since that time a number of implementations for microcomputers have appeared, including two for the IBM PC and compatibles, and two for the Macintosh.

For the IBM PC:

PCTeX
Personal TeX
20 Sunnyside Ave., Suite H
Mill Valley, CA 94941
(415) 388-8853
Suggested retail: $249

MicroTeX
Addison-Wesley
Jacob Way
Reading, MA 01867
(617) 944-6795
Suggested retail: $295

For the Macintosh:

MacTeX
FTL Systems, Inc.
234 Eglinton Ave. E, Suite 205
Toronto, Ontario Canada M4P 1K5
(416) 487-2142
Suggested retail: $750

TeXtures
Addison-Wesley
Jacob Way
Reading, MA 01867
(617) 944-6795
Suggested retail: $495

The DeskSet program is based on the Horizon Composition Management System, a program for controlling Compugraphic and Varityper phototypesetters. DeskSet runs on the IBM PC, PC XT, or PC AT (or compatible) and requires 512K of RAM and a Hercules graphics card for the previewing program (a version for the IBM EGA should be available by the time you read this). A mouse is recommended but not required. The author wishes to thank David Price of G. O. Graphics for his kind assistance. For further information, contact:

G. O. Graphics
18 Ray Avenue
Burlington, MA 01803
(617) 229-8900
Suggested retail: $995

JustText was written by William Bates. To run the program, you need a Macintosh Plus, a 512K Mac or a Mac XL. Since the program generates PostScript code, you will also need a printer that has a PostScript interpreter. For further information, contact:

Knowledge Engineering
G.P.O. Box 2139
New York, NY 10116
(212) 473-0095
Suggested retail: $195

Bibliography

Baxter, John. *Macintosh Desktop Typography*. 1986.

Craig, James. *Designing with Type*. New York: Watson-Guptill Publications, 1980.

Crider, W. "Typeset like a Pro." *Publish*, Volume 2, No. 2 (March 1987). A review of G. O. Graphic's DeskSet.

Edwards, Stephen. "DeskSet: Low-Cost System for Quality Composition." *The Seybold Report on Desktop Publishing*, Volume 1, No. 5 (January 26, 1987), pp. 21–34.

Furuta, Richard and Pierre McKay. "Two TeX Implementations for the IBM PC." *Dr. Dobb's Journal,* Volume 10, Issue 9, September 1985, p. 68ff.

Knuth, Donald E. "Mathematical Typography." In: *TeX and Metafont, New Directions in Typesetting*. Bedford: Digital Press, 1979.

———— *The TeXbook*. Addison-Wesley, Boston, 1982.

Liang, Frank. *Word Hy-phen-a-tion by Com-put-er.* Technical Report STAN-CS-83-977, Stanford Department of Computer Science, Stanford, California, 1983.

Southhall, Richard. "First Principles of Typographic Design for Document Production." In *TUGBoat* (journal for the TeX Users Group), Volume 5, No. 2, 1984, pp. 79–90.

Varian, Hal. "PCTeX and MioTeX." *BYTE,* Volume 11, Number 4, April 1986, p. 267ff.

KEYWORDS:

• Device In-
  dependence

• Page Descrip-
  tion Language

• Operator

• Coordinate
  System

• Rotation and
  Translation

Mitchell Waite is a coffeecake hound who spends most of his time in bistros flirting with women and dreaming of being a famous publishing magnate who lives on a beach in the Bahamas. He is the well-known originator of the "parachute" look, and claims to be able to go hang-gliding just by waving his arms.

Essay Synopsis: PostScript is the standard page description language that is built into most of the printers used in desktop publishing today. If you are a programmer or desktop publishing power user, you can benefit from understanding Post-Script and how to use it. Ultimately, the printing software will convert all your documents to Post-Script code before it sends them to the printer, so understanding the rich command structure of PostScript can give you greater mastery over your printed output.

In this essay the author explains how Post-Script and other page description languages work and presents the important concept of device in-dependence followed by a tutorial on writing PostScript programs. You will learn about the most important PostScript operators, page coordinate system, font definition and caching, shading and filling, rotating and translating im-ages, and getting special effects.

19

Introduction to PostScript

Mitchell Waite

PostScript is a new computer "language" created by Adobe Systems, Inc. PostScript is not a general purpose high-level computer language, like Pascal or FORTRAN, but rather a language for printing both high-quality text as well as graphics special effects on high-resolution laser and phototypesetting printers. PostScript, as we shall learn in this essay, is a "page description language" or PDL. PDLs have revolutionized the way application programs deal with printing text and graphics. Coupled with the new breed of low-cost laser printers, PDLs (such as PostScript and others) allow a new idea in printing called device independence, which is one of the primary driving forces behind the desktop publishing boom.

This essay provides an overview of some of the features and power of the new PostScript page-composition language that is quickly becoming a standard in the industry. This is not a complete language tutorial but an overview followed by a fish-eye view of the fundamental graphic effects that can be accomplished with the PostScript language. Along the way we will learn more about what a page description language is, using PostScript as the example.

PostScript has some particularly important features. It allows arbitrary shapes to be constructed from commands (Adobe calls them operators) that produce straight lines, arcs, and curves. PostScript has routines that allow a shape to be outlined with

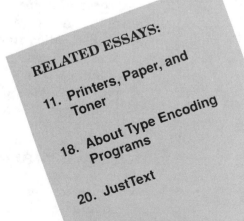

RELATED ESSAYS:

11. Printers, Paper, and Toner

18. About Type Encoding Programs

20. JustText

any line thickness, filled with any color (PostScript is already set up to handle color and shades, however most laser printers allow only black and white right now), or used as a sort of window to crop or isolate any of the other PostScript drawing commands (called a clipping path). Text may be treated as graphic objects and operated on by any of the PostScript graphics commands. PostScript has an *x-y* coordinate system that supports various combinations of scaling, rotation, reflection, skewing, and linear translation. In this essay we will cover drawing lines, drawing graphic objects (such as rectangles), filling with shades, rotation and translation, paths, printing, and imaging. Due to space limitations/considerations we will not cover some of the more esoteric or less often-used aspects of PostScript including arcs; curves; clipping; arrays; transforms on fonts, dashes, and miter joints; or modifying fonts. We also are not going to cover the more advanced operators in PostScript; they are more likely to be used only by a very motivated graphics designer, and belong in a programming book.

It is important to keep in mind that PostScript has over 250 operators that can manipulate graphics images. This is far more than most classic programming languages like Pascal, BASIC, and C. For example the C language has about 20 commands, while BASIC has about 50 to 100. In PostScript, practically all of these commands are devoted to manipulating graphics and text, whereas classic languages are more general purpose and are designed to manipulate all kinds of variables and objects. Therefore, PostScript is lacking in ways that would make it useful for general-purpose programs and is best viewed as "a page description language with general-purpose programming language underpinnings" as described in the *PostScript Language Reference Manual* (Addison-Wesley, 1985).

PostScript's syntax most resembles the FORTH language, which has somewhat of a cult attraction among programmers due to its extreme efficiency. PostScript (and FORTH) uses what is called postfix notation: Operations on numbers are given after the numbers (postfix is also called Reverse Polish Notation or RPN). So to add two numbers, you type 2 2 +, rather than the familiar 2 + 2. The examples given in this essay are so simple, you won't have to worry about postfix; but keep in mind that if you decide to learn to program in PostScript, this notation will take some getting used to.

Before We Start: Why Bother To Learn PostScript?

While we don't believe that PostScript programming will become as popular as desktop publishing tools such as PageMaker or Ventura

Publisher, we do think it will often be desirable to use a special-effect routine written in PostScript, or to understand some PostScript code so it can be modified. Indeed, a market for PostScript special effects is already developing, and some word processors, such as Microsoft Word 3.0 for the Macintosh, allow PostScript procedures to be inserted into the text. Therefore, by understanding the big-picture aspects of Post-Script you can easily move these special effects in and out of your text, modify them, and tweak them to fit your special needs.

For example, with a little knowledge of PostScript you can confidently type in the code from the page of a magazine that contains a PostScript special effect, such as a starburst effect, output it to your printer, and fix any glitch or bug that comes up. If you can figure out how the code works, you can modify it so, for example, the starburst has more radial lines or a smaller diameter. Or how about PostScript templates for forms, newsletters, and the like? You can go in and change these with your programming skills, so that the headline of a newsletter, for example, contains the name of your company instead of the dummy one, and is printed in a different point size.

PostScript: A Page Description Language

A page description language (PDL) is a set of commands that control the way text and graphics appear on a printed page. (There are signs that PDLs also may be suitable for drawing to a screen, and some companies, such as Sun Microsystems, are inventing PostScript–based operating systems using this idea.) A PDL interpreter is usually placed inside the printer in Read Only Memory (ROM). Along with a controlling microprocessor, the PDL in ROM executes commands that are sent to it, such as **144 72 lineto**, which draws a line; **/Times-Roman findfont**, which changes the font to Times Roman; and **(Pizza) show**, which prints out the word Pizza in the Times Roman font. Much of what we will say about PostScript applies to other PDLs as well.

PostScript, and for that matter any PDL, is capable of forming high-quality text fonts, such as the type found in newspapers and books, by using special mathematical functions. Although we won't go into the fine details of how this process works, you can think of Post-Script as taking incoming commands, such as **lineto** and **arc**, converting them to dots, and then "painting" these dots on an electronic page. The page of dots is actually stored in another memory device inside the printer. When the laser printer prints, it uses the information in the memory to figure out where to place a black dot on the page. The dots are represented as tiny electric charges placed over the paper as it moves through the laser printer. The charged paper passes through a cloud of graphite, and the graphite is attracted to the electric charges. The result is little black dots so close together you need a magnifying glass to see them. A similar set of events occurs with the phototypesetting printer device, but instead of dots of graphite a tiny beam of light is used to expose photosensitive paper, which is later developed. This technique leads to resolutions of up to 4,400 dots per inch.

One of the main beauties of printing to a PDL-type printer is that the printing application (such as the word processor or spreadsheet) does not have to be concerned about what the resolution of the printer is. The PDL output will print at the highest quality of the printer, and if the program outputs to a different printer, no special programming must be done. This is called device independence. This may not seem profound at first, but up until now there has been no way to print high-resolution graphics without completely modifying the program to fit each printer device. This has slowed down the development of applications. We'll say more on this shortly.

It is important to understand that today's application programs don't produce PostScript automatically. They must be modified to create a valid PostScript program. But for programs that output chiefly text, this is not a complex modification, and a simple driver may be created to convert the native output of an application so it can drive a PDL printer. Most PDL printers have a default mode that lets them emulate a Diablo 630 impact printer, allowing such features as double strike, bold, and underline.

Figure 19-1 shows the steps as the output from an application, such as a word processor or drawing program, goes into the PDL driver and then into the laser printer. The PostScript code is sent from the driver to the PostScript interpreter, which does the work of converting the graphic commands to actual dots in the bit map. Finally the laser engine turns the dots in the bit map into ink dots on the page.

You may be wondering why manufacturers would go to so much trouble to put the PDL inside the printer. Why not just build the PDL function into the application program and make the program, rather than PostScript, build the bit map? Wouldn't this make the printer cheaper because it would not contain a large amount of memory, the microprocessor, and ROMs?

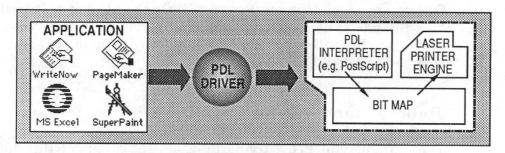

Figure 19-1. Following text from application to printing.

Device Independent PostScript

Putting a PDL inside a printer allows an old but important idea to finally come of age: device independence. As we said earlier, for the first time the new PDLs, such as PostScript, allow the application to ignore the type and resolution of the printer. This means that the application can output its PDL code, and the attached printer will simply perform the functions to the best of its ability: The resolution of the final output will be as high quality as the printer can accomplish. If you can send a PostScript file to a 300-dot-per-inch laser printer or a 4,000-dot-per-inch phototypesetter, no change in the PDL code sent to the printer needs to be made. This means that if you write a program that outputs PostScript code, the program will work with any printer — regardless of manufacturer or resolution — that understands Post-Script. This is why it is a good idea to put PostScript inside the printer. It allows the application programmer to forget the printer compatibility problem and to get high-quality output through high-level language statements, rather than having to worry about bit-map conversion. Basically, PostScript inside the printer saves each application programmer many man-years of development time; the Adobe developers have already done all the work and perfected the code (Post-Script is almost 100 percent bug free).

Device independence also means that there is a universal way to transport and store computer graphics output. The PostScript language is a new intermediary in the graphics industry — a program with no output device can output the PostScript code to a file. This file can then be taken to a remote printer that is compatible with Post-Script, and the output can be printed. Or the file can be transferred over the telephone lines and printed at a remote laser printer for a customer, eliminating the need for hard copy to be mailed and somewhat simulating a FAX machine.

Today's Standards for Page Description Language

There are several PDLs trying to attain the status of the standard PDL — the one that most printer manufacturers embrace and the one that most applications talk to. The one farthest ahead and already adopted by a large majority of printer manufacturers is PostScript, which was created by Adobe Systems early in the development of the laser printer technology. Apple Computer was the first company to license PostScript in 1976; they placed it inside the Apple LaserWriter printer. Coupled with the Apple Macintosh computer, the LaserWriter allowed beautiful high-quality results with certain software products (such as MacDraw and PageMaker) and was the beginning of the desktop publishing revolution. This was a major coup for Adobe Systems, and eventually more than 25 printer manufacturers adopted PostScript, while all the major software companies began making their programs output PostScript code. The biggest coup came in early 1987 when IBM endorsed PostScript, sending a clear message that it was the new standard.

The second significant PDL comes from a company called Imagen. Called DDL for document description language, DDL works much like PostScript and even accepts PostScript files, only it has a few special tricks. It has been adopted by Hewlett-Packard as the standard page description language for their LaserJet line of laser printers. One thing DDL offers that PostScript doesn't is font tables with definitions in several, rather than one, font size. PostScript uses a single font character table for each font that contains a mathematical description of the font. PostScript applies transformations to it to come up with all other font sizes. This means that the same template is used for the 8-point version as for the 80-point version. DDL uses several tables to hold font descriptions in different point sizes, which allows the font information to be optimized for different sizes, giving higher-quality characters. Hewlett-Packard has thrown itself behind DDL and is offering a PC add-in board that will control its LaserJet series of printers. Since IBM and Apple are behind Adobe, one can only wonder why

Hewlett-Packard choose DDL. Perhaps because it did not want to be considered "part" of that alliance. DDL offers the user the same features as PostScript, but offers programmers more confusion as now there are two kinds of printer languages to support. Since DDL can accept PostScript code this may be an issue only when a developer wishes to take advantage of DDL's special features. *(Hewlett-Packard recently announced it will offer PostScript in its new printers. — Ed.)*

The third important PDL is the command language built into the Hewlett-Packard LaserJet printer, called PCL for printer command language. The LaserJet was the first low-cost laser printer on the market and today most laser printer manufacturers offer PCL as a default, calling it the HP emulation mode. PCL differs from PostScript and DDL in the way fonts are created and in the amount of control that users have in manipulating graphic images. DDL and PostScript create outline fonts; PCL creates bit-mapped fonts. PCL stores patterns of the bit-mapped fonts in ROM cartridges in particular font sizes. PCL can't create odd font sizes like DDL and PostScript, and therefore is not as powerful. PCL requires that the application programs do a lot of the work compiling a complex page. PCL is good for traditional word processing and simple desktop publishing, while PostScript and DDL are better for complex page layouts.

Introduction to PostScript: Some Basics

Now that you have the basics of PDLs in mind, let's learn a few fundamentals of PostScript so that you can follow the program examples. We'll look at the way PostScript lays out a page, the way PostScript acts as a language, and some terminological details.

Organization and Layout of the PostScript Page

Recall that we said that PostScript is used to draw on an electronic page. This is an ideal way to visualize the operation performed by the PostScript code. You use the commands to build up a series of dots on the electronic page. Then when you instruct the printer to print the page with the PostScript **showpage** operator (we'll show all the PostScript commands in bold from now on), the dots you built up become black dots on the final page that comes out of the printer. Thus, when you send a command to PostScript to draw a line, PostScript will draw the line as a series of dots. The entire page's resolution is dependent on the printer in use. In the case of the Apple LaserWriter, with a resolution of 300 dots per inch, an 8½ by 11 inch page is made up of a grid of dots, with 2,550 horizontally and 3,300 dots vertically. This is a total of 2,550 by 3,300 or 8,415,000 dots on the page! Eight million is a pretty large number. A one-megabyte MacPlus has 16 million bits of memory, so you can figure a LaserWriter must have at least the equivalent of a MacPlus in memory capacity (actually the LaserWriter Plus has eight megabytes of ROM, much more than the MacPlus or Macintosh SE with 128K and 256K respectively). If you could hand draw one dot on a page every second, it would take you about 97 days to fill the entire page.

Of course if the printing device is a Linotronic L-300 phototypesetting machine, the resolution can be as high as 2,400 dots per inch. In this case, the print quality will be fantastic and graphic objects will be super sharp. On more complex printers a dot can be set to a particular shade of gray.

Drawing Graphics Objects in PostScript

PostScript can draw objects of all kinds, including lines, arcs, boxes, polygons, and circles. In this section we will see how to draw a line, a rectangle, a filled box, and a group of gray-shaded boxes. From this simple set of graphics programs you can see the basic techniques that are used almost all the time.

A Simple Program — Draw a Line

We are going to take an approach to teaching you PostScript that is unlike the traditional programming tutorials, where a ton of fundamentals are presented, followed by techniques for using them. Usually you forget all the fundamentals and the examples seem overwhelming. Instead we will present the language via examples, letting the new concepts be introduced at that point. Here is an example that draws a vertical line one point wide in PostScript:

```
% Example 19-1: Draw a one point wide line.
% Author: Mitchell Waite.
% Date: April 9, 1987.

gsave
newpath
```

```
    144 72 moveto
    144 432 lineto
stroke
grestore
showpage
end
```

The first few lines of the program preceded by the percent signs are "comments" in PostScript and have no effect on the program other than taking up space. They are to let anyone using the program understand what it does, who wrote it, and when. There can be more comments, but this should be the minimum.

The first PostScript command is **gsave**, pronounced *gee-save*. This command makes PostScript save the current state of the graphics environment. There is a matching graphics statement, **grestore** (pronounced *gee-restore*), that restores the state. The environment refers to the state of the PostScript coordinate system, how much it has been rotated, translated, scaled, and what previous paths may have been defined. (We'll get to paths in a moment.) When we use **gsave/grestore** we are making sure our program is nonintrusive on any previous conditions that the last program may have set up (should it not have used a **gsave/grestore** first). For example, if the last person using the laser printer set up a certain coordinate system with a PostScript file and did not use **gsave/grestore**, our program would end up using that old coordinate system, which would probably mess up our output. If we use a **gsave/grestore** we avoid this potential problem.

Coordinate System for PostScript Revisited

Every device that has a built-in PostScript interpreter has its own unique coordinate system that is used to access all the points on the page. There are 72 points in an inch, thus the top of the 8½ by 11 inch page is at 792 (72 x 11), the left side of the page is at 612 points (72 x 8.5), and the center of the page is $x=306$ points, $y=396$ points. Figure 19-2 shows the standard PostScript coordinates. Note that this is the coordinate system expressed in standard typograph points (where one point equals ½ inch).

The built-in coordinate system is called the device space and it varies from printer to printer. The device space origin can be anywhere on the page; paper moves through different printers in different directions; and devices have different resolutions. Coordinates

Figure 19-2. The coordinate system for PostScript.

specified in PostScript refer to an ideal coordinate system that always bears the same relationship to the current page regardless of the output device on which printing will be done. This space or coordinate system is called the user space, as it is the coordinate system that the program refers to. PostScript automatically makes the transformation from the user space to device space and the programmer rarely has to consider device space (again, this is device independence).

PostScript can manipulate the user space in three ways. It can move the coordinate system's origin to any other point in the user space, even outside the limits of the page. Thus 0,0 can be moved to the center of the page, making the lower left-hand corner a negative position. The axis of this origin can be rotated to any degree from 0 to 360. Finally the coordinate system may be scaled differently in the x and y directions; so for example, moving two units in x is the same as one unit in y.

Getting back to our vertical line example, the next statement after **gsave** is **newpath**. A path is an invisible outline of an object and is the basic way that PostScript handles objects and fonts. PostScript can build paths, and then once they are built it can fill these with a pattern or color, or stroke the path, which means to give it a specific line thickness and line pattern.

The **newpath** operator tells PostScript to initialize a path, which means setting it to empty (no pattern or line thickness defined for it) and having no starting point. You will see **newpath** used often.

The next statement, **144 72 moveto**, causes PostScript to move its "current location" to the coordinates x=144, y=72, which is at the bottom of the page. Current location is the coordinates of the last operation that PostScript performed. As an analogy you can think of **moveto** as moving a mouse cursor but not doing any drawing. The next statement, **144 432 lineto**, causes a path to be drawn from x=144, y=72 to x=144, y=432 which is a vertical path. Most graphics are first drawn as a path. The next command, **stroke**, actually draws our line in the PostScript bit map, filling it with the current color which is always a default of black, but could be white or invisible.

The final program statement is **showpage**. This instructs the PostScript printer to process the program and run the actual page of paper through its laser engine. The bit-map information in the memory of the printer is used to transfer images to the page. Figure 19-3a shows the output from the vertical line program.

The three steps to almost every PostScript drawing you will see over and over are:

- Construct a path made up of newpath, moveto, and lineto.
- Stroke (or paint) that path.
- Print the page with showpage.

Draw a Box and Fill It

This next example shows how to draw a box and vary the border width.

```
% Example 19-2: Draw a box and change border width.
% Introduces relative movement.
% Author: Mitchell Waite.
% Date: April 9, 1987.

gsave
newpath
   270 72 moveto
   0 72 rlineto
   72 0 rlineto
   0 -72 rlineto
   -72 0 rlineto
4 setlinewidth
stroke
grestore
showpage
end
```

This program should be easy to figure out. The output, as shown in Figure 19-3b, is a simple box with thick sides. The first **moveto**

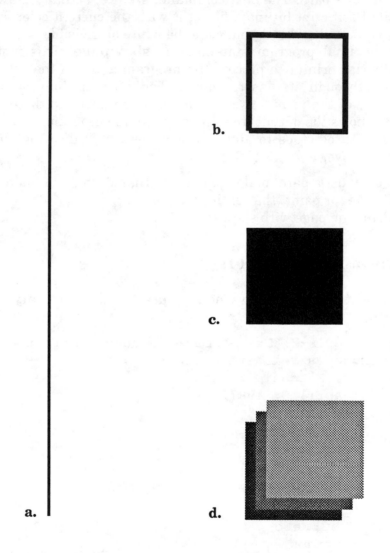

Figure 19-3. Drawing rules and boxes using PostScript.

statement locates the starting position for the box. Four **rlineto** statements are used to make the path for the box. The **rlineto** statement means relative move, so its two values are displacements, rather than absolute coordinates as in the **moveto** and **lineto**. Thus the statement **0 72 rlineto** makes a path for stroking 0 points from x and 72 points from y. Thus the line is drawn up from $x=270$, $y=72$ to $x=270$, $y=144$.

After the path for the box is set by the four consecutive rlineto's, the **setlinewidth** statement is executed with a 4, which means make the line width 4 points wide, which is ¼₇₂ inches, about ⅟₁₈ inch. Finally, the **stroke** command fills the current path with black and **showpage** prints it. Note that the **gsave** and **grestore** make sure that our change in line width is local to our program and leaves the current width at its default 1-point width. Now you can see that stroking a path means filling the path (in this case a rectangular path) with a solid black line, in this case 4-points wide. The path is a ghostlike entity that floats over the coordinate system waiting for a command to materialize.

Did you notice the notch in the lower left corner of the box? This is caused by the fact that we have not set the endcap of the lines. PostScript is set up so the path is in the center of any line you draw; increasing the thickness adds it from the middle outward, but the end of the line ends abruptly. So when the paths finally end, there is a unit square that does not get filled in. We will see how to fix this in the next example.

Draw a Filled Black Box

In the next example we draw a box and fill it with black. The program is almost exactly like the previous program, except for the commands **closepath**, **setgray**, and **fill**, and the fact that one of the **rlineto** commands is missing. The path for this square is started at a different location with a **moveto**, then three **rlineto** commands make the paths for three legs of the square. The last leg is closed with the **closepath** command, which simply draws a straight line segment to the first point of the path but uses a mitered joint, which eliminates the notch. You can also add the statement **2 setendcap** to the beginning of Example 19-2, which will make the default end of the lines a mitered joint instead of a butted joint.

```
% Example 19-3: Draw a filled black box.
% Author: Mitchell Waite.
```

```
% Date: April 9, 1987.
gsave
newpath
    270 216 moveto
    0 72 rlineto
    72 0 rlineto
    0 -72 rlineto
closepath
0 setgray
fill
grestore
showpage
end
```

The command **0 setgray** sets the fill color to black (0 is black, 1 is white, and values in between are shades of gray). Now a path has been drawn similar to the path we drew for the outlined box. Instead of stroke, we use the fill command so the current path is filled with the current color, giving us a black box. Fantastic, no?

Shades of Gray

In this example we draw three boxes and fill them with different shades of gray. Although the program is longer, it is not much more complex.

```
% Example 19-4: Draws three boxes — fill with shades.
% Author: Mitchell Waite.
% Date: April 9, 1987.
gsave
newpath
    270 360 moveto
    0 72 rlineto
    72 0 rlineto
    0 -72 rlineto
closepath
.2 setgray
fill

newpath
    278 368 moveto
    0 72 rlineto
```

```
   72 0 rlineto
   0 -72 rlineto
closepath
.4 setgray
fill

newpath
   286 376 moveto
   0 72 rlineto
   72 0 rlineto
   0 -72 rlineto
closepath
.6 setgray
fill

grestore
showpage
end
```

This program should be easy to figure out because there are no new statements. Three boxes are drawn, each eight points above and to the right of the one before it. Each box is drawn with a different shade of gray by using the **setgray** command. The **setgray** command is used to control the current color parameter, with intermediate two-digit decimal values corresponding to intermediate shades of gray. Note in the final output that each box we paint completely paints over the box underneath it; the result of opaque paint only in PostScript. If PostScript had provided a transparent paint we could do interesting mixes of shades and patterns. This will be especially missed on upcoming color laser printers. The fill and stroke commands are opaque; that is, they have no transparency and none of the color or shades underneath show through.

Sidelobe Issue: Color Is Built into PostScript

There are two other PostScript color control statements called **sethsbcolor** (set the hue, saturation, and brightness) and **setrgbcolor** (set the red-green-blue percentages). We won't go into them here, but it is nice to know that PostScript is set up for not one but two different color models, and when color laser printers appear, PostScript will work with them. Moreover, if companies start using PostScript to display graphics to the screen (as Sun Microsystems has done with NeWS), it will be easy to make these graphics in color.

In our program we use the values .2, .4, and .6 for the grayness in the **setgray** command. The whole story on how many different shades of gray you can get using PostScript is quite involved. Gray is made by controlling the spacing and number of dots in a unit area on the printed page, and because this is at a limited resolution, the gray pattern is not a perfect rendition of gray. On a LaserWriter, halftones are particularly rendered poorly, and shades of gray are not as high-quality as you would want. Certain PostScript gurus have figured out how to get many more possible combinations of gray out of PostScript using some special math. You can read more about this in the Adobe manuals and PostScript journals.

Figure 19-3d shows the final output from the Shades program. The trick to doing shadows in PostScript is hidden in this program. To do a shadow you simply redraw the object several times, moving it a tiny amount and filling it with a different shade of gray each time. The final time you draw the object, you draw it in white **(setgray=1)** — draw its outline so it covers all the other shades from the previous drawn objects, thus leaving just a trail of gray changes behind it. We will see how to exploit this soon with text.

Text in PostScript

Manipulating text in PostScript is very much like drawing graphics. You can think of PostScript text characters as graphic-outlined paths that can be filled, outlined, both filled and outlined, scaled, rotated, and translated (we will see this later). Note we did not say print text. It's funny, but even though PostScript outputs to paper, the word "print" is not even in the PostScript language definition.

The definitions that make up a font in PostScript actually are kept in a dictionary. A dictionary contains definitions of how to draw character shapes in a specific typeface. For example, the Times Roman dictionary tells PostScript how to draw characters in the Times Roman font. For each font typeface only one standard set of shapes is stored in the dictionary. More exactly, a PostScript font dictionary contains the mathematical definitions for a font that is one unit high, which is one point (or $\frac{1}{72}$ inch). In other words, each letter is one point tall. Why? Because PostScript can then get any point size from this unit font by scaling it mathematically. This is accomplished with the **scalefont** command. So, for example, the PostScript command **15 scalefont** would take the unit-size-selected font and scale it up to a 15 point size. A font is made current by giving its name preceded by a slash (/).

Also contained in the font dictionary is the width of each character of a font. The **show** command positions each character according to this width.

Font Caching

When the name of a font is encountered by the PostScript interpreter, it caches the font. This means that PostScript copies the unit font descriptions from a ROM and calculates the newly scaled, sized font in its particular style through a process known as scan conversion. Scan conversion produces a pixel map of the font. It then stores the pixel map in a temporary memory. This conversion consumes a fair amount of processing time because of all the math involved. If a scan conversion had to be done each time a new character changed its font metrics, printing might be very slow. The PostScript caching mechanism is based on the idea that a page usually contains many repetitions of the same character in a given font, size, and orientation. The number of distinct characters is very much smaller than the total number of characters. So once a font is cached, typically it is 1,000 times faster to draw than scan conversion from the character description in the font. *(Two excellent books on the topic are* Principles of Interactive Computer Graphics, *William M. Newman and Robert F. Sproull, McGraw-Hill, Inc., 1978 and* Fundamentals of Interactive Computer Graphics, *James D. Foley and A. Van Dam, Addison-Wesley Publishing Company, Inc., 1982.* Principles *is the perfect starting point for anyone who wants to understand raster scanning and graphic algorithms.* Fundamentals *lacks the simplicity and clarity of writing of the Newman/Sproull book, but makes up for it with incredible detail on many more subjects. — Ed.)*

Printing a Font

Printing a font is extremely simple in PostScript, as Example 19-5 shows. This example selects the Times Roman font from the font dictionary with the statement **/Times-Roman findfont**. It then sets it to 15 point, moves to the location $x=36$, $y=144$ and then displays (prints) the word **typo.icon.ography** with the show command. Note that the name of the font in the program must match exactly the name of the font inside the printer or font cartridge, and these names usually do not match their counterparts display in the font menu of a program.

For example, you see the name Times on the Apple font menu for MacWrite, not Times Roman. Likewise, Bookman on the Apple Mac-Write menu is called Bookman-Demi in the Apple LaserWriter. (The fonts on the screen of the Macintosh are bit-map approximations of the font dictionaries that are in PostScript. The Macintosh screen is 72 dots per inch and the LaserWriter is 300 dots per inch, so the screen fonts can't exactly match the final spacing of the PostScript fonts that are printed.) You can find out the exact names stored in the printer by using another PostScript command or by looking them up in the standard Adobe font catalog.

```
% Example 19-5: "Showing" a font.
% This example prints (shows) the word
typo.icon.ography
% in 15 point Times-Roman type
% Author: Mitchell Waite.
% Date: April 9, 1987.

gsave
/Times-Roman findfont 15 scalefont setfont
36 144 moveto
(typo.icon.ography) show
grestore
```

The output of this program is shown in Figure 19-4a.

Changing Font Size

Printing text in different point sizes and differing locations is straight-forward in PostScript, and produces very high-quality output on a 300-dots-per-inch laser printer. Example 19-6 is made up of statements that print the word **typo.icon.ography** in four point sizes from 75 points to 5 points. The output is shown in Figure 19-4b. Note that jaggies are minimized, so the only obvious ones in this figure are the ends of the top of the horizontal part of the 75 point letter *T*.

This program uses a "procedure" to make it easier to understand and take less code. A procedure in PostScript is like a subroutine in BASIC. You can call it by name and it will do a specific task and return back to your calling program. In Example 19-6 we have defined the procedure **showstuff**. The rule is to precede the procedure name with a slash (/), and then to enclose the procedure commands in braces followed by the word **def**. The **showstuff** procedure does a **moveto** using the last numbers fed to PostScript, then prints the

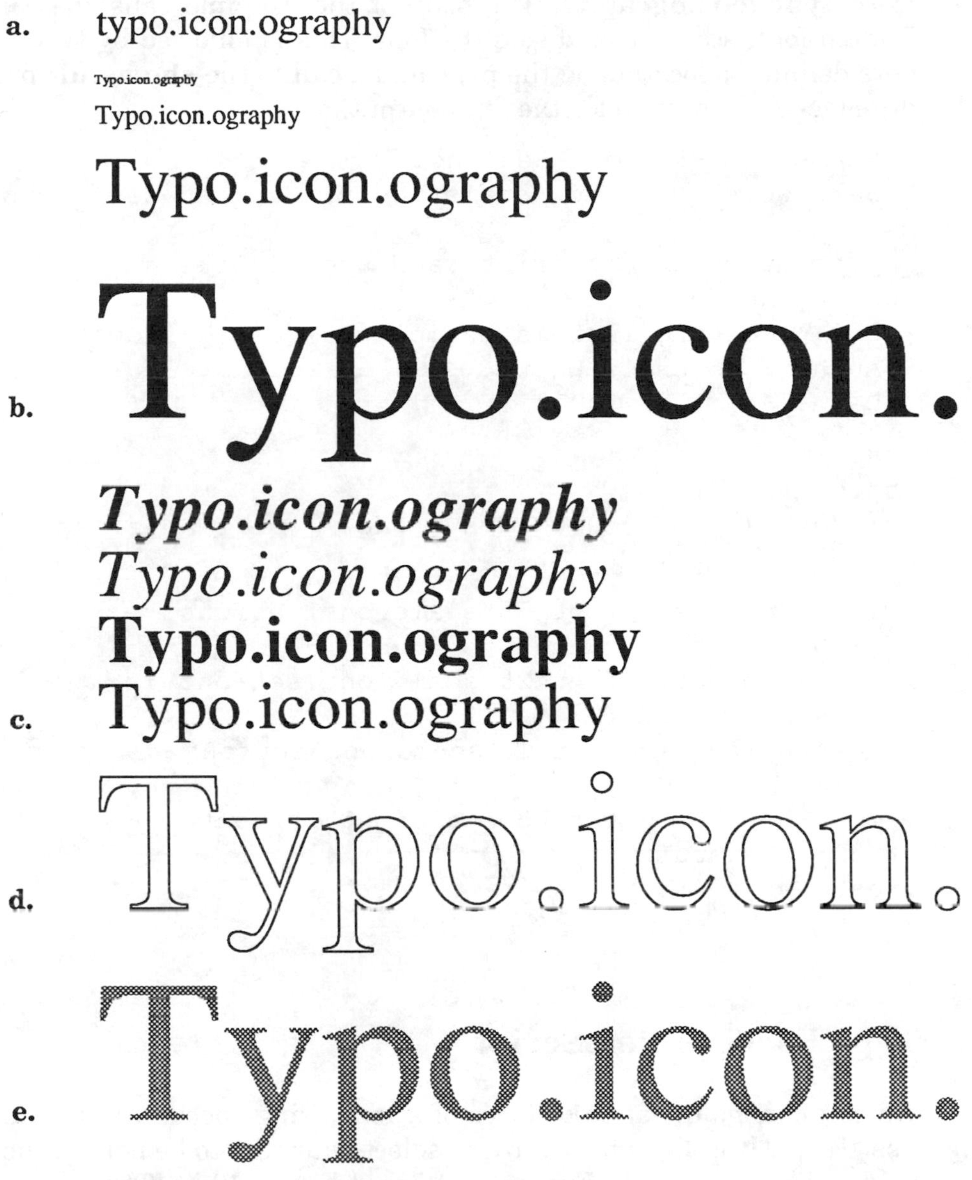

a. typo.icon.ography

Typo.icon.ography

Typo.icon.ography

Typo.icon.ography

b.
Typo.icon.

Typo.icon.ography

Typo.icon.ography

Typo.icon.ography

c. Typo.icon.ography

d.
Typo.icon.

e.
Typo.icon.

f.
Typo.icon.

Figure 19-4. Simple typographic variations using PostScript.

word **typo.icon.ography**. The body of the example calls the Times Roman font, scales it, and sets the font. This is followed by two numbers defining a location on the page and a call to the **showstuff** procedure (see Figure 19-4b for the final output).

```
% Example 19-6: Font Scaling.
% Here we show to how scale fonts. You can define your
own
% procedure in PostScript, and use it like a
subroutine in BASIC.
% The procedure in this example is called showstuff.
% Author: Mitchell Waite.
% Date: April 9, 1987.

gsave
/showstuff
{ moveto (Typo.icon.ography) show } def % defines
procedure

/Times-Roman findfont 75 scalefont setfont
36 200 showstuff
/Times-Roman findfont 25 scalefont setfont
36 280 showstuff
/Times-Roman findfont 10 scalefont setfont
36 310 showstuff
/Times-Roman findfont 5 scalefont setfont
36 325 showstuff
grestore
```

Type Faces in PostScript

We can change the style or faces of a font using special commands in PostScript. It is straightforward to select your text to be bold, italic, or bold italic, as shown in Example 19-7 and Figure 19-4c. The way PostScript selects the desired typeface is exactly the same as the way it obtains the desired plain version of the font, which is what Times Roman is. The Times Roman bold font is actually another font definition/ description stored in a ROM with the printer, as are the italic and bold italic fonts. (We haven't mentioned it, but it is possible on some laser printers to send a font definition from the computer to the printer and define a new font. The Apple LaserWriter allows this feature. It's called downloading fonts.) The names of these fonts are Times Bold, Times Italic, and Times Bold Italic. There is no underline font because underlining is not used in typesetting; it is a typewriter trick for communicating format to an editor or reader. Typically underline means make the underlined word italic. To get an underline you must calculate its position and draw it using **lineto** and **moveto**.

```
%Example 19-7: Faces.
% Note that there is no underline font defined in
PostScript.
% understand we are using the defined showstuff
procedure.
% Author: Mitchell Waite.
% Date: April 9, 1987.

gsave
/Times-Roman findfont 25 scalefont setfont
36 350 showstuff
/Times-Bold findfont 25 scalefont setfont
36 375 showstuff
/Times-Italic findfont 25 scalefont setfont
36 400 showstuff
/Times-BoldItalic findfont 25 scalefont setfont
36 425 showstuff
grestore
```

Drawing an Outline Font

PostScript defines its fonts with outline paths. If you think about this, it means that you can fill the font with any shade of gray (since it's an object like a rectangle). And you can stroke the font and thereby give it a solid outline. Example 19-8 shows how to draw the outline of the word **typo.icon.ography** in a 75-point height Times-Roman. The output is shown in Figure 19-4d. The thickness of the outline is set with the **setlinewidth** command; in this case its set to ½ point (.5). The statement **(Typo.icon.ography) true charpath** tells PostScript to obtain the character path, much like **show** does, but rather than paint the string, to append it's path to the current path. This yields a result suitable then for filling, stroking, or clipping. The word **true** is used to distinguish what to do if the character is a stroked font, such as Courier, but this can be ignored for this level of discussion.

```
% Example 19-8: Outlined font.
% Outlining a font is a bit tricky because of the way
PostScript
% defines fonts.
% Author: Mitchell Waite.
% Date: April 9, 1987.

gsave
/Times-Roman findfont 75 scalefont setfont

36 475 moveto
.5 setlinewidth
(Typo.icon.ography) true charpath
stroke
grestore
```

Filling an Outline Font

Once we have defined a character path outline, it is a simple matter to fill that path with a shade of gray, as Example 19-9 shows. This program is almost exactly similar to the previous one, except that instead of the **stroke** command coming after the charpath definition, we set the gray level to 50 percent with **.5 setgray**, and follow this with a **fill** command. Note that the output of Figure 19-4e shows that there is no outline around the filled font. Why not? Because we removed the **stroke** command.

```
% Example 19-9: Filled font.
% Here we just fill the font path
% Author: Mitchell Waite.
% Date: April 9, 1987.

gsave
/Times-Roman findfont 75 scalefont setfont

36 550 moveto
.5 setlinewidth
(Typo.icon.ography) true charpath
.5 setgray fill   % this used to be "stroke"
grestore
```

Fill and Stroke a Font

You might think it would be a simple matter to both stroke and fill a font (see Figure 19-4f). It is a simple matter, but there is a small "gotcha." Since both the **fill** command and the **stroke** command destroy the font's path, we must use **gsave** and **grestore** to restore the path after one of these commands is used. Example 19-10 shows how this is done: After the string's path is set up with **charpath**, we do a **gsave** right before the fill, and a **grestore** after it. Thus, even though the **fill** kills the path, the **grestore** restores it so we can follow with a **stroke** command and still have a path to stroke. With all hats off to Adobe, it is strange that the software would not save the path somehow after a fill or stroke, or have an option that would allow turning the save path mode on and off or default to always doing a **gsave/grestore** after a fill or stroke.

```
% Example 19-10: Filled and Outlined font.
% Here we fill the font, then stroke it so the outline
shows
% It shows that with all its goodness even PostScript
has
% faults - the fill and stroke commands destroy the
path so you
% have to gsave/grestore all the time.
% Author: Mitchell Waite.
% Date: April 9, 1987.

gsave
/Times-Roman findfont 75 scalefont setfont

36 625 moveto
.5 setlinewidth
(Typo.icon.ography) true charpath
gsave .5 setgray fill grestore % we must
gsave/grestore because
stroke   % fill kills the old path
grestore
```

Further Out Fonts

You can do a lot more than we have just shown with fonts in Post-Script. You can make custom fonts. You can control the pattern a font is filled with. You can control the kerning of a font (the spacing between character pairs) and the leading (the amount of space above and below characters).

You can also get inside a special matrix that allows several parameters called the font matrix to be controlled. This matrix contains six elements that define how font coordinates are to be transformed in regard to the scale, orientations, and position of the x and y axes. The **makefont** command implements the values in the font matrix and allows you to produce characters that are condensed, extended, oblique to right, oblique to left, flipped horizontally, flipped vertically, and flipped both horizontally and vertically. The Adobe manuals make this clear.

Looping and Shadows

It is possible to perform special effects in PostScript using its interactive or "looping" functions. If you execute some small PostScript effect over and over the result can be very dramatic. Example 19-11 shows how a PostScript "for loop" can be used to draw (make) a shadow behind some text. The output is shown in Figure 19-5.

```
% Example 19-11: Translation and Looping.
% This program shows how you can add a shadow to text
% and it shows how a general purpose for loop works.
% Author: Mitchell Waite.
% Date: April 9, 1987.

gsave
/Times-Italic findfont 72 scalefont setfont

/printShade % procedure to draw text
{ 0 0 moveto (Shade) show } def
72 720 translate

.95 -.05 0 % Loop start value, increment value and end
value
{ setgray printShade -1 .5 translate } for

1 setgray printShade
grestore
```

The program sets up the font to be 72 point Times Italic. A procedure is defined called **/printShade**. Its job is to move to location 0,0 with a **moveto**, then to draw the path for the string "Shade" with the **show** command. The command **72 720 translate** moves the user space origin to a new position, leaving everything else about the coordinate system unchanged. So in this case we translate the coordinates to $x=72$, $y=720$, and this becomes the new 0,0 for our user space.

Next, a simple for loop is entered. The values .95, -.05, and 0 are the initial value of the loop, the step size or increment value and the value, at which to end the loop. The statement **{ setgray printShade -1 .5 translate } for** is where the basic work takes place. The values that are fed to **setgray** are the values the loop produces each time it increments. So it starts at setting gray to .95, then to .90, .85, and down to 0 (100 iterations). The **printShade** is called each time, which draws the text at the current position. Each time through the loop, -1 and .5 are fed to the translate operator, which moves the origin over 1 unit to the left and .5 units up the page. The next time we execute **printShade**, it will do a **0,0 moveto**, which will start the next text moved slightly up and over from its last printed position. The result of doing this over 100 times and changing the gray level each time is a shadow or what is also called a fountain. The last statement **setgray printShade** is used to print the string one more time in full white, which covers all the black behind it except for the trailing shadow as shown in in Figure 19-5.

Simply setting the gray scale is only one way to control the pattern for filling objects. PostScript has a nifty operator called the image operator. We won't go into detail on how to use the image operator because it is fairly advanced programming and is covered adequately in the PostScript manuals. Basically, image takes a string of ASCII characters, decodes them into a bit pattern, and uses this pattern to fill an object.

Figure 19-5. Making a shadow with a loop in PostScript.

Summary

Okay, now you are a PostScript apprentice, ready to go out and make the world a more illustrative place to live. You should know enough about PostScript to do simple things like write a program that draws a ruled line box around your text and prints out your company name in 128 point, outline, Bookman Demibold type. There are so many things that can be done with this language that it boggles the mind. We think you will see more and more PostScript programs appearing, and that writing PostScript will become more important over the next five years. In fact, Microsoft recently signed an agreement with Sun Microsystems to license Sun's NeWS operating system. This operating system is based on PostScript and uses it to draw to the screen as well as the printer. You can expect that Sun and Microsoft may offer an alternative to the Macintosh interface by porting the Windows standard to the Sun WorkStation running under PostScript.

Other PostScript Learning Sources

If you are real gung ho on learning PostScript programming there are two books available that were written by Adobe Systems Incorporated and published by Addison-Wesley (*PostScript Language Tutorial and Cookbook*, 1985, 243 pages, ISBN 0-201-10179-3 and *PostScript Language Reference Manual*, 1985, 321 pages, ISBN 0-201-10174-2). These books are well put together and will teach you a lot about using and programming PostScript. There is also an excellent journal available for programmers that includes how-to articles, product reviews, advanced programming techniques, and a tips and tricks column. Published quarterly by Pipeline Associates, Inc. the *PostScript Language Journal* is $15/year, Canada and Mexico add $2/year; overseas add $4/year for surface mail. Address all correspondence to P.O. Box 5763, Parsippany, NJ 07054; (201) 334-0772.

KEYWORDS:

- Leading

- Kerning

- Hyphenation

- Columns

- Rules

- PostScript Pass Through

Peter Lin is a lover of beautiful women, cute children, and fine type. He is a self-taught Macintosh, PostScript, and JustText user. In the tradition of his forebears, he and his wife operate a small typesetting sweatshop in Oakland, California.

Essay Synopsis: JustText is a Macintosh-based type encoding system that creates PostScript files. The program offers an easy-to-learn command format that provides control over leading (the distance between lines of text), kerning (the space defined between specific letter pairs), hyphenation of words at the end of a line, and much more, including special effects such as drop caps and a way to access the actual PostScript codes in the output file.

In this essay you will learn about the important type codes used in JustText and how they adjust leading and kerning, create effects, format text in complex columns, and more.

The author used JustText to typeset this book.

20

JustText

Peter Lin

JustText, a word processing program from Knowledge Engineering, offers high-quality page production in a Macintosh product that retails for less than $200. Unlike PageMaker, MacWrite, or Microsoft Word, JustText is not a WYSIWYG (What You See Is What You Get) product. Instead, the user embeds typesetting codes into text files. The text files may come from any source, typed in or imported from another word processor. JustText converts the combined text and embedded codes into a PostScript file, ready to send to any PostScript output printing device.

JustText offers automatic dictionary and algorithm hyphenation, kerning (automatic, manual, and track), multiple column layouts that are redefinable at will, reverse leading, and some powerful typographic features, such as true drop caps, rules of any length and width, boxes, and typographical style tabs. Just-Text offers direct access to PostScript code and a page preview feature so users have some idea of how their page looks before it is printed. In addition, it comes with some useful utilities for converting MacWrite documents into text files, and for converting MacPaint, Thunderscan, and MagicVision documents into PostScript files. The resulting PostScript files may then be manipulated to create special effects.

While JustText is code-driven, the codes are mnemonic in approach. For example, the code to set point size is {pn} where the

RELATED ESSAYS:

3. Features of Conventional Typesetting Systems

8. About Type Encoding Programs

19. Introduction to PostScript

n is an integer. (Half points are not allowed, but point size can be from 1 to 256 points, and higher if you access the PostScript file directly.) The beginning user will find the code-drive approach difficult; users who have typesetting experience or experience with code-driven word processors, such as WordStar, will find the approach direct and easy to master.

For the graphics professional, exact control over all aspects of the placement of type and graphics elements is essential in a page layout program. The program must be able to place text and graphics at any location with precision down to the point (in traditional typesetting, a point is $\frac{1}{72.27}$ inch; Adobe Systems rounded this to $\frac{1}{72}$ inch, thus in PostScript a pica is $\frac{1}{6}$ inch and a point is $\frac{1}{12}$ pica). Because one limitation of WYSIWYG systems is their inability to place blocks of text so precisely, it is an important feature that JustText offers this kind of control.

Leading

JustText allows the user to play with different amounts of leading, which is the space between lines of text. In the days when type was set using cast letters, lead strips were used between the lines to set the lines apart, thus the term. Leading, then, refers to the amount of space between the baseline of the line above and the baseline of the line below. Ordinarily, type size and leading are set together. In Just-Text, the commands for 12-point type with 14 points of leading would be **{p12}{l14}**. Leading may be set smaller, the same as, or larger than the point size. In this example, a 12-point typeface will be set vertically centered on a line that is 14 points high.

Microsoft Word and PageMaker offer similar leading features, but they have taken some control away from the user; in some situations the results of setting leading and point size manually can be unfortunate and uncorrectable. For example, one typesetter tried to set a raised capital letter at the beginning of a block of type using Page-Maker and ended up having to set the leading for the entire line to a number larger than the point size of the raised cap. JustText will obediently do as the user wishes. If the result is that the line above is overwritten by the raised capital, the program assumes that this is what the user wanted (you can avoid overwriting by using the advance command, **{an}**, discussed below).

The amount of leading can radically alter the readability of a page. Too much leading and the eye tends to wander, too little leading and the lines of type seem to sit on top of each other, so the eye tires.

Typefaces with longer ascenders and descenders need more leading in order to be readable; others need less. Certain special effects, for example, text set in all caps, work well with leading set smaller than the point size. By making point size and leading manual, JustText encourages experimentation and decisions on the part of the user.

In the early days, a typesetter's apprentice might spend at least one day setting the same text in the same typeface, varying the combinations of point size and leading. This might be a useful exercise even for someone without a lifetime commitment to typesetting, because knowledge of how various sizes look with various amounts of leading can be invaluable in creating beautiful pages. Anyone who has ever been to an art supply store and looked at books on type speccing has seen pages of typefaces set in various point and leading combinations. With computer technology, users need not buy such books; checking out a new look is a matter of changing a couple of point and leading codes and running the page again.

Kerning

No single feature distinguishes typesetting from typing (or word processing for that matter) more quickly than kerning, the ability to adjust space between letter pairs. The need for kerning is probably felt most strongly when setting headlines, because it is in headlines that the large holes and irregular spacing between letters become most obvious.

Even today, the majority of typewriters type letters that are all the same width. Readers have come to accept an *m* that is the same width as an *i* and a large space between a capital *T* and a little *o* in the word *To*. Computer word processors and electronic typewriters have changed some of that by allowing fat letters to be fat and skinny letters to be skinny (proportional type), but as yet none afford the user control over how much space will occur between letters. Readers must accept large holes as part of the natural order of things.

Typesetters, on the other hand (especially high-end typesetters), have long expected kerning to be an integral part of producing quality work. Professionals have come to expect that kern pairs (such as *r.* or *WA*) will be kerned and that the typesetting house will be able to open text up by adding space between all letters as well.

JustText also supports track and manual kerning. Track kerning, which controls the amount of space between all letters in a block of text, can radically alter the readability of a block of text. While the decisions made by the original typographer are probably the right ones, particular users may want to add space for their own purposes. One type-speccing book claims that each typesetting house should have its own track kerning as part of its special look. Perhaps, but the client should be able to specify alternative kerning as needs change.

The JustText track kerning instruction is "allow kerning," **{akn}**, where *n* is a three-digit number between -999 and +999. Notice that this is a microspace measure, and very flexible. The cancel command is "cancel kerning," **{xk}**.

JustText also offers a manual kerning facility that allows the user to take out space between a particular pair of letters based on the final appearance of the work. For example, a user might manually take out space in every occurrence of "To" to improve the appearance of that particular pair of letters. (JustText has a very fast global search and replace function, by the way.) Or, if a user were to set a capital *T* in 24 point and the remainder of the word in 18 point, more kerning would be necessary than would happen automatically. This is a typographical problem that is best handled manually. The command is "minus a unit space," **{-u}**. The size of this space is determined by the current point size.

From a typographical perspective, the most important feature of JustText is its ability to kern specific pairs of letters automatically every time they appear. The number of possible kern pairs is enormous once you get into it, and users' tastes will vary as to what should be kerned and by how much. One JustText user reportedly has a file for a single font that includes 500 different kern pairs. Because manually kerning each pair of letters in an entire document like a book would drive typesetters crazy, this facility must be automatic.

In JustText, not only is the kerning automatic and "pair-wise," it is also "font-specific," meaning that the amount kerned between letters depends on the font being used. This makes sense for exactly the same reason that certain fonts need more leading than others for optimum readability.

Changing or adding kern pairs is a fairly simple process for which the documentation provides clear instruction. When Adobe Systems codes a font, they create what is called the Adobe Font Matrix (AFM) file, which is unique to that font and included on the disk with the font itself. Among the various bits of information in the file is kern pair information that tells the user which specific pairs of letters should be kerned and by how much. This information is already on-line in Just-Text, but if the user is unhappy with Adobe's decisions or if the user wishes to take out or add other kern pairs, the user edits the AFM file and then downloads that information to JustText (this command is a menu item).

For example, if a careful inspection of a block of text reveals a particular pair of letters that needs kerning and for which there is none, the user can easily add that pair to the list and decide how much kerning to allow. Space between letter pairs can also be added, by the way. For some reason, the spacing after the lowercase *t* in Helvetica always results in very tight interletter spacing. This is a place for some added space. Once the user has made these kerning changes, these kerns will happen automatically every time JustText sets type. If you do not save your edits of the AFM file, then you can easily return to the original file simply by reopening the (original) file and downloading it again.

Hyphenation

Very few programs on the market offer automatic hyphenation. Again, from years of looking at pages done without automatic hyphenation, we have come to accept large amounts of space between words in fully justified, multicolumn layouts simply because that's the way we have always seen them done. But a careful look at a newspaper or glossy magazine will reveal that, in fact, such large holes in the text are not acceptable at a professional level. When JustText justifies a line, it does so by adding space only between words, not by adding space between letters as some high-end typesetters do.

JustText offers both manual and automatic hyphenation. The automatic hyphenation follows the rules of TeX, a typesetting program developed by Donald Knuth. They are (in order): First, don't hyphenate anything less than five letters; second, break between words with a capital letter in them (e.g., LaserWriter); third, look at the exception dictionary; fourth, break at suffixes and prefixes; and fifth, break between double consonants. The user is free to add entries to the exception dictionary but is forewarned that very large dictionaries slow the program down tremendously. Anyone who has ever used a spelling checker has had this experience. One possible alternative might be particular dictionaries for particular applications. These automatic hyphenation rules are conservatively based on the theory that it is easier to add hyphens than to take them out.

The user can add hyphens manually with a simple hyphen command and prevent bad word breaks with a similar command. For example, impos{-}sible would insert an optional hyphen and {-}impossible would prevent hyphenation. The problem with English is that no matter how conservative the rules, there will always be an exception. So, unfortunately, users will still need to look over their finished copy closely to remove or add hyphens before going to print.

Columns

JustText allows the user to define up to four columns on a page using the command {cn,m,m,m,m} (again, notice the mnemonic *c* used for column), where the first *n* is a number from one to nine and the following four *m*'s are the measure of the column in points in this order: top of the column, measured from the bottom of the page; left of the column, measured from the left side of the page; bottom of the column, measured from the bottom of the page; and right side of the column, measured from the left side of the page. All of the measures are in points.

Columns are numbered from one to nine. When JustText has finished filling column one with text, it automatically "jumps" into column two and so on; or if it is in the last column on the page, it moves to the first column on the next page. The user can jump at will, however, using the column jump instruction, {cjn}, where the *n* is the number of the column you want to jump to. The starting point is always at the top of the column less the current point size, although by using the advance, {an}; y-save, {ys}; and y-restore, {yr}; commands; users can start anywhere in the column they want. While JustText allows only nine columns, the columns may be redefined at any time.

Adjusting Columns

JustText allows the user to flexibly move the *current point* up and down the page with an "advance," **{an}**, and "back," **{bm}**, command. The measure here is points (typesetters and graphics professionals please remember that in PostScript systems, one point is $1/72$ inch). Advance and back are important commands for many reasons. There are times, for example when the previous paragraph ends early in a line and the line following has a large indent, where less than the normal amount of space between paragraphs is important. Or, for example, in multicolumn layouts it is important that all the columns end at the same vertical position.

In a typewritten, word-processed world, most people never even think about the amount of space to be inserted between paragraphs.

And yet extra care taken to set pages can make a difference in appearance. One or two points added between paragraphs to even out the columns is nearly invisible to most readers.

JustText does not adjust column lengths or get rid of widows and orphans automatically; the designer will have to do this manually. Some users may prefer to be able to make these decisions based on the appearance of the finished product, but other users may find the lack of these features irritating.

Rules

Of course, beautiful pages are not made of type alone. There are times when the page designer would like to draw a box around a body of text in order to set it off from other sections of the page, or draw a thin-line rule down the page between two columns in order to give a sense of rest between columns (all this, of course, must flow from the page design because columns with a very narrow gutter will look quite odd with a line between them, and yet a narrow column and a wide gutter would similarly look quite odd). But the ability to control the placement of lines and boxes and their widths is an important tool. The command for a rule between columns is **{crn,m}** or "column rule between column n and column m." The width of the rule is set with the command "line width n points," **{lwn}**; n may be a number as small as $\frac{1}{10}$, the thin line rule.

JustText also provides a way for users to set baseline rules, rules centered in the current column, of any width. For example, in order to set out a pull quote, the user might draw a 5-point baseline rule the width of the column, set the following text in a large point size with more leading, centered in the column in boldface instead of regular type, cancel the hyphenation, and then set another baseline rule in a smaller line width and go back to the original settings. The syntax for the baseline rule command, **{brn.m}**, is in "picas.points," so a user who wants a rule to be exactly 37 points wide can have that kind of control (it would be **{br3.1}** — by the way, 3 picas is 36 points plus 1, which makes 37).

One interesting rule line is wider on one end than on the other. This kind of rule can be set by combining a baseline rule and a plain rule. To do this, set a narrow baseline rule, go back up the page using the "back" command (discussed above), and then set a plain rule in a wider width. Then go back again, issue a PostScript command to print white, and set white type inside the wider black rule. The amount to go back might take some trial and error, but once you get it right, it can be repeated on each occasion (but be careful to change back to print black before going on — white type on a white background is very difficult to read).

There are some limits to what can be done with rules within Just-Text. Experienced graphic artists may find the old pasteup method easier sometimes. There is nothing wrong with that, but those who are willing to learn the program will be able to do a great deal using the PostScript pass through **{ps}** command (more later).

The JustText method of creating rules is much more direct than that of PageMaker or Ready,Set,Go!. Because all the rules are in points and picas, JustText allows very precise control over the length, placement, and width of the rules. PageMaker, for example, limits a user's choices of line width.

Including Art

One lesson we learned as children, often easy to forget, is that pages of type need to be broken up by pictures. For the graphics professional, however, the 300 dots-per-inch (dpi) resolution available with low-end scanners may be inadequate for complex graphic material such as photographs with continuous gray tones. But for simple black-and-white material, 300 dots per inch is more than adequate.

JustText provides a number of quite useful tools to the page designer working with such material. The program comes bundled with three utilities that convert art in the MacPaint, Thunderscan, or MagicVision formats into pure PostScript code. Each utility allows the user to control the precise location of the visual on the page, to scale the image, and to crop, rotate, and lay a bounding box around the visual. There is also a way to preview the visual before putting it on the page by dumping it off to a PostScript printer. These images will appear as rectangles on the page, but by removing the **clip** command in the PostScript file, setting type after the graphic has been set, and using JustText's indent and force justify commands, it is possible to do a very nice wrap manually.

In JustText, there is also a way to insert MacPaint visuals directly into your page and then wrap text around them so that the text follows the outline of the artwork. The command is "paint include," **{pi}**, and results in a very nice one-pica border around the art.

As mentioned above, you can manually do wraps and runarounds using the indent commands (indent left, **{iln.m}**, and indent right, **{irn.m}**) and then manually break lines using the force justify command {**fj**} (assuming that you're fully justifying the rest of the text). In a book-length piece this kind of approach would be difficult, but in a situation where the designer is setting each page individually, this kind of painstaking preparation is entirely practical. The main difficulty is getting the peaks and valleys of your wrap right. Once those are set, getting a continuous line of text between them is simple. With laser-generated pages being as cheap as they are, this is a serious alternative approach to doing some very elegant art wraps.

Incorporating Various Type Sizes

In a large block of text it is often difficult to distinguish between more important and less important ideas. One way to do this visually is to set off sections with heads and subheads. A head might be set in double the normal point size (e.g., 24 point instead of 12) and in boldface. A subhead might be set in the normal point size but using boldface and adding space all around.

Another useful device for breaking off a section from the text around it is the drop cap. In JustText, drop caps are a simple four-stroke command. As an example, {**dc2T**} will set a *T* two lines high and then indent the text following around it automatically, ending the indents at the second line. The user can further distinguish sections by setting some of the following text in boldface; this is a common practice in newspapers. Or you can set the head text in 13 point with 14 point leading, breaking into 10 point with 12 point leading as the article progresses. The size of the drop cap varies with the point size and leading of the text.

One attractive approach involves setting a three-column layout but setting the first paragraph in a larger point size as a single column of twice the width. This kind of layout is really quite simple using Just-Text, because columns are redefinable at will. In addition to the column definition summarized above, JustText allows the user to define a column where the top of the column is at the current vertical position on the page. The definition reads {**cn,y,k,l,m**}, where everything is the same as a normal column except that JustText automatically sets the top of the column to the current vertical position on the page. In the example described above, the user might define three columns on the page. The first and third columns could start at the top of the page, but at the end of the first paragraph, a new first column would replace the original, and the user could add a second using the same *y* as its top.

Postscript Pass Through

One tool that typesetters do not have available, but which can be extremely powerful in willing hands, is access to PostScript. Without delving too much into the powers of PostScript, JustText allows the user to "pass through," {ps}, PostScript commands that may range from the very elementary to the extremely complex. The PostScript pass through ends with a set of double uppercase *Q*'s. In the PostScript Cookbook and Tutorial (Addison-Wesley), the user will find programs to do various kinds of screen manipulations.

JustText is, in fact, a PostScript interpreter. When the user tells JustText to print, the first thing JustText does is to convert the text and code into PostScript. For the truly brave, JustText includes a "Make PostScript Window" that allows the user to see the actual PostScript code before it is sent off. This can be an intimidating experience. A careful reading, for example, will reveal the automatic hyphenation at work as well as the column redefinition and so on.

Having access to the actual code has certain advantages. For one, if you can find the locations in the code for your particular area of interest, you can take those out and manipulate just those leaving the rest of the code intact. Setting large bodies of text in PostScript directly, though, is a Herculean task, not for those who are faint of heart or interested in life after typesetting.

One important point to note about JustText's PostScript conversions is that the resulting PostScript file contains no special commands to confuse the user. The PostScript conversion that goes on inside of Apple's own QuickDraw routines, for instance, is not legal PostScript; a user who captures this stuff will be entirely unable to decipher it, and its conversion to printing requires that a special translation driver be downloaded to the printer before printing can begin. Users who have printed files using MacDraw have perhaps run up against the message "Reinitializing Printer" when they send their document to the laser. This reinitialization is necessary because that special driver must be downloaded before printing can begin. By the way, this limits the amount of memory inside the LaserWriter available to downloadable fonts; therefore, JustText users have more downloadable fonts available to them.

The hanging bullet is a very useful tool. It sets a bullet (basically a round dot) three point-sizes larger than your current point size (a matter of taste, the regular bullet appeared too small to Bill Bates who wrote JustText), inserts an en space (a space the width of an *n*), puts an indent at that point, and indents all the text that follows to that point until you issue a command to end a paragraph (a quad command).

JustText Weaknesses

JustText comes up short of the current standard in the area of headers and footers and footnotes, which has to do with its handling of standard page setup. In JustText page setups happen through two Post-Script routines, one called *pagesetupproc* and one called *footerproc*. The first, pagesetupproc, is intended for doing such things as "nonprinting changes to the graphics state," by which the documentation means such acrobatics as rotating every page, scaling every page, or setting up pages for tiling or doing thumbnails.

The *footerproc* is a procedure for doing such things as laying down headers and footers. JustText includes some sample page setups with header and footer procedures, but all of them are in PostScript, so the user must understand at least a little programming. The footer procedure does include a method for varying the layout of the elements on a page from the left to right side. So at least that much is taken care of.

In his own defense (and anticipating my criticism) Bill Bates argues that using this PostScript approach is "powerful" and "general," meaning that the user can design headers and footers for literally any situation. There is the difficulty of anticipating the needs of every user; headers and footers vary tremendously between applications. Included with the page procedures is one for setting page numbers in Roman numerals.

Another problem area for JustText is that there is no footnote procedure and none is anticipated in future versions. The user must decide where footnotes are to go, generate them manually, and then set type so that they occur at the right place. This could drive a user to drink if precision layout in a long manuscript is involved.

Summary

JustText is a word processor for the Macintosh that offers a capable typesetting environment and direct access to the PostScript page description language. The major features are flexibility in leading, kerning, hyphenation, columns, and rules. JustText provides some very convenient tools for including graphics on a page, including simple drop cap and bullet commands as well as utilities to incorporate art from MacPaint, Thunderscan, and Magic Vision files. Just-Text does not provide powerful header and footer tools, and will prove cumbersome for very long manuscripts with extensive footnotes, elaborate running heads, or other difficult formatting problems. Despite these limitations, JustText provides a powerful typesetting and word-processing environment for a low price.

IV

Techniques and Special Applications

About This Section

As desktop publishing tools mature, they are moving into specialized areas, with each geared towards mastery over a specific medium. In this section the authors explore their experiences in using a wide variety of desktop publishing tools for the production of newsletters, forms, magazines, comics, posters, and even sheet music, revealing that all is not perfect in this new world. The first essay, on newsletters, warns us not to toss out our scissors, white-out, or glue, for it is sometimes most effective to use desktop publishing tools in combination with traditional pasteup techniques. The following essay, on forms, shows how a publishing application can depend on a database program. In a magazine environment, general-purpose desktop publishing software is pushed to the limit, and the next essay shows how to recognize the many points of diminishing returns. The essays on comics and music show us more applications with requirements that demand specialized software. The final essay offers the almost poetic creation of a poster using a digitizer, paint program for touching up, and page composition program for final sizing and printing.

KEYWORDS:

- Pica Stick

- Proportion Wheel

- E-Scale

- Opaque

- Pasteup

- Photographs

James Karney is assistant technical director with Mantech Services in Oak Ridge, Tennessee, working with Oak Ridge National Laboratories coordinating research in electronic publishing. He has operated his own desktop publishing business, is a speaker at seminars and conferences related to desktop publishing, is a contributing editor with *Personal Publishing Magazine*, and has more than ten years experience in print journalism.

Essay Synopsis: In this era of high-technology publishing tools it is easy to forget traditional production tools such as T-squares, white-out, and rub-on letters. These products are often ignored when they could easily solve a deficiency of a page layout or graphics program.

Newsletters, one of the most popular applications of desktop publishing, are often produced on a shoestring budget with inexpensive tools. In this essay the author discusses the production process of creating a newsletter and presents tips and techniques for using traditional pasteup devices such as T-squares, glue, white-out, scissors, pressure-sensitive typefaces, and other physical layout tools. You will learn how to handle photographs and other hard-copy artwork. You will also learn how to use proportion wheels to make reduction estimates, style sheets to control writing consistency, and drafting pens and opaque to fine-tune computer-generated art.

384

21

Newsletters

James Karney

In the current heyday of computerized desktop publishing, let's not forget the tried-and-true graphics tools that have been used for years by layout and production people. Combined with computer desktop publishing tools, traditional, low-tech graphics methods may well hold their own in speed, accuracy, and professional results.

This essay is for those of you using very low-cost microcomputer systems, an inexpensive printer, a word processor, and little else. Such a system does not normally allow you to create graphics and merge them with text in a single, printable disk file. We will show you how to combine such things as projection wheels, magnifiers, and T-squares with word processors and dot matrix printers to produce high-quality printed material. This hybrid method is not full-blown desktop publishing, but it is a way to publish from your desktop, on the cheap. We have chosen the newsletter form to present examples of these methods, but they will work well for any printing project. You may even keep some of these tricks when you graduate to a more sophisticated system.

Several thousand newsletters are published in the United States every month. Countless organizations publish newsletters including churches, colleges, neighborhoods, clubs, political parties, and special interest groups. As desktop publishing tools become increasingly common, we're likely to see a glut of newsletters that will result in heightened competition for readership and

RELATED ESSAYS:

1. Printing Production

4. Copyright Law

23. Producing a Magazine

funding. Those publications that survive will be well designed and have a character of their own, and, more importantly, will contain well-written, timely information. If you plan to produce a successful newsletter, you had better know your field, learn how to create an appealing design using type and graphics, and get a good mailing list.

Those of you who are undertaking to publish a newsletter ought to familiarize yourselves with the following concepts and tools. Successful publishing involves considerable forethought, good writing skills, and a working knowledge of the tools of the trade.

Planning: Budget and Time

Newsletters have to be completed on time and within a budget. First, decide when your newsletter must be in the hands of its readers. In order to set realistic deadlines for having writing, editing, layout, and printing completed, estimate how long each step will take and work backward from the delivery date.

Second, decide how it will be distributed — by bulk or first-class mail, or picked up from a regular location. First-class mail takes about three days and costs twenty-two cents per five-page newsletter. Bulk mail takes about three weeks and costs about twelve cents per newsletter. Newsletters that depend on timeliness should, obviously, go first class.

Third, find out how much time the print shop will need to run the job. A one-color job will require two to three days. If you use a second color, a special ink, or special paper, the printer may need extra time, but usually no more than five working days.

Fourth, find out how long it will take to put the art and copy together for a camera-ready mechanical (this is the term for the paste-up board with everything in place, ready for the printing shop to photograph it and make printing plates).

The real test of planning comes in estimating production — layout and pasteup. If everything is written and all the art is prepared, pasting up a four-page, three-fold newsletter may take a whole day. Something larger and more elaborate may take as long as a week.

Assuming first-class delivery and a two-day printing schedule, you'll need five business days. Better leave two more days for folding, stapling, and stamping. Now add your production time (layout and pasteup), and you have what the industry calls the drop dead date: All the writing and art must be finished by this date.

Design

The design of your newsletter communicates your intent and ability to the reader before that person reads a single word. The design should invite the reader to explore the contents. Good design doesn't have to be expensive — but it should be simple and appealing, with enough variety to be interesting but not cluttered. For example, a typed sheet may look more like a letter than news, while a jumble of columns and typefaces may confuse rather than entice.

The best place to learn about design is by studying other newsletters (or whatever kind of product you're working on). Make notes about what you like and keep tear sheets of pages you find attractive. The ground rule of good design is to keep it simple and consistent; beginners especially should start with a simple format and refine it over time.

Begin by designing your page layout. Remember that the eye moves from the upper left corner of a page to the lower right, so plan your layout and arrange design elements (illustrations, headlines, sidebars) with that in mind. How many and what size columns will you allow? If your page is approximately eight inches across, use only one or two columns. If you use two, make one wider to add visual impact.

Type can be set justified or ragged. Justified type usually refers to type set evenly down the side of the column, whereas ragged type is not. Generally, a justified left, ragged right column format works best. The problem of justifying both right and left margins is that some word processors must add spaces between words to make them fit exactly into the even margins. The results are haphazard, unsightly, and often difficult to read. Whatever your decision, be consistent throughout the entire publication. If the layout is dramatically different from one page to another, your readers will have difficulty following the flow of a story. The visual appearance of the printed page is as important as the text in communicating your message to the reader.

Illustrations: Drawings, Charts, and Photographs

Add impact to the data presented in your newsletter by illustrating it with drawings and charts. You can create them with software, such as Microsoft Chart, Lotus 1-2-3, or an electronic paint program, or you can use ready-made clip art. Clip art is a collection of cartoons and drawings, and it is a good source of illustrations for a publisher without an artist. Art stores sell books of clip art that are very useful for a desktop publisher. Clip art is also available on disk.

A simple design rule to follow when placing advertising or other separate graphics is the pyramid style, which means placing them so that they use the lower half of the page and rise toward the center of two pages side by side.

The snappiest kind of illustration to use in a newsletter is a photograph. Photos provide a lot of information in a small amount of space and with a one-line caption can tell an entire story. A helpful rule of thumb on photo background is to keep it simple; the simpler the better. A white wall is an excellent background for a portrait, a full bookcase is not.

When handling a photo, don't write on the front or back. Use the largest size of Post-its® (gummed note pads). Write the caption line, figure number, page number, reproduction size, and other information on the sticky side of the Post-it, then attach the Post-it to the back of the photo so that the information is visible below the photo and readable as you look at it. Many publications include photographer credits in tiny print that is rotated 90 degrees along the side.

Some people photocopy pictures and get washed-out results. For photos to be reproduced well, they must be converted into halftones. A print shop or full-service copy shop can take a picture of your photo using a graphics camera with a screen in place over the work. The screen breaks up the tones into a pattern of dots that will reproduce with the appearance of shades of gray. The number of dots per inch will affect the quality of the resulting halftone. The more dots per inch, the better the resolution. Be careful not to use too fine a screen or the ink on the final printing will run together. For newsprint paper, use a screen of 85 dots per inch. Most newsletters printed on bond paper can take advantage of 100 dots per inch.

If you want to do it yourself, make a photographic enlargement of the negative with a halftone screen covering the paper. Another alternative is to photocopy the print with a screen laid on the glass in front of the picture.

If you reuse a photo that has been clipped from a printed page, it probably is a halftone. Be careful not to repeat the process of making a halftone of a piece of art that is already a halftone, for it will very likely generate a moire pattern — a set of geometric curves superimposed on the image by the offset of the second screen over the dots of the first.

Page Budget

Because you have limited space, you will need to correlate the length of an article with a page budget. Here's how to do it. Determine the width of a column to find the length of the lines in it. Calculate how many characters fit on your line, then divide by six to get the average number of words on a line (six characters per word is the commonly accepted average). Multiply the average words per line by the number of lines per column inch to get average words per column inch. Now your job is to budget a certain number of column inches to each story or article. Multiply the number of column inches by the average number of words per column inch and you get the number of words needed for the article.

Writing

Most newsletters are a sort of small-scale newspaper, so a tight journalistic style is usually necessary: Keep the story to the point. When you're planning an issue, the best way to make sure all the points are covered is to work from a "news budget" or assignment sheet. This is a list of stories outlining who will write the copy, what photographs and artwork are needed, and when it is due to be completed. An assignment sheet allows an editor to see what copy is expected and how much space to allot based on a topic's importance.

Also, using a style sheet can save you hours of decision making as well as ensure consistency from your writers. A style sheet dictates formal considerations including the form in which articles should be submitted, the use of type variations (such as bold and italic), and consistency of terms. Your style sheet will evolve out of your own purposes and needs, but you can begin by following the guidelines in one of the many widely used reference manuals for styles and usage, such as the *Chicago Manual of Style*. See below for a partial list of items controlled by a style sheet.

Submission requirements
Hardcopy, double-spaced printed pages and MS-DOS disk, files in ASCII format. Art must accompany manuscripts.

Numbers
Spell out numbers between zero and one hundred; use numerals for numbers 101 and higher.

Dates
Spell out months, numerals for days and years.

Punctuation
Serial comma, always: we'll tell Joe, Jeanne and John, and Billy.

Abbreviations
Do not allow acronyms with the following exceptions: desktop publishing, dtp; dot matrix printer, dmp; AT&T; IBM

Hyphenation and spelling
Use *Standard Handbook for Secretaries*

Italics, Capitalization, Cities, States
Use *Chicago Manual of Style*

Spelling
Use *Webster's New World Speller* or *Webster's Collegiate Dictionary*

The Basics of Layout

Set up a work space. You'll need a good worktable that has a straight edge to at least one of its sides so you can run the tail of a T-square against it. You'll create your layout on a pasteup board, which is a sheet of stiff cardboard with lines printed in nonreproducing blue ink. You can find boards sized in 8½ by 11 inches, in standard tabloid size, and full newspaper broadsheet in bulk quantities. You can also find boards in a number of different column widths so you can use them with a variety of formats.

To "square off" your art, mount a piece of pasteup board by taping its corners to the tabletop. Lay the T-square on the pasteup board so that the T-square tail fits snugly against the straight edge of the work table. Draw a horizontal line across the bottom of your work. Now place a triangle on the work so it rests on the T-square, with one edge of the triangle at 90 degrees to the T-square. Draw a vertical line along the triangle edge. Using the T-square and triangle combination you can draw crop marks, column rules, boxes, and other set-up lines. Paste up your text and art using these lines as a reference. Remember that your work will not necessarily be square to the edges of the pasteup board unless you've lined up the edges of your pasteup board to the T-square.

Pens

A common problem is a rule line that didn't go far enough. A fineline or drafting pen can touch it up. It's a good idea to get several different widths of pens. You can also use them to smooth graphics or headlines generated by dot matrix printers that print with jagged edges.

In addition, use a pen filled with nonreproducing blue ink because it will not show up on a photocopier or on a plate for the printing press. An editor can use it to label spaces for art and halftones, or to confirm page numbers and folds. Nonreproducing pens are handy for proofing because the ink stands out on the page, and you can see where edits have been made. For rough drafts a red editing pen works fine, but many newspapers use the nonreproducing blue for both initial corrections and pasteup pages. When all corrections are made in the same blue tone, it becomes a familiar flag: Fix this!

Measuring Tools: Let's Be Precise

The key to exact measurement is a good set of rulers. Yes, more than one. Other measuring tools that should be near at hand include a pica stick, proportion wheel, an E scale, and a clear rule.

The Schaedler Precision Rules are a cherished possession of the professional graphic artist. They are traceable, which means they are exact to the official inch. These rulers can be used on both hard copy and the screen of a computer monitor because they are photoset on a flexible, translucent Cronar emulsion. Two sets of scales are included in the set, which costs about $17. One has metric and inch rules, while the other provides points, picas, and agate lines. There are also bullet and rule scales from hairline to 30 points wide.

A pica stick is a firm metal ruler with 6- and 12-point lines, showing points, inches, and agates. If you have to figure the number of inches of type a page can handle or fit a photographic halftone into an exact amount of space on a page, this tool is a gem.

A proportion wheel is an instrument used to size a photo or other graphic element. To use it, first measure the width of the column and that of the artwork to be placed. Next find the number matching the size of the original on the inside scale of the wheel. Now turn the wheel until the number is lined up with the dimension of the column width on the outer scale. The percentage of enlargement or reduction will be visible under the arrow in the window. For example, a picture 5 inches (30 picas) across that is to go into a 2¼ inch (14 pica) column will have to be reduced to 47 percent of its original size. If the picture is 7 inches tall, the reproduction height will be 3¼ inches tall. That may call for cropping the image, cutting some of the accompanying story, or moving other elements of the page around a bit. A pair of L-shaped pieces of cardboard is a handy device for cropping (covering up) the parts of the illustration to be eliminated. Draw crop marks on the edges to indicate where the crop is to be made. You will probably have to fiddle with the cropping in order to get the photo to reduce correctly. Be careful neither to cut too closely on the subject nor to allow too much background. Once you have determined the amount of space needed to include the graphic, you can draw a box or other mark on the screen to note its position.

An E scale is a clear sheet or rule with a series of capital E characters. By lining them up with a capital letter in the body of type, you can figure out the point size of the text type or get an idea of what point size to use for a headline. One thing to remember about E scales (or the less common C scales) is that the letter E has no ascenders or descenders, so don't use a letter that does have them as a match, such as a *y* or a *q* in some fonts.

A clear rule has a zero point in the center and a grid pattern with increasing numbers on both sides. Sizing boxes is easier with a clear rule because the grids can be used to count the number of characters that will fit in a column.

Magnifiers: An End to Eyestrain

Traditional tools help when you have to inspect fine lines and small type. A linen tester is a magnifying lens with a folding stand. It is great for making precise brush strokes on an illustration, applying opaque, or just getting a close look at the edges of your type.

A loupe is another instrument for close inspection. This is a lens set in a circular base. Agfa makes an eight-power model with a translucent base which allows light to reach the work area when the loupe is placed on the page.

About White-Out

When you find a hairline rule that runs too long or a shadow from a photocopier, remember white-out! Instead of fussing with the electronic graphics kit, print the page and clean it up with Liquid Paper®.

There is a red-labeled version for photocopies that works great on laser output.

Another traditional tool is opaque, a clay in white, black, and red, which is stocked by art supply stores and publishers houses. Opaque can be used much like Liquid Paper and is better for covering large sections. The black variety comes in handy when a reversed area does not have an even, dark tone.

Tips for Pasting

Until every part of a layout can be done in the computer, and until scanners become both less expensive and capable of higher resolution, we will still have to paste parts of a publication together. Some people use two-sided tape, but there are better ways to get the job done.

One effective way to paste a publication together is with wax. Commercial printshops have large waxers costing hundreds of dollars, but you can buy a small, hand-held waxer for less than $50. You insert small wax cubes (sold at art supply stores), and the waxer melts them. You can then roll the wax onto the back of your type and graphics. It dries quickly, but retains enough adhesion to stick to boards. The copy can be lifted and moved easily, but then burnished with a roller for a more permanent bond when it's in final position. One caution in using wax with laser printer output: Be careful not to get any wax on top of your type or the toner may smear.

FaberCastel makes the UHU Stic, which has a washable glue in a lipstick-type container. Coated objects can be adjusted for a few seconds after being placed on the page before the glue sets down tight.

Spray adhesive also works well, as does good old rubber cement (as long as you don't put it on too thick, in which case you will end up with wrinkled copy). Beware of fumes from both products. The federal government once considered a permanent ban on rubber cement because of its toxicity. Use products like these in a well-ventilated area and follow precautions on the labels. Also, be careful that the spray does not get on top of your work, or it will collect lint and dust.

Columns

The easy way to print columns is to adjust your word processor's margin settings to match the column width; you'll get a good WYSIWYG representation of the text. Leave room for headlines and art. You may have to print columns out more than once to get it right.

Use a word processor to compose text in columns. Some word processing programs (such as WordPerfect and Microsoft Word) offer the ability to produce multiple columns on a single page. Column formats can be combined with halftones for a simple newsletter. A little practice with tabs can provide spaces for photographs and drawings.

Typefaces

If you have different fonts available, use a serif type (such as Times Roman) for all of your body copy (the stories), and a sans serif type (such as Helvetica) for headlines. Italics and boldface can be used for emphasis. You can create columns as well as make headlines and special typefaces with an inexpensive program such as Fontasy from Prosoft, which costs only $49.95. Fontasy supports most dot matrix printers, and the latest upgrades are provided with some laser printer support. Because this program is constructed for use with a dot matrix printer, it offers an option for those on a low budget.

Fontasy offers a large selection of fonts and the ability to use files from word processors. The program works by having the user enter "dot prompt" codes into a word processor file, but you have to define fonts when you place them; you can't just go back and change your mind. You can also type text while in the program. Fontasy also offers kerning, microjustification, and the ability to wrap text around a graphic; plus it offers on-line help. And because the screen shows the actual size, you can see what you are going to print. Not bad for $50 on an IBM PC or clone.

As good a value as Fontasy is, it is not perfect. Because it works in a bit-mapped mode, small fonts are ragged. Another major omission is the lack of hyphenation, which can make for a lot of space between words in a narrow column. You'll have to hyphenate words manually for good results.

Fontasy needs a large amount of memory. A page of information stored in bit-map form needs at least 700K of memory. That means a standard 8088 type of PC (limited to 540K) can't produce a full-size page. Because margins are white space needing commands to define their borders, specifying larger margins will cut down the load. If you set margins to match the width of a single column, you'll reduce the load by half for a two-column page. But you may need an above-board memory card to maximize your use of Fontasy.

Headlines Attract Attention

Headlines can really catch the eye of the reader — much more so than regular typefaces that match your text. You can create headlines by generating expanded fonts with printer commands to your dot matrix printer. You can get large or special fonts from a laser printer on an occasional basis.

But if you want a special font or a fancy border for only occasional emphasis, it's hardly worth buying an entire laser font for just one use. Press-on letters also offer you different typefaces or point sizes that your program or printer can't produce. Chartpak and Letraset both manufacture lines of transfer letters and fancy rules, usually containing characters, numbers, and punctuation for a given font. They are on a special waxed sheet, and you can select and rub the letters onto a page one at a time. Be careful that you apply them along a line — it's easy to get them slightly crooked.

Rules, Lines, and Boxes

Rules are straight lines of various styles and thicknesses. They can be used to create sidebars of information, to set off a box around a coupon, or simply to create an attractive border. The ability to create rules is available with some printers in combination with some word processing programs. Some of these programs offer pleasing results on a high-quality printer, while others fall far short of the traditional method of using a tape that is placed on the page during layout.

Among the tools at your art supply store you'll find fancy rules on rolls of tape. A rule line on tape that is coated with acetate is easy to place, but it's shiny and doesn't copy well. "Non-acetate" tapes are a little trickier to place than acetate tapes, but the rules look better when copied because they don't produce glare. Try each to see which you prefer.

Rule tapes are available either as straight lines or corners. You will need each to construct boxes. Make sure you buy the same style and thickness of each roll. Most art stores have catalogs showing the choices available.

A simple method for placing a taped box rule is to use the lines on the layout board as a guide. Place a horizontal line by drawing the tape out between your thumbs and trimming both ends to a 45-degree angle with an X-Acto knife. Then place the second horizontal line to match and trim the same way. Now draw out one of the vertical lines and trim the edges so that they complete the box neatly. If you are using a border tape with fancy corners leave room for the angles and match them after the four lines are placed. Then use a burnishing tool to rub the rules firmly in place.

Summary

We have presented this discussion of traditional graphic tools because there are times, for lack of money, time pressures, or a need for higher quality, that you may find these helpful. Publishing a newsletter, even on a budget, is a lot of work, but the process can be fun. The most important thing to remember is to produce your newsletter regularly and on time. Remember to keep your design simple; you can improve it as you learn. Some well-respected newsletters are produced simply; it's the content that makes them worthwhile. Practice makes perfect. Good luck.

KEYWORDS:

- **Data Fields**

- **Data Base**

- **Data Entry**

- **Screen**

Christophe Meneau is president and founder of Graphics Development International (GDI), in San Rafael, California. GDI develops and markets forms generation software for laser printers and scanners. Christophe Meneau has extensive experience in international distribution, mainframe, and microcomputer programming. He received the "Bourse de la Vocation," a prestigious French award, for his innovative advancements in musical and Braille software. He has a master's degree in applied mathematics and a Ph.D. in computer sciences from Lille University in France.

Essay Synopsis: Creating forms is a different process from creating newsletters, manuals, or posters. Forms combine labels with boxes, lines, and shading to define text entry areas. Forms are also closely tied to database information; for example, a sales flyer lists inventory on hand for sale, and a medical form presents data on a patient's health in an accessible format.

In this essay the author explores the graphic requirements that differentiate forms generation from other desktop publishing applications. You will learn how an automated forms generating system can minimize the costs associated with customizing, changing, and upgrading business forms.

22

Forms Generation Software

Christophe Meneau

Forms are a part of everyday life in a technical society. We fill in forms to order merchandise, to obtain loans, and to express opinions. Specialized forms provide checklists, guide analysis, and measure knowledge. Forms can vary from small registration cards to complex, multipage labyrinths like income tax returns. One can scarcely imagine running a business, dealing with a government agency, or sustaining any organization without forms. The basic purpose of forms is to gather information, organize it, store it, and make it available for future reference.

In the past, forms have been designed by hand, typeset, and printed on printing presses. This process is expensive and frequently too slow to keep up with immediate and changing needs. Now, some desktop publishing software facilitates the design of forms on a computer. The printed forms can be filled out on the computer screen and then printed or merged with a data base. A form can be designed on a computer and printed on a laser printer in far less time than when typesetting, layout, and mechanical printing are required.

Although designing a form may seem a simple task, most word-processing and page layout software does not facilitate the job. This essay outlines the special technical requirements of forms design, and lists the features of a good forms generator. It discusses three areas of function as they re-

RELATED ESSAYS:

12. Image Scanning and Processing

25. Music Desktop Publishing

late to the design and production of forms on a computer: text and graphics, speed of printing on a laser printer, and data base merge.

Some software packages are advertised as "forms-generation software," with claims that they are specialized for the design and processing of forms. Similarly, much desktop publishing software is billed as just the tool for laying out pages and designing brochures. Increasingly, software developers are combining page-layout and forms-generation features into a single, more comprehensive package. Therefore, those interested in desktop publishing must look closely at each package to discover if the particular capabilities it possesses will suit their particular needs.

Designing a Form

From a design point of view, a form is a combination of words, lines, boxes, shading, and blank space on paper. It is used interactively: The form asks questions and you fill in answers, check boxes, circle numbers, or shade in the area between parallel lines.

In a form, text and graphics are closely integrated and interdependent. Lines and text are positioned in close relationship to each other. Lines serve two functions in forms: They can separate elements from each other or they can function as the data entry areas for specific pieces of information (such as name and address).

For example, on a loan application form, "Name" is always followed by a long line, while "Zip Code" is followed by a much shorter line. The name and address elements must always stay near each other and be separated visually from other areas, such as the credit history area. Therefore, the algorithms for reformatting must be very specific about the position of each element and character. By contrast, in a newsletter or brochure, a picture might be appropriately placed anywhere on a page, without particular relation to individual words in the surrounding text (see Figure 22-1).

Saving Space and Time

Forms created with a computer offer many advantages. Chief among these are speed of design and printing. If only a few copies are needed, the cost is not prohibitive. The form can be easily modified or adapted to special situations. When changes are made, there are no leftover reams of outdated forms to discard (with concomitant absorption of wasted printing expense). No storage space is required if the forms can be printed as needed, and no one need make frequent inventory checks to assure that the supply isn't about to run out.

When time comes to print a long run of records on a computer-designed form, such as an invoice, there is no need to align forms on the printer and then watch carefully to be sure the registration (the placement of the printed information on the page) doesn't go out of alignment.

How the forms generator communicates with the laser printer controls how fast each form is printed. There are two types of laser printers — those with a parallel or serial interface, and those with a RAM interface. Parallel or serial interface printers are attached in the same manner as dot matrix printers. The Hewlett Packard LaserJet, Laser-Jet Plus, Canon, and PCPI Laserimage printers are in this category. For RAM interface printers, the printer control board is inside the PC. This method allows faster transfer of data from the computer memory or disk to the printer. Cordata, the AST laser printer, Kyocera, and Lasermaster have been the first printers in the category.

Speed of printing is an important issue. A single page of print is a considerable amount of data. Consider a printer that prints at a resolution level of 300 dots per inch. An 8½ by 11 inch sheet of paper represents 8,415,000 pixels! (300 x 300 x 11 x 8½ = 8,415,000).

At 9,600 baud (the usual speed of the LaserJet printer), the time required to cover an entire page with dots would be 15 minutes if the characters and images were sent to the printer one pixel at a time. This method uses a bit map, or a set of specifications for the placement of each pixel in each character or image.

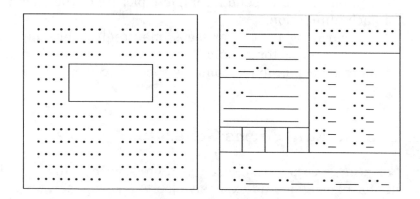

Figure 22-1. In each of the above pages, dots represent text; lines and boxes represent fields and graphic elements.

The use of a character set will speed character transmission to the printer. For example, characters may be printed from the ASCII code in the desired font and attribute, which may include underline or boldface.

For graphic elements such as lines, boxes, or shaded areas, vector graphics transmission makes it possible to send an entire line to the printer as a single command rather than as a sequence of pixels. A four-by-six-inch shaded area, stored as a bit map, requires 270K of storage and takes between four and five minutes to transmit to a printer. Software that uses vector graphics transmission can store the same area in ten bytes and send it to the printer in one hundredth of a second. This kind of speed is required if many forms and complex images are to be printed on a regular basis.

Vector graphics affords two other advantages: reduced storage requirements for forms, and the ability to expand and compress the size of forms. Storing a line as a single command requires a small fraction of the disk storage space that a bit map for the same line would occupy. Because vector graphics stores images as sets of commands, the entire form can be enlarged or reduced simply by changing two parameters — vertical and horizontal spacing — for the form. Thus, a form can be shrunk to fit on a smaller page without any need to redesign it.

If the laser printer has macro storage capability, another way to speed the printing of forms is available. The forms generator should automatically store the unchanging parts of the form as a macro in the laser printer during printing. Only the variable information (such as the individual fields being changed) is then sent from the computer for each copy of the form. Printing time is therefore much faster than if the computer had to send a complete picture of the form to the printer for each impression.

Special images, such as logos, may require bit-map transmission. The forms generator should be able to integrate bit-map and vector graphics transmission to combine speed and flexibility in handling images.

Centralizing Forms Generation

For a large corporation, such as a bank with many branches, managing forms is a big and expensive job. A forms generator can reduce the cost and increase the efficiency and consistency of forms management. A form can be designed on a computer at the central office and sent via communications devices to the branch offices. In this way, all branches have instant access to the latest version of the form. The possibility that people will continue using the older, obsolete version of a form is eliminated if there are no paper copies of the old version lying around. Instead, a loan officer calls up a form by name on the computer and the latest version appears on the screen.

When paper forms are used, any change to a form requires typesetting and printing. In addition, programs may be altered to fit the new version of the form. With a forms generator, fields can be added to the form, moved to a new location, deleted, or otherwise changed in a few minutes at the computer screen. Since the forms generator controls which fields are printed on the form and where they appear, there is no need to write new programs integrating the form with a data file.

Making Changes

A new small business, although its capital reserves are limited, may want to create a professional impression with forms, such as invoices and purchase orders, that help introduce the company to customers and vendors. The costs of having a graphic designer design all the pieces and then having them typeset, pasted up, and printed in small quantities is prohibitive. The forms generator allows inexpensive production of forms with a strong graphic appearance, multiple fonts on a page, and even the company logo.

Things change rapidly for a small company. Typically, the start-up business is staffed by a few people wearing lots of hats, and policies emerge from individual incidents. Decisions about product names, company image, and marketing strategy are still in process. It is hard to justify ordering 1,000 or more brochures or price lists when they may require revision before the hundredth copy has gone out. Customers may assume they have 30 days to pay an invoice until someone realizes the need to add the terms of payment (such as "net 10 days") on the invoice. Therefore, the invoice should be easy to modify by the future CEO who may now be functioning as controller, accountant, billing clerk, and forms designer.

Merging with Data Bases

In addition to making it possible to do faster and more inexpensively what can already be done with paper forms, computerized forms generation also offers capabilities that traditional paper forms cannot.

These result primarily from how the forms generator interacts with a data base.

Forms-generation software can integrate paper forms with a data base more completely than has been possible in the past. On the computer, you can design a form that also acts as a data entry screen. You can fill out the form on the screen and then simultaneously print the filled out form and add the information to a data file as a new record. You can modify the form by adding or deleting fields or by adding text, without having to change your data base file.

The forms generator adds to a data base merge function the ability to give some typographic design to the information merged from the data file. For example, on an invoice you can print the customer's name and mailing address, which will show through the window on the envelope, in 10-point Times Roman; the items purchased and amounts owed can be printed in smaller type or in a different typeface (see Figure 22-2).

The computer-designed form can be developed to match a paper form or vice versa. The two can be modified together to keep them in sync. For example, fields can be added or deleted, or field lengths can be changed. Data can be entered into the data base and printed on paper in exactly the same format.

Some companies, such as a record distributor, need to keep customers up-to-date on their rapidly changing specialized music offerings. The forms generator, because it combines data base merge with graphic and typographic design capabilities, is well suited to the development of price lists.

INVOICE

To: ABC Company
        123 Main Street
        Belleville, OH 44105

Qty	Item	Price	Ext.
1	Drafting table	250.00	250.00
2	T squares	20.00	40.00

Figure 22-2. A simple invoice with the customer's name positioned for a see-through mailing envelope.

Names, descriptions, specifications, and prices of items may be stored in a data file that is constantly updated. The information changes so rapidly that large print runs of price lists quickly become obsolete, but small runs are too expensive. With the forms generator, the staff can design the price list with a heading at the top and an attractive border around the edge of the page. A box contains a paragraph describing the ordering procedure. The rest of the page lists the information from the data file: the items and their prices. The staff can control where on each line the item name, description, and price are to appear by tying each position to a field in a data file. Each file can be printed in a different font. Album titles might appear in larger type than the descriptions; they also might be underlined. Prices are placed flush right. A dotted line (dot leader) fills the space from the item name to the price, although this space may be different for each item.

When it's time to print the price lists, the boxes, borders, text, and data fields are all printed at the same time. The price list contains only current information from the most recent update of the file. Runs of 20 or 50 copies can be made on the laser printer in a few minutes.

The ability to include memo fields (variable length text fields that contain comments or other information) in the data base merge with the form adds even more flexibility. For example, a record distributor can issue a monthly catalog that includes the title, artist, label, price, and song list for each album. Since lists of song titles can vary enormously in length, they are well suited for storage in a memo field. This field can be included in a special form that prints camera-ready catalog pages. The information about the albums is pulled from the data file and printed according to the page layout and font specifications in the form.

Choosing Features

Not all desktop publishing software is ideally suited to designing forms. The remainder of this essay explores the particular points that characterize a form as a published piece and indicates what features desktop publishing software should have if it is to be extensively used for designing forms and merging data base files to print filled-out forms.

Graphic Capabilities

Horizontal and vertical lines may be drawn with cursor movement keys. If the forms generator supports a mouse, freehand drawing may be possible. Since forms rarely require diagonal or curved lines, a freehand drawing function may not be important to you.

Lines can vary in width and composition. Narrow lines may be solid or broken. Wide lines can be made up of shading patterns. Double or triple lines offer variety and emphasis (see Figure 22-3). If line attributes need to be modified, you can easily change the thickness of a line or the type of shading that makes up a wide line.

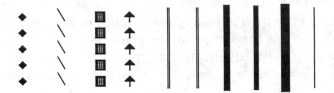

Figure 22-3. Variations of line thickness with other symbols.

Any variety of lines can constitute the border of a box. Box interiors can be shaded in a number of patterns. Check how many shading patterns are available and how flexibly you can design shaded areas. See if text or numbers can be printed against a shaded background (see Figure 22-4).

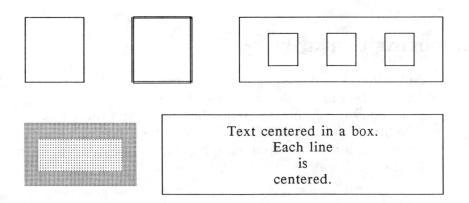

Figure 22-4. Control of boxes, shading, and text is especially important in creating forms.

Check also whether other kinds of graphics functions are available. Some packages enable you to make a bit map of a graphic image (such as a logo) and print it in various sizes on your forms. Check the levels of resolution available for printing such images.

The recent introduction of form-scanning software means that it is possible to produce, merge, and print complex forms without having to design them on the computer. Form-scanning software supports a hardware scanner that scans a printed form. The software displays the form image on the computer screen, where it can be modified, stored as a form and then merged with a data base file and printed. For insurance companies and other organizations that depend on long and complex forms, scanning a form — instead of creating it word by word and line by line — can save considerable time and money.

Text

Check what word processing functions the forms generator itself offers. Also find out whether documents prepared with other word processing software, such as WordStar or WordPerfect, can be copied into forms and then manipulated.

Layout capabilities should include precise positioning of all elements. Since forms and the elements within them often must conform to exact dimensions, it is important to know how close lines and words are to each other and where a given element appears on the form.

Forms are laid out in columns and rows or lines. Columns may be measured in picas, inches, or centimeters. Line width can be determined in point size (i.e., the height of the letters or numbers to be printed, plus the space between the lines). Some forms-generation software shows you the location of the cursor on the form in any of these units of measurement.

Text placement options should include the ability to center text within a box and to right-justify text. Either of these options should be available in proportional or fixed position fonts. Columns of numbers, for example, must be right-justified to keep the ones, tens, and hundreds properly aligned. Whether this facility is available with proportional fonts should be checked carefully.

The typographic possibilities offered by the forms generator must be considered in the context of the fonts offered by the laser printer that the forms generator is to work with. All fonts supplied by the manufacturer of the laser printer should be supported. Some packages include a utility that makes it possible to add soft, or downloadable, fonts that are compatible with the printer. These are fonts, frequently supplied by companies other than the printer manufacturer, that are stored as software on your computer and downloaded to the printer as needed. The forms-generator utility stores information about the spacing requirements of each character in a given font.

Data Base Merge

The ability of the forms generator to merge with a data file and print each record on a separate form is one of its strongest advantages. Therefore, the relation of the forms generator to your data base software should be carefully investigated.

As an output adjunct to some software, such as dBase, the forms generator can enable you to print any information on any form in any numbers of copies. Records can be retrieved, automatically merged with a form you have designed, and printed. You also may be able to insert comments or other text around the data base field values. This information can be added and printed without being saved to the data base.

You should know what file format is required for the forms generator. Frequently, the forms generator reads an ASCII delimited file that you produce with the file utility in your data base software. Similarly, when you fill out forms on the screen, they update an ASCII delimited file, which you then append to a data file created with your data base software.

If you can embed forms-generator commands or macros in a data base query program, you can join the record sorting and selecting functions of the data base software with the design and printing functions of the forms generator.

Disk Functions

Disk functions include the saving and storing capabilities of the forms generator. A directory function should be available to make it easy to locate forms you may have saved in directories other than that in which the forms generator resides. The disk facility should also enable you to save a portion of a form and copy it easily into another form by means of a cut-and-paste facility.

Some forms generators include a library of forms ready for use or modification. These may include invoices, purchase orders, or even a current 1040 federal tax form (see Figures 22-5 and 22-6).

The Printer

If you already have a laser printer, find out if the forms generator supports it. If you don't, you can evaluate the printer and the software together. A laser printer represents a significant investment and therefore merits careful appraisal. The forms-generator software, which is likely to cost a fraction of what the printer does, may seem a minor investment by comparison. However, it should be evaluated in terms of how thoroughly it enables you to exploit the value of the printer.

Summary

Many desktop publishing software products are suitable to some degree to forms production, and they bring the important benefit of reduced inventory expense and flexible design upgrades. But, as can be expected, general purpose packages lack some of the power of a dedicated forms generator.

The key benefits of a forms-generating software package are production speed and database merge capabilities. Production speed derives from the built-in features that tie directive elements (shading, fill-in blanks, lines, boxes, and textual instructions) together to support text entry. Database merge capabilities enable great output convenience, for as a database is updated, all changes immediately can be incorporated in subsequent forms, with the added benefit of by-passing the registration problems of outputting database information onto preprinted forms. As forms generators become linked to scanning systems in the near future, they will be further differentiated as a class of software that serves a specific publishing need extremely well.

GRAPHICS DEVELOPMENT INTERNATIONAL

20-C Pimentel Court, Suite 4
Novato, California 94947
415/382-6600

INVOICE NUMBER: 10093

CUSTOMER CODE:

BILL TO:
  Main Offices

SHIP TO:
  Main Offices

DATE	SHIPVIA		FOB		TERMS	
04/20/87						

PURCHASE ORDER NUMBER		ORDER DATE	SALES PERSON		OUR ORDER NUMBER	
Verbal			00			

QUANTITY			ITEM	DESCRIPTION	UNIT PRICE	EXTENDED PRICE
ORDERED	SHIPPED	BACK OR	NUMBER			
1	1	0	MISC	Miscellaneous Invoice	0.00	0.00

	Sub-Total	0.00
	Tax	0.00
	TOTAL	**0.00**

Customer Copy

Figure 22-5. A standard, full-sized invoice form can include automatic invoice number and date fields.

1040	Department of the Treasury-Internal Revenue Service				

1040 Department of the Treasury-Internal Revenue Service
U.S. Individual Income Tax Return **1984** (O)

For the year January 1-December 31, 1984, or other tax year beginning February 1	,1984, ending January 31	.1985	OMB No. 1545-0074

Use IRS label. otherwise please print or type.	Your first name and initial (also give spouse's name and initial) Peter O.	Last Name **Meara**	Your social security number 204 43 1155
	Present home address (Number and street, including apartment number, or rural route) **1122 Lafayette Square**		Spouse social security number
	City, town or post office, State, and ZIP code **Whitestone, KB 41991**	Your occupation **Taxi Driver** Spouse's occupation	

Presidential Election campaign	Do you want $1 to go to this fund?	Yes	X	No	Note: checking will not increase your tax or reduce your Refund.
	if joint return, does your spouse want $1 to go to this fund?	Yes	X	No	

Filing Status

1	X	Single	For Privacy and Paperwork Reduction Act Notice, See instruction
2		Married filing joint return(even if only one had income)	
3		Married filing separate return. Enter Spouse's social Security No above.	
4		Head of household (with qualifying person). (See Page 6 of instructions). If the qualifying person is child but not your dependent, write child's name here.	
5		Qualifying widow(er) with dependent child (Year spouse died 19). (See page 6 of instructions.	

Exemptions

Always check the box labeled Yourself. Check other boxes if they apply.

6a	X	Yourself		65 or over		Blind	Enter number of boxes checked on 6a and b	2
b		Spouse		65 or over		Blind		
c	First names of your dependent children who lived with you						Enter number of children listed on 6c	0

d Other dependents: (1) Name	Relationship (2)	(3)Number of months lived in your home	(4)Did dependent have income $1,000 or more?	Did you provide more than 1/2 of dependent support	Enter Number of other dependents	0
					Add numbers entered in boxes above	2

e Total number of exemptions claimed (also complete line 36)

Income

Please attach copy B of your Forms W-2, W-2G, and W-2P here.

If you do not have a W-2, see page 5 of instructions.

7	Wages, salaries, tips, etc.		7	186,233
8	Interest income (also attach Schedule B if over $400)		8	11,887
9a	Dividends (attach Schedule B if over $400)	,9b exclusion		15,271
c	Subtract line 9b from line 9a and enter the result.		9c	
10	Refunds of State and local income taxes, from worksheet on page 10 of instruc. (do not enter an amount unless you deducted those taxes in an earlier year.		10	1,200
11	Alimony received or (loss) (attach Schedule C)		11	
12	Business income or (loss) (attach Schedule C)		12	-47,006
13	Capital gain or (loss) (attach Schedule D)		13	-73,601
14	40% capital gain distributions not reported on line 13 (See P 10 instruc.)		14	
15	Supplemental gains or (losses) (attach Form 4797)		15	
16	Fully taxable pensions, IRA distributions, and annuities not reported on 17.		16	
17a	Other Pensions and annuities, Total received	17a		
b	Taxable amount, if any, from worsheet on page 18 of instructions.		17b	
18	Rents, royalties, estates, trusts, etc. (Attach Schedule E)		18	8,180
19	Farm income or (loss) (Attach Schedule F)		19	660
20a	Unemployment compensation (Insurance).	20a		
b	Taxable amount, if any, from worksheet on page 18 of instructions.		20b	
21a	Social Security Benefits. See page 10 of instructions	20a		
b	Taxable amount, if any, from the worksheet on page 11 of instructions.		21b	
22	Other income. (State nature and source-see page 11 of instructions)		22	3,000
23	Add lines 7 through 22. This is your total income.		23	112,473

Adjustments to income

(See instructions on page 11)

Please attach check or money order here.

24	Moving expense (Attach Form 3903 or 3903F)	24	23,445		
25	Employee business expenses (Attach Form 2106)	25	56,231		
26a	IRA Deduction, from worksheet on page 12.	26a	4,000		
b	Enter here IRA payments you made in 1984 that are included in 26a above.				
27	Payments to a Keogh (H.R.10) Retirement plan.	27			
28	Penalty on early withdrawal of savings.	28			
29	Alimony paid.	29			
30	Deduction for a married couple when both work.	30			
31	Add lines 24 through 30. These are your total adjustments.			31	83,676

Adjusted Gross Income

32	Subtract line 31 from line 23. This is your adjusted gross income. If this line is less than $10,000, see "Earned Income Credit" (line 59) on page 16 of instr. If you want IRS to figure your tax, see page 12 of instructions		32	28,797

- Printed on **HP LASERJET** Laser printer *(B Cartridge)* Graphics Development International -

Figure 22-6. An IRS 1040 form, digitized and stored as a Form Easy File.

411

KEYWORDS:

- Page Layout

- Design

- Page Budget

- Master Pages

- Production

Jay Kinney is a San Francisco–based writer and illustrator. He has worked with the Macintosh since 1984, and uses PageMaker to produce *Gnosis*, a quarterly magazine about Western spiritual and occult traditions. His reviews of Macintosh software have appeared in *Macworld*, *Publish!*, and the *Whole Earth Review*.

Essay Synopsis: Magazines that contain a wide variety of formats, typefaces, and graphic elements present extremes of production problems. Magazines typically run on tight budgets and short time schedules. Desktop publishing tools are put to a real test in such an environment.

In this essay the author examines desktop publishing hardware and software in the context of magazine production. He discusses how to use a spreadsheet to set up a page budget and cast off characters, how a manuscript travels through production, how a page layout program is set up as small files of master pages, when and when not to depend on page layout and graphic software, what are the limitations of output devices, and more.

23

Producing a Magazine

Jay Kinney

Desktop publishing is commonly associated with newsletters or brochures, modest quality publications that involve relatively few pages and simple formats. If you've been producing an eight-page club newsletter using an electric typewriter, double-stick tape, and a mimeo or photocopier, publishing on a personal computer is a godsend. Not only is the job easier, but the new final copy looks terrific compared to the old one.

However, if you are publishing a magazine with dozens of pages, a complex production schedule, finicky advertisers, and a production staff trained in traditional methods, then converting to desktop publishing is a riskier business. The following three considerations are important when evaluating your desktop publishing needs.

First, using page layout programs on your personal computer will save you pasteup time and typesetting costs. If you've mastered the necessary skills and software, the pages that roll out of the printer will be already typeset and pasted up. This is bad news to professional typesetters and pasteup artists who see their jobs evaporating before their eyes, but it is good news to your budget. Or is it? If the person who spends hours shuffling type around on the computer screen is a highly paid art director or editor, the money saved in pasteup may be lost in editing and design. This is particularly true if your designers have a penchant for perfection. It

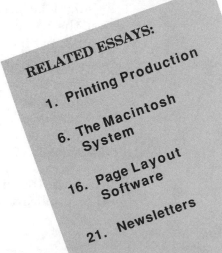

RELATED ESSAYS:

1. Printing Production

6. The Macintosh System

16. Page Layout Software

21. Newsletters

is very easy for people to dive into the self-contained world of the computer to "correct a few errors" or "try one more design" and not emerge until many hours later. Computer programmers are legendary for compulsively fiddling at the keyboard until four in the morning, so beware! Of course, questions of who spends time doing what (and how long it takes them) are less significant with small publications, such as newsletters, where one or two persons have traditionally done everything anyway.

Second, designing publications on a personal computer lets you (or your art director) have more control over the whole design process, including the much-vaunted bonus of being able to try out alternate layouts quickly. Yet, do you really want all that control and the added responsibility that comes with it? Are you interested in simultaneously overseeing questions of margin sizes, typefaces and text speccing, hyphenation, point rule size, headline placement, and page numbering? If you put out a small publication with a three-person staff, that may be appropriate. But if you have a bigger operation with carefully delineated jobs, you may soon find that desktop publishing plays havoc with job descriptions in unexpected ways. Suddenly, editors find themselves making typesetting decisions, art directors end up making copyediting and hyphenation decisions on the fly as they pour type in and out of layouts, and people with little aesthetic training (or too much!) find themselves pulled toward default design decisions by the rules and logic built into the page layout programs. With easy access to the programs, staff members sitting at other computers are easily tempted to alter the elements on a page or to make other changes that are far outside their province.

Third, publishing on a personal computer has the potential to give you thoroughly professional results that are in many respects indistinguishable from those obtained by the "good old ways." However, as might be predicted with a field still in its infancy, you'll discover that the route to seamless results is strewn with more obstacles and Catch-22's than the slick promotional materials ever let on. For instance, computers and page makeup programs don't replace the need for top-notch designers. Rather, they call for good designers who are savvy about hardware and software or who are very good learners.

Characteristics of Magazines

What are the unique characteristics that distinguish magazines from other publications, and how do these affect your approach to desktop publishing? To begin with, there is the element of size. Magazines usually have a minimum of 32 to 48 pages, but often may number their pages in the hundreds. Also they often have odd trim sizes, such as 8⅜ by 10¾ inches. Depending on how your software handles things like page and margin size, you may find yourself making some odd math calculations in order to get the results you want. This is because desktop publishing programs are usually set up for standard 8½ by 11 inch or 11 by 17 inch pages.

For instance, because PageMaker determines text column widths through the backhanded method of asking you to specify margin and gutter widths, you have to subtract the total measurement of your intended columns from the width of a 8½ by 11 inch page in order to determine the margin and gutter widths as they would be on a standard page, not as they will actually be on your custom-trimmed pages. Confused? So was I the first time I had to figure that out!

Another characteristic to consider is format. Many magazines vary their text font from section to section, use a wide variety of headline fonts in varying point sizes, and change page layouts from article to article. They may also run book excerpts or long articles that are continued to the "back of the book" amidst pages partially filled with ads. This can complicate matters considerably.

With multiple type fonts in use, your laser printer may run out of memory halfway through a job. An ever changing variety of page layouts will call for constant customizing of page settings, making it more difficult to rely on previously worked up page design templates. And articles that are continued from one part of the magazine to another will probably have to be produced without using the automatic page numbering features of most desktop programs. (This is because such features generally assume that all pages in a file are consecutively numbered, and do not allow for jumps in numbering.)

Aesthetics is yet another element to take into account. In magazine publishing, where phototypesetting has long been the norm, laser output will suffice only for proofs. Final page printouts must be printed by digital phototypesetting equipment, such as the Allied Linotronic series that read files produced by page makeup programs. Depending on the prices at your local Allied-equipped printer or copyshop, you may save a bundle — or mere pennies — on this form of phototypesetting. (Per-page rates from Allied machines range from $5 to $12. Only time will tell whether this range will remain the norm.)

And lastly, it is important to assess the impact of desktop publishing on your staff. The size of your magazine staff may vary anywhere from three to a couple of dozen workers, including editors, copyeditors, proofreaders, art directors, production artists, and managers. Introducing desktop publishing will affect them all, and not all will like it. Some of your best workers may turn out to be adamant computerphobes who resist the process every step of the way. Conversely, some staff members may take to the new system like ducks to water, happily spending hours on end getting a detail just right that would have taken five minutes to solve the old way. In either case, switching to a desktop system may cost you more time and money than you've anticipated.

Is Desktop Publishing Appropriate for Your Magazine?

The following description of the procedures used to produce a magazine should enable you to make an informed decision. The system used in this example included a Macintosh Plus, a DataFrame 20 hard disk, a DataSpace DS800 external double-sided disk drive, an Apple LaserWriter, and Aldus's PageMaker 1.2. No matter which hardware or software you end up using, most of the procedures discussed here will apply.

Stage One: Laying the Groundwork

The key to efficient desktop publishing is to complete as much of the work as possible before you even open the page layout program! This follows normal publishing procedure. A good editor will see that all of the copyediting, word counts, and editorial changes are made before sending an article into production. Similarly, a good art director has planned how an article in the magazine can best be presented before sending it off to be typeset. Since opening a page layout program is the equivalent of starting typesetting and production, there are a number of tasks to polish off before diving into page design. These include word processing, copyfitting, and typeface selection.

Things work best if all manuscripts have been typed using the same word processing program or have been ported into that program in ASCII form (from another computer or word processor). In my work with the Macintosh, I use Microsoft Word because it allows the line spacing to be set more exactly than MacWrite does, eliminating an extra step of work in PageMaker.

I recommend saving each article and sidebar as a separate file on a common file disk. (If you have a hard disk, these files should all be placed together in a designated folder or directory.) This will come in handy later on when having each piece of writing filed (and poured into PageMaker) as an independent element will let you shift the pieces around without distorting the rest of your layout. Keeping all the text for a single issue together on one disk also alleviates confusion as things proceed through the editorial process.

As the next step, the files should be copyedited and proofread while they are still in double-spaced, easily-read form. They should also be saved on a backup disk as insurance against unexpected disasters or mistaken deletions. It's also a good idea to take each article and do an exact word or character count (MicroSoft Word provides the latter), and run that figure through a copyfitting calculation. Such formulas multiply the number of words or characters in an article by the amount of space each word or character takes up when typeset (see Figure 23-1). In this example, I've worked up a simple copyfitting grid in Multiplan that automatically provides estimates for story lengths in different typefaces and point sizes.

The third step is to create a simple Multiplan template to tally the lengths of all the articles in the issue into a page budget. If you, as editor, have 56 pages to fill, your page budget will tell you how much space is filled currently and what space is still available. Figure 23-2 shows a spreadsheet-based copy-fitting table. Calculations take average number of characters per line and multiply times number of lines in manuscript. This total is then divided by average number of characters per column inch, a 10 percent adjustment is added to cover for error margin and the number of pages of typeset text is discovered. This is then multiplied according to a ratio of art to text and the final estimate of illustrated article space is shown. With this information, you can draw a map for the issue showing which articles will follow each other and what will be their general placement in the magazine as a whole. Many publications work this out on a large map posted on the wall for all to see. If you are determined to run everything through the computer, you can concoct an issue map using a visual database, such as Business Filevision. Such a database might involve a diagram of the issue's pages, with icons or visual symbols on the pages representing different types of articles. By clicking the mouse on different pages, files detailing that page's contents and characteristics could be summoned to the screen. This is an example of one of the clever uses of the computer that Macintosh owners love to point to. The ques-

    File   Edit   Select   Format   Options   Calculate

| R15C4 | ⊗ | 0.5 |

Page Budget

	1	2	3	4
1	PAGE BUDGET for GNOSIS #1			
2				
3	Article Title	Author	Illustrations	pgs. alloted
4				
5	World acc. to Valentinus	Fideler	charts	7
6	"Franz Kafka" by Borges	Greenburg	H. Robins	5
7	Interview w/ Gilles Quispel	Farmer	photos	3
8	Rumi's Poetry	ibn Yusuf	?	6
9	Philip K. Dick article	Kinney	photos	6
10	Excerpts from Exegesis	P.K. Dick	ex. xerox?	2
11	Valentinus' relevance	Hoeller	?	4
12				
13	Reviews			
14	Natureword by de Lubicz	Cutsinger		0.6
15	The New Gnosis by Avens	Beizer		0.5

Figure 23-1. Portion of Page Budget for magazine developed with Multiplan. Bottom of spreadsheet (not shown) has total of pages currently allotted and also indicates number of unfilled pages, if any.

    File   Edit   Select   Format   Options   Calculate

| R11C3 | =R11C2/361.6 |

Copyfitting Calc.

	1	2	3	4	5	6
5	ch/line:	86	lines/pt. A:	289		
6	ch/line:	0	lines/pt. B:	0		
7						
8	pt. size	total # of ch	total col.in.	adj. total in.	pgs. of text	pgs. text & art
9						
10	TIMES					
11	"8" pt.	24854	68.73	75.61	2.80	3.72
12	"9" pt.	24854	82.85	91.13	3.38	4.49
13	"10" pt.	24854	68.70	75.56	4.20	5.58
14						
15	HELVETICA					
16	"8" pt.	24854	78.87	86.76	3.21	4.27
17	"9" pt.	24854	101.53	111.69	4.14	5.50
18	"10" pt.	24854	75.24	82.76	4.60	6.12
19						

Figure 23-2. Sample of copyfitting table for magazines developed with Multiplan.

tion remains whether or not setting up such a database might gobble up far more time than it would ever save.

Stage Two: Design

Going from the editorial to the design phase brings you into one of those zones of potential job overlap in desktop publishing. This overlap doesn't have to be troublesome as long as you and your co-workers are aware of it and work out a division of labor. The issue of choosing typefaces is one example. While still within the word processing program, your articles are now ready to be converted into the typefaces and point sizes that will be used on the magazine pages themselves. In traditional terms, this conversion is the equivalent of "speccing" (specifying) the type, which is usually done by the art director prior to sending copy out for typesetting. However, if your magazine has a standardized format that uses only one or two type faces and sizes (such as 10-point Times Roman with 11-point leading), it may be simplest to have someone in the editorial department convert all the files to the proper font and point size prior to turning them over to the art director.

Once the text files have been converted they are ready as raw material for use in PageMaker. It is a good idea to work up some no-frills page layout templates in PageMaker that can be used at this juncture for running out preliminary galleys. If the articles in your magazine are usually set in two 21-pica-wide columns per page, while your news section and letters pages are always three 13-pica columns per page, templates matching those formats can be used over and over (see Figure 23-3). Text files transferred (or poured) into these templates, saved as separate working files, and printed out on the LaserWriter provide the art director with the basic elements for tighter page layouts. These galleys can also be proofed for typesetting errors that might have crept in during file conversion (see Figure 23-4).

But hold on a moment! What's this about using laser printed galleys for tighter page layouts? Isn't desktop publishing supposed to do away with such old-fashioned methods as cutting up galleys and moving them around on tissue paper over a blue pasteboard grid? Maybe, but maybe not. Some programs, such as PageMaker, are touted as letting you do the whole page design process on screen, thus eliminating scissors, tape, knives, and wax. However, at this point, Macintoshes, as well as other personal computers, still have small

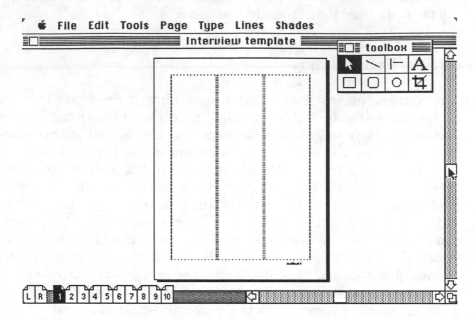

Figure 23-3. Stock three-column template in PageMaker developed by magazine designer. Correct margin size, column width, gutter width, and placement of page numbers are already in place.

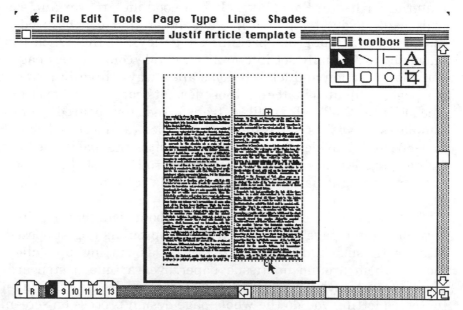

Figure 23-4. "Galleys" of text being poured into PageMaker. Sample runout of text on laser printer at this stage provides art director with the basics with which to further refine the article design.

screens that show only a portion of the page at a time. Employing reduced whole page shots on screen only helps up to a point, and I'll wager that your art director will end up doing some layouts on paper, even if you've spent $10,000 on fancy hardware. This is even more likely if your art director prefers to concentrate on design and leaves the job of making PageMaker jump through hoops to an assistant.

At this initial layout stage, certain elements — such as drop caps, headlines, wraps around pictures, and changes in type point size for credit lines — can be indicated and drawn in on the galleys and layout sheets by the art director. These will be guidelines that the designer or an assistant will use when returning to PageMaker for final layouts.

Stage Three: Production

Now it's time to get down to the real heart of desktop publishing: turning the raw material into tightly designed pages on screen. You have two choices as to how to go about this. If your proofreaders found a large number of typos, or if your art director decided to change the font or point size in an article, you may want to go back to your text file and make the changes there. Then, using the art director's layouts as guides, you can repour the corrected text into PageMaker, producing such things as drop caps and headlines as called for.

If no major changes are called for, however, it will be most expedient to go back to your already poured galley pages and readjust the text to fit the art director's layouts. Again, there is likely to be some job overlap here, since hyphens may have to be inserted or sentences edited to make the text fit well. If an art department person is making these corrections to the file, that person should have some editorial knowledge or writing background. Otherwise you may find some new errors introduced while these corrections are made!

I've found that it is easiest to save each article in an issue as a separate PageMaker file, or if you have two or three single-page layouts following each other (such as a masthead page, letters page, and editorial), save them together as one file. The reasons are very simple: First, much of the convenience of PageMaker lies in creating "master pages" that specify such details as column widths, vertical rules, and headers for all the pages in a file. However, if you have several articles with distinctly different layouts included in one file, these master pages would be useless and would fail as a timesaving device because you'd end up customizing each article's details on its own.

What's more, long files take longer (sometimes far longer) to save, and in a program such as PageMaker where you should save constantly, the delay can add up. While PageMaker version 1.0 through 1.2 was roundly criticized by reviewers and competitors for limiting files to 16 pages, I've rarely found it convenient to have a file exceed eight pages in length! On the contrary, even with a hard disk, "save" times have sometimes been so sluggish that I've divided up documents filling nine magazine pages into two files.

Adding Visual Elements

Unless your magazine consists of page after page of text, you'll be working with photos and illustrations in your page layouts. This is an area where you'll again run into the limitations of the desktop publishing dream. While there are constantly new developments in digitizing images, computer-generated art and charts, and many disks of prepared art ready to drop onto your PageMaker pages, the fact remains that few magazines will want to use those resources. The resolution of detail available with digitized images and computer clip art is still too crude for most professional publishing. Therefore, you'll likely find yourself putting in black rectangular windows on your pages to indicate where screened art or photos will be stripped in at the printers (see Figure 23-5). This may not look as striking on screen as painstakingly crafted MacPaint drawings, but your art department will confirm that it certainly beats cutting windows out of rubylith or red Zipatone with X-Acto knives, which was the previous method for indicating art.

A word of caution when creating headlines or drop caps: It is usually simplest to create these large type elements in PageMaker itself, using the "drawing board" area outside of the boundaries of the page designs (see Figure 23-6). By doing this to make a headline, you can type across the entire page. (If you type within the page design you will be limited to a narrower single column width that is set according to the page specs.) This enables you to make headlines that span more than one column. But it also means that you may run into overlapping text block areas if you have headlines, bylines, drop caps, and text columns in close proximity. There is nothing more frustrating than attempting to adjust the placement of a dropcap only to find yourself yanking your text halfway across the page by mistake, or vice versa. The best way to avoid this time consuming fiasco is to become very familiar with the "Bring to front" and "Send to back" commands under the Edit menu and make sure that what you want to move is the text block on top.

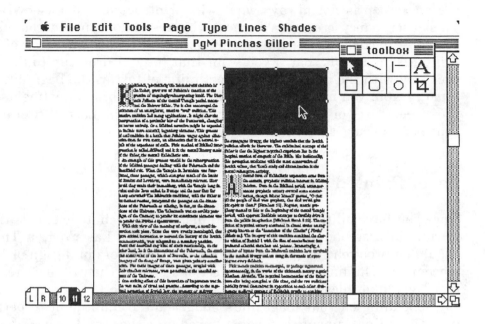

Figure 23-5. Black rectangles can be used to indicate "windows" for printer to insert screened negatives of photos or detailed art.

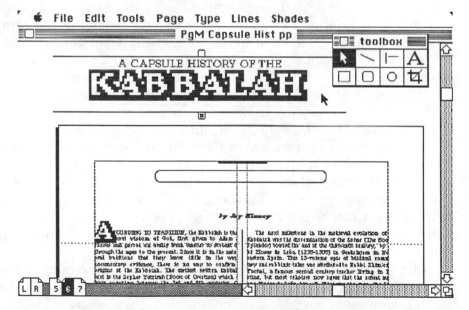

Figure 23-6. Headlines and other text spanning the width of the page is best typed in on the "drawing board" area outside of the boundaries of the page design. It can then be dragged onto the page and placed properly.

When handling large-size type elements, remember that what you see on screen is not always what will print out of the LaserWriter. This discrepancy creeps in because the resolution on the computer screen — particularly for large point sizes — is cruder than that of the printer. This means that if you want that large *A* drop cap to line up precisely with the bottom of the fourth line of text at the beginning of a paragraph, you may need to make incredibly subtle adjustments on the screen three or four times and run a proof on the LaserWriter each time before you get exactly what you want.

Laser Printed Proofs

Once you have all the final layouts finished for each article, it is time to run out a second set of complete proofs on the LaserWriter. These should be proofread again and scoured for any errors in design or text placement. The final round of corrections should then be inserted in the PageMaker files and a set of final runouts made.

Depending on your magazine's budget and commitment to perfection, these final runouts can be produced on either the LaserWriter or a compatible phototypesetter such as the Allied Linotronic family of machines. If you opt to stick with the LaserWriter you can get the sharpest, cleanest output by using the best quality paper that will run through the printer. I've obtained excellent results from Simpson Opaque 70-weight, a smooth finish, long grain paper that is available by the ream (500 sheets) for under $10. An even better result is possible with Karma Text White 80-pound paper, which has a very smooth coated surface. However, you may have to obtain this from a printer or paper company in 23 by 35 inch sheets and have it custom cut into 8½ by 11 inch paper at considerable expense.

For the very best results, you'll want to make your final runouts from an Allied or Linotronic or similar machine. Prices on these runouts from copy shops seem to range from $5 to $12 per page. Depending on such factors as schedule and staff flexibility, a magazine staff member can do the runouts (at a self-service shop) or they can be done by the copyshop staff. Even at this stage there are possible pitfalls.

The phototypesetting equipment that reads Macintosh or other PostScript-generating files is basically identical in operation to the digital equipment used by many professional typesetters. This means that it utilizes photosensitive paper and a chemical processor. If the copyshop you use is lazy about changing their chemicals, or if you make runouts at the end of a long day of equipment use, the output may be more gray than usual, and details may drop out when the negatives or printing plates are made. If you are using the equipment on a self-serve basis, you should check this output quality on the first page you run out.

You'll run into another possible pitfall if your art director has used numerous fonts that are not already embedded in the printer's memory and must be downloaded from the System folder of your PageMaker disk. If this is the case, and if you've used the copy-protected fonts published by Adobe, you'll have to use copies of those font files that are initialized for use with that specific printer. This means making sure that the fonts you've used are available for printing at the copyshop, getting the right initialized files from them, and copying the files into your System folder, which is a time consuming process. Laser type fonts from other companies — such as Casady Co., Century Software, or Image Club — don't have this machine-specific limitation, but they will still require that you have their printer font files inside your System folder before you go to print.

Another pitfall arises from the advanced capabilities of page layout software. For instance, PageMaker lets you lay in areas of gray screen on the page, including gray screens over blocks of type. Theoretically this is a big expense-saver because it lets you use design elements, such as laying a 20 percent screen on top of a column of text, without having to go through the expense of having the printer "double-burn" a screen tint onto the type when the negatives are shot for printing. The problem that arises here is that the screen percentages indicated by PageMaker (e.g., 20 percent, 40 percent, 60 percent) are not always reliable. As I've learned (twice!) to my chagrin, what is shown as a 20 percent screen in PageMaker (and on the LaserWriter) comes out of the Linotronic 100 as a 10 percent screen and ends up dropping to a 5 percent screen when the page is shot into negatives. What is even worse is that this is not always the case, so one is constantly tantalized with the possibility that maybe this time it will come out right! However, I've concluded from bitter experience that to get a reliable 20 percent screen on the printed page, a rubylith overlay still needs to be cut on the pasted up page, and so the printer must drop in the screen.

Final Stage: Tying Up the Loose Ends

Once you have your crisp final printouts in hand you are almost done, but not quite! Desktop publishing may eliminate pasteup if you are doing a newsletter or flyer where you can hand a few laser-printed pages to the printer and let them do the rest. A fatter and more complex magazine, however, requires pasted up pages on boards showing page order and trim-marks. The good news is that desktop publishing can reduce this step considerably. The bad news is that it may still take longer than you think. This is because there are still various loose ends to tie up in pasteup.

If you've left black rectangles as windows for art or photos to be dropped in by the printer, you'll still have to size the art and label it by page or window. If you've made photostats of line art, these will have to be positioned and pasted in. If your magazine runs display advertising, the ad art will have to be pasted in or indicated for the printer. And last, but not least, you may find yourself (or your art department) wielding an X-Acto knife and shifting type around to get it just right — despite all the time you've spent jiggling it around on screen! The letterspacing on some headlines may have suffered from the kerning limitations of your page layout program and require you to move single letters or parts of words to the left or right. Paragraphs may need to be shifted slightly or — most bothersome of all — rules (particularly at the bottom of pages) may not be quite square. You may reasonably ask, with $40,000 worth of equipment, Why are the rules still not square? Such things cause pasteup artists to smirk in their coffee, and publishers to get ulcers. Once all these things are done and the printouts are all securely down on the boards, then you can relax and contemplate life on the cutting edge of publishing.

Is Desktop Publishing the Route for Your Publication?

In order to answer this question you should ask yourself a few other questions first. Are you satisfied with your present (nondesktop) method of production? If you are, and if things are going smoothly, there is no sin in continuing with this method. "If it ain't broke, don't fix it," is good advice most of the time, especially when you are constantly running a tight schedule.

Do you have a big, thick publication or a small one? Desktop publishing with the Macintosh or IBM PC can be a boon to a small magazine that wants to look as professional as possible on a minute budget. However, until full-page and two-page-spread sized screens become common and inexpensive enough for your budget, you may find that the partial page view allowed by most present systems cramps your publication's style and slows things down noticeably. If time is of the essence, desktop publishing may eat up more time than you have.

Is your staff morale high? Are they looking for new challenges? If not, introducing a totally new way of doing things may introduce more chaos than your magazine can handle. One small quarterly magazine with which I'm familiar switched from an IBM composer to the Macintosh and LaserWriter and had to skip an issue because the changeover took far longer than anticipated.

Summary

The computer and desktop publishing magazines are full of excitement over the prospect of doing everything with a Macintosh or other personal computer. Ads for the appropriate hardware and software feature spiffy pages where everything from the type to digitized photos to pie charts have been computer-generated and come rolling out of the laser printer. It is a seductive vision — you might even call it utopian — but be forewarned that it is a nerd's utopia. Much of the hype associated with desktop publishing would have you believe that squeezing everything through the computer (no matter how many hours it takes) is somehow superior to doing anything by hand. This simply isn't so, and if your first commitment is to getting the best results in the shortest amount of time with the least cost, you will still discover that pasting a simple $6 photostat in place on the pasteup board often beats two hours of careful digitizing, pixel touch-up, and PageMaker picture juggling. Desktop publishing may solve some problems, but for magazine production it isn't a panacea.

KEYWORDS:

- Sequential Storytelling

- Panel

- Caption

- Balloon

Mike Gold is senior editor at DC Comics, U.S. correspondent for the British edition of *MacUser* magazine, and a contributor to *Personal Publishing Magazine*. He has been in print and broadcast media for 19 years and was the original editor of *Shatter*.

Essay Synopsis: Comic strip publishing relies more heavily on the use of graphic art than most other forms of publishing and has unique requirements such as mixing graphics with captions and text balloons. Not surprisingly, developers have designed software to cope with these special needs.

In this essay the author examines the nature of comic strip art along with a brief history of the use of computers in this field, and then shows how paint and draw programs, word processors, page layout programs, and dedicated comic-generating software work together. He discusses tricks to using various products to transfer and manipulate electronic art easily, limitations to page layout software, and how working artists choose to mix traditional graphic techniques with the use of Macintosh-based software.

24

Comics and Cartooning

Mike Gold

Like the rest of the publishing industry in the United States, the comic art field is beginning to feel the impact of the ongoing microcomputer revolution. It's about time: Comic art has been used to tell stories about people who were on the cutting edge of technology, yet the comics themselves have been produced by the same technology used since the Great Depression.

First, some definitions are in order. The term "comic art" is an unfortunate misnomer because it refers to the graphic storytelling form that is more appropriately called sequential storytelling. It isn't necessarily comic in tone, and many comic books tend to be deadly serious.

Compared to comic strips and single-panel cartoons, comic books and graphic novels have the ability to tell longer stories of a fantastic scope over a larger space. Panels can be divided in such a way as to control pacing and time, and to provide stronger visual impact than comic strips. Indeed, comic books are unique in their ability to control time and space through this visual pacing, giving the comic book writer and artist storytelling powers undreamed of by more traditional authors.

Comic strips generally consist of three or four panels (eight or nine panels for Sunday strips) of roughly the same size. To the extent that there may be the need for storytelling, it occurs in a very linear way. Strips are more dependent on captions

RELATED ESSAYS:

12. Image Scanning and Processing

15. Graphics Fundamentals

25. Music Desktop Publishing

(such as "meanwhile..." and "the next day...") to establish timing and pacing.

Of course, there are single-panel comics as well, which are often referred to as cartoons. This type of comic is frequently seen in the *New Yorker* magazine, for example. Since comic strips and comic books evolved from the single-panel cartoons of the 1800's, bringing computer techniques to this particular form presents an ironic challenge.

We can be humorous, we can tell stories of epic proportions, we can probe deeply into the human condition, and we can speak to audiences of all ages — occasionally all at the same time! In the comics field, we are as much magicians as we are storytellers, and, as we all know, there is a direct connection between magic and computers.

History of Comics and Computers

To understand how to use desktop publishing techniques in the production of comics and cartoons, we will start by taking a look at what has been done and how it was done.

Microcomputers had their greatest impact on comics in early 1985 with the highly successful comic book series *Shatter,* written by Peter B. Gillis and drawn by Mike Saenz. The entire first issue of *Shatter* was drawn the preceding year with a Macintosh 128K computer using Apple's MacPaint software and a single disk drive. It was printed on an ImageWriter I printer. By today's standards, that's like chiseling artwork into blocks of stone.

In producing 29 pages of black-and-white art (including the cover), Saenz established himself as a true pioneer in both the comic art medium and the computer graphics field. Quite simply, he pulled off something amazing, something nobody had ever done before. Saenz opened both worlds to new techniques.

Under Saenz, all the artwork in subsequent issues of *Shatter* was drawn on the Mac. In those dim days before laser printers, the 72-dots-per-inch printouts were touched up by hand. After leaving *Shatter,* Saenz went on to co-create ComicWorks software for MacroMind and to work on establishing systems to produce both high-resolution computer art and color separations. He presently is drawing a one-shot for Marvel Comics employing the latest techniques with their popular character *Iron Man.*

In the midst of its success, *Shatter* quickly revealed the central difficulty in using microcomputers as a drawing medium: The artist is limited to comparatively low resolution — in this case, 72 dots per inch. Whereas the art's high-tech look to the art has quite an impact on readers (similar to, say, sneaking a print of Star Wars into a Frank Capra film festival), the style imposes a severe limitation on the story itself.

Indeed, without a solid story worth telling, computer art is reduced to a gimmick, and all gimmicks wear thin after a while. The writer must come up with a story that plays into the technique, and people already are tiring of high-tech stories going hand in hand with the high-tech art.

It is easy to use technique to overwhelm, but the gifted storyteller will discover a way to use the same technique to enliven as well. The true challenge to the computer storyteller will be in creating stories that are as impressive as the medium itself.

After Saenz's departure, *Shatter* was drawn by more conventional pencil-on-paper techniques, digitizing the art to give it the computerized appearance. Shortly after writer/co-creator Gillis returned to the series, a new computer artist was brought into the project, and the digitized line art approach was abandoned.

More recently, artist Jim McGreal brought NAPLPS graphics techniques (North American Presentation Level Protocol Standard) from his work in the videotext field to a new comic book, *Vector.* Whereas the AT&T Frame Generation System could hardly be referred to as a desktop computer, *Vector* serves as still another approach to the use of computers in sequential storytelling. McGreal combines traditional line art, using computer art only when the story demands. This mixed media approach has proven quite effective.

Saenz's embryonic work helped establish the Macintosh as the microcomputer standard of the comics industry. At least three major publishers use Macintoshes in-house, and more writers and artists own Macintoshes than any other PC.

Quite a number of talented and successful artists, including John Byrne, Jim Starlin, and Bruce Patterson, have been using the Macintosh in still another way: to generate limited art for special effects, weird backgrounds, and unusual objects to enhance their more traditional storytelling. Their work has been seen in such best-selling DC and Marvel Comics as *Superman, Green Lantern,* and *Dreadstar.*

Approaching a New Medium

Before you begin to use a microcomputer to draw comics, you first must understand who is in control. Computers do not draw comics, just as word processors do not write text: The microcomputer simply is a medium in which to work. The artist selects computer tools in the same manner as selecting the type of brush, pen, or paper.

Drawing

In order to draw, you can use either a mouse (a small, hand-held box that rolls on a giant rubber bearing) or a graphics pad (an electronic pen and a special drawing surface). Even though the pad is far more expensive, it has a more natural feel for the artist who is used to traditional drawing implements. In either case, the way you manipulate the device tells the computer where you want your lines and dots to go.

Most graphics software includes a palette with various tools that allow you to draw, edit, shape, and mold your art. You can select the width of your line, or draw circles, boxes, and straight lines without a template. You can clean up or edit either by using an electronic eraser or by enlarging the pixels (going to "fat bits," in Macintosh parlance) and adding or eliminating them on a one-by-one basis.

You will never have to erase anything, and you'll never have to glue a patch over something that didn't work out quite right. It's a wonder more grammar school art teachers haven't lobbied for the machines.

One of the fastest ways of drawing is by using the smooth, irregular-shaped line tool on the palette called regions, which allows you to draw complete objects freehand. You'll have to try it before you understand its potential, and don't be too surprised if everything you draw at first looks like something Picasso might doodle on Publisher's Clearinghouse Sweepstakes envelopes.

To add shading to traditional line art, you painstakingly cut up sheets of "tones" (Ben Day effects, most popularly known as Zip-A-Tone™, although many companies provide sundry substances and techniques). In the computer art medium, your microcomputer adds it all for you, allowing you to fill enclosed spaces (or backgrounds) instantly with different types of tones — dot screens, line screens, or patterns (see Figure 24-1). The better graphics programs will allow you to design your own patterns as well.

Using Existing Images

When using reference material in traditional art, you would have to find a photograph of your object (e.g., the Taj Mahal) and trace it onto your artboards. By using a digitizer, you can take a drawing, a photograph, or a freeze-framed image on video tape, run it through a scanner, and get a computerized version of your image.

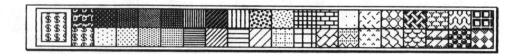

Figure 24-1. Examples of shadings (patterns).

You then can open it up as a graphics document, take portions of the image, alter them, improve on them, clean them up, and change them to your specific desires. Once digitized, you can turn the ancient Taj Mahal into a futuristic location on another planet, or hide a gigantic ape behind one of its turrets.

Of course, there can be a fine line between digitizing and plagiarism. This is not a problem that is unique to the computer artist. For decades, artists have traced photographs and have even pasted up photocopies and halftones as part of "their" art. The field has yet to come to grips with the ethical issues here; certainly, there is a difference between swipe and reference. In any event, digitizing allows the artist to have a greater personal impact on the reference material.

When adding dialogue to line art — generally accomplished after the art is pencilled but before it is rendered in ink — a calligrapher is brought in to ink the panel borders (the frames that contain the art are called panels) and to letter the job. Again, in the computer art medium the microcomputer can take care of both tasks for you.

Using the straight-line and the box tools from the palette and selecting the desired line width, you can have your computer automatically ink your panel borders, going into your software's edit mode to specialize your work. Some graphic art software will create unique types of panel borders as well (see Figure 24-2).

Adding Text

Words are carried in caption boxes and in balloons. There are various types of balloons: the round ones that suggest ordinary speech, bubbly

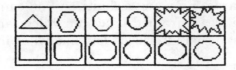

Figure 24-2. Panel shapes (from ComicWorks).

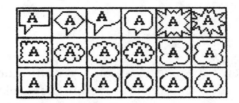

Figure 24-3. Balloon shapes (from ComicWorks).

ones that suggest thoughts, and pointy ones (called bursts) that suggest exclamations or exceptionally loud or aggressive speech.

You can draw captions and balloons with any graphics application and the dedicated comics applications will do it for you (see Figure 24-3). In some programs, it may be difficult to have specific words stand out in bold type without going back and "pasting over" new type.

Many microcomputers offer the potential for custom-designed fonts (families of type). Copy within balloons and captions should be readable and allow for differing types of emphasis — bold words, italics, underline — but a number of display fonts should be available for titles, sound effects, and the like.

New fonts are being designed every day of the week. There is software out there for you to design your own (Fontastic, for the Macintosh, perhaps is the most popular); but beware, it is extremely easy to design fonts that are too designy for your own good. A handful of the more unusual — but highly readable — fonts are shown in Figure 24-4.

There is a negative side to using desktop computers in the creation of your work: You will never have any original art. Most successful artists command some decent money for their originals, but with a microcomputer, the "original" pixels disappear when you turn your machine off! What you have saved to your floppy disk is a duplication of your original instructions. As always, being a graphic arts guerrilla carries its price.

Figure 24-4. Font display.

Selecting Your Tools

To begin with, keep in mind that sooner or later all types of software are imitated for most major systems, and often they are adapted for sundry hardware by the original publishers themselves. The lion's share of professional-quality software is available for the Macintosh, but most of the items discussed here should be available in some form for other systems before too long.

Choosing a Graphics Program

First, you need a good, reliable, easy-to-learn basic graphics program to allow you to master the technique of drawing with a microcomputer. MacPaint is the entry-level program, but FullPaint is an equally simple but more powerful and useful expansion of the seminal Macintosh graphics program. Either will allow you to draw anything for printout on a good dot matrix or laser printer, and both offer a full range of useful palette tools.

FullPaint has the significant advantage of allowing you more screen space on which to draw without moving your art, and it is geared for larger-than-screen-sized images. It will also allow you to keep up to four different files (a file contains one page) on screen at a time.

MacDraw is not well suited for drawing sequential line art per se because it sees figures as objects as opposed to groupings of pixels, and it is difficult to edit objects. However, if you are into architecture or graphs, MacDraw is ideally suited for these demands. Eventually, MacDraw will offer you opportunities that FullPaint does not, so don't dismiss the program out of hand — just don't start with it.

SuperPaint combines the qualities of both MacPaint and Mac-Draw. Again, I recommend starting out with MacPaint or FullPaint and mastering the basics first.

Page Layout Programs

Next, you might want to consider a page layout program — particularly if you have access to a laser printer or you need large-size printouts. Here, MacDraw can be particularly useful because it offers the largest work space of any such program. You can transport images and even completed panels over from FullPaint and electronically paste them up in whatever position or location you desire.

More sophisticated — and, of course, more expensive — page layout programs, such as PageMaker, can be extremely useful in virtually all personal publishing areas except sequential art storytelling. However, if your work is of a more illustrative nature where you are likely to combine sequential art with blocks of copy (including statistics and graphs for your more avant-garde board meetings, for example), these types of programs will be extremely useful.

Comic Generating Software

As noted above, there are a number of dedicated comic-art-producing programs. ComicWorks is among the best and probably is the best known. A complicated but inexpensive program, ComicWorks is so comprehensive that its largest potential audience actually is computer artists with no desire to produce sequential art. This audience failed to flock to ComicWorks, however, due to misperceptions caused by its name. When MacroMind and its publishing company Mindscape understood the limitations of the name ComicWorks, they came out with an almost exact copy called GraphicWorks, which is equipped with clip art files of a more serious nature.

When Mike Saenz co-created ComicWorks, he started out with the mental wishlist generated during the time he spent working on *Shatter*, and it shows. Just about everything a comics artist might want is in this program. Its main advantages include automatic captioning, ballooning, and an air brush emulator that alone is worth the price of the program. Built into its palette, the air brush tool allows you to paint fields of black or white in much the same manner as a real air brush. This is not surprising because Saenz was an accomplished air brush artist before discovering the Macintosh.

ComicWorks' main disadvantage is in its lack of PostScript support. On a LaserWriter, it could take nearly a half hour to print out a dense page of graphics. It also takes more time to learn than your average Macintosh program, and Macintosh owners tend to be an impatient lot.

Unlike its GraphicWorks counterpart, the ComicWorks package includes a couple of disks full of artwork — mostly from Mike Saenz (see Figure 24-5) — which may be useful as part of your clip-art collection.

There is a counterpart to ComicWorks for the newspaper comic strip field. Comic Strip Factory is somewhat easier to learn but it doesn't have as many features. Most important, ComicWorks allows you to draw anything you like in whatever panel configuration you desire, whereas Comic Strip Factory is more limited inasmuch as newspaper comic strips are limited in panel arrangements and size. This is not to say that Comic Strip Factory is less useful. On the contrary, it — and programs like it for other systems — might be more useful for your needs. As with all software decisions, you should shop and experiment before you buy.

Utilities and Clip Art

There is a wonderful little program called Glue that will allow you to paste virtually anything created on one program into almost anything you are creating on another. This allows you to use exactly whatever software fits your needs at the moment, as long as you are willing to

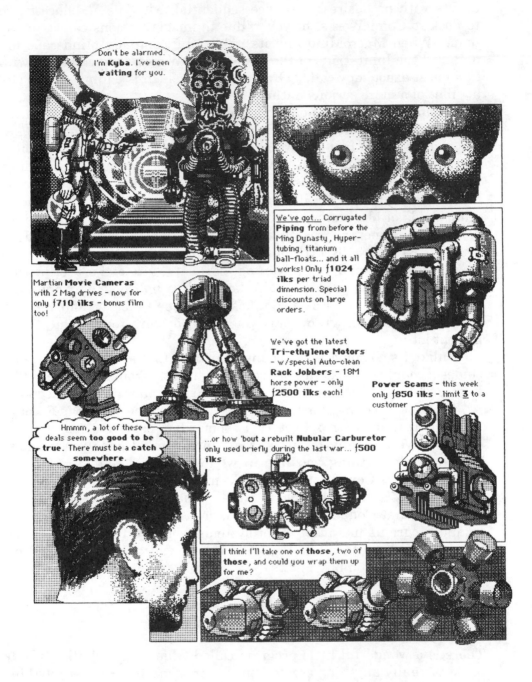

Figure 24-5. ComicWorks page by Mike Saenz.

assemble your various items later. Luckily, such assembly work is a quick and painless task — once you have some experience.

There are any number of other accessories that can supplement your software. The busy folks at MacroMind have an extremely useful tool called Art Grabber that runs in conjunction with most Macintosh graphic programs and allows you to "grab" images from MacPaint and FullPaint files (and, doubtlessly, others as well). Whereas you can always clutter your screen with additional files or, if necessary, (inhale!) close down your working file, open another, select the image you wish to borrow, copy it, close down the file, reopen your original file, and paste the image in (gasp!), Art Grabber does it all in one clean operation without ever closing down your working file.

Of course, other companies have programs similar to Art Grabber on the market, and some work better with larger images, but improvements on all successful software are constantly being made. This basic tool is essential, and you can use it to copy your own art. For example, there is no reason to draw the same building over and over, particularly when you can resize, edit, and alter your copied image. But you also have the opportunity to borrow other people's work without running the risk of copyright violation. There are literally hundreds of clip-art disks on the market full of all sorts of designs, drawings, digitized photos, graphs, icons, and doodads. Look carefully at the catalogs and the ads in the computer magazines; you'll be amazed at what you can find.

Then again, clip art is a commercial shortcut: It isn't really your work and the art won't reflect your own style. If you are putting your own artistic personality into your assignment, you first should try and draw it yourself. If that fails, consult the hundreds of clip-art files — but try to edit and personalize the image.

The Macintosh has a built-in method of generating your own art files. You can create a MacPaint file of whatever is in the active window on your screen by pressing "command-shift-3." The Mac will take a snapshot of the window and store it as a file that you can open with MacPaint or FullPaint.

Again, you have to be careful to avoid using graphics that were created by others and are under copyright, but the snapshot technique is an instant method for preserving your own creations — particularly those created with the assistance of various public domain games and desk accessories.

You also can use the snapshot technique in your word processing program to create solid blocks of type, such as ersatz newspapers. Microsoft's latest Macintosh version of Word, 3.0, allows you automatically to box in blocks of type. In conjunction with the snapshot technique this can be a speedy way of transferring captions from your script to your art.

FullPaint includes image-altering techniques built into the package, but you can install these options into MacPaint with Click-Art Effects. Either way, you can take groups of pixels and stretch, bend, rotate, and/or drop them into perspective (see Figure 24-6). If used with restraint, you can give a unique touch to various objects in your design.

However, there is one problem with image-altering software: You must be careful to avoid adding shading to these items before you are done manipulating them. Otherwise you will be stretching the shading out of proportion, and it will look extremely weird (see Figure 24-7). Experimenting with these procedures can be a lot of fun, and occasionally you might get something that is both weird and useful.

Computer Environments

The fact that the Macintosh is the industry standard is its main advantage to the would-be comic book computer artist. The Macintosh is as powerful and as fast as anything around. Although it presently does not provide on-screen color, there are plenty of color-blocking and color-printing programs available and even a major color-separation system is in development.

The various high-resolution full-page monitors available for the Mac are quite a boon to the graphic artist. They are a great deal of fun. If you are used to desktop computers with standard-sized monitors, seeing a full-page monitor is like walking straight from an elevator into a Boeing 747.

While the Amiga and the Atari ST offer color, both are crippled by an overwhelming lack of software and peripherals in the United States. Both have been on the market long enough to attract more support. Interestingly, the Atari ST is far more successful overseas, and if you live or work in Europe or Britain, you might want to give this system a closer look. No matter where you live, the ST offers a great deal of value for your money.

The Apple II — particularly the Apple II GS — can be configured to be a junior-level Macintosh with color. The main advantage of the Apple II series is that it is the microcomputer of choice in the majority of schools across the nation. If you have a child in school, you may very well have an Apple II expert living under your own roof. If you are in your teens, you already may be an Apple II expert!

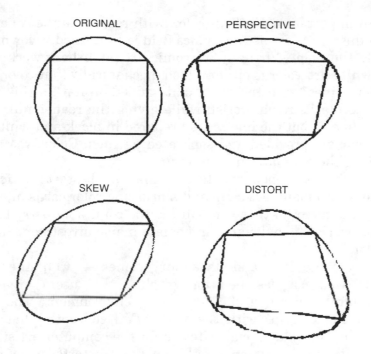

Figure 24-6. Altered images.

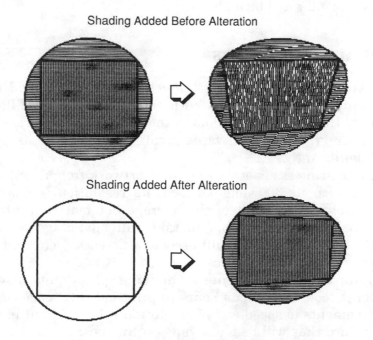

Figure 24-7. Shading altered images.

An important note about color, with respect to the American comic art industry: As far as the comics field is concerned, color monitors are beside the point. Virtually all comic art publishers work with black-and-white art; color is either added mechanically (flat color) or painted on "blue-lines" with the black plate added on top. In this latter manner, the blacks remain crisp while giving the reader full color at the same time — but the line art is prepared in black-and-white. Rarely is full color art provided and separated as such. Color was air brushed "behind" the dot matrix art in *Shatter*.

So when the open-architecture Macintosh starts enticing outside vendors into manufacturing and marketing color cards and color monitors, it is doubtful that you will see the comics industry breaking the sound barrier to make any immediate major investment in upgrading to color.

As for the IBM and its sundry clones — well, the famous PC simply was not designed for graphics. PC users are stuck with Microsoft Windows, a slow operating environment. The PC doesn't quite come to grips with the WYSIWYG concept (What You See Is What You Get — a crucial criterion for the computer artist). What you work with on the screen should not be a distorted view of your art. And, by the time you've added the mouse, the graphics card, the high-resolution monitor, and all the necessary cables to your PC, you've got a slow, second-rate Macintosh.

Printers and Digitizers

A desktop computer isn't worth much without a printer. New printers come out virtually every day. With its massive RAM and its PostScript support, the LaserWriter Plus, although expensive, presently is best suited for graphics. As it faces greater competition, its price should drop significantly.

Laser printers generate the finest artwork from a desktop computer; and with its 300 dots-per-inch, its resolution is more than four times greater than that of the average dot matrix printer. As more software becomes available to take full advantage of this greater resolution, laser printers will become a necessary element in the production of computer graphics.

However, all laser printers handle graphics quite slowly. For example, it took nearly four hours to print out a 29-page *Shatter* story. Improvements in speed and in resolution will come, but in the foreseeable future they will be found only on the most expensive laser printers.

At 72 dots per inch, the ImageWriter II offers multicolor printing, solid resolution and speed, and — most important — when the print head overheats (and it will if you are using a lot of solid blacks or a lot of dense artwork) the machine stops until it cools off. By the way, the ImageWriter I doesn't have this built-in safeguard. *Shatter* burned out at least one ImageWriter I print head — mine.

There also is an ever-growing variety of digitizers on the market. Here your best bet is to follow the specifications carefully. Do you need 72 dots per inch or something greater? Do you need the ability to pick up images that are freeze-framed on a videocassette recorder (do you even have a VCR capable of freeze-framing)? What about a video camera pick-up for digitizing static real-life images? How much control over the finished image do you desire? Remember, digitizers do not produce halftone resolution, and it is silly to acquire a digitizer that will generate graphics files to a resolution higher than the standard employed by the rest of your hardware.

Summary

Overall, the comic art field has just scratched the surface of the potential of microcomputer capabilities. How it evolves in the future depends on what present and upcoming artists bring to the attention of the publishers.

The positive reception to *Shatter, Vector,* and other uses of computer-generated art in comic art storytelling is clear: There is a willing and enthusiastic audience out there, waiting to see more. As a would-be computer comics artist, it is your duty to give it to them.

KEYWORDS:

- **Standard Notation**

- **Score**

- **Beams**

- **Clef**

- **MIDI**

- **Sonata Font**

James J. Romeo of Cambridge, Massachusetts, a Ph.D. in music composition from Harvard University and full Writer Member of A.S.C.A.P., has composed scores for stage, film, and television, developed the music software Ear Training Expert (published by Techno-Arts) for university-level study, and is the founding editor of *SoundWaves*, the newsletter of the Boston Computer Society Computers and Music Group.

George F. Litterst of Newton, Massachussetts, has a Master of Music degree in Piano Performance from the New England Conservatory of Music, is the music editor of *MACazine*, and teaches piano and music theory and history privately at Northeastern University.

Essay Synopsis: Compared with the typical mix of text and graphics, Standard Music Notation is specialized, something like merging English with a language from Mars.

In this essay the authors discuss the problems of desktop publishing Standard Music Notation and present the variety of note forms, beaming and phrasing between notes, dividing phrases by measures, adding accents, slurs, and other instructions available for the music transcriber. They explain the MIDI standard of communication between music devices, capturing music directly from instruments and autoconversion to notation on a staff, editing electronic music files for playback, and more.

25

Music Desktop Publishing

**James J. Romeo and
George F. Litterst**

The music industry is a continually evolving field with participants from every part of our diverse culture. It has been estimated that there are over 50 million people who play one musical instrument or another. Nearly every member of society can be called a listener; indeed, more than 400 million radios have been sold in the U.S. alone. Total annual sales of musical instruments and related accessories recently topped the two billion dollar mark.

The music industry includes records, tapes, compact disks, sheet music, rock/jazz concerts, symphony orchestras, nearly continuous music on television and radio, film music, music education, dance, and musical theater. And there is one common thread that unites nearly every second of this vast quantity of music: musical notation, a complex written language.

In the late 1970's the total sales of published, printed music topped the 300 million mark. Even traditionally non-notated music like rock, fusion, and jazz improvisation has taken part, with sales of transcribed solos and arrangements in sheet music form at a new high.

In the Roman alphabet there are 26 letters; a typical computer keyboard can produce around 120 symbols for writing. In the musical alphabet there are well over 600 different symbols, not including symbols for avant-garde music, text with music, or pre-Baroque music, all of which are com-

RELATED ESSAYS:

22. Forms Generating Software

24. Comics and Cartooning

mon. (See Gardner Read, Music Notation, *Index of Notation Symbols,* Crescendo Publishing Co., Boston, Massachusetts, 1969.)

In the past, music publishing was monopolized by a few large publishing houses with expensive equipment. However, with the advent of personal computers in the 1970's and music desktop publishing software in the 1980's, the music publishing industry has begun a process of profound change, gradually making room for the rapidly expanding field of music desktop publishing.

In 1987, a complete, top-of-the-line music desktop publishing setup can be purchased for less than $12,000, and a budget configuration can be set up for as little as $2,400. Printed music that is created using these systems can match the current standards of quality for commercial music publications. Music desktop publishing capabilities include piano scores with both polyphonic and chordal complexity (Figure 25-1), lead sheet notation for jazz and popular music (Figure 25-2), music with lyrics (Figure 25-2), multistave chamber and orchestral scores (Figure 25-3), and instructional material with mixed text, graphics, and music notation (Figure 25-4).

The Music Desktop Publishing Breakthrough

In 1501, Ottaviano Petrucci published the *Odhecaton,* the first book of music printed from moveable type. Block printing with engraved plates was also a common technique in early music publishing. Engraving with the use of punches (developed in the early 1700's) further facilitated publication. Lithography was developed and employed around 1800. Remarkably, with the exception of these few developments, for nearly 500 years, from 1501 to 1984, the way music was published remained basically unchanged. A photolithographic process using plates engraved by punches is still in use at the major music publishing houses today.

Several decades ago the development of xerography and the commercial manufacture of the photocopier provided for a new but limited form of music publishing. Composers could take a master hand copy of their music, photocopy it, and distribute it themselves to performers, libraries, and sales outlets. However, this was and still is a time-consuming and costly process; accurate notation by hand is so time-consuming that $5,000 for the professional copying of an original orchestral score with parts is not unusual. Composers must compete with each other for funds for score copying and reproduction from government grants and private sources. Consequently, many compositions never reach the public.

Figure 25-1. Cadenza for Mozart's Piano Concerto in D Minor, K466. Created using Deluxe Music Construction Set, Version 2.0 and the Sonata font from Adobe Systems.

Figure 25-2. Peaceful Night, jazz lead sheet. Created using Deluxe Music Construction Set, Version 2.0 and the Sonata font from Adobe Systems.

Figure 25-3. Sextet, contemporary chamber work. Created using Performer, Version 1.2 and Professional Composer, Version 2.0.

With recent breakthroughs in music desktop publishing technology, all this has changed. Now, a composer can put a score into a computer and at the touch of a button print out the score; press another button and print out a separate set of parts. A composer of vocals can click a mouse and transpose a copy of a song for high, medium, or low voice in seconds. For musicians involved with musical research and scholarship, the effect of music desktop publishing is far-reaching and permanent. For example, it will soon be simple for any teacher to prepare a unique edition of any musical work that can be used to teach private students and to instruct classes. Conductors could easily prepare the bowings and articulations of orchestral parts on disk, then print them out (saving time and money). And coaches could prepare special performance editions of chamber music from which to teach.

Music Desktop Publishing Software

The music desktop publishing scene is unique in that even the simplest musical notation communicates with a highly complex symbolic-graphic language. As an illustration of the richness of musical notation, consider just the first two measures of Figure 25-2. In this short, simple opening there are over a dozen different symbols, including staff lines, a clef, a meter signature, a dynamic marking, chord symbols, noteheads, stems, beams, a rhythmic dot, a rest, a tie, a flag, not to mention letters and numbers.

A sentence handwritten in greatly varying styles, spoken by many different voices, will still be understandable by nearly everyone. A corresponding musical passage, if not properly notated in accordance with specific written and unwritten rules, will usually be unplayable by musicians. The profound difficulty of solving this problem has unfortunately resulted in many companies producing products that create poor and unusable musical notation. Hence there are many products on the market that can only be regarded as diversions or toys, and not suited for high-quality professional work.

Of the products that are sophisticated enough for serious musical notation, the best are available for the Apple Macintosh and the IBM. Many of the so-called smaller computers (such as the Commodore 64/128 and Apple II) do not have the speed or power necessary for professional-quality music printing. The important basic capabilities of music printing, such as crisp, on-screen WYSIWYG display and sophisticated cut-copy-paste, cannot be handled adequately by computers with slower microprocessors and smaller memories.

IBM Software

There are several products for IBM computers and compatibles that offer good results. RolandCorp has a sequencer (music entry editing/performing software) for the IBM AT called MPS (Music Processing System), which has recently been updated as a product called MESA (Music Editor Sequencer Arranger). There is also MIDI Textures for the IBM PC, by Roger Powell. Although this does not have printing capabilities (it is a sequencer that manipulates sounds only), there is a product called The Copyist published by Dr. T's Music Software that interfaces with MIDI Textures. The Copyist provides score-printing, editing, and transcription, and it supports the LaserJet Plus printer.

Finally there is Personal Composer for the IBM PC, by Jim Miller. This is possibly the best product of those mentioned so far with regard to music printing. It has insert, delete, copy, and move. It accepts data entry from a music keyboard. It lets the user transpose music, and it extract parts from a complete score. Text and chord symbols can be added to the score, which can be up to 64 staves. Its only drawback is the actual printed quality of the music symbols. The notation (the actual shapes of the symbols and the calligraphy) is good but not perfect. Be that as it may, Personal Composer and both of the other products mentioned above work well and allow the user to get fair-quality music printout.

Macintosh Software

The Macintosh is currently the music desktop publishing computer of choice for many people. The advantages of using a Macintosh include its capability for display and manipulation of the exact layout on the screen prior to printing, exceptionally good screen graphics (72 dots per inch), the option of large monitors (such as E-Machine's Big Picture that can display up to 12 staves at a time in full size), compatibility with the Apple LaserWriter (300 dots per inch) and the Allied Linotype printers (1,000 or more dots per inch), a PostScript music font for engraved-quality printing of music symbols, a high-speed processor for handling the complexities of music notation, and file compatibility between sophisticated notation and page layout programs.

Figure 25-4 shows a sample page from a music theory textbook that was created on the Macintosh and printed on the LaserWriter. In this one example, there is text, a screen dump from a music program, and a musical example. The ability to integrate musical examples with text and other graphics currently sets the Macintosh apart from other systems. Virtually engraved-quality notation produced with the Macintosh and LaserWriter can be found in Figures 25-1 and 25-2. These examples were created with the Deluxe Music Construction Set, which supports the PostScript music font called Sonata from Adobe Systems. This font was released in the fall of 1986.

One of the most significant features of the Macintosh and its music software is the intuitive user interface that can be learned by musicians without extensive training. A musician normally can enter notes and other symbols either by selecting them and positioning them on the staff with the mouse, by typing on the Macintosh keyboard, or by using a combination of typing and pointing and clicking of the mouse. In the case of the program pictured in Figure 25-5, notes can even be entered by clicking on an on-screen keyboard with the mouse. Other features that are standard with most Macintosh programs (such as cut, copy, and paste) can be combined with specific music commands (such as transpose, change key, change clef, change rhythm) to generate a lot of music after entering only a few notes.

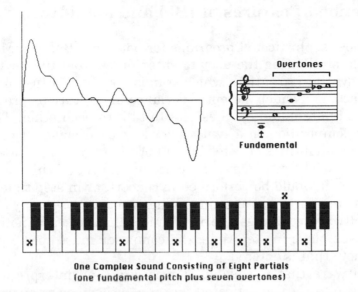

One Complex Sound Consisting of Eight Partials
(one fundamental pitch plus seven overtones)

Figure 25-4. Ear Training Expert, instructional material. Created using MusicType, FullPaint, screen dump from Ear Training Expert programs, and Chicago font.

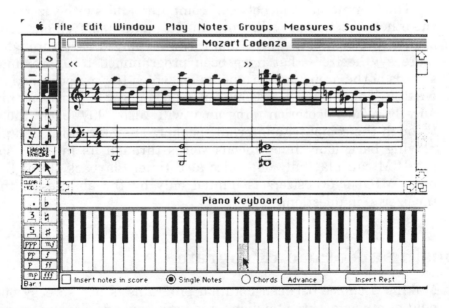

Figure 25-5. Screen dump of Deluxe Music Construction Set. Notice the use of pull-down menus, palates of music symbols, and an on-screen keyboard of note entry with the mouse.

Advanced Features of IBM and Macintosh Systems

The most sophisticated programs for both the IBM and Macintosh are capable of allowing the user to enter notes from the keyboard of any MIDI synthesizer. MIDI, which stands for Musical Instrument Digital Interface, is a widely accepted serial communications protocol that allows computers and synthesizers to talk to each other. The ability to play a composition on a synthesizer keyboard makes it possible to enter large quantities of notes into a notation program. The composer often has the choice of playing a piece in real time, which is to say more or less as it would be performed in concert, or in step time, which is to say one note or chord at a time. When the composer plays in real time, the software computes the rhythmic values of each note. When the composer plays in step time, the composer must specify the value of each note that is entered.

Software that is capable of recording and interpreting real time input is often so sophisticated that it is written as a separate program, which is generically known as a sequencer. Sequencing software not only records a performance but also offers a variety of editing features for "cleaning up" the composer's input. Once a sequencer file has been purged of wrong notes and rhythms, the file is converted to the appropriate file structure of a particular notation program.

The communication between computer and synthesizer works in the other direction as well. Once musical data has been entered into a sequencing or notation program, it can be played back through one or more synthesizers that have been programmed to approximate the sounds of the acoustic instruments for which the composition has been written. This makes it possible for the composer to proofread his work aurally. Many notation programs will also play back the music through the computer's internal speaker. The Macintosh is capable of playing back four simultaneous voices through its internal speaker; the IBM can play only one voice at a time. Playback through one or more MIDI synthesizers is limited only by the abilities of the synthesizer(s) in question.

Choosing a Notation Program

Making a choice between notation programs is not an easy one. The field of music desktop publishing is very new and developers are constantly adding new features. No software has all of the features that one might desire. As an an example of the trade-offs involved in purchasing software, consider the chart below which compares the two best music desktop publishing programs for the Macintosh: Professional Composer from Mark of the Unicorn and Deluxe Music Construction Set from Electronic Arts. One person might chose Professional Composer because of its superior scoring abilities (see Figure 25-3). Someone else might choose Deluxe Music Construction Set for its support of the Sonata font (see Figures 25-1 and 25-2) and its ability to export musical examples easily to page-layout programs, such as PageMaker, where music can be combined with text and graphics.

Table 25-1   Product Comparison Chart

	Professional Composer (version 2.0)	Deluxe Music Construction Set (beta version of 2.0)
Note Values	128th - dotted double whole	32nd - dotted whole
Key Signatures	all 15	all 15
Time Signatures	1-99	1-99
	1, 2, 4, 8, 16, 64	1, 2, 4, 8, 16
# of Staves	40	8
# of Clefs	8	4
# of Ledger Lines	up to 45 above and 45 below	up to 8 above and 11 below
Tuplets	duplets to 99-tuplets	triplets and quintuples
Beams	horizontal	slanted
Beam over Bar Line	no	no
Beam over Rests	yes	no
Flip Stems	yes	yes
Double Sharps	yes	no
Double Flats	yes	no
Text	yes	yes
Text Fonts and Styles	yes	yes
Brackets/Braces	yes	yes
Staff Size*	21 pixels high	25 pixels high
Allow extra notes in measure	yes	no
Multimeasure Rests	yes	no
Note Density Control	yes	yes
Line Break Control	yes	indirect**
Page Break Control	yes	indirect**
Title Page	yes	no**
Headers	yes	no**
Footers	yes	no**
Guitar Symbols	no	yes
Jazz Symbols	yes	no

Table 25-1   (cont.)

	Professional Composer (version 2.0)	Deluxe Music Construction Set (beta version of 2.0)
String Symbols	yes	no
Percussion Symbols	yes	no
Hide Rests	yes	no
Hide Tuplets	yes	no
Transposition	diatonic or by any interval or by 8ve	diatonic, by half step,
Print Separate Parts	yes	yes
Print to MacPaint	yes	no
Supports Sonata Font	not yet***	yes
Supports Clipboard Transfer to Word Processing or Page Layout Programs	no	yes
Direct MIDI Input	no	yes
Direct MIDI Output	no	yes
Compatibility with Sequencing Software	yes	yes

* Staff size can be larger or smaller when printing is done on a PostScript machine.

** Deluxe Music Construction Set is enhanced if used in conjunction with a page layout program, such as PageMaker.

*** Professional Composer has the most complete set of music symbols and the most sophisticated features for extracting parts, merging staves, checking instrumental ranges, checking rhythm, etc. Although it does not currently support the Sonata font, this is an expected addition.

Pricing a Complete System

The needs of individual composers vary considerably. The field of published music ranges from lead sheets to keyboard scores to multistave scores and instructional materials. A composer who wants to do straightforward formatting and printing of scores has one set of needs that are distinct from an educator, for example, who needs to combine musical examples with text and other graphics in the creation of instructional materials.

At the moment, a complete scoring system for either the IBM or the Macintosh would be comparably priced if the features offered were similar. The least expensive setup would cost around $2,400 and would include a computer with the minimum required memory, monitor, dot matrix printer, and synthesizer. The price would be somewhat lower if a synthesizer were not required. A full-featured system that included more computer memory, a laser printer, and a high-quality synthesizer would start at around $11,200. Were engraved-quality output desired, such a top-of-the-line system would have to be a Macintosh system at the moment because the Macintosh is currently the only computer with software that supports the Sonata music font from Adobe.

Most musicians, from band leaders to choir directors to arrangers of pop music, would find that a budget system such as the one shown below would be quite adequate for quickly producing highly legible scores. Anyone interested in producing martketable scores for a living would more than likely need a more expensive system, such as the top-of-the-line system shown subsequently.

If page-layout features are desired (the ability to combine music with text and graphics), a Macintosh system would be necessary as things stand at the moment. Other computer/software setups will, no doubt, offer similar music-pagemaking abilities in the future. The additional hardware and software costs necessary to add page-making features to either the budget or top-of-the-line scoring systems mentioned above would range from $225 to about $700. Page-layout features are a must for authors of instructional music books, composers of music for children, teachers who need to create tests and other instructional materials, and any musician who needs to combine music and text in advertising brochures.

Table 25-2 Configuration for Straightforward Score Printing

Prices are approximations based on list price and commonly available discounts as of October 1, 1986.

Top of the Line	
Hardware	
$2,000-$4,000	Computer: Macintosh with 1 megabyte or more of memory, internal 800K drive, and internal hard disk, external SCSI hard disk, or external 2-megabyte RAM drive
$2,000	Monitor: Large black and white (1040 by 808 pixels or greater)
$5,000 on up	Printer: LaserWriter Plus or Allied Linotype printer
$125	MIDI Interface (if using keyboard input); many from which to choose
$1,500 on up	Keyboard (if using keyboard input): MIDI synthesizer or controller keyboard with 88 full-size keys and weighted action
Software	
$300-$600	Notation Software: Professional Composer and (optionally)

Table 25-2   (cont.)

Top of the Line

	Deluxe Music Construction Set (As this is being written, Professional Composer does not support Adobe's Sonata music font for PostScript compatible printers, but that is expected to change soon. Many users may prefer the Deluxe Music construction Set to Professional Composer for keyboard scores if the other limitations of DMCS are not a problem.)
$80 and up	PostScript Fonts: Sonata Font and other desired text fonts
$200	Sequencing Software (optional): MegaTrack XL/ MIDIWorks, MIDIMAC, or Performer. (Sequencers can be used to input data in either real or step time. As of this writing, MegaTrack XL/MIDIWorks and MIDIMAC did not convert sequencer files to Professional Composer or Deluxe Music Construction Set, but new versions that do this conversion are planned for release. Performer will only convert to Professional Composer. Currently, each independent line of music on each staff must be recorded as a separate track using a sequencer.)
$0	Multitasking Software: Switcher or Servant
Total Price:	$11,205 minimum

Budget Configuration

Hardware	
$1,500	Computer: 512K Mac with second disk drive $400 Printer: Imagewriter (Many copying services offer LaserWriter printout of disk files for a reasonable cost per page.) $125 MIDI Interface (if using keyboard input): many from which to choose $300 Keyboard (if using keyboard input): Casio CZ 101 or similar MIDr
Software	
$80	Notation Software: Deluxe Music Construction Set (Deluxe Music Construction Set will accept step time input from a MIDI keyboard directly without the use of sequencing software.)
Total Price:	$2,405 minimum

Additional Hardware and Software for Music Publishing with Page Layout

Top of the Line

Hardware	
$175-$450	Video Digitizer (optional if additional graphics capabilities are required); many from which to choose
Software	
$450	Page Layout Software: PageMaker
$60-$185	Graphics Software: FullPaint and (optionally) MacDraw
$25	Font Editor (optional): Fontastic
Total Additional Price	$710 minimum

Table 25-2   (cont.)

Budget Configuration

Hardware	
none	
Software	
$40	Music Font (If a bit-mapped graphics program (such as MacPaint or FullPaint) is used extensively for page layout, a music font (such as MusicType) is almost indispensable for creating musical examples. A font editor is also useful for making the MusicType characters exactly match those of the music notation program you are using, or vice versa. The font editor can also be used to customize MacPaint's brush shapes as music symbols. Note that any font becomes a bit-mapped image when it is introduced into MacPaint.
$100-$135	Page Layout Software: Ready,Set,Go!, MacPublisher II, or MacWrite
$60-$125	Graphics Software: MacPaint and/or FullPaint (FullPaint is definitely a better choice than MacPaint as far as features and price go. However, with only 512K of RAM, MacPaint can be run in Switcher with MacWrite but FullPaint cannot.)
$25	Font Editor (optional): Fontastic
Total Additional Price	$225 minimum

The Future of Music Desktop Publishing

Music desktop publishing can be broken down into three stages: massive data entry, editing, and printout. Massive data entry is most easily accomplished by real-time performance at a piano-style keyboard, with the performance being transmitted to the computer through a MIDI interface. Sequencing software will receive this data and transcribe it into musical data (i.e., during this stage the computer data is transformed from numbers to on-screen musical notation). Editing, which comes next, is the process by which the user alters the musical notation from a rough draft to a perfectly notated work. Finally, the composition gets printed out in hard copy.

All the elements for this three-stage process are currently available, as has been pointed out in this essay. Of these three stages, most progress has been made in the area of music printout. In fact, with the printout quality of the Sonata font on the Apple Laserwriter, this can virtually be considered a solved problem (see Figures 25-1 and 25-2). With recent advances in MIDI (an electronic music communications standard) and computer-synthesizer communications, the problem of massive data entry is also well under way to being solved. The real area of music desktop publishing that needs serious improvement is editing.

Music Editing

Editing can be divided into four categories: playback (e.g., for aural error-checking of pitch and rhythm), auto-correction (e.g., instrumental ranges, proper duration-total per measure), manipulation (e.g., page layout, cut-copy-paste), and block modification (e.g., pitch transposition, rhythmic alterations). Each of these areas of editing is intimately linked with the subtleties of music notation.

Music notation is complex, yet logical. Since proper music notation can be summarized by a set of notational rules, it would seem that music notation itself would be naturally programmable. Unfortunately, there are a lot of rules. Furthermore, even if a programmer *did* include 600 music symbols and the correct rules for their interplay, that would not be enough to create a great music notation program. Musical notation relies on careful bending and breaking of the rules for the power of its communicability. For example, the standard beaming (connecting stems of notes with straight lines) of eighth and sixteenth notes in a piece for a given time signature enables a performer to follow the beat. But composers often choose irregular groupings to show, for example, where phrases start or which hand should play which note on the piano. This is analogous in speech to having standard rules for accentuation in a sentence such as "I saw you at the *store* today." For purposes of expressiveness, these rules are often broken, such as "I saw *you* at the store today." Similarly, a difference in beaming can change a simple passage of music in four-four time into an asymmetric, jazzy rhythm.

Because music notational rules are really designed to be broken, a music program would ideally know not only all the symbols and their strict rules, but also be a sophisticated musical interpreter. Clearly, for such a growth in sophistication, new data-editing software must incorporate artificial intelligence programming. This, in turn, demands computers with greater memory, greater speed of data manipulation, and increased power of musical-digital communication. This also demands increased communication between musicians and programmers in the design stage of music desktop publishing hardware and software.

Summary

Although there is still room for growth and development, it can undeniably be stated that in this decade music publishing underwent a profound and permanent change. The development of the MIDI standard, faster and cheaper computers, products like sequencers and synthesizers, the Sonata Font, and the LaserWriter, all have contributed to the birth of music desktop publishing. Now, through music desktop publishing, composers, performers, and music educators have a new and powerful means of musical expression: affordable personal score creation for communication with a wide audience. The era of Music Desktop Publishing has arrived.

Products Mentioned

Big Picture, E-Machines Inc., 7945 SW Mohawk St.,
Tualatin, Oregon 97062; (503) 692-6656

Casio CZ-101, Casio, Inc., 15 Gardener Rd.
Fairfield, NJ 07006; (201) 575-7400

Deluxe Music Construction Set, Electronic Arts, 1820 Gateway Dr.
San Mateo, CA 94404; (415) 571-7171

Ear Training Expert, TechnoQArts, 28 Daniel St.
Newton Centre, MA 02115; (617) 498-2198

Fontastic, Altsys Corp., 720 Ave. F #108
Plano, TX 75074; (214) 424-4888

FullPaint, Ann Arbor Softworks, Inc., 3082 S. State St.
Ann Arbor, MI 48104; (313) 996-3838

Imagewriter, LaserWriter, Macintosh Computer, MacPaint, MacWrite,
Apple Computer, Inc., 20525 Mariani Ave.
Cupertino, CA 95014; (408) 996-1010

LaserJet Plus, Hewlett-Packard Co., 11000 Wolfe Rd.
Cupertino, CA 95014; (800) 367-4772; (415) 330-2500

Linotronic 100, Linotronic 300, Allied Linotype Co., 425 Oser Ave.
Hauppauge, NY 11788; (516) 434-2016; (415) 785-9100

MacPublisher II, Boston Software Publishers, 19 Ledge Hill Rd.
Boston, MA 02132; (617) 267-4747

Megatrack/MIDIworks, Musicworks, 18 Haviland St.
Boston, MA 021116; (617) 266-2886

MIDIMAC, Opcode Systems, 707 Urban Lane
Palo Alto, CA 94301; (415) 321-8977

MPS, MESA, RolandCorp US, 7200 Dominion Circle
Los Angeles, CA 90040; (213) 685-5141

MusicType, Shaherazam, P.O. Box 26731
Milwaukee, WI 53226; (414) 442-7503

PageMaker, Aldus Corp., 411 First Ave. S. #200
Seattle, WA 98104; (206) 622-5500

Personal Composer, Jim Miller, P.O. Box 648
Honaunau, HI 96726; (808) 328-9518

Professional Composer/Performer, Mark of the Unicorn, 222 Third St.
Cambridge, MA 02142; (617) 576-2760

Ready,Set,Go!, Manhattan Graphics, 163 Varick St.
New York, NY 10013; (212) 989-6442

Sonata Font, Adobe Systems, 1870 Embarcadero Rd.
Palo Alto, CA 94303; (415) 852-0271

Texture II, MusicSoft, P.O. Box 274
Beekman, NY 1257; (914) 724-3668

The Copyist, Dr. T's Music Software, 66 Louise Road
Chestnut Hill, MA 02167; (617) 244-6954

KEYWORDS:

- **Thunderscan**

- **Fatbits**

- **ClickArt Effects**

- **MacPaint**

- **MacDraw**

- **PageMaker**

Patrick Brinton, founder and partner in Interface (the first desktop publishing business in Fairfax, California, and one of the first in the country), became interested in computers in 1977 when he wrote a large program in BASIC for the Community Memory Project. When the Macintosh was introduced in 1984, he ordered one of the first off the production line to help him organize his bookshop/cafe. Nine months later, seduced by the Mac, he divorced himself from the cafe and has lived happily ever after as a desktop publisher.

Essay Synopsis: This brief essay describes the complete process of making a poster for a dance event. The dancer for whom the poster was being made was watching, and, curious about the process and having never used a computer to make art, she began to play with the images with surprising success.

The author of this essay used a Thunderscan scanner to digitize the image of a photograph and then used Macintosh paint and draw programs to make changes to the scanned image. Other elements were added to complete the composition, and it was finally moved into PageMaker for sizing and printing. Because of the brevity of the essay, you get a bird's-eye view of the process of creating a desktop publishing project from start to finish.

26

The Oriental Dance Poster

Patrick Brinton

The Oriental Dance poster (see Figure 26-1) came about when Nancy Rose, a well-known figure in the San Francisco Bay Area ethnic dance world, asked me to design the poster for her upcoming concert in Marin. She had a picture of an Oriental arch she wanted to use, and also a picture of herself dancing. Other than that, she had no particular preconception of what the poster should look like.

First I scanned both pictures using Thunderscan. The arch came out looking good, but the mosaics looked fairly rough, and the vertical lines were not uniformly straight. I therefore proceeded to redraw in MacPaint the left-handed half of the arch, keeping only the curved decorative border on the inside of the arch. First I counted the pixels horizontally and vertically, and divided the results by the number of squares I needed. Then I set up a grid and laboriously filled in the appropriate black squares to form the mosaic, copying the original pattern. I had to cheat slightly to make the mathematics come out, and sharp eyes will detect that some of the rows of squares are slightly "squashed." I copied and flipped the left half of the arch to form the right half. Since this was in the old days of not being able to select more than a MacPaint windowful, this was a tricky move!

Seeing that the arch now looked a little plain, I decided to reverse out the upper half; this area was all white in the original. I designed an oriental-looking "curtain," and filled in everything above it with black, also in

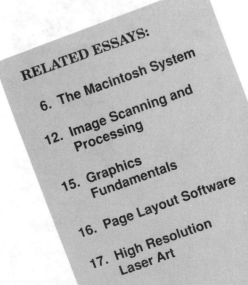

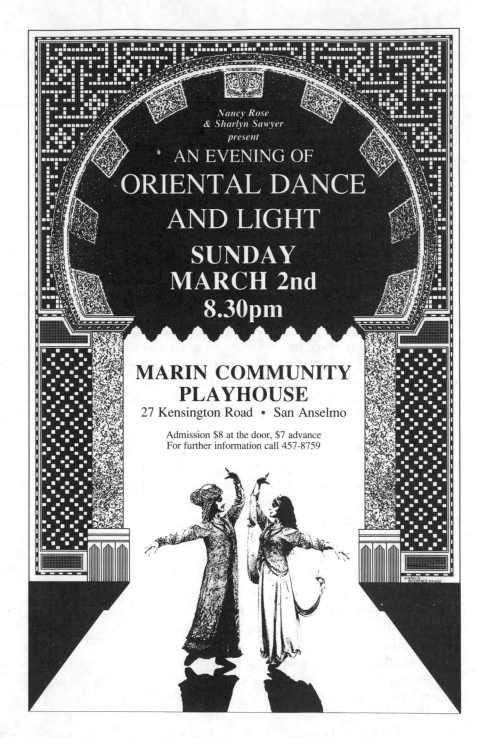

Figure 26-1. The Oriental Dance poster.

MacPaint. Now the arch was looking good, and I turned my attention to the dancer.

Nancy Rose, who had been observing with fascination the progress of the arch, wanted to try her hand at improving the dancer scan. I showed her the basics of MacPaint, and she worked in Fat bits to make it exactly what she wanted; she is a considerable artist as well as a very fine dancer and the end result was a vast improvement on the original scan. When she had finished it to her satisfaction, we saved it. Then she decided to have some fun after all the painstaking detail work, so she did what almost anyone would probably do: She drew a moustache on her own face! Then she added a turban and was in fits of laughter when I looked over her shoulder and said, "Hey, we could use that in the poster!" After some hours of work making a female figure into a male (notice she even made him a little taller to enhance the effect), she turned it over to me. I flipped it and added shadows to both figures by copying the lower halves, flipping them, and filling in with black. I achieved the perspective effect on the shadows in ClickArt Effects (this was before the days of FullPaint).

Now I had an arch and two dancers with shadows, and needed shadows for the arch to give some depth to the picture. I was not satisfied with the result I got in MacPaint, since the edge of the shadow was saw-toothed (being diagonal). I therefore pasted the whole arch into MacDraw, and drew the shadows there using black-filled polygons.

Time to assemble the whole poster and add the lettering. Switching to PageMaker, I placed the arch with its shadows from MacDraw, and adjusted the size to fill the page. Unfortunately, MacDraw has a problem with the sizing of bit-mapped images, and the shadows did not quite match up with the bottom of the arch, although they looked fine on the screen. I had to place the arch from MacPaint, and place the shadows separately from MacDraw, and resize and crop them so that they matched exactly. Many printouts and adjustments later, I was ready to add the dancers (which went without a hitch) and type in the lettering, using white type for the top half and black type for the rest. Finally I realized that something was needed to keep the eye from going off the page at the bottom, so I added a hairline to complete the poster.

The final camera-ready copy was printed out on a Linotronic 300, and we shipped the whole thing off to the printer, breathing a huge sigh of relief that we had the poster out before the concert!

Index